MOON

ICELAND

JENNA GOTTLIEB

Contents

Discover Iceland **6**
  10 Top Experiences 10
  Planning Your Trip 16
  • Chasing the Northern Lights 19
  Iceland Weekend Getaways 22
  • Winter Wonders 23
  • Best Wildlife-Watching.......... 24
  • Best Day Hikes................. 26
  • Get Yourself in Hot Water........ 28
  • Local Iceland 29

Reykjavík **30**
  Itinerary Ideas 32
  Sights 36
  Sports and Recreation............ 46
  Entertainment and Events......... 48
  Shopping 52
  Food 57
  Bars and Nightlife 67
  Accommodations 70
  Information and Services 73
  Getting There and Around 74
  Around Reykjavík 76

**Reykjanes Peninsula and the
  South** **84**
  Itinerary Ideas 88
  Reykjanes Peninsula 90
  The Golden Circle 99
  The South Coast 108
  Heimaey 130

**Snæfellsnes Peninsula and the
  Westfjords**.................... **134**
  Itinerary Ideas 137
  Akranes and Inland 139
  Snæfellsnes Peninsula............. 151
  The Westfjords 164

North Iceland **178**
  Itinerary Ideas 182
  Húnaflói Area 184
  Skagafjörður 187
  Tröllaskagi 192
  Grímsey....................... 199
  Akureyri....................... 203
  Around Akureyri 213
  Mývatn Region 215
  Húsavík 222
  Jökulsárgljúfur (Vatnajökull National
    Park—North)................. 227

East Iceland and the Eastfjords 230
Itinerary Ideas 233
Vopnafjörður 235
Fljótsdalur Valley 238
The Eastfjords 244
The Vatnajökull Region 259

The Highlands 268
Route F26 (Sprengisandur) 272
Route F35 (Kjölur) 277

Ring Road Road Trip 281
Planning the Drive 283
Day 1: Reykjavík and the Blue Lagoon . 287
Day 2: The Golden Circle 288
Day 3: The South Coast 290
Day 4: The Glacial East 291
Day 5: The Eastfjords to Mývatn 292
Day 6: Detour to Húsavík 293
Day 7: The North 294
Day 8: Driving to Snæfellsnes 296
Day 9: Snæfellsjökull National Park and Borgarnes 298
Last Day 299

Background 300
The Landscape 300
History 304
Government and Economy 306
People and Culture 308

Essentials 311
Transportation 311
Visas and Officialdom 315
Recreation 316
Festivals and Events 317
Food 318
Accommodations 319
Health and Safety 321
Practical Details 322
Travel Tips 325

Resources 328
Glossary 328
Icelandic Phrasebook 328
Suggested Reading 332
Internet Resources 333

Index 334
List of Maps 345

Iceland

Scale soaring mountaintops. Dive into some of the clearest water in the world. Explore crystalline ice caves and mineral-rich lava tubes. Hike the rim of a remote volcano that rises from an arctic desert. Witness a rainbow materialize over a thundering waterfall. Iceland is a place not just to see, but to experience.

Iceland is revered for its breathtaking landscapes, unrivaled trekking, and arctic wildlife. Three national parks and a dozen smaller reserves protect these resources. Vatnajökull National Park makes up 13 percent of the country and contains the largest glacier in the world outside the poles. Geothermal pools, like the famous milky waters of the Blue Lagoon, bubble up from beneath the earth and provide a place to soak away your worries.

If city life is more your speed, Reykjavík is waiting for you. Stroll the capital's streets and explore the galleries, coffeehouses, intimate concert venues, and music shops—you can't help but feel the city's creative energy. Handcrafted local beers replace specialty coffees as the drink of choice come evening time, when low-key daytime hangouts morph into pulsing parties that fuel a thriving nightlife scene.

Clockwise from top left: fireworks over Akranes; puffins; annual Viking Festival in Hafnarfjörður; Harpa in winter; an Icelandic horse; Goðafoss.

In summer, the days seem endless—the sun shines for nearly 24 hours around the solstice—and it's the ideal time to embark on an epic drive around the Ring Road. And winter tourism is increasing, with visitors lured by the chance to hunt the northern lights, yet another of Iceland's spectacular natural wonders. Watching the lights flicker in the sky, changing colors, disappearing and popping up again stronger and brighter, makes braving the wind and cold worth it.

For scenery and adventure, Iceland is unmatched.

Clockwise from top left: Jökulsárlón Glacier Lagoon; Mývatn Nature Baths; Strokkur geyser; pipe organ inside Hallgrímskirkja.

10 TOP
EXPERIENCES

1 Taking in wondrous waterfalls like **Goðafoss** (page 215) and **Dettifoss** (page 228).

2 Soaking in one of Iceland's **pools and hot springs,** from the milky blue waters of the **Blue Lagoon** (page 95) to less famous pools, frequented by locals (page 28).

3 Exploring mountains, volcanoes, lava fields, and valleys on well-maintained **hiking trails,** from the famous four-day **Laugavegurinn Trail** (page 120) to less ambitious **day hikes** around the island (page 26).

4 Observing Iceland's rich **wildlife,** from reindeer and puffins to seals and whales (page 24).

<<<

5 Hitting the road on a **scenic drive** to enjoy the country's nature and culture, whether you're touring the entire **Ring Road** (page 281) or the famous **Golden Circle** (page 99).

>>>

6 Strolling through artsy, vibrant **Akureyri,** unofficial capital of the north (page 203).

<<<

7 Watching the green and white lights of the **northern lights** dance and flicker in the sky (page 19).

8 Strolling through Iceland's three majestic **national parks,** which are free to enter and explore (pages 99, 151, 227, and 264).

<<<

9 Sailing along the gorgeous glacier lagoon **Jökulsárlón,** where icebergs calve from the glacier's edge and drift by (page 263).

>>>

10 Experiencing the large selection of bars and music venues that make up **Reykjavík's legendary nightlife** (page 67).

<<<

Planning Your Trip

Where to Go

Reykjavík

Home to two-thirds of Iceland's population, the **capital city** is the **cultural and social hub** of the country, with an energy distinct from the rest of the island. Here you'll find chic hotels, eclectic restaurants, and top-notch shopping on the main street, **Laugavegur**—not to mention a thriving **art scene** and vibrant **nightlife.** Pay a visit to the distinctive church **Hallgrímskirkja,** the placid pond **Tjörnin** near city hall, and, for a taste of history, the **National Museum of Iceland.** A trip to the **old harbor** is also a must—take in a concert at the striking glass hall **Harpa,** or head out on a **whale-watching** tour.

Reykjanes Peninsula and the South

Outside of Reykjavík, the **Reykjanes Peninsula** and the natural sights in South Iceland get the most traffic on the island. The Reykjanes Peninsula is home to charming fishing villages, **Keflavík** airport, and the **Blue Lagoon,** where you can take a healing dip in the heated water. The **Golden Circle** route encompasses three key sights: the powerful waterfall **Gullfoss,** bubbling geothermal phenomenon **Geysir,** and history-steeped national park **Þingvellir.** Some of the best **hiking** trails in the country are in the South. A favorite is the **Laugavegurinn Trail,** where you'll see towering mountains, vast glaciers, hot springs, roaring rivers, and stunning waterfalls.

the town of Akureyri

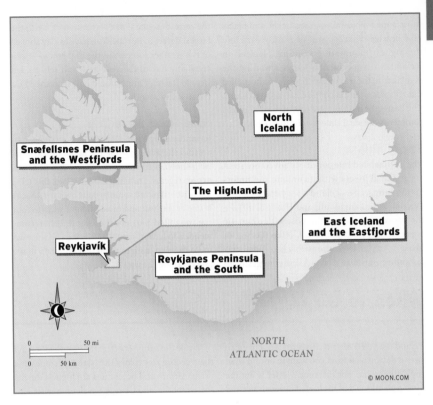

North
Iceland

Snæfellsnes Peninsula
and the Westfjords

The Highlands

East Iceland
and the Eastfjords

Reykjavík

Reykjanes Peninsula
and the South

0   50 mi

0   50 km

NORTH
ATLANTIC OCEAN

© MOON.COM

Snæfellsnes Peninsula and the Westfjords

Called "Iceland in miniature" by locals, the **Snæfellsnes Peninsula** has a bit of everything: quaint fishing towns, spectacular mountains, hiking, whale-watching, and even a glacier you can walk on—**Snæfellsjökull**, world famous as the starting point of Jules Verne's *Journey to the Center of the Earth*. Endless coastlines, offbeat museums, and beautiful rocky landscapes await in the **Westfjords**. For outstanding birdwatching, visit the **Látrabjarg cliffs** in summer to check out thousands of nesting puffins.

North Iceland

Iceland's "second city," low-key **Akureyri** offers beautiful botanical gardens, first-rate hotels and restaurants, and a booming art scene.

It's the perfect place to base yourself for a visit to the North. The **Mývatn region** lures visitors with its birdlife-rich lake, gorgeous hiking trails, vast lava fields, enormous craters, soaring mountains, and soothing **Mývatn Nature Baths**. Jökulsárgljúfur, part of **Vatnajökull National Park,** offers a number of treasures, including the gigantic canyon **Ásbyrgi** and **Dettifoss,** the largest waterfall in Iceland. **Húsavík** has some of the best **whale-watching** opportunities on the island, with a chance to see as many as 12 species of whales.

East Iceland and the Eastfjords

Looking for the "ice" in Iceland? Head to East Iceland, where the giant white **Vatnajökull glacier** will take your breath away. Drive or hike close to the glacier's edge in **Skaftafell,** home to snowcapped mountains, green fields, and black-sand beaches. Hikers can scale **Mount Snæfell,** the highest mountain (excluding glaciers) in Iceland, with spectacular views spanning the highlands to the sea. Weave through the unspoiled **Eastfjords,** where each fjord has its own charm. The East is the most remote part of the island, and summer is the ideal time to tour this region.

The Highlands

The uninhabited interior draws adventure seekers and avid hikers with its unique and unforgiving landscape. Iceland's **largest glaciers** (Vatnajökull, Langjökull, and Hofskjökull) are the backdrop to the highlands, with dramatic scenery cut by wind and ice. Hike the rim of **Mount Askja,** a volcano with a lake-filled crater and sensational views. Askja emerges from the eerie, desolate **Ódáðahraun lava field,** the largest desert in Europe. You have to stay abreast of the weather forecast in the highlands—it can snow any day of the year here and self-guided trips to the highlands should only be planned for the summer months.

Ring Road Road Trip

Iceland's Ring Road **(Route 1)** is a scenic loop around the island, revealing some of the most well-known attractions in Iceland as well as unexpected gems. Traveling the entirety of this 1,332 km (828 mi) paved route in your own **rental car** is one of the best and most popular ways to tour the inhabited parts of the island. It is recommended to have at least **10 full days** on the road to do the trip justice, as there is so much to see and do along the way.

When to Go

Iceland is a **year-round destination,** but when to visit depends on what you want to do and what you'd like to see. For instance, winter is not the time to go hiking, but the lure of lower airfare and hotel prices, as well as the northern lights, draw many people over this season.

Summer (June-August)

The summer is the **high season** and offers the **best weather** to explore all of Iceland's **outdoor activities** such as hiking, diving, whale-watching, glacier-walking, bird-watching, and swimming. Average temperatures in the summer range between 10-25°C (50-76°F). The landscape is green and lush and the days long. The **midnight sun** has to be seen to be believed. June-August is also the best time to embark on a **Ring Road trip,** as the roads are the best this time of year, and the weather is not likely to cause many problems. That said, it's important to closely monitor the weather forecast for wind or heavy rain.

While the summer offers the best weather and the freedom to explore the island, it comes at a price. Airfare and hotel rates are highest during these months, and there is a rush of tourists.

Autumn (September)

Autumn is quite short in Iceland, and attracts travelers who want to **avoid the tourist crush** of summer but still explore some of the countryside and enjoy outdoor activities. There remains plenty of daylight, and **hiking** is viable in the fall, but you must monitor the weather because storms can pop up. It's also possible to see **northern lights** this time of year; check the forecast at www.vedur.is.

September is perfect for a long weekend in **Reykjavík.** This time of year is also known for local festivals in the capital city, such as the Reykjavík International Film Festival. Average temperatures in September and October range between 2-10°C (36-50°F). The winds can make it feel colder.

Chasing the Northern Lights

The biggest winter attraction in Iceland is the northern lights. People travel from around the world to catch a glimpse of the green, white, blue, and red lights dancing in the night sky. The phenomenon is caused by solar winds, which push electronic particles to collide with molecules of atmospheric gases, causing an emission of bright light. Seeing the lights comes down to a mix of timing, location, solar conditions, and some luck. Here are some **tips** to maximize your chances for a glimpse of the dancing auroras.

- **Pick the right month:** Timing is essential since the northern lights are visible from mid-September to mid-March.

- **Monitor the forecast:** To see northern lights, you'll need clear skies and solar activity. Before you head out on a northern lights hunt, check the aurora forecast at **www.vedur.is.**

- **Dress appropriately:** It can get cold out there, so be prepared. Dress in warm layers and carry a hat, scarf, and gloves.

- **Find darkness:** For optimum visibility, get away from bright city or town lights. Tours take you out of town, or if you are self-driving, find a dark place, safely out of the road. Do not park next to the road with your headlights off; find a suitable location.

- **Have a good dose of patience:** It's not like turning a switch. It can take time for the lights to appear even if the forecast is favorable. You may have to wait several hours.

- **Take a tour:** Northern lights tours are offered by companies like **Reykjavík Excursions** (www.re.is).

the northern lights

Though all you really have to do to see the northern lights when they're on is venture outside a city area and look up, here are some particularly excellent places to see the lights in all their splendor:

- **Akranes Lighthouse:** The lighthouse is far from the town lights and is perfect on a dark night (page 139).

- **Grótta Lighthouse:** Grótta is probably the best spot in Reykjavik to catch the lights (page 76).

- **Þingvellir National Park:** The park is lovely in all seasons and is a favorite for local photographers capturing the aurora (page 99).

Winter (October-April)

Iceland's **low season,** winter, isn't a bad time to visit if you're willing to go with the flow, as the weather can be unpredictable at best and punishing at worst. Pluses are that airfare and hotel prices are the lowest of the year, you won't battle any crowds, and this is the best time to catch a glimpse of the **northern lights.** Popular outdoor activities during the winter include **riding snowmobiles and horses** and **skiing** in the North. Temperatures tend to hover around freezing with averages of -3 to 3°C (26-38°F). The winds make it feel colder.

The downside to winter travel is, unsurprisingly,

the **changeable, challenging weather.** You will likely encounter wind, rain, snow, sleet, and everything in between. Travel to the countryside is limited in the winter as **many roads are closed,** and even open roads can have tough conditions. Also, **many establishments outside Reykjavík close** for the winter.

Spring (May)

April and May fall in between the low winter season and high summer season and are good options for **budget-conscious** travelers. You have a crack at **decent weather** without paying the higher summertime prices. That said, the weather is unpredictable, so a visit in April can feel like winter—it's **hit or miss.** But if the weather is pleasant enough, you can enjoy hikes, horse riding, whale-watching, and all that Reykjavík has to offer. The temperatures for April and May range between 0-8°C (32-47°F).

Before You Go

Money and Budget Tips

The official currency of Iceland is the **króna** (abbreviated kr or ISK). For credit cards, Iceland uses the chip and PIN system, which requires a **4-digit PIN** for transactions, including at unmanned gas stations (common on the Ring Road). If your card does not have a PIN, contact your credit card issuer to set one up (and memorize it!) before traveling to Iceland.

Pulling off a budget trip to Iceland is difficult, as the country routinely ranks as the most expensive destination in Europe. However, there are some ways to save money.

- Consider staying in **hostels, apartments,** or **guesthouses** with shared facilities instead of hotels.

- Shop in local **grocery stores** and self-cater instead of dining out every day.

- Plan a **camping trip** in the summer and stay in budget-friendly designated campsites.

- Splurge on a couple of activities like a glacier walk or snorkeling tour but be sure to take advantage of the **free attractions.**

- Skip the Blue Lagoon and swim like a local in **heated public pools** and **hot tubs.**

- Bring a **water bottle** with you and never pay for water, as Iceland's water is some of the cleanest and best tasting on earth.

Visas and Officialdom

Visitors to Iceland must arrive with a valid **passport** that expires no sooner than three months after your intended departure date. Travelers from the **United States, Canada, Australia, New Zealand, South Africa,** the **United Kingdom,** and **Ireland** do not need a visa for trips shorter than 90 days. However, if you would like to stay longer, you need to procure a permit from the **Directorate of Immigration** (www.utl.is), which is very difficult to get. There are different, more lenient rules for residents of European Union and European Economic Area countries.

Reservations

As Iceland is a sparsely populated island with limited accommodations, it's strongly recommended you **book accommodations in advance.** For summer trips, plan to book hotels and guesthouses at least six months in advance to get the best choices at the most favorable prices. For the rest of the year, plan to book rooms at least three months in advance. **Campervans** and **motorhomes,** which should only be rented during the summer months for safety reasons, should be booked far in advance as well, at least five months before your arrival date.

The **Blue Lagoon** must be booked in advance through its website, www.bluelagoon.is. Be sure to reserve as soon as possible because time slots

camping in Iceland

frequently sell out, even in the winter. If you're considering any **private or small-group tours,** be sure to book those in advance. It's also recommended to make **dinner reservations during the Christmas season** because there are limited options, and it's necessary to book **New Year's Eve dinner reservations** far in advance (think July/August).

Getting There and Around
GETTING THERE
Flying into Iceland is a pretty seamless experience. The country's main carrier, **Icelandair** (www.icelandair.com), serves more than 30 destinations in the United States, Canada, and Europe. Iceland's accessibility has been the island's main selling point as a travel destination, as the country is just over five hours from New York City and about three hours from London.

For those traveling from mainland Europe, a **ferry** can be a great option, especially if you want to bring a car, camper, or bicycle for the trip. **Smyril Line** (www.smyril-line.fo) runs a ferry to Iceland from Denmark and the Faroe Islands. The ferry drops you off in Seyðisfjörður in East Iceland, which is convenient if you're traveling with a car and want to spend time in the countryside. If you want to stay in the South, where Reykjavík and the Golden Circle attractions are, a ferry may not be the best option.

GETTING AROUND
Having access to a **car** gives you the ultimate freedom in seeing the island on your own schedule (but with insurance, expect to pay dearly). If you plan to stay in Reykjavík for most of your trip, or want to do short day trips in the southern or western parts of the country, it's not necessary to rent a car as you can book **tours.** Public transportation is not ideal for tourists as the buses in the countryside connect towns and villages, and do not travel to tourist attractions.

Iceland Weekend Getaways

If you don't have a lot of time, it's possible to see some of the country's highlights in four short days. Short stopovers are very common, as Iceland is just five hours from the East Coast of the United States and about three hours from London.

The Best Long Weekend in Iceland

DAY 1

After landing at **Keflavík International Airport,** either pick up your rental car or take the FlyBus into **Reykjavík.** If you are arriving in the morning or afternoon, make a stop at the **Blue Lagoon** near Grindavík for a soothing soak. Head to Reykjavík and check into your accommodation. Explore the town, including the landmark church **Hallgrímskirkja,** the **Reykjavík Art Museum,** and the **National Gallery of Iceland.** Have a delicious dinner at **Fish Market,** followed by some of Iceland's

nightlife by taking in a concert at **Harpa** concert hall or having a couple of drinks at **Kex Hostel,** a favorite among locals and tourists alike. Spend the night at **Grand Hotel Reykjavík.**

DAY 2

From Reykjavík, get in your rental car and kick off your drive of the famous **Golden Circle** route. Make your first stop **Þingvellir National Park,** an ideal introduction to the Icelandic countryside due to its historical and geological significance. Next, drive to the Haukadalur geothermal area for a look at **Geysir,** the original geyser, and its spouting neighbor **Strokkur.** Have lunch at the **Geysir Center** before continuing to **Gullfoss,** the golden waterfall. Gullfoss is one of the most photographed attractions in Iceland, and its beauty never disappoints. After spending some time exploring the area around Gullfoss, drive to the small village of **Fluðir** and take a dip

Harpa in Reykjavík

Winter Wonders

a glacier walk tour

Sure, Iceland's winter weather can be challenging. But you'll be rewarded with truly unique experiences that make it all worthwhile.

- **Hunt for northern lights:** The main season to see northern lights is October-February. Book a guided tour or venture out on your own (page 19).

- **Soak in the Blue Lagoon:** This is the most popular tourist attraction in Iceland for a reason, and is just as special in the winter. It's soothing and beautiful to soak during light snowfalls or while watching northern lights dance above on clear nights (page 95).

- **Tour the Golden Circle:** Iceland's number one tour is available year-round. Book a bus tour or drive the attraction-heavy route yourself. The frozen **Gullfoss** falls and rocky landscape are gorgeous when mantled in winter white (page 99).

- **Take a glacier walk:** Tour operators offer the unique opportunity to hike on a glacier. They supply all the necessary equipment and provide pickups at your hotel or guesthouse. **Icelandic Mountain Guides** (www.mountainguides.is) offers a year-round guided tour walking on a glacier in Skaftafell (page 264).

- **Ride majestic Icelandic horses:** Icelandic horses are hardy creatures that are beautiful to ride along the snowy landscape. Akureyri-based tour company **Saga Travel** (www.sagatravel. is) offers horse-riding day tours from Akureyri and Mývatn (page 208).

- **Go cross-country skiing up north:** Iceland isn't known for its skiing, but it does have a well-maintained ski area in its North, not too far from Akureyri. The **Hlíðarfjall** ski area (www. hlidarfjall.is) has more than a dozen well-kept trails (page 207).

- **Ride snowmobiles:** It's spectacular to glide atop the pristine white snow on crisp, clear winter days. **Vatnajökull Travel** (www.vatnajokull.is) features a year-round tour that includes snowmobile rides on Vatnajökull glacier, the biggest glacier in Europe (page 263).

- **Embark on an art museum crawl in Reykjavík:** If the weather outside is frightful, head indoors to explore Iceland's modern artists, like Erró, and old masters such as Jóhannes Kjarval at the **Reykjavík Art Museum** (page 36).

Best Wildlife-Watching

WHALES

Several whale-watching tour companies operate around the island. Some head out year-round, while others are restricted to the summer. The main whale-watching destinations are in the South (Reykjavík), West (Grundarfjörður), and North (Dalvík and Húsavík).

- **Reykjavík:** Operating from Reykjavík's harbor, whale-watching tours offer opportunities to see minke, blue, and fin whales as well as dolphins and porpoises (year-round) (page 46).

- **Grundarfjörður:** This western town is your best shot at catching a glimpse of orcas (it's possible to see orcas year-round, but is more likely during the winter months) (page 159).

- **Dalvík:** You may see humpback whales, minke whales, blue whales, harbor porpoises, and dolphins on tours leaving from the harbor of this small northern fishing town (year-round) (page 193).

- **Húsavík:** The unofficial whale-watching capital of the island has several species off its shores, including minke, humpback, pilot, northern bottlenose, sperm, sei, fin, orca, and blue whales (mid-May-late Oct.) (page 223).

PUFFINS

From May through August, it's possible to see puffins in several parts of the country.

- **Heimaey:** Thousands of visitors flock to this island off the South Coast to walk along the sea cliffs and spend time with its puffin population (June-Aug.) (page 132).

- **Látrabjarg:** In West Iceland, trails allow you to access the colossal Látrabjarg cliffs, where puffins gather to nest in intricate crevices (May-Aug.) (page 172).

- **Borgarfjörður Eystri:** Get a close-up view of puffins at this fjord in East Iceland, which has an observation platform connected to a small islet that the birds love (mid-Apr.-mid-Aug.) (page 245).

puffin in northern Iceland

SEALS

Six species of seals have been spotted off the coast of Iceland. Most commonly sighted are **gray seals** and **harbor seals.** The remaining four species (hooded, harp, bearded, and ringed seals) are hit or miss. In the summer, you have a good chance of spotting gray seals and harbor seals around the **Vatnsnes Peninsula** in the North. The peninsula is also home to the **Icelandic Seal Center,** which contains wonderful exhibits about these creatures. The center's staff has information on the best sites for seal-watching opportunities.

REINDEER

Iceland's reindeer herds live only in **East Iceland.** The best places to view them during the summer are the areas around **Mount Snæfell.**

in the **Secret Lagoon,** a smaller and more intimate bathing experience than the Blue Lagoon. After you're refreshed, head back to Reykjavík for dinner at **Grillmarkaðurinn** and spend another night at Grand Hotel Reykjavík.

DAY 3

Spend a day in the **Snæfellsnes Peninsula** exploring charming fishing villages and the mighty **Snæfellsjökull glacier,** which appeared in Jules Verne's classic tale *Journey to the Center of the Earth.* Make a stop at **Djúpalónssandur,** a vast black sand beach on the southern edge of Snæfellsjökull before continuing to the town of **Grundarfjörður.** Have lunch at **Bjargarsteinn** before going on a whale-watching tour with **Laki Tours.** This region is your best chance to see Orca whales off the coast of the island. Drive the 2.5 hours back to Reykjavík and have dinner and drinks at **Mathöll Hlemmur.**

DAY 4

Before your flight, wander Reykjavík's numerous **cafés, galleries,** and **shops.** You can pick up gifts and quality clothing at top-notch stores like **66 North** and **Geysir** and take a break at **Mokka** or **Café Babalu.**

Getaway for Outdoor Adventurers

DAY 1

After landing at **Keflavík International Airport,** pick up your **rental car** and head into **Reykjavík.** If you are arriving in the morning or afternoon and feeling up for it, drive to **Esja** for an easy hike. Just outside Reykjavík, the mountain is a great introduction to hiking in Iceland. The hike is eight kilometers (5 miles) round-trip and relatively easy, and you will be treated to a beautiful view from the top. Spend the evening in Reykjavík.

Djúpalónssandur beach in Snæfellsjökull National Park

Laugavegurinn Trail

Iceland is undeniably a hiker's paradise. The mountainous landscape begs to be climbed, lava fields invite you to explore, and the highlands offer the adventurous a place to conquer.

- **Mount Esja** is the picture-perfect backdrop to Reykjavík and a favorite hiking destination for locals and tourists. The hike is eight kilometers (five miles) round-trip and relatively easy, but it does get steeper toward the top. Along the way, you'll see a placid stream and gorgeous scenery. The vista from the top is breathtaking, with views of Reykjavík across the bay (page 78).

- Hike to the summit of **Mount Hekla** via a moderately challenging seven-kilometer (four-mile) trail crossing lava fields and you'll be rewarded with gorgeous views, which, on clear days, include Vatnajökull glacier (page 116).

- Looking for a challenging day hike? Consider the **Fimmvörðuháls Trail,** which some tackle over two days but which can also be done in a long day hike of around 8-10 hours. Along the way you see gorgeous lava fields, glaciers, and waterfalls (page 123).

- In the West, **Mount Akrafjall** offers moderate hiking, with two paths from which to choose. The shorter climb (about two hours) gains 555 meters (1,855 feet) in elevation and offers a lovely view of the outskirts of Akranes. If you're up for a longer climb (about five hours), the more strenuous path climbs 643 meters (2,110 feet), and on clear days you can see Snæfellsjökull glacier (page 141).

- For those who make it to the highlands, hiking the rim of **Mount Askja** is a must. The approximately two-hour trek is moderate, and the trail is well maintained and sees a bit of traffic from hikers. It offers special views of looming mountains, lava fields, and the spectacular Víti crater (page 274).

- Hiking in **Hveradalir,** a geothermal area, is a popular option. For those seeking a taste of the highlands without committing to an all- or multi-day hike, a three-kilometer (1.9-mile) loop trail near Neðri-Hveradalir (Lower Hveradalir) takes you through the glacial landscape, juxtaposed with bubbling hot springs and the muted hues of the desert-like earth (page 279).

- Though it takes several days, embarking on the **Laugavegurinn Trail** is one of the most popular summertime hikes of the interior. The trail, which runs between Landmannalaugar and Þórsmörk, offers varied landscapes ranging from stark lava fields to colorful rhyolite mountains to bubbling hot springs. Hikers can choose to stay at mountain huts (booked in advance) or designated camping sites along the way (page 120).

DAY 2

From Reykjavík, drive south, where you will be based the next two nights. Stop in Þingvellir National Park for the chance to go snorkeling with Dive Iceland (www.dive.is) in the Silfra ravine and explore the park after. Next, continue to Hveragerði to hike the Reykjadalur trail and bathe in the hot river at the top. The hike is about 1 hour each way. Spend the night in Selfoss at Hotel Selfoss.

DAY 3

Get ready to see the Westman Islands today! Board the ferry from Landeyjahöfn harbor, with your rental car. Once on the island, you can hike Eldfell, go on a puffin watching boat ride (in the summer) with Viking Tours (www.vikingtours.is), and visit the new Beluga whales in the Beluga Whale Sanctuary. Have dinner at Slippurinn before heading back to the ferry. Spend another night in Selfoss.

DAY 4

Before your flight, return your rental car and stop by the Blue Lagoon for a rejuvenating soak in the milky geothermal water.

Relax and Unwind

DAY 1

After landing at Keflavík International Airport, pick up your rental car and drive to the Blue Lagoon Silica Hotel near Grindavík, where you will stay for the next two nights. Spend your first day soaking in the milky blue water and have dinner at the Lagoon's Lava Restaurant.

DAY 2

After a healthy breakfast, treat yourself to an in-water massage at the Blue Lagoon before checking out of your hotel. Spend the rest of the day exploring the Reykjanes Peninsula, including the geothermal region of Krýsuvík and the Bridge Between the Continents. Drive to Reykjavik for the evening.

Blue Lagoon

Get Yourself in Hot Water

Blue Lagoon

From waterfalls to boat trips to hot springs, water is a constant tourist attraction in Iceland.

- A trip to Iceland would not be complete without visiting the **Blue Lagoon** (page 95) just outside of Grindavík. Against a backdrop of lava fields, the man-made hot spring soothes and exhilarates at the same time. And that goes for any weather conditions—rain, snow, or sunshine. Soaking within the deep mist is a unique and slightly eerie experience, one you will remember—and talk about—for ages.

- Up North, the **Mývatn Nature Baths** (page 215) feel secluded in comparison to the Blue Lagoon, with fewer people and more room to wade. The water comes from the National Power Company's borehole in Bjarnaflag, scorching when it arrives at the basin next to the man-made bathing lagoon but cooling significantly before filtering into it. The bottom of the lagoon contains minerals beneficial to the skin. The bathing experience is divine, relaxing every inch of your body.

- In the South, the **Secret Lagoon** (page 107) is a popular stop for tourists driving the Golden Circle. Located in the small village Fluðir, the Secret Lagoon is small and less touristy than the Blue Lagoon, offering a more intimate experience. Surrounded by a landscape of lush moss and hot springs, the Secret Lagoon is a perfect place to relax after logging some hours on the road.

- Tourists who visit **local swimming pools** will quickly see how integral they are to Icelandic culture. It's common to see families, friends, and coworkers relaxing in a hot tub and talking about politics, music, or the latest movies. The pools are also a great alternative to outdoor activities when the weather is particularly bad—which can happen in Iceland at any time, in any season. Almost every town has its own local pool.

An important note: You must **shower** before entering pools or hot tubs. Icelanders shower, sans bathing suit, in gender-divided locker rooms prior to taking a dip, and you're expected to do the same. Just go with the flow.

Icelandic culture is relaxed yet quirky, with a heavy dose of appreciation for the arts and the outdoors. Below are some ideas on how to **live like a local** while on vacation.

- Enjoy **ice cream** any month of the year, in any weather. Seriously, ice cream is very popular here. Some lovely places in Reykjavík are Valdís and Skúbb.

- Take advantage of the **local swimming pools.** While the Blue Lagoon is great for first-time visitors, swimming pools are where you will find the locals. There's a local pool in almost every town.

- When in Reykjavík, go to a concert at local hotspots like **Mengi, Kex Hostel,** or **Harpa Concert Hall.**

- **Rent a bike** and ride down to the **Grótta lighthouse** in Reykjavík, one of the locals' favorite ways to spend a Saturday.

- **Chase the sun.** If you are visiting in the summer and camping, base your itinerary on the weather and travel where the sun is shining. Icelanders like to keep things flexible.

- Visit **breweries** here like Ægir Brewery and Bryggjan Brúgghús to sample the beer, or go on an epic **pub crawl** in Reykjavík.

Grótta lighthouse

DAY 3

Spend today exploring the main sights of the Golden Circle—**Gullfoss, Geysir,** and **Þingvellir**—before driving to the **Secret Lagoon** for a relaxing swim. Stop by **Friðheimar** to check out the **greenhouses** and enjoy a non-alcoholic Bloody Mary before driving back to Reykjavík.

DAY 4

Enjoy an early morning soak at the local pool **Laugardalslaug** before picking up some last-minute souvenirs in downtown Reykjavik, and returning to Keflavik International Airport for your flight.

Reykjavík

Itinerary Ideas 32
Sights 36
Sports and Recreation. . 46
Entertainment and
    Events 48
Shopping 52
Food 57
Bars and Nightlife 67
Accommodations 70
Information and
    Services 73
Getting There and
    Around 74
Around Reykjavík 76

Reykjavík is having a moment. Relatively afford-
able airfares are drawing weekenders from both sides of the Atlantic,
giving Iceland's capital city a chance to show off its urban appeal and
individualistic style.

Reykjavík's history dates back to AD 874, when Ingólfur Arnarson
from Norway established the first settlement in Iceland. The city slowly
grew over the centuries, and in 1786, Reykjavík was established as an
official trading town.

Today, Reykjavík has a lot of people, cars, and trees, in stark contrast to the rest of the country. Roughly 230,000 of Iceland's 360,000
residents live in the capital city. Though it's small, its energy mimics
that of bigger cities like Berlin. Reykjavík residents are known to have

Highlights

Look for ★ to find recommended sights, activities, dining, and lodging.

★ **Hallgrímskirkja:** The "Church of Hallgrímur" is a striking national monument dedicated to one of Iceland's most cherished and celebrated poets. Its tower boasts spectacular views of the city (page 37).

★ **National Gallery of Iceland (Listasafn Íslands):** The largest collection of Icelandic art on the island has everything from classic portraits to gorgeous landscapes (page 42).

★ **Tjörnin:** Close to Reykjavík City Hall, this pond is a lovely place to take a stroll and enjoy the birdlife (page 42).

★ **Harpa:** This striking concert hall features individual glass panels that light up during the darkness of winter (page 44).

★ *Sun Voyager* **Sculpture (*Sólfar*):** The large boat sculpture by the sea has been delighting photographers and tourists for decades (page 44).

★ **Perlan:** This unique dome-shaped building has one of the best views of Reykjavík from its outdoor deck (page 45).

★ **Reykjavík Nightlife:** Whether you're up for some live music, want to dance, or are interested a classic pub crawl, Reykjavík will not disappoint (page 67).

★ **Hiking Esja:** An easy climb on basalt rock climaxes with gorgeous views out to sea (page 78).

two lives: They work by day, and by night become musicians, artists, novelists, or poets. While strolling on Reykjavík's main street, Laugavegur, you'll see street art among the high-end shops, musicians playing impromptu concerts outside coffeehouses, and small art galleries boasting original "Icelandic Design." It's undeniably a creative city.

While Reykjavík can seem quite urban with its galleries and restaurants, nature is never too far away. The air is unbelievably clean, and whales can be seen passing by the harbor during the summer.

ORIENTATION

Reykjavík is the most compact capital city in all of Europe. Its **downtown** and the **old harbor** are situated in the northern half of the city, and the **main bus station** (BSÍ) for intercity and tour buses is in the south. Most of the hotels, museums, shops, and restaurants are also in the northern half. The main street in central Reykjavík is **Laugavegur,** which starts in the east. As you move west,

it eventually becomes **Bankastræti,** which ends as **Austurstræti.** The streets tend to have long names, and there isn't a grid system in place, but the city is small enough that you won't get too lost. **Hlemmur bus station** on the east end of Laugavegur is a main depot downtown for Strætó, the city bus company. It can connect you to just about anywhere in central and greater Reykjavík.

PLANNING YOUR TIME

Given its small size, Reykjavík can be experienced in 1-2 days depending on your level of interest. Some travelers treat Reykjavík as their starting point, given its proximity to **Keflavík International Airport,** before heading out on the **Ring Road** or booking day trips into the countryside, while others travel to Reykjavík specifically for the nightlife and art scene. The most central neighborhood in Reykjavík is the post code 101, which is close to shops, restaurants, bars, and landmarks.

Itinerary Ideas

THE BEST OF REYKJAVÍK

With quaint museums, cool music venues, and top-notch restaurants, small Reykjavík makes a big impression.

Reykjavík on Day 1

Explore downtown Reykjavík and all the shops, galleries, restaurants, and coffeehouses the city has to offer.

1 Walk down the street Skólavörðustígur to the landmark church **Hallgrímskirkja** to check out the amazing interior, beautiful organ, and view from the top.

2 Grab coffee or lunch on Skólavörðustígur at **Café Babalu,** which makes tasty lattes and light meals like crepes and panini.

3 Down the street, you can pick up a traditional Icelandic sweater at the **Handknitting Association of Iceland.**

Previous: colorful downtown Reykjavík; Hallgrímskirkja; coffee at Mál og Menning.

4 Walk down the main street, **Laugavegur,** and pop into Hrim store for Icelandic design and Mál og Menning for books, T-shirts, and other tourist wares.

5 Walk toward city hall and stroll around the man-made pond **Tjörnin,** where you can check out swans, ducks, and other birds.

6 For dinner, consider trendy **Fiskfelagid** for the freshest catch of the day.

7 Reykjavík nightlife is epic, and **Kiki Queer Bar** is perfect for checking out local DJs or live bands and dancing the night away.

Reykjavík on Day 2

Reykjavík's harbor has a lot to see.

1 Have breakfast at **Deig,** then watch boats enter the harbor.

2 Sign up for a whale-watching or bird-watching excursion with **Elding Whale Watching** for a chance to spot minke whales, dolphins, fin whales, blue whales, and seabirds (depending on the season).

3 Once back on land, walk to the **Saga Museum** to learn about Iceland's history and enjoy a coffee and snack or light meal at the in-house restaurant, Matur og Drykkur.

4 Walk over to **Harpa** concert hall to take in a concert or just check out the amazing interior and architecturally striking exterior.

5 Walk back downtown and explore the **Reykjavík Art Museum.**

6 Next have dinner at wildly popular sushi restaurant **Osushi.**

7 Stop by **Mengi** to hear some local live music.

Reykjavík Like a Local

1 Stop by **Mokka** café on Skólavörðustígur for breakfast—the waffles with homemade jam and fresh cream are delightful.

2 Go for a relaxing swim at **Laugardalslaug** and soak in a hot tub next to Icelanders.

3 Then visit Reykjavík's best record shops: Head to **12 Tónar,** and Lucky Records near Hlemmur Mathöll.

4 Check out **Hlemmer Mathöll,** a new food hall, for lunch and a drink: try Fuego for tacos and Skál! for a cocktail.

5 Head to **Perlan** for the exhibitions, then walk one of the trails by the museum, a wonderfully forested area that is a favorite among locals.

6 Take in a movie at **Bío Paradís,** Reykjavik's art house cinema.

7 Finish the day with dinner at **Gló.**

8 Start your night with drinks at **Bravó.**

Itinerary Ideas

© MOON.COM

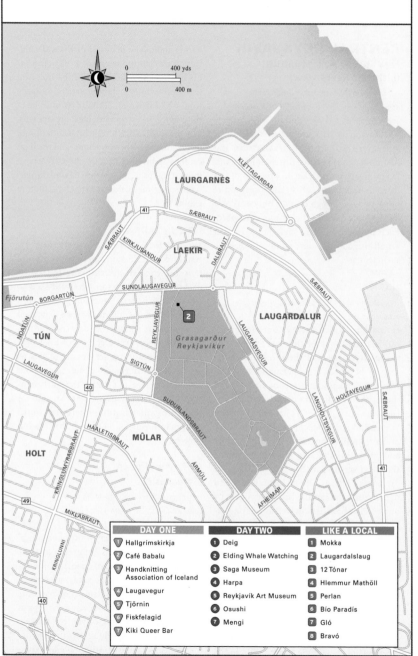

DAY ONE	DAY TWO	LIKE A LOCAL
1 Hallgrímskirkja	1 Deig	1 Mokka
2 Café Babalu	2 Elding Whale Watching	2 Laugardalslaug
3 Handknitting Association of Iceland	3 Saga Museum	3 12 Tónar
4 Laugavegur	4 Harpa	4 Hlemmur Mathöll
5 Tjörnin	5 Reykjavík Art Museum	5 Perlan
6 Fiskfelagid	6 Osushi	6 Bio Paradís
7 Kiki Queer Bar	7 Mengi	7 Gló
		8 Bravó

Sights

CENTRAL REYKJAVÍK
Reykjavík Art Museum
(Listasafn Reykjavíkur)

tel. 354/411-6410, https://artmuseum.is, 10am-5pm daily, adults 1,800ISK, students 1,100ISK, children and seniors free

The Reykjavík Art Museum is actually three museums (Hafnarhús, Kjarvalsstaðir, and Ásmundarsafn) in three different locations. If you purchase a ticket to any one of the three museums, you also gain access to the other two—although entry is only available on the same day your ticket was purchased. Each museum is fairly small, and you can hit all three in one day; an hour at each is sufficient.

HAFNARHÚS

Tryggvagata 17, tel. 354/590-1200, https://artmuseum.is

Hafnarhús, which focuses on contemporary art and has three floors of exhibitions, is the crown jewel of the three museums, in part because of its permanent collection of paintings and prints by Erró, one of the most celebrated modern Icelandic artists, who currently splits his time between France and Spain. His pieces displayed here range from light pop art with bright colors and interesting characters to samples of line sketches from his earlier work. While the art can be playful, Erró also tackles political and social issues. Hafnarhús also houses works by other Icelandic artists, as well as rotating exhibitions of foreign painters, designers, and visual artists.

KJARVALSSTAÐIR

Flókagata 24, tel. 354/517-1290, https://artmuseum.is

Kjarvalsstaðir explores the works of Icelandic painter Jóhannes Kjarval (1885-1972), best known for his dark and moody paintings of Iceland's landscapes. Kjarval was a master of capturing the country's raw nature in the winter light. The majority of Kjarval's collection was left to the city of Reykjavík after his death. The other wing of the museum features various Icelandic artists, ranging from well-known modern artists to some of the country's best and brightest art students. The museum is one level with a coffeehouse in the middle of the two wings, and the high ceilings and wall of windows here creates an interesting space. A large field behind the museum sometimes serves as a spot for sculpture exhibitions.

ÁSMUNDARSAFN

Sigtún 105, tel. 354/553-2155, https://artmuseum.is

Ásmundarsafn is an impressive sculpture museum exclusively featuring the works of Ásmundur Sveinsson (1893-1982), who worked with materials including wood, copper, and iron. Ásmundur's work is housed in a gorgeous stark-white domed building. An exhibit features a replica of his workshop and contains renderings of projects, as well as his masterpiece, a chair carved out of wood; the level of detail in the craftsmanship of the chair is spectacular. An outdoor sculpture garden features interesting works of human forms among trees, shrubs, and flowers.

Culture House
(Safnahúsið)

Hverfisgata 15, tel. 354/545-1400, www.culturehouse.is, 10am-5pm daily, adults 2,000ISK, students 1,000ISK, children free

Culture House is a stately white neoclassical building that opened as a museum in 1909. It is home to significant medieval manuscripts, including unique sagas, narratives, and poems from early settlers. Guided tours of exhibitions on Mondays and Fridays at 3pm last about an hour, or you can tour on your own. Rotating exhibitions throughout the year can include paintings, photography,

Reykjavík Walking Tour

Reykjavík is a small, walkable city with a lot to see. While spending at least one day in Reykjavík is recommended, you can see quite a bit in just an hour, which is approximately how long this walk takes without stops. It's ideal to complete this five-kilometer (three-mile) walking tour in the early afternoon, but monitor the weather and decide when it's best for you to go.

- Start your leisurely self-guided walking tour at **Hallgrímskirkja,** where you can explore the interior and head to the top of the tower for a fantastic view over the city.

- Then walk down Skólavörðustígur, the street directly across from the church entrance, to check out some quirky shops and cafés. **Café Babalu** is a nice stop on Skólavörðustígur for a cup of coffee and slice of dynamite carrot cake.

- Continue walking down Skólavörðustígur until you hit **Laugavegur,** the city's main drag and center of life in downtown Reykjavík, and turn left. Proceed until you meet Lækjargata street, where you'll turn left and head to **Tjörnin,** a pretty pond where you can watch ducks and swans.

- Walk clockwise around the perimeter on a pondside path, and loop past **Reykjavík City Hall** at the pond's northwest corner.

- Follow Tjarnargata street from here for one block, turning right on Kirkjustræti to see Iceland's Parliament House, **Alþingishúsið,** near Austurvöllur square.

- Then it's time to head toward the harbor; backtrack slightly the way you came, heading west down Kirkjustræti, and turn right onto Aðalstræti, continuing on it as it becomes Vesturgata. Turn right on Mjóstræti and left onto Tryggvagata, crossing the road here and heading east on Geirsgata. In about 400 meters (1,300 feet) you'll link up with the Sculpture & Shore Walk, a waterfront path that leads to **Harpa** concert hall, a striking architectural gem.

- After some time exploring the building or taking pictures, head 600 meters (2,000 feet) farther southeast along the waterfront walkway to see *Sólfar,* a popular sculpture and another excellent photo opportunity.

- Next, cross Sæbraut at the pedestrian crossing east of the sculpture and turn left onto Skúlagata, continuing about 150 meters (500 feet) until you see **Kex Hostel** on the right. Stop for a coffee, beer, snack, or chance to chat with locals and other tourists at this hip and wildly popular spot's bar and lounge area.

- Afterward, exit the hostel to the left and head south on Vitastígur for a couple of blocks, turning right back onto Laugavegur to check out more shops like **Hrím** design shop and **Mál og Menning** bookshop. You're back in the center of town and will soon connect with the portion of Laugavegur covered earlier in the walk.

or literary works. The exhibits do an excellent job of placing the manuscripts, literature, and artwork in context, giving visitors a great overview. Be sure to check the website to see what's on view. Culture House also plays host to conferences, gatherings, and readings throughout the year, including Reykjavík's annual design festival, DesignMarch, in the spring. The cafeteria serves light meals, and the traditional meat soup is delicious.

★ Hallgrímskirkja

Hallgrímstorg, tel. 354/510-1000, www. hallgrimskirkja.is, 9am-9pm daily May 28-Sept. 30, 9am-5pm daily Oct. 1-May 27

Hallgrímskirkja is one of the most photographed, and most visited, sites in Reykjavík. The "Church of Hallgrímur" is a national monument dedicated to Hallgrímur Pétursson (1614-1674), a poet cherished and celebrated by Icelanders. Hallgrímur is best known for 50 hymns that he wrote, *Hymns of*

Reykjavík

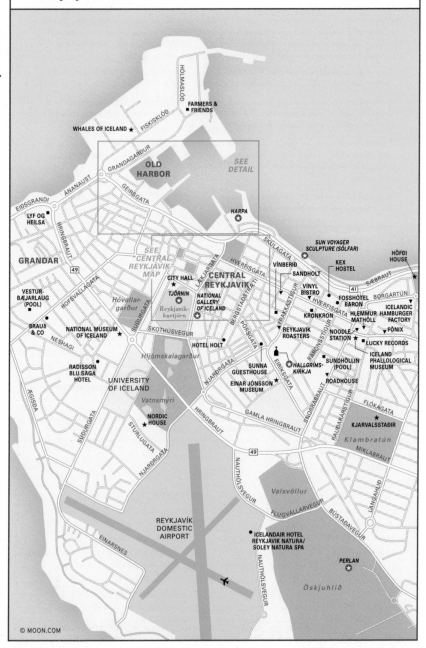

WHALES OF ICELAND ★

FARMERS &
FRIENDS ■

HÓLMASLÓÐ

FISKISLÓÐ

GRANDAGARÐUR

OLD
HARBOR

ANANAUST

SEE
DETAIL

GEIRSGATA

EIDSGRANDI

LYF OG ■
HEILSA

HRINGBRAUT

HARPA
✪

SUN VOYAGER
SCULPTURE (SÓLFAR)

SKÚLAGATA

HÖFDI
HOUSE ★

GRANDAR

49

HOFSVALLAGATA

SEE
CENTRAL
REYKJAVÍK
MAP

CITY HALL

LÆKJARGATA

HVERFISGATA

VÍNBERIÐ

CENTRAL
REYKJAVÍK

SANDHOLT

KEX
HOSTEL

SÆBRAUT

VESTUR-
BÆJARLAUG ■
(POOL)

SUDURGATA

TJÖRNIN
✪

NATIONAL
GALLERY
OF ICELAND

BERGSTAÐASTR.

VÍNYL
BISTRO ▼

41

FOSSHÓTEL
BARON

BORGARTÚN

Hóvallar-
garður

Reykjavík-
kurtjörn

ÞÓRSGATA

HVERFISGATA

HLEMMUR
MATHÖLL

ICELANDIC
HAMBURGER
FACTORY

BRAUÐ ●
& CO

NESHAGI

NATIONAL MUSEUM
OF ICELAND ★

SKOTHÚSVEGUR

KRONKRON

REYKJAVIK
ROASTERS ●

NOODLE
STATION ★

FÖNIX ▼

HOTEL HOLT ●

LUCKY RECORDS ■

Hljómskalagarður

NJARÐRGATA

ÆGISDA

RADISSON
BLU SAGA
HOTEL ●

SUÐURGATA

UNIVERSITY
OF ICELAND

Vatnsmýri

STURLUGATA

NJARÐRGATA

SUNNA
GUESTHOUSE ●

EINAR JÓNSSON
MUSEUM ★

HRINGBRAUT

EIRÍKSGATA

HALLGRÍMS-
KIRKJA ✪

BÁRÓNSSTÍGUR

SNORRABRAUT

SUNDHÖLLIN
(POOL)

ROADHOUSE

RAUÐARÁRSTÍGUR

ICELAND
PHALLOLOGICAL
MUSEUM

FLÓKAGATA

KJARVALSSTADIR ★

Klambratún

NORDIC ★
HOUSE

GAMLA HRINGBRAUT

49

MIKLABRAUT

SUÐURGATA

NAUTHÓLSVEGUR

REYKJAVÍK
DOMESTIC
AIRPORT

Valsvöllur

FLUGVALLARVEGUR

BÚSTAÐAVEGUR

LANGAHLÍÐ

EINARSNES

ICELANDAIR HOTEL ●
REYKJAVIK NATURA/
SOLEY NATURA SPA

PERLAN
✪

NAUTHÓLSVEGUR

Öskjuhlíð

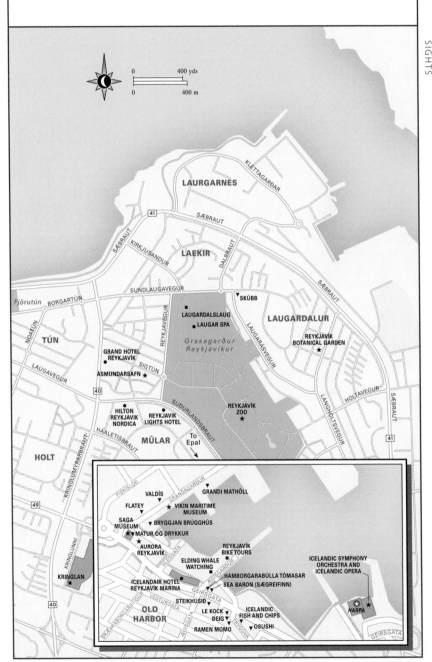

LAURGARNES

LAEKIR

SKÚBB

LAUGARDALUR

LAUGARDALSLAUG

LAUGAR SPA

Grasagarður
Reykjavíkur

REYKJAVÍK
BOTANICAL GARDEN

Fjörutún BORGARTÚN

TÚN

GRAND HOTEL
REYKJAVÍK

ASMUNDARSAFN

LAUGAVEGUR

REYKJAVÍK
ZOO

HILTON
REYKJAVIK
NORDICA

REYKJAVIK
LIGHTS HOTEL

MÚLAR

To
Epal

HOLT

HOLTAVEGUR

VALDÍS

GRANDI MATHÖLL

FLATEY

VIKIN MARITIME
MUSEUM

SAGA
MUSEUM

BRYGGJAN BRÜGGHÚS

MATUR OG DRYKKUR

AURORA
REYKJAVÍK

REYKJAVÍK
BIKE TOURS

ELDING WHALE
WATCHING

ICELANDIC SYMPHONY
ORCHESTRA AND
ICELANDIC OPERA

KRINGLAN

ICELANDAIR HOTEL
REYKJAVÍK MARINA

HAMBORGARABÚLLA TÓMASAR

SEA BARON (SÆGREIFINN)

STEIKHÚSID

OLD
HARBOR

LE KOCK

DEIG

ICELANDIC
FISH AND CHIPS

RAMEN MOMO

OSUSHI

HARPA

GEIRSGATA

Central Reykjavík

GARDASTRÆTI

TÚNGATA

OLDUGATA

BRÁÐGATA

NÝLENDUGATA

SUDURGATA

HRANNARGATA

GARDASTRÆTI

HRANNARGATA

MJOSSTRÆTI

REYKJAVÍK MUSEUM OF PHOTOGRAPHY ★

STOFAN CAFÉ ▼

FISCHERSUND

FISCHER ▼

TAPAS BARINN ▼

FISKFELAGID ▼

HAFNARHÚS/ HARBOR HOUSE ★

FISH MARKET ■

CENTRUM PLAZA HOTEL ●

RESTAURANT REYKJAVÍK ▼

Ingólfstorg

HLOLLABÁTAR ▼

THE VIKING ▲

GRILLHÚSID ▼

REYKJAVÍK CITY HALL ★

ADALTRÆTI

VALLARSTRÆTI

AUSTURSTRÆTI

NAUSTIN

VÍKINGSTRÆTI

HÓFSVALLAGATA

Reykjavíkurtjörn

HARNARGATA

ALPINGISHÚSID ★

Alpingisgarðurinn

KIRKJUSTRÆTI

MICRO BAR ■

EYMUNDSSON ■

THE ENGLISH PUB ▲

PÓSTHÚSSTRÆTI

B.ÆJARINS BEZTU PYLSUR (THE TOWN'S BEST HOT DOGS) ●

KOLAPORTID ■

0   300 yds
0   300 m

TJÖRNIN

VONARSTRÆTI

TEMPLARASUND

BERGSSON MATHÚS ■

KVOSIN HOTEL ●

KIRKJUTORG

SKÓLABRÚ

HOTEL BORG ●

ICELANDIC BAR ■

THE SECRET CELLAR ■

HRESSINGARSKÁLINN HRESSO ▼

GRILLMARKET (GRILLMARKAÐURINN) ▼

RADISSON BLU 1919 HOTEL ●

HORNID ▼

GANDHI RESTAURANT ▼

GERÐSGATA

41

41

FRIKIRKJUVEGUR

NATIONAL GALLERY OF ICELAND (LISTASAFN ÍSLANDS) ★

LAUFÁSVEGUR

SKÁLHOLTSSTÍGUR

BÓKHLÖDUSTÍGUR

MIDSTRÆTI

ÞINGHOLTSSTRÆTI

LÆKJARGATA

MESSINN ■

CENTRAL REYKJAVÍK

THE LOBSTER HOUSE ▼

LÆKJARBREKKA ▼

SKÓLSTRÆTI

ANTMANNSSTÍGUR

BANKASTRÆTI

Lækjartorg

Arnarhóll

LINDARGATA

CINTAMANI ●

AURUM ■

ICELANDIC OPERA ★

SKÓLAVÖRÐUSTÍGUR

BERGSTADSTRÆTI

INGÓLFSSTRÆTI

HALLVEIGARSTÍGUR

REYKJAVÍK4YOU APARTMENTS ●

SUSHI SOCIAL ▼

KAFFITÁR ▼

LOFT HOSTEL ★

101 HOTEL ●

SUSHIBARINN ▼

ELDUR OG ÍS ▼

MOKKA ■

66° NORTH ●

CULTURE HOUSE ★

ÞJÓÐMENNINGARHÚSID

INGÓLFSSTRÆTI

MENGI ▲

BASTARD BREW & FOOD ▼

KAFFIBARINN ▼

ÍTALÍA ▼

THE LITTLE CHRISTMAS SHOP ●

NATIONAL THEATER OF ICELAND ★

ÞJÓÐLEIKHÚSID

HVERFISGATA

SMIÐJUSTÍGUR

SÖLVHÓLSGATA

GEYSIR ■

YEOMAN ▼

12 TÓNAR ■

MAL OG MENNING ■

ROOM WITH A VIEW ●

VÉBUD ▼

TÝSGATA

SKÓLAVÖRÐUSTÍGUR

VEGAMÓTASTÍGUR

REYKJAVÍK RECORD SHOP ■

GLÓ ▼

BLUE LAGOON ●

HOTEL KLOPP ●

CAFÉ BABALÚ ▼

HANDPRJÓNASAMBAND ÍSLANDS ■

GARÐURINN ▼

LEBOWSKI BAR ▲

KIKI QUEER BAR ▲

SÚMAC GRILL + DRINKS ▼

BRAVÓ ▲

SPÚTNIK ■

HOTEL FRON ●

KRIA THAI ▼

BOSTON ▲

DILLON ▲

HRÍM ■

PUBLIC HOUSE GASTROPUB ▼

SMEKKLEYSA (BAD TASTE) RECORD ■

KLAPPARSTÍGUR

GRETTISGATA

41

41

LAUGAVEGUR

FRAKKASTÍGUR

VATNSSTÍGUR

BARÓNSSTÍGUR

© MOON.COM

the *Passion,* about the passion of Christ. These hymns are familiar to all Icelanders, and are read annually on Icelandic radio before Easter. The church is a modern structure, made out of concrete, with basalt-style columns at the bottom coming to a point at the top. Standing 73 meters (240 feet), the Lutheran church was designed by state architect Guðjón Samúelsson. Work started on the building in 1945, and was completed in 1986. Still an active church that holds services, Hallgrímskirkja is a must-see for tourists. The interior is home to a gorgeous organ constructed by Johannes Klais Organworks in Germany, as well as beautiful stained glass windows. Concerts ranging from choirs to organ performances are frequently held; be sure to check the website for upcoming concerts. An annual Christmas concert features traditional songs sung in English.

The highlight of a trip to Hallgrímskirkja for many is a visit to the top of the **tower** (1,000ISK), which has spectacular views of the city. An elevator takes you up.

Einar Jónsson Museum

Eiríksgata 3, tel. 354/561-3797, www.lej.is, 10am-5pm Tue-Sun, 1,000ISK, free for children under 18

This Museum houses the works of one of Iceland's most celebrated sculptors, Einar Jónsson (1874-1954). Situated across the street from Hallgrímskirkja, the museum features work ranging from Christian-themed sculptures to those depicting Iceland's rich folklore. Einar worked almost entirely with plaster, which was rare for the period. The outdoor sculpture garden is beautiful, whether the sun is shining or if it is under a layer of snow. The garden makes the museum a very special visit. Plan to spend about an hour checking out the art inside, and if the weather is nice, spend additional time outside in the garden.

Icelandic Phallological Museum
(Hið Íslenzka Reðasafn)

Laugavegur 116, tel. 354/561-6663, www.phallus.is, 10am-6pm daily, 1,700ISK

The Icelandic Phallological Museum is just as weird as it sounds. Guests can view the penises of 200 animals, including the arctic fox, walrus, seal, and polar bear. After the museum was moved to its current location in Reykjavík (from Húsavík in North Iceland) in 2011, the curator unveiled his latest acquisition—a human member. The museum has members on display in glass cases, and preserved bones of certain mammals are hanging on the wall. The highlight is also a unique photo op: the huge whale specimen on display. Some people find the museum humorous, while others are a bit freaked out. Looking for unique postcards, T-shirts, and souvenirs? Look no further.

National Museum of Iceland
(Þjóðminjasafn Íslands)

Suðurgata 41, tel. 354/530-2200, www.nationalmuseum.is, 10am-5pm daily, 2,000ISK

Reykjavík's main heritage and history museum houses everything from tools and clothing of the settlement era to models of Viking-era ships. This is the best museum in the city to get insight on the history of the Icelandic nation and its people. The artifacts and exhibitions are well presented with clear information in English. Budget about two hours to take in all the exhibits.

Nordic House
(Norræna Húsið)

Sturlugata 5, tel. 354/551-7030, www.nordichouse.is, 10am-5pm daily, free

Nordic House is home to a library, café, and numerous cultural events during the year. Literary and film festivals are held at the building, as well as fashion and music events. Most tourists visit Nordic House for the structure itself. The building, which was opened in 1968, was designed by noted Finnish architect Alvar Aalto, and several of his signature traits are reflected in the design, including the use of tile, white, and wood throughout the building. The one-story building's exterior features a blue ceramic roof.

Reykjavík Museum of Photography
(Ljósmyndasafn Reykjavíkur)

Tryggvagata 15, tel. 354/563-1790, www.
photomuseum.is, 10am-6pm Mon.-Thur., 11am-6pm
Fri., 1pm-5pm Sat.-Sun., 1,000ISK

The Reykjavík Museum of Photography has an extensive collection of photographs, as well as items and documents related to the practice of photography, from professional and amateur photographers in Iceland. The collection is divided into three categories: landscape, press, and portrait photography. The museum is small, but there are a lot of treasures to be found, including the oldest photo in the museum's collection, a landscape photo dating from 1870. Iceland's most famous landscape photographer, Ragnar Axelsson, regularly has photos on exhibit.

★ National Gallery of Iceland
(Listasafn Íslands)

Fríkirkjuvergur 7, tel. 354/515-9600, www.listasafn.is,
10am-5pm daily, 2,000ISK

If you have time for only one art museum, make it the National Gallery of Iceland. The National Gallery has a large and varied collection, and houses the country's main Icelandic art. It places particular emphasis on 19th- and 20th-century Icelandic and international art. Here you will see everything from traditional landscape paintings to art depicting the sagas to works by modern Icelandic artists. Works from international artists on display include some from Pablo Picasso and Richard Serra. The stately white building is a stone's throw from Tjörnin (the Pond), so if the weather is fair, taking a leisurely stroll after visiting the museum is quite nice.

Reykjavík City Hall
(Ráðhús Reykjavíkur)

Tjarnagata 11, tel. 354/411-1111, www.visitreykjavik.is,
8:30am-4:30pm daily

Reykjavík City Hall is more than just a building that houses the mayor and other officials. Built in 1992, the large white structure has a wall of windows overlooking the Pond. On the ground floor, visitors will find a large hall that is often used for art exhibitions and markets, and a huge model of Iceland is a favorite among tourists and worth a visit.

★ Tjörnin
next to Reykjavík City Hall

Tjörnin (the Pond) is a small body of water, rich with birdlife, situated next to Reykjavík City Hall. The scenic strip of colorful houses surrounding the Pond begs to be photographed. When the weather is nice, a walk around the Pond, which is about 1.5 kilometers (1 mile) around, is delightful. Sculptures and benches dot the perimeter. Birdlife is plentiful, with arctic terns, ducks, gulls, and swans. Feeding the birds is not allowed, so don't be that tourist who empties a bag of stale bread at the edge. In the winter, the water freezes and it becomes a popular spot for ice-skating.

Alþingishúsið

Alþingishúsið, or Parliament House, is the meeting place of the national parliament members of Iceland. Iceland's democracy dates back to the year 930, when parliament members met at Þingvellir; the parliament was moved to Reykjavík in 1844. Situated near Austurvöllur park, the stone building was designed by Danish architect Ferdinand Meldahland and built in 1881. Currently, only the debating chamber and a few small meeting rooms are actually located in the building. Offices of most of Alþingi's members are in other buildings in the area around Austurvöllur, which is actually the address of the building. It's not possible to attend sessions of parliament.

OLD HARBOR (GRANDI)

Reykjavík's old harbor has been undergoing a transformation over the past few years, and it's become a dynamic place to visit, with

1: Reykjavík Lighthouse 2: view of the Reykjavík harbor from Harpa 3: Hallgrímskirkja 4: the National Gallery of Iceland and Tjörnin

shops, museums, new hotels, and the Ólafur Elíasson-designed Harpa concert hall.

Saga Museum

Grandagardi 2, tel. 354/511-1517, www.sagamuseum. is, 10am-6pm daily, 2,200ISK

The Saga Museum has 17 exhibits covering everything from Iceland's first inhabitants to the nation's conversion to Christianity to the Reformation. Special emphasis is placed on important characters in Iceland's history, such as Ingólfur Arnarson, who is believed to have been Iceland's first settler. There are interactive displays and artifacts on view and even a Viking dress-up area that is great for kids. An audio guide in English, German, French, or Swedish is available to accompany your walk around the museum. The in-house restaurant, **Matur og Drykkur,** serves traditional Icelandic food with a modern twist. Budget two hours for this museum.

★ Harpa

Austurbakki 2, tel. 354/528-5000, www.harpa.is, 9am-10pm daily

A striking glass structure, Harpa hosts rock concerts, operas, the Icelandic Symphony, and international conferences. Designed by Icelandic-Danish artist Ólafur Elíasson, the hall's exterior features individual glass panels that light up during the darkness of winter, sometimes blinking in a pattern or simply changing colors, and the building's waterside location lends itself to lovely reflections. Since opening its doors in 2011, Harpa has been lauded by design organizations and magazines around the world. Daily 30-minute guided tours of the building are available (1,750ISK, year-round) six times a day mid-June-August and three times a day from the end of August to mid-June. It's also just a fun place to explore and take pictures of, even if you're not going to attend a concert or conference. **Bergmál** (10am-6pm daily), a café on the bottom floor, serves coffee, soft drinks, light meals, and cakes, and **Kolabrautin** (5pm-10pm daily), a formal restaurant on the 4th floor, has stunning views of the harbor.

Höfði House

Borgartún 105

Höfði House (Borgartún) is one of Reykjavík's most historically significant buildings and worth a photo or two. Built in 1909, the stately white building was initially used as the French consulate, and later served as a sort of guesthouse for famous folks passing through including Winston Churchill, Queen Elizabeth II, and even actress Marlene Dietrich. Perhaps its most famous use was as the backdrop for a 1986 meeting between U.S. president Ronald Reagan and the head of the Soviet Union, Mikhail Gorbachev. Today, Höfði is owned by the city of Reykjavík and is used for official receptions and meetings. Although the house is not open to the public, visitors are welcome to explore the exterior of the building.

★ Sun Voyager Sculpture (Sólfar)

Sæbraut

Situated near a coastal path popular with cyclists and runners, *Sólfar* (by Sæbraut Street) is a huge stainless steel sculpture described as a dreamboat. Before Harpa was built, *Sólfar* was the top spot to take photos near the harbor. It remains a big draw for tourists and is definitely worth a visit. Icelandic sculptor Jón Gunnar Árnason (1931-1989) wanted to convey a sense of undiscovered territory, hope, progress, and freedom, and built the piece as an ode to the sun, hence the name. The sculpture was unveiled in 1990, just months after the artist's death. The view of Mount Esja, the sea, and passing boats is a perfect backdrop for photos. On clear days, you can see the town of Akranes across the bay.

Reykjavík Lighthouse

Sæbraut

A small bright yellow lighthouse was built near *Sólfar* in 2019. The lighthouse has become a tourist attraction since opening, but it has an official function to guide sailors coming into the harbor. It sits on a platform that overlooks the water, and it's a lovely spot to take photos.

Aurora Reykjavík

Grandagarður 2, tel. 354/780-4500, www.

aurorareykjavik.is, 9am-9pm daily, 1,800ISK

Aurora Reykjavík gives you a chance to check out northern lights in any season. If you can't make it to Iceland in the wintertime, this is the next best thing. The multimedia exhibition gives a history of the aurora borealis, relates stories of northern lights from around the world, and provides an introduction to northern lights photography. The highlight of the center is a 13-minute film that shows some of the most majestic northern lights displays over the island.

Viking Maritime Museum

Grandargarður 8, tel. 354/517-9400, www.

borgarsgusafn.is, 10am-5pm daily, 1,700ISK

Vikin Maritime Museum is Reykjavík's main museum devoted to the city's fishing history. The exhibitions show the progression from rowboats to modern trawlers and describe the vessels used, trading routes, and the construction of Reykjavík's harbor. There are daily tours of the coastal vessel *Odinn* available at 11am, 1pm, 2pm, and 3pm that last about an hour. The exhibitions cover the city's fishing history from the settlement to the present day. The museum café has great views of the harbor and offers an outdoor eating area when the weather cooperates.

Whales of Iceland

Fiskislóð 23-25, tel. 354/571-0077, www.

whalesoficeland.is, 10am-5pm daily, adults 2,900ISK,

children 7-15 1,500ISK, children under 7 free

Whales of Iceland is a large museum near the harbor dedicated to Iceland's gentle giants. The museum is home to 23 life-size models of different whale species found off the coasts of Iceland. There are also interactive displays where you can learn about the whales, and a film. There's a small café inside for snacks.

OUTSIDE THE CITY CENTER

Reykjavík Zoo

(Fjölskyldu- og Húsdýragarðinum)

Laugardalur, tel. 354/575-7800, www.mu.is,

10am-6pm daily June-late Aug., 10am-5pm daily

late Aug.-May, 900ISK adults and teenagers, 680ISK

children 5-12, children 4 and under free

The Reykjavík Zoo is more park than zoo. You won't see monkeys or polar bears, but instead horses, pigs, goats, sheep, and other farm animals. The main attraction is a pair of seals. It's a pleasant place to walk around and bring children, but it isn't much of a tourist destination; if you're not on a long trip with small children, you can skip the zoo and not feel bad about it. Inside is a tiny aquarium that houses mainly fish. In the summer months, you'll see Icelandic families taking a stroll, looking at the animals, and visiting a small play area for children. There isn't an official petting zoo, but it's common to see parents holding their children up to pet horses in a penned area.

Reykjavík Botanical Garden (Grasagardur Reykjavíkur)

Laugardalur, tel. 354/411-8650, www.grasagardur.

is, 10am-10pm daily May 1-Sept. 30, 10am-3pm daily

Oct. 1-Apr. 30, free

The Reykjavík Botanical Garden is a beautiful spot tucked away in a quiet part of the city. East of downtown Reykjavík, the neighborhood is more residential. During the summer months, the garden is chock-full of bright flowers, hardy plants, peaceful ponds, and thriving birdlife. The café within the garden, Café Flora, is a little-known spot among tourists. You will find locals sipping on coffee drinks and enjoying light meals while taking in the view from grand windows. If you're not visiting in the summer, you can skip the garden.

★ Perlan

Öskjuhlíð, tel. 354/562-0200, www.perlan.is,

9am-10pm daily

Perlan, "the Pearl," is the distinctive, dome-shaped structure in Reykjavík's skyline. It offers one of the best views of the city skyline from its **outdoor viewing platform** (9am-10pm daily, 890ISK), where you can walk the perimeter and get a perfect panorama. The interior underwent a significant renovation in 2017, and the public building now hosts exhibits (3,990ISK), kicked off by an installation on glaciers and ice caves. There is also a planetarium and northern lights exhibition in the building as well as a café that serves coffee and light meals and a souvenir shop.

Sports and Recreation

WHALE-WATCHING, BIRDWATCHING, AND FISHING

ELDING WHALE WATCHING

Ægisgarður 5, tel. 354/519-5000, www.elding.is, year-round, tours adults 10,990ISK, children 7-15 5,495ISK, children 6 and under free

Whale-watching is in some ways the best part of natural Reykjavík, in that you get to see a slice of nature just minutes from shore. Elding Whale Watching, which has 12 boats in Reykjavík, offers tours year-round and boasts a 95-percent chance of seeing whales in the summer, and 80 percent chance in the winter. Guides are enthusiastic, and the business is one of the oldest at the harbor. Tourists relish the sightings of minke and humpback whales, dolphins, porpoises, and various seabirds, including puffins and arctic terns. Make sure you dress warmly, even in the summer, as it can get quite cold on the open waters. Tours are about three hours, and the company has environmentally responsible whale-watching policies.

For sea angling tours, Elding Whale Watching offers a tour with a "gourmet" twist, where you can cook and eat your catch on board the boat. The tour is available May 1-Sept 20. The tour is about three hours, departs daily from Reykjavík harbor, and costs 14,900ISK.

SPECIAL TOURS

Ægisgarður 13, tel. 354/560-8800, www.specialtours. is, year-round, 10,990ISK per person, one-hour boat tour adults 5,900ISK, children 2,995ISK

Special Tours has a fleet of five boats of different speeds and sizes and runs year-round tours from Reykjavík harbor, with five daily departures May-August and 1-2 daily departures the remainder of the year. Tours are about three hours, and the company also has environmentally responsible whale-watching policies.

For bird-watchers, the "Puffin Express" tour, which leaves from Reykjavík harbor May through mid-August, is operated by Special Tours. The owners have been running bird-watching tours since 1996, provide binoculars on board, and the company says they have a 100-percent sighting success rate. The guides have a soft spot for the funny black and white birds with the brilliant beaks and take great pride in telling you all about them.

BIKING

REYKJAVÍK BIKE TOURS

Ægisgarður 7, tel. 354/694-8956, www.icelandbike. com, bike rentals start at 3,500ISK for 4 hours

Reykjavík is a wonderful city to see by bicycle—that is, when the weather holds up. Over the past few years, there has been an initiative to designate more bike lanes and establish more places to lock up your bicycle along the streets. This isn't Amsterdam, but Reykjavík has come a long way. If you're in town and would like to rent a bike for an independent ride, or join a tour, Reykjavík Bike Tours will get you going. Its "Classic Reykjavík Bike Tour" (7,500ISK) covers about seven kilometers (four miles) and takes a good 2.5 hours. Along the tour, you will see the University of Iceland campus, Reykjavík's Catholic cathedral, the parliament house, the old harbor, and more.

Walking Tours for Everyone

Reykjavík is a compact capital city, perfect for walking tours. A number of niche tours have popped up in recent years.

- **The Pub Crawl** (www.citywalk.is, 2,500ISK) is a three-hour tour that takes you to three top watering holes in city center. The tour doesn't include drinks but offers a 20-30 percent discount and happy hour deals on beer, wine, shots, and cocktails. Please note that the drinking age is 20 in Iceland.

- Foodies will rejoice over the **Reykjavik Food Walk** (www.thereykjavikfoodwalk.com, 13,900ISK), where you get to see landmarks of the city while sampling food at five or six Icelandic restaurants. During the tour you will get to taste local lamb, fish, cheeses, homemade ice cream, and Iceland's famous hot dogs.

- Local music journalist and radio host Arnar Eggert Thoroddsen runs the popular **Reykjavík Music Walk** (www.reykjavikmusicwalk.arnareggert.is, 4,800ISK) that focuses on Reykjavík's pop and rock history. Guests will get to see music venues, artist hangouts, practice spaces, and other landmarks important to an array of musicians including Björk and Sigur Rós.

- The **Reykjavík Queer City Walk** (www.funkyiceland.is, 4,500ISK) is a fun 90-minute walking tour that gives insight into the LGBTQ history of Iceland. You will learn about the struggle for LGBTQ rights, visit important landmarks like Kiki Queer Bar, and stop by the permanent street rainbow in the heart of downtown.

- The free 90-minute **Old Harbor Brewery Tour** (www.freewalkingtour.is) takes you to explore and learn about the old harbor area of Reykjavík before visiting Ægir Brewery, where you can try a selection of craft beers. Please note that the drinking age in Iceland is 20.

- The **Icelandic Mythical Walk** (www.yourfriendinreykjavik.com, 3,900ISK) gives you a chance to learn about Icelandic sagas, and the stories of elves and trolls that have been passed down over the centuries. You will visit two graveyards, see an elf stone, and learn about the 13 Santas of Iceland (the Yule Lads).

SWIMMING

Swimming is a central part of Icelandic culture, and if you don't visit a pool or two during your stay in Iceland, you're missing out. Icelanders treat the pools as places for social gatherings. You'll see friends and families in the pools and relaxing in hot tubs, chatting, laughing, and catching up. Each pool has its own character and local flavor, and some pools are more child-friendly than others, with slides and bigger areas designated for children. And, for roughly $5, it's a great way to spend a few leisurely hours. The pools listed here are recommended.

LAUGARDALSLAUG

Sundlaugavegur 30, tel. 354/411-5100, 6:30am-10pm Mon.-Fri., 8am-10pm Sat.-Sun., 1,000ISK

Laugardalslaug is the biggest pool facility in Reykjavík, and the one that gets the most tourists. The heated 50-meter (164-foot) outdoor pool is a big draw, along with the hot tubs, steam bath, and sauna. It's very crowded in the summer months (June-August) and can be loud because the giant waterslide in the children's pool is a favorite among local kids.

SUNDHÖLLIN

Barónstígur, tel. 354/551-4059, 6:30am-10pm Mon.-Fri., 8am-10pm Sat.-Sun., 1,000ISK

The only indoor pool in Reykjavík is popular among locals and tourists alike. The outdoor sundeck overlooking Hallgrímskirkja is a great spot to spend a couple of hours when the sun is shining. Sundhöllin also has a steam room and two hot tubs. Given its proximity to the city center, the pool gets a lot of traffic.

VESTURBÆJARLAUG

Hofsvallagata 104, tel. 354/566-6879, 6:30am-10pm Mon.-Fri., 8am-10pm Sat.-Sun., 1,000ISK
Vesturbæjarlaug is situated in a quiet neighborhood west of the city center. If you're looking to beat the crowds and experience the pool culture among locals, this is the spot. Facilities include a 25-meter (82-foot) pool, a few hot tubs, and a sauna.

SPAS

If you're after something more luxurious than a local swimming pool, there are a couple of spas in Reykjavík where you can relax and get treatments. Many tourists opt to spend an afternoon at the **Blue Lagoon** near Grindavík, and several buses depart from the bus station BSÍ (www.bsi.is). But if you want to beat the crowds, a local spa is a great option.

LAUGAR SPA

Sundlaugavegur 30A, tel. 354/553-0000, www.laugarspa.is, 6am-11pm Mon.-Fri., 8am-9:30pm Sat.-Sun., 5,500ISK
Laugar Spa is Reykjavík's largest private spa, offering an extensive menu of treatments including facials, body massage and scrub, tanning treatments, waxing and nail services,
and clay wrap treatments. The spa is marketed as an "aquatic heaven," and it's as good as it sounds. The entrance to the spa is reminiscent of a cave, with the soothing sound of water drops falling from a six-meter-wide (20-foot) waterfall. Inside, six sauna rooms are kept at different temperatures, each with its own unique theme. The treatment rooms feature muted hues and calming music. There is an on-site gym, as well as a café serving fresh, healthy meals.

SOLEY NATURA SPA

Nautholsvegur 2, tel. 354/444-4085, www.icelandairhotels.com, 10am-8pm Mon.-Fri., 10am-7pm Sat., noon-5pm Sun., hotel guests 3,000ISK, nonguests 4,900ISK
Icelandair Hótel Reykjavík Natura's Soley Natura Spa has an earthy atmosphere with natural hues and lots of wood furnishings. Guests have access to a heated pool, hot tub, and sauna before and after treatments. Massage options include lymphatic massage, hot stone massage, reflexology, and pregnancy massage. Beauty treatments include waxing services, manicures and pedicures, and facials. Access is 3,000ISK for hotel guests, 4,900ISK for nonguests. The spa is only open to guests 16 years of age and older.

Entertainment and Events

PERFORMING ARTS

ICELANDIC OPERA
(Íslenska Óperan)

Ingólfsstræti 2A, tel. 354/511-6400, www.opera.is
The Icelandic Opera has been thriving since productions moved in 2011 to the exquisite Harpa concert hall by the harbor. Productions have become more elaborate, and entire runs have been selling out. If you are an opera fan, check the website to see the current and upcoming shows. Past performances include *Carmen*, *Il Trovatore*, *La Boheme*, and *The Magic Flute*.

ICELANDIC SYMPHONY
ORCHESTRA
(Sinfóníuhljómsveit Íslands)

Austurbakki 2, tel. 354/545-2500, www.sinfonia.is
The Icelandic Symphony Orchestra consists of 90 full-time members and performs about 60 concerts each season, including subscription concerts in Reykjavík, family concerts, school concerts, and recordings, as well as local and international tours. Based in the Harpa concert hall, the symphony has performed works by Igor Stravinsky, Sergei Rachmaninoff, and Pyotr Tchaikovsky.

NATIONAL THEATER OF ICELAND
(Þjóðleikhúsið)

Hverfisgata 19, tel. 354/551-1200, www.leikhusid.is

The National Theater of Iceland has been a Reykjavík mainstay since its opening in 1950. The emphasis is on Nordic and Scandinavian plays and musicals, but some foreign works are translated into Icelandic. In 2019, the theater put on productions of *The Great Dictator* and *A Midsummer Night's Dream* in the 500-seat main stage. The exterior is a cold, concrete-gray building, but inside is a different story. The interior is modern, the theater is comfortable, and there's a lovely lounge area with plush seats and small tables where you can have a drink and wait for the show to begin.

THE SECRET CELLAR

Lækjargata 6a, 7pm-1am Sun.-Thur., 7pm-3am Fri.-Sat.

The Secret Cellar, Reykjavík's first and only comedy club, features nightly performances in English. Comedy in English is very new to Iceland, but the club draws a lot of Icelanders, so it's not strictly for tourists. Shows start at 9pm, happy hour begins at 8pm, and karaoke is nightly at 11pm to closing. Performers include Icelandic comedians, immigrants, and visitors, and this is a great night out in Reykjavík. Come for the comedy and stay for the karaoke.

FESTIVALS AND EVENTS

Spring

DESIGNMARCH
(HönnunarMars)

www.designmarch.is

Coinciding with the Reykjavík Fashion Festival is DesignMarch, a broader event that covers everything from product design to graphic design. With pop-up stores around the city and exhibitions held in museums and open-air spaces, the festival attracts people from around the world to check out the latest and greatest in Icelandic design.

REYKJAVÍK BLUES FESTIVAL
(Blúshátíð í Reykjavík)

www.blues.is

You may not expect Reykjavík to be a blues town, but don't tell that to locals. The Reykjavík Blues Festival is a weeklong event held in early April. It mixes local talent with acclaimed international acts like Michael Burks, Lucky Peterson, Pinetop Perkins, and Magic Slim and the Teardrops.

EVE FANFEST

www.fanfest.eveonline.com

Gamers rejoice! The EVE Fanfest takes over the city every April or May, celebrating the beloved video game *EVE,* which is the creation of local company CCP. Thousands of gamers and curious locals gather, attend roundtable discussions, play live tournaments, and indulge in a pub crawl.

REYKJAVÍK INTERNATIONAL LITERARY FESTIVAL

www.bokmenntahatid.is/en

Every April, Reykjavík celebrates local and international authors during this five-day festival. The program includes discussions, readings, workshops, meet and greets, and lectures. Past participants have included Maja Lunde, Ian Reid, Yoko Tawada, and Hallgrímur Helgason.

Summer

REYKJAVÍK ARTS FESTIVAL
(Listahátíð í Reykjavík)

www.artfest.is

Delighting locals and tourists since 1970, the Reykjavík Arts Festival manages to keep the program fresh, showcasing visual and performance artists from around the globe. The festival spans two weeks over late May and early June and holds events in different cultural venues as well as outdoor exhibitions.

REYKJAVÍK PRIDE
(Hinsegin Dagar)
www.hinsegindagar.is/en

Reykjavík Pride is a citywide celebration of human rights, diversity, and culture. It garners a huge turnout every year. Each August, the city hosts rainbow-themed events ranging from concerts to guest speakers. It's known as the highest-profile event for Iceland's gay, lesbian, bisexual, and transgender community. Hundreds of volunteers organize the event, and people from around the country congregate to celebrate their fellow citizens.

REYKJAVÍK JAZZ FESTIVAL
(Jazzhátíð Reykjavíkur)
www.reykjavikjazz.is

Since 1990, the Reykjavík Jazz Festival has been delighting horn section enthusiasts. International artists like Aaron Parks and Chris Speed are invited to put on concerts and jam with locals over five days in mid-August. There are off-venue free events throughout the city for this popular festival among the locals. Headline concerts take place at the concert hall Harpa.

REYKJAVÍK DANCE FESTIVAL
www.reykjavikdancefestival.com

Independent choreographers launched the Reykjavík Dance Festival in 2002, and the annual event is still going strong today. The focus is on bringing contemporary dance closer to the people. The weeklong event held every August showcases local talent as well as international dancers.

REYKJAVÍK CULTURE NIGHT
(Menningarnótt)
www.culturenight.is

Reykjavík Culture Night has the darling slogan "come on in," which is a reference to the island's old-fashioned customs of hospitality. Culture Night actually starts during the day, with select residents opening up their properties to offer waffles and coffee to their neighbors and visitors. Hundreds of events around the city range from cultural performances to free museum events. The festival culminates with a huge outdoor concert that features some of the biggest names in Icelandic rock and pop music. It's held at the end of August.

SECRET SOLSTICE
www.secretsolstice.is

Each June, during the summer solstice, locals and tourists descend on downtown Reykjavík for a weekend of music and fun. Past international headliners include the Foo Fighters, the Black Eyed Peas, Robert Plant, Radiohead, Slayer, and Wu-Tang Clan. You can always count on impressive local artists as well, including Gus Gus, Agent Fresco, Samaris, and FM Belfast.

Fall
REYKJAVÍK INTERNATIONAL FILM FESTIVAL
www.riff.is

Beginning at the end of September, the Reykjavík International Film Festival takes place over 11 days, during which films from more than 40 countries are screened. They range from short films to full-length features and documentaries, and the festival is a great venue to discover new talent. Invited special guests have included American director Jim Jarmusch, English director Mike Leigh, and American actor John Hawkes.

ICELAND AIRWAVES
www.icelandairwaves.is

Iceland Airwaves has been delighting music lovers since 1999. The five-day festival, held in late October/early November, has hosted an impressive list of performers, including Sigur Rós, Björk, and Of Monsters and Men, as well as international artists including Robyn, Kraftwerk, and The Flaming Lips. There are also off-venue performances held for free in bars, bookstores, record shops, and coffeehouses—so if you don't score tickets to the festival, you can still check out some amazing

1: rainbow road for Reykjavík Pride 2: Winter Lights Festival 3: Reykjavík Culture Night

music. A detailed off-venue schedule is published along with on-venue appearances.

Winter
REYKJAVÍK FOOD & FUN FESTIVAL
www.foodandfun.is
This annual food festival showcases the culinary exploits of world-renowned chefs collaborating with local Icelandic chefs. There are competitions, exhibitions, and lots of eating. It takes place at the end of February.

WINTER LIGHTS FESTIVAL
www.winterlightsfestival.is
Reykjavík is lit up during the dark winter days and nights of February with outdoor light exhibits as well as concerts, art exhibitions, workshops, and discussions.

Shopping

Reykjavík may not strike you as a shopping destination, but there are quite a few local brands, like clothing labels 66 North and Cintamanti, that are quite popular. If you're up for some shopping, be sure to take a stroll on **Laugavegur.** The street is chock-full of design shops, jewelers, boutiques, and bookstores.

CENTRAL REYKJAVÍK
Art/Design
AURUM
Bankstræti 4, tel. 354/551-2770, www.aurum.is, 10am-6pm daily
Aurum is the place to go for unique Icelandic jewelry. Shoppers are treated to an impressive display of rings, necklaces, and earrings made from silver, gold, or lava stones. Aurum's jewelry is distinctively Icelandic, with pieces inspired by the raw nature of the island. An adjoining section is dedicated to modern toys, knitwear, accessories, and home goods.

EPAL
Laugavegur 70, tel. 354/551-3555, www.epal.is, 10am-8pm Mon.-Sat, noon-8pm Sun.
The original design store in Iceland, Epal stocks everything from furniture to light fixtures to bedding and small goods. At Epal, which was founded in 1975, you'll find Icelandic designers as well as international brands, including Fritz Hansen, Georg Jensen, Marimekko, OK Design, and Tin Tin. Other than the downtown Reykjavík store, Epal has three other stores at Skeifan, Keflavík International Airport, and Harpa concert hall.

FISCHER
Fischersund 3, www.fischersund.com, noon-6pm Mon.-Fri., noon-4pm Sat.
Fischer is a small shop housed in a black house owned by Sigur Rós frontman Jón Þór "Jónsi" Birgisson and run by his sister. The shop features unique products that can't be found in other shops in Reykjavík, including shampoo bars with activated charcoal, natural deodorant, loose Icelandic tea, special edition vinyl records, art prints, and candles. This is a niche shop to satisfy those looking for something other than a stuffed puffin doll to take home.

HRIM HÖNNUNARHÚS
Laugavegur 25, tel. 354/553-3003, www.hrim.is, 10am-6pm Mon.-Sat., 1pm-5pm Sun.
Hrim Hönnunarhús is where you go for one-stop shopping for design lovers, whether you're looking for accessories, playful paper goods, or housewares. There is an emphasis on Icelandic design, especially when it comes to jewelry and home goods, but there are also foreign-made items as well. For instance, Hrim has an impressive Lomography camera display for those looking for lo-fi film or a new Diana plastic camera. The staff is friendly and eager to help you find that perfect purchase.

Bookstores

Reykjavík was named a UNESCO City of Literature in 2012, and locals like to boast that 1 in 10 Icelanders will publish a book in their lifetime. Iceland has the highest number of Nobel Prize winners for literature per capita. That would be one winner—Halldór Laxness for *Independent People*. Due to the importance of literature to the city and the exceptionally high literacy rate of its citizens, Reykjavík boasts an unusually large number of bookstores.

EYMUNDSSON

Austurstræti 18, tel. 354/540-2000, www. eymundsson.is, 10am-10pm daily
Eymundsson is the oldest and largest bookstore chain in Reykjavík, dating back to 1872. The main shop on Austurstræti has four levels, with an impressive magazine section, tourist books on Iceland, and a large English-language book section.

MÁL OG MENNING

Laugavegur 18, tel. 354/515-2500, www. malogmenning.is, 9am-10pm daily
Mál og Menning, which means "Language and Culture," is a favorite among Reykjavík locals. The three-level store sells fun tourist wares on the ground floor next to the magazine section. Upstairs is a collection of art and photography books, along with hundreds of English-language novels and nonfiction reads. The top floor also houses a café, where people sip lattes as they flip through magazines and newspapers.

Music

Icelandic music is more than Björk and Sigur Rós, and a few choice music shops will help you discover local favorites as well as up-and-coming Icelandic artists.

12 TÓNAR

Skólavörðustígur 15, tel. 354/511-5656, www.12tonar. is, 10am-6pm Mon.-Sat., noon-6pm Sun.
A lot more than a record shop, 12 Tónar is a place to mingle with other music lovers and sample new Icelandic music with private CD players and headphones, all while sipping on a complimentary cup of coffee. The shop was founded in 1998 and is an integral part of Reykjavík's music culture; the owner also runs an independent music label, and the shop is often used as a music venue during Reykjavík's annual autumn music festival, Iceland Airwaves. This is a landmark, a cultural institution.

LUCKY RECORDS

Rauðarárstígur 10, tel. 354/551-1195, www. luckyrecords.is, 10am-6pm Mon.-Fri., 11am-5pm Sat.-Sun.
If you like vinyl, Lucky Records is the place for you. The shop has the largest collection of new and used vinyl in the city, with an extensive Icelandic selection as well as foreign rock, pop, hip-hop, jazz, soul, and everything else you could imagine. Bands and DJs frequently play free concerts at the shop, and it's a fun place to spend a couple of hours. There's a turntable and headphones, with which you're welcome to sample used records.

SMEKKLEYSA (BAD TASTE) RECORDS

Skólavörðustígur 16, tel. 354/534-3730, www. smekkleysa.net, 11am-6pm Mon.-Fri., 11am-4pm Sat.
Smekkleysa (Bad Taste) Records was born from the legendary Smekkleysa record label that has released albums from the Sugarcubes (Björk's former band), Sigur Rós, and scores of other Icelandic artists. Its record shop, while small, has a great collection of Icelandic music on CD and vinyl, as well as a DVD section, box sets, and classical music on CD.

REYKJAVÍK RECORD SHOP

Klapparstígur 35, tel. 354/561-2299, 11am-6pm Mon.-Fri., 11am-8pm Sat.
Reykjavík Record Shop is a small shop specializing in vinyl that has an impressive selection of local music as well as international artists. You can browse new and used records, as well as CDs, books, and T-shirts.

Clothing/Knitwear

66 NORTH

Bankastræti 5, tel. 354/535-6600, www.66north. com, 9am-9pm daily

Perhaps Iceland's best-known and oldest brand, 66 North has been keeping Icelanders warm since 1926. You will find hats, rainwear, gloves, fleeces, vests, and parkas in colors ranging from basic black (a favorite among Icelanders) to lava orange. Heavy parkas cost an arm and a leg (around 50,000ISK) but you pay for the Thermolite insulation and design details. If you're not looking to make a fashion investment, you can grab a hat for about 3,000ISK.

CINTAMANI

Bankastræti 7, tel. 354/533-3390, www.cintamani.is, 9am-9pm daily

Cintamani has been dressing Icelanders in colorful, fashionable designs since 1989. Ranging from base layers to outerwear, Cintamani is a bit more playful than 66 North, with more prints and brighter colors. The emphasis is not just on style but on warmth as well, with top-notch insulation.

GEYSIR

Skólavörðustígur 16, tel. 354/519-6000, www.geysir. com, 10am-7pm daily

Geysir features clothes that combine beauty with the utility of Icelandic wool. Warm sweaters, cardigans, capes, and blankets are on offer at the flagship Reykjavík shop, not too far from Hallgrímskirkja. The clothes have a traditional look with some modern twists.

YEOMAN

Skólavörðustígur 22, tel. 354/519-8889, www. hilduryeoman.com, 11am-6pm Mon.-Sat.

Hildur Yeoman is a well-known fashion designer who has won numerous design awards in Iceland and has dressed celebrities including Taylor Swift and Björk. Her womenswear label, which is young and playful, includes dresses, blouses, and scarves. Her fabrics are delicate and her prints can be whimsical.

SPÚÚTNIK

Laugavegur 28, tel. 354/533-2023, 10am-6pm Mon.-Fri., noon-6pm Sat.-Sun.

A trendy secondhand store, Spúútnik is perfect to dig through for that perfect vintage '80s or '90s item. You will find everything from denim to leather bags to military jackets and faux fur coats.

HANDKNITTING ASSOCIATION OF ICELAND

Skólavörðustígur 19, tel. 354/552-1890, www. handknitted.is, 9am-10pm Mon.-Fri., 10am-6pm Sat.-Sun.

Handknitting Association of Iceland (Handprjónasamband Íslands) is a collective of Icelanders that knit and sell sweaters, scarves, shawls, hats, mittens, and other woolen goods. If you are looking for an authentic, traditional Icelandic sweater, and are willing to pay top dollar, this is your place. There are a lot of colors and patterns to choose from in an array of sizes.

KOLAPORTIÐ

Tryggvagata 19, tel. 354/562-5030, www.kolaportid. is, 11am-5pm Sat.-Sun.

Kolaportið is Reykjavík's only flea market and, boy, do they go all out in this space. You can find everything from secondhand traditional Icelandic sweaters to used CDs and vinyl records to books and even fresh and frozen fish. A very popular place, it's usually packed, regardless of the weather or season.

KRONKRON

Laugavegur 63b, tel. 354/562-8388, www.kronkron. com, 10am-6pm Mon.-Thur., 10am-6:30pm Fri., 10am-5pm Sat.

KronKron is a hip shop that focuses on up-and-coming designers. Fashions for men and women range from fun and flirty to chic and modern. You can find elegant dresses, fashion-forward sweaters, and unique accessories. The clientele ranges from teens to

---

1: the Handknitting Association of Iceland
2: Hrim Hönnunarhús

young professionals, which shows the variety of duds available.

Gifts and Souvenirs
BLUE LAGOON

Laugavegur 15, tel. 354/420-8849, www.bluelagoon. com, 10am-6pm Mon.-Sat., 1pm-5pm Sun.

Blue Lagoon is a tiny shop on the main street that carries all of the Blue Lagoon's skin-care line. If you can't make it to the actual Blue Lagoon near Grindavík, don't fret, because you can take home some of the essence that makes the site so special. The shop is decked out in cool blue hues and lots of lava stones, and the shelves are filled with everything from a nourishing algae mask to mineral bath salts.

THE LITTLE CHRISTMAS SHOP

Laugavegur 8, tel. 354/552-2412, 9am-6pm Mon.-Fri., 10am-5pm Sat., 10:30am-2pm Sun.

The Little Christmas Shop is a small shop where it's Christmas all year round. A pair of stone Santa shoes outside the store draws you into a world of Christmas tree ornaments, ceramic Yule Lads figurines, soft toys, dishes, and just about everything with a Christmas theme. No matter what the season, it's a joyous shop to visit and will get you buying Christmas ornaments in July.

POLAR BEAR GIFT STORE

Laugavegur 38, tel. 354/578-6020, www.isbjorninn.is, 10am-10pm daily

Polar Bear Gift Store is bound to catch your attention with its huge toy polar bear models outside the store. While polar bears are not indigenous to Iceland, don't let that fact stop you from checking out the cute wares inside. You can pick up T-shirts, hats, magnets, keychains, and other souvenirs.

THE VIKING

Hafnarstræti 3, tel. 354/551-1250, www.theviking.is, 9am-8pm Mon.-Fri., 9am-9pm Sat.-Sun.

The Viking is exactly what you would expect from a souvenir shop in Reykjavík. T-shirts, mugs, stuffed puffins and polar bears, wool products, Viking helmets, and just about

everything in between can be found here. If you're looking for unique and sophisticated trinkets, this isn't your spot. But, if you're up for fun and affordable items, you will likely find them here.

VÍNBERIÐ

Laugavegur 43, tel. 354/551-2475, 9am-6pm Mon.-Fri., 10am-6pm Sat., noon-5pm Sun.

This sweets shop is stocked with everything from chocolates to rhubarb toffee. There's a good mix of local and foreign brands, and it would be almost impossible to not find something you like. Gift options include treats wrapped in pretty packaging. In the back there are spices and baking products, and in the summer there is frequently a mini outdoor fruit market just outside the shop. One sweet that is wildly popular among Icelanders is black licorice. You can find a selection of licorice candies with or without a chocolate coating.

OLD HARBOR (GRANDI)
Clothing/Knitwear
FARMERS & FRIENDS

Laugavegur 37, tel. 354/552-1960, www. farmersmarket.is, 10am-9pm Mon.-Fri., 11am-7pm Sat.-Sun.

Farmers & Friends is the flagship store of the wildly popular Farmer's Market clothing label. If you are looking for sweaters other than the traditional garb available at Handprjónasamband Íslands (Handknitting Association of Iceland), Farmer's Market offers everything from cardigans to capes in stylish colors and patterns. The label, which was launched in 2005, is focused on combining classic Nordic design elements with a modern aesthetic.

OUTSIDE THE CITY CENTER
Shopping Malls
KRINGLAN

Kringlunni 4-12, tel. 354/568-9200, www.kringlan. is, 10am-6:30pm Mon.-Wed., 10am-9pm Thur., 10am-7pm Fri., 10am-5pm Sat.-Sun.

Kringlan resembles just about any mall in

America. There are clothing stores, a bank, a movie theater, and a food court packed with teenagers and shoppers. If the weather is particularly bad and you want to get some shopping done, it's a good destination. There's a 66 North shop in Kringlan, as well as some other Icelandic brands. Kringlan is a five-minute drive east from downtown Reykjavík, and it can be reached by Strætó bus numbers 1, 2, 3, 4, 6, 13, and 14. One-way bus fare is 470ISK and it takes about 10 minutes from downtown Reykjavík.

Food

Reykjavík's culinary charm may be surprising to some. While there are traditional Icelandic restaurants serving up fresh fish and tender lamb fillets, there are also fantastic eateries specializing in food you may not expect to see in Iceland. For instance, there's an impressive collection of Asian and Mediterranean restaurants, which have authentic menus that incorporate the great ingredients found in Iceland. If you're in the mood for tapas, there's a place to have an exquisite meal. Craving sushi? You will not be disappointed. As for Icelandic cuisine, there are upmarket restaurants catering to foodies as well as fast-food joints offering quick, affordable bites.

CENTRAL REYKJAVIK
Icelandic
BERGSSON MATHÚS
Templarasund 3, tel. 354/571-1822, www.bergsson.is, 7am-10pm daily, 2,400ISK
Bergsson Mathús is known for its fantastic brunch menu and light, flavorful dishes. Try the roast beef on a bed of salad or the spinach lasagna. The eatery is also a popular coffee spot for locals.

ICELANDIC BAR
Ingólfsstræti 1, tel. 354/517-6767, www.islenskibarinn. is, 11:30am-1am Sun.-Thur., 11:30am-3am Fri.-Sat., entrées from 2,600ISK
Icelandic Bar (Íslenski Barinn) takes classic Icelandic ingredients like lamb, whale, and puffin and puts a creative spin on the dishes with interesting flavor combinations. For example, the restaurant serves a sweet and savory dish of grilled puffin with blueberries,

pickled red onions, *skyr,* and herbs. Guests can also order items like local salmon, traditional lamb meat soup, and the famous Icelandic hot dog. The reindeer burger is highly recommended.

RESTAURANT REYKJAVÍK
Vesturgata 2, tel. 354/552-3030, www. restaurantreykjavik.is, 11:30am-10pm daily, entrées from 3,790ISK
Restaurant Reykjavík is known for its fantastic fish buffet (6,450ISK), which starts every day at 6pm. This is a favorite among tourists looking to sample traditional Icelandic fish dishes as well as international classics. The restaurant is housed in a huge yellow building with lots of seating, so you're not likely to have to wait for a table. The fish buffet features everything from salmon, cod, lobster, fish balls, trout, and caviar to shrimp and crab specialties. An à la carte menu offers beef, lamb, fish, and vegetarian options.

★ LÆKJARBREKKA
Bankastræti 2, tel. 354/551-4430, www. laekjarbrekka.is, 11:30am-10pm daily, entrées from 4,290ISK
Lækjarbrekka occupies a historic building that dates back to 1834. Today, Lækjarbrekka is one of the best-known downtown restaurants catering to tourists. Fresh fish dishes are on the menu alongside some of Iceland's most adventurous cuisine. You'll find fermented shark, whale meat, puffin, and Icelandic horse fillets on offer. For tamer choices, the pan-fried fillet of lamb and arctic char are splendid.

Seafood
★ MESSIN

Lækjargata 6, tel. 354/546-0095, www.messinn.com, lunch 11am-3pm daily, dinner 5pm-10pm daily, fish pans from 3,890ISK

Messinn does fish very well, and it's the only food on the menu. You can choose from fish pans featuring plaice, redfish, salted cod, Atlantic wolffish, Arctic char, or salmon. Other courses include lobster salad, fish burger, and creamy fish soup. The décor is simple and the atmosphere relaxed, with the food taking center stage. This is a favorite place among locals.

FISKFELAGID

Vesturgata 2a, tel. 354/552-5300, www.fiskfelagid.is, 11:30am-10:30pm Mon.-Thur., 11:30am-11:30pm Fri., 5pm-11:30pm Sat.-Sun., entrées from 4,900ISK

Fiskfelagid (Fish Company) has a striking, chic interior with modern wooden tables and chairs, candleholders throughout the space, and personal notes and photos adorning the walls. There are comfortable couches in the lounge, where you're welcome to sip a cocktail while waiting for a table. The food is flawless, ranging from pan-fried prime lamb and oxtail with artichoke puree to blackened monkfish and fried langoustine with lobster spring rolls.

★ FISH MARKET

Aðlstræti 12, tel. 354/578-8877, www. fiskmarkadurinn.is, 5:30pm-10:30pm daily, entrées from 4,990ISK

Fish Market stands out among a number of fantastic seafood restaurants in Reykjavík. What makes Fish Market special is the way the chef combines ingredients. The grilled monkfish comes with crispy bacon, cottage cheese, tomato yuzu pesto, and crunchy enoki mushrooms. It's a vision, as is the salted cod with lime zest with potato puree, dried cranberries, and celery salad.

Asian
KRUA THAI

Skólavörðustígur 21, tel. 354/551-0833, www. kruathai.is, 11:30am-9:30pm daily, 1,600ISK

Krua Thai has all your favorite Thai classics, ranging from chicken pad thai to spring rolls and noodle soups. During weekdays, the restaurant has a three-course lunch special for just 1,400ISK.

NOODLE STATION

Laugavegur 103, tel. 354/551-3198, 11am-10pm daily, 1,680ISK

Noodle Station is a popular spot for Reykjavík natives, students, and tourists. People flock to the tiny shop for one of the tastiest and cheapest meals you can find in downtown. Noodle soup is available with chicken or beef or as a vegetarian option. The smell of spices wafting down Laugavegur will draw you in.

SUSHIBARINN

Laugavegur 2, tel. 354/552-4444, www.sushibarinn. is, 11:30am-10pm Mon.-Sat., 5pm-10pm Sun., rolls from 1,990ISK

Sushibarinn has not only sushi roll staples like California, volcano, and shrimp tempura rolls, but also some creative combinations, including the Rice Against the Machine roll, which has salmon, cream cheese, red onions, and chili. For those who are inclined, whale sushi is on the menu as well.

FÖNIX

Bíldshöfði 12, tel. 354/567-7888, www. fonixveitingahus.is, 11am-2pm and 5pm-9pm Mon.-Fri., 11am-9pm Sat., 5pm-9pm Sun., 2,190ISK

It was hard to find good Chinese food in Reykjavík until Fönix opened. You can sample all the classics here including wonton soup, lo mein, egg rolls, sweet and sour pork, and dumplings. There are vegan entrees on the menu as well as a kids menu.

GANDHI RESTAURANT

Posthusstræti 17, tel. 354/511-1691, www.gandhi.is, 5:30pm-10pm daily, entrées from 3,400ISK

Gandhi Restaurant features the creations of two chefs from southwest India. Combining local Icelandic ingredients with traditional Indian spices, the menu offers authentic dishes like chicken vindaloo and fish masala as well as vegetarian options. The food is fresh and perfectly spiced. The butter chicken is gorgeous, rivaling that of the top Indian restaurants in London.

SUSHI SOCIAL

Þingholtsstræti 5, tel. 354/568-6600, www. sushisamba.is, 5pm-11pm Sun.-Thur., 5pm-midnight Fri.-Sat., rolls from 3,490ISK

Sushi Social combines Japanese and South American elements to create inventive and delicious sushi rolls and entrées. You'll find traditional fresh seafood like tuna, salmon, crab, lobster, and shrimp, along with South American influences like spicy salsa, jalapeño mayo, and chimichurri. Main entrées include baked vanilla-infused cod and grilled beef tenderloin with mushroom sauce, jalapeño, and coriander.

SUMAC GRILL + DRINKS

Laugavegur 28, tel. 354/537-9900, www.sumac. is, 5:30pm-10pm Tues.-Thur., 5pm-11pm Fri.-Sat., 3,990ISK

Sumac Grill + Drinks is a stylish addition to the restaurant scene in downtown Reykjavík. Opened in 2017, the menu is a fusion of Lebanese and Moroccan dishes created from seasonal Icelandic ingredients, resulting in some surprising yet delicious courses. On the menu you will find Tahini-glazed cod, lamb ribs with lentils, grapes, and almonds, Shawarma chicken thighs, and an array of vegan dishes. There is also a seven-course menu to share with the entire table for 8,990ISK per person.

Mediterranean
HORNIÐ

Hafnartsræti 15, tel. 354/551-3340, www.hornid.is, 11am-11:30pm daily, large pizzas from 1,890ISK

Hornið, with its yellow and blue walls, looks like a bistro from the outside, and the interior reveals a relaxed atmosphere with friendly service and yummy pizzas. Classic pizzas include pepperoni, four cheese, and vegetable, but there are also adventurous creations like the Pizza Pecatore, which

has shrimp, mussels, and scallops on top. If you're not up for pizza, entrées include salted cod with risotto and fillet of lamb with vegetables.

ÍTALÍA

Laugavegur 11, tel. 354/552-4630, www.italia.is, 11:30am-10pm daily, pasta dishes from 3,100ISK

This is a cute Italian restaurant right on the main street, Laugavegur. The menu offers classics like spaghetti Bolognese, lasagna, and mushroom ravioli as well as options that incorporate local ingredients, like smoked salmon with toasted bread and pan-fried salted cod with onions. Pizza and calzones are also on the menu.

TAPAS BARINN

Vesturgata 3b, tel. 354/551-2344, www.tapas.is, 5pm-11:30pm Sun.-Thur., 5pm-1am Fri.-Sat., entrees from 4,990ISK

Tapas Barinn has many delightful choices, but if you'd like to taste its best Icelandic dishes, go for the "gourmet feast" in which the chef prepares dishes with smoked puffin, Icelandic sea trout, lobster tails, grilled Icelandic lamb, minke whale with cranberry sauce, and pan-fried blue ling with lobster sauce. The seven plates, along with a shot of the famous Icelandic spirit Brennivin and a chocolate skyr mousse dessert, will only set you back 8,990ISK. If you would like more traditional tapas, there are lots of options, including salmon and bacon-wrapped scallop bites.

Steak Houses
★ GRILLMARKET

Lækjargata 2a, tel. 354/571-7777, www. grillmarkadurinn.is, 5:30pm-10:30pm daily, entrées from 4,590ISK

Grillmarket (Grillmarkaðurinn) is an upscale restaurant specializing in all things meat. Expect dishes like grilled rack of lamb, dry-aged rib eye steaks, and beef tenderloin. But the restaurant also offers spectacular fish courses like salmon, cod, and fresh langoustine tails. The decor is modern yet rustic with

Food Trucks Arrive in Reykjavík

Street food is pretty new to Reykjavík, but the number of trucks grows each month. Be sure to check the trucks' Facebook pages or websites to see where they are parked when you are visiting, as the trucks move around the city.

- **Fish and Chips Vagninn** (tel. 354/840-4100, www.fishandchipsvagninn.is, 11am-9pm daily) serves up delicately battered cod fish and chips (1,790ISK).

- **Lobster Hut** (tel. 354/691-3007, 11:30am-8pm daily, from 1,500ISK) specializes in all things lobster. There's lobster soup, lobster sandwiches, lobster salads, and lobster hot dogs.

- **Tacoson** (tel. 354/777-5855) serves pork, chicken, chili con carne, and vegan tacos for the unbeatable price of 650ISK per taco. Quick eats at a cheap price.

- **Fish & Co.** (tel. 354/823-1667, noon-9pm daily) offers delicious, fresh pan-fried cod with a side of tomatoes for 1,000ISK, a price that's hard to beat.

Lobster Hut

- **Vöffluvagninn** (tel. 354/626-2882, 11am-7pm daily, 890ISK) is for those with a sweet tooth—and craving waffles. You can choose from classic waffles to cinnamon with cream, caramel, chocolate and cream, and a number of syrups including rhubarb, blueberry, and even licorice syrup (for the brave).

Scandinavian design and a lot of wood. If you are after a top-notch carnivore's dinner, this is your place.

Vegetarian
GARÐURINN
Klapparstigur 37, tel. 354/561-2345, 11am-8pm Mon.-Fri., noon-5pm Sat.

Garðurinn is a lovely café inhabiting a quiet corner downtown. It has an eclectic rotating menu of vegetarian meals including items like curry, vegetable chili, and lentil patties, all at affordable prices. You can also expect soups, sandwiches, cakes, teas, and coffee.

VÍNYL BISTRO
Hverfisgata 76, tel. 354/537-1332, 3pm-11pm Mon.-Fri., 11am-11pm Sat.-Sun., 1,600ISK

Vínyl Bisro is a café and one of the hippest places to hang out in downtown Reykjavík. Music is always playing, and artists and musicians mingle among tourists and locals. Stop

by to enjoy tasty coffee drinks, beers, and light meals. There are several vegetarian options.

★ GLÓ
Laugavegur 20b, tel. 354/553-1111, www.glo.is, 11am-10pm daily, 1,690ISK

Gló has a spectacular menu featuring not just vegetarian and vegan options, but also a killer raw food selection. Expect to see staples like tofu and hummus served in creative ways, and there's also an excellent salad bar. The meat dish option can be great if you're traveling with a carnivore. The decor is modern and chic and the staff friendly.

Fast Food
★ BÆJARINS BEZTU PYLSUR
Tryggvatagata 1, tel. 354/511-1566, www.bbp.is, 10am-1am Sun.-Thur., 10am-4:30am Fri.-Sat., 450ISK

You have to visit Bæjarins Beztu Pylsur (The Town's Best Hot Dog). Even if you don't eat hot dogs, you should get a look at the tiny shack that has long been delighting tourists, locals, food critics, and even U.S. President Bill Clinton. Located close to the harbor, the hot dog stand serves up lamb meat hot dogs, with fresh buns and an array of toppings. If you're out for a late-night bar crawl and get hungry, the stand is open until 4am on weekends.

HLÖLLABÁTAR

Ingólfstorg, tel. 354/511-3500, www.hlollabatar.is, 11:30am-10pm daily, sandwiches from 1,595ISK

Hlöllabátar has hot and cold hero/hoagie sandwiches on offer, including barbecue, curry, ham and cheese, and veggie boats. It's a great place to get something quick and fuel up before you continue exploring the city.

ROADHOUSE

Snorrabraut 56, tel. 354/571-4200, www.roadhouse. is, 11:30am-9:30pm Mon.-Thur., 11:30am-11pm Fri.-Sat., noon-9:30pm Sun., burgers from 2,195ISK

Roadhouse does its best to depict an American-style hamburger joint. It's kitschy, cute, and familiar, with Americana hanging on the walls, ranging from old license plates to Elvis Presley posters. The food is exceptional "fast food," with choice burgers featuring everything from crumbled blue cheese to jalapeños and fried onions. A favorite among Icelanders is the Texas mac-and-cheese burger, with a patty, macaroni and cheese, bacon, and barbecue sauce piled on top. The pork baby-back ribs are memorable.

ICELANDIC HAMBURGER FACTORY

Höfðatún 2, tel. 354/575-7575, www.fabrikkan. is, 11am-10pm Sun.-Thur., 11am-midnight Fri.-Sat., burgers from 2,499ISK

Icelandic Hamburger Factory (Islenska Hamborgarafabrikkan) is a wildly popular hamburger joint. It has the look and feel of a casual eatery, but the hamburgers are pretty special. They range from classic hamburgers with lettuce, cheese, and tomatoes to more creative concoctions like the surf-and-turf, which combines a beef patty with tiger prawns, garlic, Japanese seaweed, cheese, lettuce, tomatoes, red onions, and garlic-cheese sauce. Other options include chicken and lamb, as well as a whale meat burger.

GRILLHUSIÐ

Tryggvagata 20, tel. 354/562-3456, www.grillhusid. is, 11:30am-10pm Sun.-Thur., 11:30am-11pm Fri.-Sat., 2,500ISK

Grillhusið is part diner, part TGI Friday's, with Americana displayed on the walls and

Bæjarins Beztu Pylsur

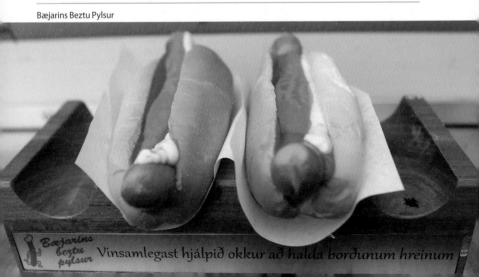

Vinsamlegast hjálpið okkur að halda borðunum hreinum

an extensive menu ranging from hamburgers to fish-and-chips to salads and sandwiches. There is an interesting array of burgers on offer, and the lamb and béarnaise burger is a personal favorite.

Gastropubs/Breweries

BASTARD BREW & FOOD

Vegamótastígur 4, tel. 354/558-0800, www.bastard. is, 11:30am-1am Sun.-Thur., 11:30am-4am Fri.-Sat.

Bastard offers fast food kicked up a notch. Some favorites on the menu are duck confit flatbread, the Fat Bastard burger with beef brisket, and pulled pork tacos. The food is good, but locals tend to come for the drinks. You can enjoy a beer tasting of four brews for 2,800ISK. Bastard brews an IPA and an amber ale, and serves beers from Tuborg, Guinness, Brió, and Borg. They also have an extensive gin menu and impressive cocktails.

PUBLIC HOUSE GASTROPUB

Laugavegur 24, tel. 354/555-7333, www.publichouse. is, 11:30am-1am daily

Public House has 10 beers on tap, a number of flavorful cocktails, and a menu with a touch of Japanese flair. You will find small plates like bacon-wrapped dates with chili jam, tuna tacos with wasabi and guacamole, and crispy duck breast with jalapeno teriyaki. On weekends you can enjoy a bottomless brunch with bottomless drinks for 4,990ISK a person.

Cafés

BRAUÐ & CO

Frakkastígur 16, tel. 354/456-7777, 6am-6pm daily

Brauð & Co is the hippest bakery in Reykjavík. You can get great pastries, breads, and cookies, as well as a delicious cup of coffee, plus do some fun people-watching in the heart of downtown. Many of the employees and owners are connected to the music industry.

SANDHOLT

Laugavegur 36, tel. 354/551-3524, www.sandholt.is, 6:30am-9pm daily

Sandholt is a lovely place to have a coffee and fresh-baked pastry, sandwich, or panini. The bakery also has fine chocolates and other packaged goodies, like jams and cookies, which make good souvenirs.

MOKKA

Skólavörðustígur 3A, tel. 354/552-1174, www.mokka. is, 9am-6:30pm daily, 500ISK

The oldest coffeehouse in Reykjavík, Mokka retains a faithful following. It's busy all day, with tourists as well as artists, writers, and other folks stopping by for a cup of coffee and Mokka's famous waffles with fresh cream and homemade jam. Art and photography exhibitions are frequently held at the coffeehouse, so stop by and have a look at the walls.

REYKJAVÍK ROASTERS

Karastigur 1, tel. 354/517-5535, www. reykjavikroasters.is, 8am-6pm Mon.-Fri., 9am-5pm Sat.-Sun., 500ISK

Reykjavík Roasters is a charming corner coffeehouse situated in a great part of town. Just a stone's throw from Hallgrímskirkja, Reykjavík Roasters is a wonderful spot to sit down for a coffee to break up a busy day of sightseeing. Decorated with vintage couches and chairs and wood tables with delicate tablecloths, the coffeehouse is packed with tourists and locals chilling out, drinking lattes, and taking advantage of the free Wi-Fi. During the summer months, when the weather is cooperating, there's an outside sitting area where guests can enjoy their drinks while soaking in the sun.

STOFAN CAFÉ

Vesturgata 3, tel. 354/863-8583, 9am-11pm Mon.-Wed., 9am-midnight Fri.-Sun., 9am-10pm Sun., 500ISK

Stofan Café, a hot spot near the harbor, has plenty of couches, chairs, and tables to accommodate its legion of fans. The café serves coffee drinks, local beers, and cakes and light meals. It's common to catch locals enjoying their drinks while curling up with a good book on a vintage armchair.

1: Café Babalu 2: Brauð & Co

KAFFITÁR

Bankastræti 8, tel. 354/511-4540, www.kaffitar.is,
7am-6pm daily, 650ISK

Kaffitár is the closest thing Iceland has to a coffee chain like Starbucks. There are locations in the city center, Keflavík airport, and a smattering of other sites. They also sell coffee beans and ground coffee in supermarkets and takeout coffee at gas stations. The city-center location is bright, colorful, and usually crowded. The coffee is fresh and the cakes and other sweets are delicious. You can't go wrong at Kaffitár.

CAFÉ BABALU

Skólavörðustígur 22, tel. 354/555-8845,
www.babalu.is, 11am-11pm daily,
1,200ISK

This charming coffeehouse is decorated with vintage wood furnishings and kitschy knick-knacks. Other than coffee drinks, the two-floor café serves light meals including soup, panini, and crepes. This is a favorite among tourists, and in the summer months, there's an outdoor eating area on the 2nd floor.

Ice Cream
ELDUR OG IS

Skólavörðustígur 2, tel. 354/571-2480,
8:30am-11pm Mon.-Sat., 10am-10pm Sun.,
500ISK

Eldur og Is offers soft-serve and Italian-style ice cream with flavors including the basics: vanilla, chocolate, and strawberry, as well as coffee, pistachio, and several others. A crepe bar inside has delicious combinations, including the Nutella and nut special crepe. This place has a central location and a good reputation, so it can be a bit crowded. The sofas and armchairs inside make it very comfortable.

Food Halls

Three indoor food halls (*mathölls*) opened in Reykjavík the past couple of years as Reykjavik's appetite for street food grows. The food halls, which are upscale food courts, have seating areas to enjoy your food and drinks.

HLEMMUR MATHÖLL

Laugavegur 107, tel. 354/577-6200, www.
hlemmurmatholl.is, 8am-11pm daily

Hlemmur Mathöll is housed in the building that used to be the main bus station in Reykjavík. It's now home to the bakery **Brauð & Co.**, Los Angeles-style taco masters **Fuego**, experimental bar and restaurant **Skál!, Flatey** pizza, and Vietnamese street food eatery **Bánh Mí.**

MATHÖLL HÖFÐA

Bíldshöfði 9, www.mathollhofda.is, 9am-10pm
Mon.-Fri., 10am-10pm Sat., 11am-10pm Sun.

This is where you will find the locals. Situated outside of downtown Reykjavík, Mathöll Höfða features Chinese food vendor **Wok On,** pizza place **Flatbakan,** Mexican restaurant **Culiacan,** and Indian fusion eatery **Indican.**

OLD HARBOR (GRANDI)
Icelandic
MATUR OG DRYKKUR

Grandagarður 2, tel. 354/571-8877, www.
maturogdrykkur.is, 11:30am-10:30pm daily, entrées
from 3,990ISK

Matur og Drykkur has an eclectic menu that includes items such as double-smoked lamb with buttermilk and nutmeg, a whole cod's head cooked in chicken stock with dulse (a type of seaweed), and rutabaga soup with red beet caviar and sunflower seeds. The restaurant, which is housed in the Saga Museum, has a casual atmosphere with reminders of the fishing industry—appropriate, because the building used to be a saltfish factory.

Seafood
ICELANDIC FISH & CHIPS

Tryggvagata 11, tel. 354/551-1118, www.fishandchips.
is, 11:30am-9pm daily, entrées from 1,390ISK

Icelandic Fish & Chips serves up a wonderful range of fresh seafood: cod, plaice, blue ling, haddock, redfish, wolffish, and shellfish. For an authentic Icelandic fish-and-chips meal, go for the cod. The biggest draws, however, are the "skyronnaise dips," in which Iceland's famous soft cheese, *skyr,* is blended with an array of spices, including basil, coriander, ginger, and tarragon. The truffle and tarragon dip is heavenly.

THE LOBSTER HOUSE

Amtmannsstígur 1, tel. 354/561-3303, www.
thelobsterhouse.is, 11:30am-10pm Mon.-Sat.,
5pm-10pm Sun., entrées from 4,300ISK
The Lobster House is the place for—you guessed it—lobster. You can't make a bad choice: grilled lobster tails with garlic butter, lobster soup, slow-cooked monkfish and smoked lobster with potato salad, lobster tempura, and lots of other options. If you're not a fan of lobster, don't fret. There are lamb, pork, and other fish options on the menu.

Asian
OSUSHI

Tryggvagata 13, tel. 354/561-0562, www.osushi.
is, 11:30am-10pm Mon.-Sat., 3pm-10pm Sun., bites
250-590ISK
Osushi is a sushi train with bites snaking their way around the restaurant on a conveyor belt. Diners are treated to everything from deep-fried shrimp tempura rolls to tuna sashimi and grilled eel bites. For kids, there are chicken teriyaki kebabs, spring rolls, and even a chocolate mousse for dessert.

RAMEN MOMO

Tryggvagata 16, tel. 354/571-0646, www.
ramenmomo.is, 11:30am-9pm Tue-Fri, noon-9:30pm
Sat, 1pm-9pm Sun, closed Mon, 1,890ISK
Ramen Momo is an adorable hidden restaurant not too far from the harbor. Owned and operated by a Tibetan immigrant, Ramen Momo serves up glorious chicken, beef, or vegetarian ramen soup and dumplings. The nondescript eatery has an authentic feel to it, and your taste buds will thank you.

Mediterranean
★ FLATEY

Grandagarður 11, tel. 354/588-2666, www.
flateypizza.is, 11am-10pm daily, pizzas from 1,750ISK
Located in the hip Grandi neighborhood, Flatey serves up delicious Neapolitan pizzas

with fresh ingredients and eclectic combinations. You can try the Padrino pie with San Marzano tomatoes, fresh mozzarella, pepperoni, pickled chili peppers, honey, fresh basil, and olive oil. Other pies include Margheritas, Parmas, a vegan pizza, and even a dessert pizza with Nutella, almond flakes, and powdered sugar.

★ SEA BARON

Geirsgata 8, tel. 354/553-1500, www.saegreifinn.is,
11:30am-10pm daily, entrées from 1,800ISK
Sea Baron (Sægreifinn) has been a Reykjavík institution for years. With its prime location by the harbor, Sea Baron is known for its perfectly spiced, fresh lobster soup, which comes with a side of bread and butter. Fish kebabs on offer include scallops, monkfish, and cod. Whale meat is also available if you're so inclined. Inside, visitors will find a hut-like atmosphere with fishing relics, photos, and equipment. A net hangs from the ceiling, and charming knickknacks are displayed.

Steak Houses
STEIKHÚSIÐ

Tryggvagata 4, tel. 354/561-1111, www.steik.is,
5pm-10pm Sun.-Wed., 5pm-11pm Thur.-Sat., steaks
from 3,990ISK
Steikhúsið offers beef rib eye, porterhouse, and T-bone cuts or lamb fillets, with tasty sauces including béarnaise, creamy pepper, and blue cheese. There are also fish entrées on offer as well as a dynamite hamburger with brie, pickled vegetables, mango chutney, chipotle, and bacon. For the adventurous, the surf-and-turf features minke whale and horse meat grilled in a coal oven.

Fast Food
HAMBORGARABÚLLA TÓMASAR

Geirsgata 1, tel. 354/511-888, www.bullan.is,
11:30am-9pm daily, burgers from 1,290ISK
Hamborgarabúllan Tómasar (Tommi's burger joint) is situated in the old harbor district, close to where the whale-watching tours depart. The food is tasty, the service quick, and the decor a little kitschy, making this a great

spot to grab a quick bite to eat. A special includes a hamburger or veggie burger, fries, and soda for 1,990ISK, which is pretty cheap for a meal in downtown Reykjavík.

★ LE KOCK

Tryggvagata 14, tel. 354/571-1555, www.lekock.is, 7am-11pm Sun.-Thur., 7am-11am Fri.-Sat., 2,100ISK

Le Kock is part dive, part foodie paradise. The chefs are creative, constantly playing with flavors. Their Nacho Lambre consists of nachos, braised lamb, grilled lamb hearts, chipotle sauce, cheddar cheese, red onions, and pickled chili. There's also beer-battered cod, burgers, and fried buffalo wings on the menu, and beer on tap in the bar.

Gastropubs/Breweries
BRYGGJAN BRÚGGHÚS

Grandagarður 8, tel. 354/456-4040, www. bryggjanbrugghus.is, 11am-11pm Sun.-Wed., 11am-midnight Thur.-Sat.

This brewery has a retro feel to it with a dash of fishing culture. The menu is simple, with the fish of the day, fish and chips, burgers, and duck legs. Their beers are brewed on site and they have fun cocktails, like the Jude Law, with pear cognac and lemon soda.

Cafés
★ DEIG

Tryggvagata 18, tel. 354/555-0434, www.lekock.is/ deigworkshop, 7am-7pm daily

Reykjavík was a bagel desert before Deig opened in 2018. Now, locals and travelers can enjoy freshly baked bagels in the heart of Reykjavík. They bake plain, sesame, and everything bagels as well as sourdough bread and some of the tastiest donuts on the island.

Ice Cream
VALDÍS

Grandagarður 21, tel. 354/586-8088, www.valdis.is, 11:30am-11pm daily, from 450ISK

Valdís draws a crowd during sun-soaked summer days and the dim, windy dog days of winter. It's always busy here and for good reason. The harbor location and its creative and delicious ice cream flavors make this a favorite among locals and tourists. Flavors include coconut, white chocolate, vanilla coffee, Oreo, and local favorites black licorice and rhubarb. During the summer, there are tables and chairs outside the shop, where scores of people enjoy their cones.

Food Halls
GRANDI MATHÖLL

Grandagarður 16, tel. 354/787-6200, www. grandimatholl.is/en, 11am-9pm Sun.-Wed., 11am-10pm Thur.-Sat.

Grandi Mathöll is the perfect place to grab something to eat when exploring the harbor area. Here you will find Korean fusion restaurant **Kore, LAX,** which specializes in sparkling wine and seafood, North American street food purveyors **Cubanos,** and pizza place **Skjaldbakan.**

OUTSIDE THE CITY CENTER
Ice Cream
SKÚBB

Laugarásvegur 1, tel. 354/767-0123, www.skubb.is, 2pm-11pm Mon-Fri, noon-11pm Sat/Sun

Skúbb is a delightful ice cream shop that has classic flavors like vanilla, pistachio, and chocolate, but some unique options as well like strawberry and basil, mango and mint, and bad brownie.

★ Bars and Nightlife

Reykjavík may be small, but its nightlife is epic. The main drag, **Laugavegur,** is ground zero for the hottest clubs and bars in town. If you are up for dancing, **Kiki Queer Bar** is your spot. If you fancy a whiskey bar, **Dillon** is the place. If you want to catch a hot Reykjavík band performing live, **Húrra** is your best bet.

Be prepared for it to be a late night and for your wallet to take a hit. Locals don't venture out until around midnight, and drinks are expensive—expect to pay upward of 1,000ISK for a pint of beer and 2,200ISK for a cocktail. Because mixed drinks are so expensive, cocktail bars are scarce, and beer is the favored beverage. But, for such a small city, you can't help but be impressed by the number of hot spots catering to different genres. Your biggest challenge will be narrowing down your options!

CENTRAL REYKJAVIK
Bars
BOSTON
Laugavegur 28B, tel. 354/577-3200, 2pm-1am Sun.-Thur., 2pm-3am Fri.-Sat.

Boston is best known as a hangout for local artists, writers, hipsters, and hangers-on. The bar has an unassuming exterior, but inside await good drinks and hot music, mainly rock. If there's a concert on the night you go, expect to stand shoulder to shoulder. It's a tight spot and doesn't take too long to draw a big crowd.

HRESSINGARSKÁLINN
Austurstræti 22, tel. 354/561-2240, www.hresso.is, 9am-1am Sun.-Thur., 10am-4:30am Fri.-Sat.

Hressingarskálinn, simply known as Hresso, is a casual restaurant by day, serving up hamburgers and sandwiches. Free Wi-Fi attracts **writers,** tourists, and locals, who are known to spend hours sipping endless cups of coffee. By night, Hresso transforms into a dance club,

with hot DJs and live bands. Expect trendy dance music.

LEBOWSKI BAR
Laugavegur 20, tel. 354/552-2300, www.lebowski.is, 11:30am-1am Sun.-Thur., 11:30am-4am Fri.-Sat.

Lebowski Bar pays not-so-subtle homage to the Coen brothers movie *The Big Lebowski.* Inside there is bowling paraphernalia, posters from the film, and even a hanging rug by the bar that brings the room together. It's a casual eatery during the day, like many of Reykjavík's bars, but at night it transforms into a pretty wild scene, playing the latest dance music. There's a dance floor in the back of the room. A White Russian, the cocktail famously featured in the film, costs 1,750ISK.

THE ENGLISH PUB
Austurstræti 12b, tel. 354/578-0400, www. enskibarinn.is, noon-1am Mon.-Fri., noon-4:30am Sat.-Sun.

The English Pub is part English pub, part sports bar. There's a nice selection of Icelandic and foreign beer, and Guinness is on tap. If there's a soccer game being played anywhere in the world, it will likely be shown on one of the many screens in the bar. If there's a Premier League game on, expect a crowd of expats, tourists, and locals.

KAFFIBARINN
Bergstaðastræti 1, tel. 354/551-1588, 5pm-1am Sun.-Thur., 3pm-3am Fri.-Sat.

Kaffibarinn has been a Reykjavík institution since scenes from the indie film *101 Reykjavík* were filmed here. Damon Albarn, the Blur and Gorillaz front man, used to own a stake in the bar. It's a tiny space, with a rich red exterior that gets jam-packed during the weekends, but it's one of those places that it's cool to say you were there. Expect trendy dance music to be blaring as you enter.

MICRO BAR

Vesturgata 2, tel. 354/865-8389, 3pm-midnight
Sun.-Thur., 3pm-1am Fri.-Sat.

Micro Bar is a beer lover's paradise. The bar carries about 80 different beers from countries including Belgium, Germany, Denmark, and the United States. The big draws are the wide selection of Icelandic beers on tap and the number of Icelandic craft beers available. Stop by and try a local stout, pale ale, or lager. The atmosphere is relaxed and relatively quiet, with dim lighting and a large wood bar. You'll find locals at the tables enjoying a beer and conversation with friends.

VEÐUR

Klapparstígur 33, www.vedurbarinn.is, noon-1am
Sun.-Thur., noon-3am Fri.-Sat.

Veður, which means weather in Icelandic, is a chic bar popular for happy hour and a casual drink with friends. On nice days there are tables and chairs outside so patrons can enjoy the sun. In addition to beer, wine, and cocktails, Veður serves charcuterie plates, cheese, and olives, as well as coffee drinks and pastries.

BRAVÓ

Laugavegur 22, tel. 354/580-8020, 11am-1am
Sun.-Thur., 11am-4:30am Fri.-Sat.

Located downstairs from Kiki Queer Bar, Bravó is a place to chill, have a cold beer, and meet with friends. There is a casual vibe, and at night local DJs routinely play, attracting a younger crowd.

Gay and Lesbian
KIKI QUEER BAR

Laugavegur 22, tel. 354/571-0194, www.kiki.is,
8pm-1am Thur., 8pm-4:30am Fri.-Sat.

Kiki Queer Bar is Reykjavík's only gay bar and was a welcome addition to the scene. Many locals will tell you this is *the* place to go to dance because it attracts some of the best local and visiting DJs. You can expect

music ranging from Lady Gaga to the latest Icelandic pop music.

Live Music
DILLON

Laugavegur 30, tel. 354/511-2400, 2pm-1am
Sun.-Thur., 2pm-3am Fri.-Sat.

Dillon looks and feels like a dive bar. Rockers, metalheads, and hipsters unite, listening to live bands and sipping from the fine collection of more than 150 whiskeys available. Guests can find Scotch and bourbon as well as small-batch Icelandic whiskeys. When there isn't live music, locals DJs keep the music flowing. The interior is a little rough, with lots of wood and not many places to sit, and the music is always loud.

KEX HOSTEL

Skúlagata 28, tel. 354/561-6060, www.kexhostel.is

Kex Hostel has become a Reykjavík institution over the past few years. The building, formerly a biscuit factory, is a great space, complete with mid-century furniture, vintage wall maps, and a lot of curiosities. A small stage in the entryway hosts up-and-coming bands while guests drink and hang out at the **bar** (11:30am-11pm daily). A back room serves as a **venue** for more formal concerts. If you're in your 20s and aren't bothered by hipsters, this is your place. Since this is a hostel, it's open 24 hours, so check listings at www. grapevine.is for concert times.

LOFT HOSTEL

Bankastræti 7, tel. 354/553-8140, www.lofthostel.is

Loft Hostel has earned a reputation as a place to see and be seen. The fourth-floor bar/café hosts up-and-coming bands, established live acts, and DJs. An outdoor deck overlooks Bankastræti and is packed with locals and tourists alike when the sun is shining during the day, and filled with mingling concertgoers at night. Since this is a hostel, it's open 24 hours, so check listings at www.grapevine.is for concert and event times.

1: Kiki Queer Bar 2: Lebowski Bar 3: Hótel Borg

MENGI

Óðinsgata 2, tel. 354/588-3644,
www.mengi.net, 11am-5pm Tue.-Wed.,
noon-11pm Thur.-Fri., 1pm-11pm Sat.,
closed Sun.-Mon.

Mengi is an exciting music and art space that showcases up-and-coming and established artists. The room holds no more than 100, so performances are intimate, making this a unique space in Reykjavik. You can see experimental musicians like Ben Frost and dj. flugvél og geimskip, or Icelandic favorites like Ólafur Arnalds and Högni Egilsson. There is also a small shop inside where you can pick up CDs, vinyl records, and art prints during opening hours.

Accommodations

Accommodations in Reykjavík fall into three categories: hotels, guesthouses, and self-catering apartments. The city isn't known for luxurious hotels, but there are a few more upmarket choices; however, they remain "no frills" when compared to other cities in Europe.

By and large, expect to pay a lot during the high season (June-August). While most of the options are downtown, there are a few outside the 101 postal code. However, given how small Reykjavík is, most options are within walking distance or a short bus ride to downtown.

CENTRAL REYKJAVÍK
Under 25,000ISK
★ KEX HOSTEL

Skúlagata 28, tel. 354/561-6060,
www.kexhostel.is,
private rooms from 16,000ISK

Kex Hostel is a lot more than a hostel; it's where music lovers, hipsters, and the beautiful people of downtown Reykjavík congregate, meeting for drinks and live music. The hostel offers options ranging from dorm accommodations to private rooms, all with shared bathroom facilities. That said, most people don't stay for the style or comfort of the rooms, but for the Kex experience. The front lounge houses vintage wall maps, mid-century furniture, and a small stage for live bands to plug in and play. The back room is a converted gym that hosts concerts, fashion and vinyl markets, and even food festivals.

★ LOFT HOSTEL

Bankastræti 7, tel. 354/553-8140, www.lofthostel.is,
private rooms from 18,000ISK

Loft Hostel has a reputation as a place to see and be seen. Rooms range from dorm accommodation to privates, but the big draw is the 4th-floor bar/café that hosts up-and-coming bands, established live acts, and DJs. An outdoor deck overlooks Bankastræti in downtown Reykjavík, and it's packed with locals and tourists alike when the sun is shining.

SUNNA GUESTHOUSE

Thórsgata 26, tel. 354/511-5570, www.sunna.is, rooms
from 20,000ISK

Sunna Guesthouse offers several types of accommodations: one- and two-bedroom apartments, studios, rooms with private bathrooms, and rooms with shared bathroom facilities. All rooms are decorated in a light, minimalist style with muted colors and wood furniture. The location is key, as it's right across the street from Hallgrímskirkja in downtown Reykjavík. Guests have access to a shared kitchen to prepare meals, and a breakfast buffet is included in the price. The breakfast accommodates vegetarians as well as those with gluten allergies.

ROOM WITH A VIEW

Laugavegur 18, tel. 354/552-7262, www.
roomwithaview.is, rooms from 21,000ISK

Room with a View is right next to the popular bookstore Mál og Menning and near all the great bars downtown. Rooms range from small singles to three-bedroom apartments for groups. Rooms are clean and modern, some with private bathroom facilities. Guests have access to two hot tubs as well as a common kitchen area. Be advised that because of the proximity of bars and restaurants, it can be quite noisy on Friday and Saturday nights. If you're looking for a quiet room on a sleepy street, this isn't it.

FOSSHÓTEL BARON

Baronsstígur 2-4, tel. 354/562-3204, www.fosshotel.is, rooms from 21,000ISK

Fosshótel Baron may not be pretty from the exterior, but it's clean, convenient, and in a good location in downtown Reykjavík. The 120 rooms range from standard singles and doubles to apartment-style accommodations that have kitchenettes and mini refrigerators. The lobby looks a little depressing, but the accommodating staff and the location make up for it. Guests have access to free Wi-Fi, free and plentiful parking, and an adequate included breakfast.

★ HÓTEL FRÓN

Laugavegur 22A, tel. 354/511-4666, www.hotelfron.is, rooms from 23,000ISK

Hótel Frón couldn't have picked a better location if it tried. Located on the high street Laugavegur, the hotel has single, double, and apartment-style studios that are clean, bright, and comfortable. The apartments come with small kitchens, and a couple of them feature Jacuzzi bathtubs. It's also conveniently close to the bars on Laugavegur—though this means it can be quite noisy on Friday and Saturday nights.

HÓTEL KLÖPP

Klapparstígur 26, tel. 354/595-8520, www.centerhotels.is, rooms from 25,000ISK

Hótel Klöpp offers fresh rooms on a quiet corner in the city center. Some rooms feature warm, bright hues including red walls, while others are stark white, clean, and cool. All rooms have hardwood floors and small private bathrooms. Guests have access to free Wi-Fi, assistance with booking tours is provided, and the friendly staff even offers a northern lights wake-up service in the winter when the aurora borealis is visible.

RADISSON BLU SAGA HOTEL

Hagatorg, tel. 354/525-9900, www.radissonblu.com, rooms from 25,000ISK

Radisson Blu Saga Hotel has a dynamite location in the city center, close to the Reykjavík Art Museum and the famous Bæjarins Beztu Plysur hot dog stand. Rooms are larger than average, many with a maritime theme that's charming. Beds are lush, and the 209 rooms are stocked with bath products from Anne Semonin. Amenities include free Wi-Fi, access to the spa and health center, and two in-house restaurants: Grillið for fine dining and Restaurant Skrudur for more casual meals.

REYKJAVÍK4YOU APARTMENTS

Laugavegur 85, www.reykjavik4you.com, rooms from 25,000ISK

The Reykjavík4You Apartments offer great spaces in a central location. Studios and one- and two-bedroom apartments are available, and all are stocked with well-equipped kitchens, spacious bathrooms, and bright decor. Apartments are clean and comfortable, with lots of light in the summer months.

Over 25,000ISK

CENTER HOTEL PLAZA HOTEL

Aðalstræti 4, tel. 354/595-8500, www.centerhotels.is, rooms from 26,000ISK

Center Plaza Hotel is in the heart of Reykjavík. Many of the 180 rooms have spectacular views of the city, but with that comes quite a bit of noise during the weekends. The rooms are cozy and sparsely decorated but clean and bright. The bathrooms are small, with a shower, and each room has a flat-screen TV and free Wi-Fi. The clientele is a mix of business and leisure travelers. A lounge downstairs tends to be sleepy because of the proximity of popular bars downtown.

★ HÓTEL BORG

*Posthússtræti 9-11, tel. 354/551-1440, www.
hotelborg.is, rooms from 28,000ISK*

Hótel Borg is a popular choice for celebrities and politicians passing through Reykjavík. Why? Built in 1930, the 56-room four-star downtown hotel is at once elegant, modern, and steeped in old-time charm. Hotel Borg's rooms have custom-made furniture, flat-screen satellite TVs, and very comfortable beds. The in-house restaurant, Silfur, is a favorite, and a café/bar serves light meals.

KVOSIN HOTEL

Kirkutorg 4, tel. 354/571-4460, www.kvosinhotel.is, rooms from 31,000ISK

Kvosin Hotel is a gorgeous modern boutique hotel situated close to the Pond and parliament in downtown Reykjavík. Rooms come in four adorably described sizes: normal, bigger, biggest, and larger than life. All rooms feature mini refrigerators, a Nespresso machine, Samsung Smart TV, and skin-care amenities from Aveda. The rooms are sleek and Scandinavian cool with accents from local Icelandic designers. A delicious breakfast is included and served downstairs at the Bergsson restaurant.

HOTEL HOLT

Bergstaðastæti 37, tel. 354/552-5700, www.holt.is, rooms from 33,000ISK

Hotel Holt offers spacious, tastefully decorated rooms, some with a balcony. Holt is one of the few hotels in downtown Reykjavík that offers room service, and its service and amenities are comparable to upscale hotels in large European cities. Guests also have free access to free parking, free Wi-Fi, and a staff eager to assist with tour bookings and recommendations for sights and restaurants.

RADISSON BLU 1919 HOTEL

Posthússtræti 2, tel. 354/599-1000, www.radissonblu.com, rooms from 34,000ISK

Radisson Blu 1919 Hotel is an 88-room hotel that occupies a central location in the capital. Built in 1919, the hotel has undergone a couple of renovations, but it has maintained a lot of its charm. The rooms are large, with hardwood floors, sizable bathrooms, comfortable beds, and free high-speed Wi-Fi. Guests who reserve a suite are treated to a king-size bed, Jacuzzi bathtub, and bathrobe with slippers. Guests also have access to a fitness center with some basic machines. The in-house restaurant is dynamite, with a menu ranging from fresh fish caught off of Iceland's shores to lamb fillets and duck breast entrées.

101 HOTEL

Hverfisgata 10, tel. 354/580-0101, www.101hotel.is, rooms from 51,000ISK

Award-winning 101 Hotel is quite posh for Reykjavík. In 2017, the *Daily Telegraph* named it one of the best luxury hotels in the city. Rooms are cozy and stylish at the same time with a black-and-white color palette, wood floors, and in-room fireplaces. And while the rooms are pricey, the amenities are pretty great. Each room has a large walk-in shower, flat-screen TV with satellite channels, free high-speed Wi-Fi, a CD/DVD player with a Bose sound dock, and bathrobes and slippers. The restaurant offers an eclectic menu with creations ranging from mussels and pommes frites to Icelandic cod with saffron risotto.

OLD HARBOR (GRANDI)
Over 25,000ISK
★ ICELANDAIR HÓTEL REYKJAVÍK MARINA

Myrargata 2, tel. 354/560-8000, www.icelandairhotels.com, rooms from 26,000ISK

Icelandair Hótel Reykjavík Marina is in a great location by the harbor district, close to the whale-watching tours, restaurants, and museums. One of the most design conscious of the Icelandair Hótels chain, Reykjavík Marina displays art throughout the lobby, restaurant, and rooms, featuring everything from murals by local Icelandic artists to impressive wood sculptures. Rooms are minimalist and modern, the staff is warm, and the hotel is home to one of the hippest hotel bars in the city, **Slipp Bar.**

OUTSIDE THE CITY CENTER

Under 25,000ISK

ICELANDAIR HÓTEL REYKJAVÍK NATURA

*Hlíðarfótur, tel. 354/444-4500, www.
icelandairhotels.com, rooms from 19,000ISK*

Icelandair Hótel Reykjavík Natura pays homage to Reykjavík's rich art culture with murals and sculptures throughout the building. Built in 1964 but renovated in 2012, the hotel has been a favorite among business travelers due to its proximity to the Reykjavík Domestic Airport and conference facilities. The in-house restaurant Satt offers a delicious breakfast buffet and meals throughout the day. The main attractions, for many, are the indoor swimming pool and Soley Natura Spa, where guests can get massages, manicures, pedicures, and facial treatments. The hotel is a 20-minute walk to downtown Reykjavík, but guests are given free passes for the city bus, which stops just outside the hotel.

REYKJAVÍK LIGHTS HOTEL

*Suðurlandsbraut 16, tel. 354/513-9000, www.
keahotels.is, rooms from 20,000ISK*

Reykjavík Lights Hotel is a concept design hotel with 105 rooms, including singles, doubles, triples, and group rooms. Just past the reception area is an airy lobby that houses a bar and the common eating area. Rooms are large, featuring Nordic-style decor and luxurious beds. The bathrooms are modern and stark white with showers. Located outside of the city center, it's about a 10-minute walk to downtown.

HILTON REYKJAVÍK NORDICA

*Suðurlandsbraut 2, tel. 354/444-5000, www.
hiltonreykjavik.com, rooms from 25,000ISK*

Hilton Reykjavík Nordica is a 252-room four-star hotel situated in the financial district, about a 10-minute walk from downtown Reykjavík. It attracts business travelers as well as families and individuals thanks to its comfortable rooms, top-notch service, luxurious spa, and memorable in-house restaurant, Vox.

Over 25,000ISK

GRAND HOTEL REYKJAVÍK

*Sigtún 38, tel. 354/514-8000, www.grand.is, rooms
from 27,000ISK*

Grand Hotel Reykjavík is a huge 311-room high-rise hotel just a few minutes from downtown Reykjavík. This is a favorite among business travelers and conference attendees because the hotel has meeting rooms and conference facilities. The rooms are large, with hardwood floors and comfortable yet uninspiring furnishings. The **restaurant** (lunch noon-2pm, dinner 6pm-10pm) offers dishes ranging from lamb fillets with mushrooms to duck breast with parsnip.

Information and Services

VISITORS CENTERS

There are currently no tourist information centers in Reykjavík.

MEDIA

The *Reykjavík Grapevine* (www.grapevine.is) is Iceland's only English-language newspaper, and it's geared toward tourists, hipsters, and music-loving locals. There are listings for bands and DJ club dates, information about what's on at museums and art galleries, and articles ranging from humorous to informative to sarcastic on what's going on in Reykjavík. To get the pulse of the city, pick up a copy in bookstores, museums, and shops, or check it out online. In summertime, the newspaper comes out every other week, and in the winter it's monthly.

EMERGENCY SERVICES

The telephone number for emergencies is **112.** If you are having a medical emergency, are stranded by car trouble, or are experiencing a safety issue or any other pressing, dire emergency, dial this number.

MEDICAL SERVICES
LANDSPITALI
Norðurmýri, tel. 354/543-1000, www.landspitali.is

Landspitali is the national hospital of Iceland. It houses day-patient units, an emergency room, and clinical services. If you are experiencing a medical emergency, dial 112 for an ambulance.

LYF OG HEILSA
Haaleitisbraut 68, tel. 354/581-2101, 8am-midnight Mon.-Fri., 10am-midnight Sat.-Sun.

For a pharmacy, visit Lyf og Heilsa. Keep in mind that over-the-counter medication and aspirin are only available at a pharmacy, not in supermarkets or convenience stores like in other countries.

Getting There and Around

GETTING THERE
By Plane
KEFLAVÍK INTERNATIONAL AIRPORT
Reykjanesbær, www.isavia.is

Keflavík International Airport (KEF) is just 50 minutes east of Reykjavík. The Flybus (tel. 354/580-5400, www.flybus.is) runs regularly from Keflavík International Airport to BSÍ, Reykjavík's main bus station, where you can get a shuttle to the downtown hotels. It takes about 50 minutes to get from Keflavík to BSÍ bus station, and buses depart about 40 minutes after flights land. One-way tickets cost 3,299ISK. (BSÍ is also the main departure site for day-tour bus trips with various companies, including Reykjavík Excursions.) Taxis are also available at Keflavík; the fare from the airport to Reykjavík is upward of 15,000ISK.

There is no shortage of companies in Iceland eager to rent you a car, and many of them make it quite easy, with offices at Keflavík International Airport. They include the following: Avis (Knarrarvogur 2, tel. 354/591-4000, www.avis.is), Budget (Vatsmýrarvegur 10, tel. 354/562-6060, www.budget.is), Europcar (Hjallahrauni 9, tel. 354/565-3800, www.europcar.is), and

Hertz (Reykjavík City Airport, tel. 354/505-0600, www.hertz.is).

REYKJAVÍK CITY AIRPORT
Þorragata 10, tel. 354/569-4100, www.isavia.is

Reykjavík City Airport is the city's domestic airport, with regional connections to towns throughout the country, including Akureyi and the Westfjords. The only international flights are to the Faroe Islands and Greenland. Strætó (www.straeto.is) bus numbers 15 and 19 stop at the Reykjavík City Airport near the Air Iceland and Eagle Air terminals, respectively. Taxis are also available on-site.

Several airlines have offices in Reykjavík: Air Iceland Connect (Reykjavíkurflugvöllur, tel. 354/570-3000, www.airicelandconnect.com), Eagle Air (Reykjavíkurflugvöllur, tel. 354/562-4200, www.eagleair.is), and Icelandair (Reykjavíkurflugvöllur, tel. 354/505-0100, www.icelandair.is).

By Car
In addition to rental car centers at Keflavík, there are convenient outposts at BSÍ bus station, and around the city. If you are planning to stay in Reykjavík for the duration of your trip, a rental car will not be necessary.

GETTING AROUND
By Bus
BSÍ

Vatnsmýrarvegur 10, tel. 354/562-1011, www.bsi.is
Reykjavík's bus system is convenient, reliable, and an affordable way to get around the city. The bus system, called **Strætó** (www.straeto.is), which means "street" in Icelandic, runs about 30 bus lines within the city center as well as to outlying areas like Kópavogur and Hafnarfjörður. The bright yellow buses cost 470ISK per ride within the city limits, and you can ask for a free bus transfer if you need to switch buses to get to your destination. You must pay with exact change; bus drivers don't make change. Buses run daily 7am-11pm. Be sure to check the website for information on holiday schedules and delays due to weather.

If you plan to use the bus a fair amount, a great option is the **Reykjavík Welcome Card,** which grants you free access to the city's swimming pools, almost all the city's museums, and unlimited city bus rides. You can purchase a card for one, two, or three days for 3,900ISK, 5,500ISK, and 6,700ISK, respectively. If you will be spending a lot of time in Reykjavík, this is a great option to save a lot of money. Cards can be purchased online and at select hotels and bus stations. You can also buy individual tickets through the Strætó app.

Strætó's blue long-distance buses depart from **Mjodd station** (tel. 354/557-7854), eight kilometers (five miles) southeast of the city center, traveling to several regions around the country.

By Taxi

The two things you need to know about taxis in Reykjavík is that they are expensive, and you have to call ahead for one (for instance, a ride from the BSÍ bus station to Harpa takes about eight minutes and costs roughly 2,000ISK). **Hreyfill** (tel. 354/588-5522, www.hreyfill.is) and **BSR** (tel. 354/561-0000, www.taxireykjavik.is) are two popular taxi companies in the city. You can also reserve taxis with Hreyfill through an app. Taxis arrive 5-10 minutes after you call, and the price on the meter is inclusive—you don't tip in Iceland. Cab prices rival those in New York City: It's rare to spend less than 2,000ISK on a taxi ride, even for short distances. There are a couple of cab stations downtown where you don't have to call ahead—just outside **Hlemmur bus station** and near **Lækjartorg,** a square in downtown Reykjavík where Lækjargata, Bankastræti, and Austurstræti streets meet. The taxi stands are hard to miss, as the cabs can be lined up 10 deep.

By Car

If your entire stay is in Reykjavík, it is not necessary to rent a car as the city is walkable, and buses are widely available. However, if you are getting out of the city, and do not want to take tours, a car rental is necessary.

Be advised that **parking** isn't easy in Reykjavík. Most locals have cars, and street parking can take some time. However, there are several parking garages and lots available around the city, and parking at a garage will cost less than 100ISK per hour.

By Bicycle

Reykjavík has made great strides in becoming more bicycle friendly over the past few years. There are new bicycle lanes throughout the city as well as new bike racks to lock up your ride outside shops. Be aware that bike theft is rampant, so be proactive and lock up your bicycle; if you leave it unattended and unlocked, it'll disappear. Other than bike theft, the only concern for cyclists is weather, which changes often. You can start your ride during calm and sunny skies, but within minutes that could change to rain and wind. You can rent bikes at **Reykjavík Bike Tours** (www.icelandbike.com).

On Foot

Reykjavík is a very walkable city—depending on the weather, of course. Because of its small size, it's a perfect place to roam, to pop into quaint shops, visit museums, and photograph the city's many statues.

Around Reykjavík

VIÐEY ISLAND

Viðey is a little gem of an island accessible by ferry. Historically, the island was inhabited by an Augustinian monastery from 1225 to 1539 and was a pilgrimage destination in the Middle Ages. It's also home to Viðeyjarstofa, one of the oldest buildings in Iceland. The island, which is just 1.6 square kilometers (0.62 square miles) in size, hosts unspoiled nature with vast stretches of grassy plains and rich birdlife, as well as the Imagine Peace Tower, an installation created by Yoko Ono.

Sights
VIÐEYJARSTOFA
www.visitreykjavik.is

One of the oldest buildings in the country, Viðeyjarstofa dates back to 1755. Over generations, it has served as a home to many of Iceland's most powerful men. The building, made from white stone with a black roof, is open to the public.

IMAGINE PEACE TOWER
www.imaginepeacetower.com

This outdoor installation was created by artist Yoko Ono in memory of her late husband, John Lennon. Ono chose Iceland because it's one of the most peaceful countries in the world. The base of the tower is 10 meters (33 feet) wide, and the words "imagine peace" are inscribed on the structure in 24 languages. A vertical beam of light shines from the structure 4,000 meters (13,123 feet) into the sky and is visible from miles away. It was unveiled on October 9, 2007, Lennon's 67th birthday. It's lit every year from October 9 to December 8, the latter of which is the anniversary of Lennon's death.

Getting There and Around
In the summer, **Elding** (tel. 354/533-5055, www.videy.com) operates a ferry with eight daily departures mid-May through September from **Skarfabakki pier, Harpa,** and **Ægisgarður pier.** Ferries run in the afternoon. During the rest of the year the ferry runs three departures on Saturdays and Sundays from Skarfabakki to Viðey. The round-trip ferry ride costs 1,600ISK for adults or 800ISK for children 7-15, and takes about 10 minutes.

SELTJARNARNES
Grótta Lighthouse
www.visitreykjavik.is

Northwest of Reykjavík sits Grótta, a lovely lighthouse you can walk to during low tide. The lighthouse is located in Seltjarnarnes, which is technically outside of Reykjavík, and has stood since 1947. In the summer, Grótta is a great spot to visit to bask in the sun and observe the rich birdlife in the area. In the winter, locals and travelers drive to the car park on clear nights and hope to catch a glimpse of the northern lights.

Getting There
To reach Grótta Lighthouse, you can take a taxi from downtown Reykjavík, which will cost about 2,500ISK, or you can take bus #11 to the lighthouse. It's about a 10-minute drive along Eiðsgrandi, which runs along the peninsula northwest of Reykjavík where Seltjarnes sits. Better yet, it's an easy cycle.

MOSFELLSBÆR
Just 15 minutes from downtown Reykjavík, Mosfellsbær is a quaint, placid town with a picturesque bay, beautiful mountains, and clean streams and rivers. About 10,000 people live in Mosfellsbær, and despite its proximity to downtown, it feels remote enough to make it seem like you're in the countryside.

Around Reykjavík

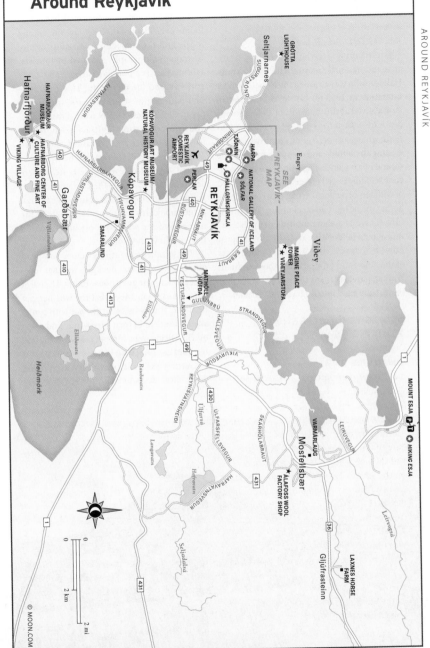

© MOON.COM

Sights
GLJÚFRASTEINN

Pósthólf 250, tel. 354/568-8066, www.gljufrasteinn.
is, 9am-5pm daily June 1-Aug. 31, 10am-4pm
Tues.-Sun. Sept. 1-May 31, 1,200ISK

Gljúfrasteinn was the home of Icelandic novelist and national treasure Halldór Laxness.
Halldór, who was awarded the Nobel Prize for
Literature in 1955 for his novel *Independent
People,* lived at this home from 1945 until his
death in 1998. It has been preserved as a museum, giving visitors a glimpse into his life, including the library and study where he wrote
several of his works. The white two-story concrete building is well preserved, but it feels lived
in with lots of personal artifacts decorating the
home, including books, clothing, and furniture. There is a short multimedia presenta-
tion about Halldór's life and work, available in
English, Icelandic, and Swedish. Guided tours
of the house and grounds take about an hour.
You can purchase many of his books at the museum, translated into English and German.

Sports and Recreation
★ HIKING ESJA

Distance: 8 km (5 mi) round-trip
Hiking time: 2 hours round-trip
Information and maps: www.visitreykjavik.is

Trailhead: Car park just off the Ring Road, signed
for Esja

Standing 914 meters (2,999 feet) high, Esja
looms over Reykjavík. It's a favorite among
locals and the subject of thousands of picturesque photographs snapped by tourists.
Hiking Esja is a popular pastime and a few
paths ascend the mountain. The most popular path begins at the car park, which is at
about 780 meters (2,559 feet). From there,
you can cross the Mógilsa stream, which
leads to a steeper stretch named "steinnin."
The hike is considered easy, but be aware that
the last stretch to the top is pretty steep; there
are handrails to lessen the challenge. When
you reach the top of this path, you can sign
a guestbook. It's fun to read through all the
names and see where people have traveled
from to climb the mountain.

Please take precautions before you head
out. Make sure you check the weather forecast and let your guesthouse or hotel know of
your plans. Remember that the weather can
be fickle. It may be beautiful out with sunny
skies, but it could turn very windy and rainy
quickly. Bring water, proper footwear, and waterproof clothing with you.

Getting to Esja is pretty easy, even if you
don't have access to a car. It's 11 kilometers

Mount Esja

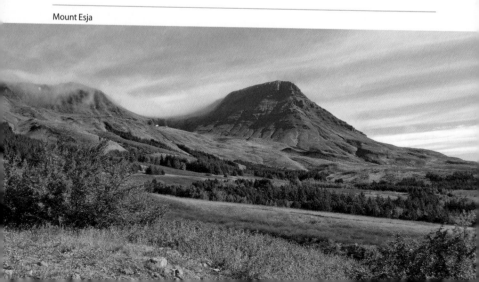

(6.8 miles) north of Mosfellsbær, about 20 minutes and accessible from Route 1. Drive through Mosfellsbær and you'll see signs pointing to the car park. You can also take the **Strætó** 57 bus (www.straeto.is) from the bus station Mjodd in Reykjavík. The bus fare is 940ISK and the bus departs 12 times a day. It's a 30-minute ride. Let the bus driver know that you are heading to the base of Esja (the bus stop is Esjumelar) and you will get dropped off at the car park.

LAXNES FARM
off Rte. 36, tel. 354/566-6179, www.laxnes.is

If you're staying in Reykjavík and want to do some horseback riding, Laxnes Farm is just a 15-minute drive northeast from downtown. Icelandic horses are available to ride year-round for different tour lengths. The staff is warm and friendly and shows a great deal of love and respect for the horses they care for. A popular tour is called the "Laxnes Special"; you will be picked up at your hotel or guesthouse in Reykjavík and taken to the farm, where you will meet your guide and horse. You are given all the gear you need, including helmets, rain clothes, and boots, and are taken on a glorious two-hour tour (11,900ISK) that has spectacular landscape views. The Laxnes Farm is close to Halldór Laxness's home, but they are not related.

VARMÁRLAUG
Þverholt 2, tel. 354/566-6754, 6:30am-8pm Mon.-Fri., 9am-6pm Sat.-Sun. in summer, 4pm-9pm Mon.-Fri. in winter, 800ISK

If you're planning to stay in town for a few hours or more, check out the local swimming pool, called Varmárlaug. The pool isn't as impressive as some of the pools in the Reykjavík city center, but the water is warm and the facilities are clean. You're likely to see locals taking a dip, but not many tourists.

Shopping
ÁLAFOSS WOOL FACTORY SHOP
Álafossvegur 23, tel. 354/566-6303, www.alafoss.is, 8am-8pm daily

The Álafoss Wool Factory Shop is home to the Álafoss wool brand, which was established in 1896 and was for decades the leading manufacturer and exporter of Icelandic wool products. The brand is still manufacturing in Iceland today. The shop is located in the old factory house by the Álafoss waterfall, which was used to drive the mills. The shop sells wool skeins, scarves, hats, sweaters, and blankets, along with some other small goods. You can also purchase a sheep skin as well as other Icelandic design products. The prices are comparable to those in downtown Reykjavík, but the selection is better and bigger. The site also includes an exhibition of old knitting machinery and photographs from the mill's early days.

Food
MOSFELLSBAKARÍ
Háholti 13-15, tel. 354/566-6145, www.mosbak.is, 7am-6pm Mon.-Fri., 8am-4pm Sat.-Sun., pastries from 600ISK

Mosfellsbakarí is a decadent bakery known for its chocolate creations. Located in the center of town, it does a roaring business. In addition to its indulgent cakes and pastries, the bakery offers light meals, including sandwiches and soup.

Information and Services
TOURIST INFORMATION OFFICE
Þverholti 2, tel. 354/566-6822, www.mosfellsbaer.is, 9am-5pm daily

Mosfellsbær's tourist information office is based inside the **Mosfellsbær public library,** which is housed in a shopping area. It's a great place to gather some tourist brochures and maps as well as buy some food at the grocery store inside the shopping center.

Getting There
Mosfellsbær is just a 15-minute drive (14 km/9 mi) from downtown **Reykjavík** via **Route 49. Street parking** is available, and it's easy to find parking spots.

You can take the **15 bus** to the **Haholt stop,** which is in the center of town. Check www.straeto.is for more bus information. Depending on the time of day, buses run every 30 minutes to every hour, and it takes 30 minutes from downtown Reykjavík to Mosfellsbær. A single ride on the bus is 470ISK.

KÓPAVOGUR

Kópavogur is a quiet suburb home to families, young professionals, and immigrants, and it attracts people traveling on business or shoppers headed to the Smáralind mall or the island's only IKEA and Costco. There are a couple of museums worth checking out for local art and history.

Sights
KÓPAVOGUR ART MUSEUM (Gerðarsafn)
Hamraborg 4, tel. 354/570-0440, www.gerdarsafn. is, 11am-5pm daily, 1,000ISK

The Kópavogur Art Museum is named Gerðarsafn in Icelandic, after sculptor Gerður Helgadóttir, who died in 1975. In 1977, her heirs donated roughly 1,400 of her works to the municipality of Kópavogur on the condition that a museum bearing her name would be opened. The museum opened in 1994. Gerður's black-iron works in the 1950s made her a pioneer of three-dimensional abstract art in Iceland. Around 1970 Gerður returned to working with plaster, terra cotta, and concrete, using simple circles with movement in many variations. Other works on display range from contemporary to landscape art. It's a pretty museum with varied works of art, and it's worth a visit if you're in the neighborhood.

NATURAL HISTORY MUSEUM (Náttúrufræðistofa)
Hamraborg 6A, tel. 354/570-0430, www.natkop. is, 10am-7pm Mon.-Thur., 11am-5pm Fri., 1pm-5pm Sat., free

The Natural History Museum is a great place to bring kids to learn about the animals and geology of Iceland. The exhibits fall into two categories: zoological and geological. The geology section, where you learn about the major rock types and minerals of Iceland, is of more interest to adults. The zoological part focuses on the mammals, fish, birds, and invertebrates of the country. It's educational and entertaining, and kids love the exhibitions on seals, foxes, and cute birds like puffins.

Sports and Recreation
KÓPAVOGUR SWIMMING POOL
Borgarholtsbraut 17, tel. 354/540-0470, 6:30am-10pm Mon.-Fri., 8am-8pm Sat.-Sun., 850ISK

The Kópavogur Swimming Pool is frequented by locals and their children and has a very family-friendly atmosphere. Amenities include a 50-meter (164-foot) outdoor pool, two smaller indoor pools, three waterslides, seven hot pots, and a steam bath. You aren't likely to see crowds or tourists, so if you're looking to just swim, this is a good spot.

Food and Shopping
SMÁRALIND
Hagasmara 1, tel. 354/528-8000, www.smaralind. is, 11am-7pm Mon., Wed., and Fri., 11am-9pm Thur., 11am-6pm Sat., 1pm-6pm Sun.

Smáralind is Iceland's largest shopping mall. You will find everything from Adidas sneakers to Levi's, but for double the price that they would be back home. However, there is a movie theater and an entertainment area with rides for kids. In addition to a food court, there are casual eateries TGI Friday's and Café Adesso, coffee shop Kaffitár, and Serrano, which serves Mexican-style food.

Information and Services
SERVICE AND ADMINISTRATION CENTER
Fannborg 2, tel. 354/570-1500

The town's service and administration center is open 8am-4pm Monday-Thursday and 8am-3pm Friday.

Getting There

Kópavogur is just a 10-minute ride, 5 kilometers (3 miles) south from downtown **Reykjavík** by car. You take **Route 40** to **Route 49**. Street parking is available and it's easy to find parking spots.

City buses go to Kópavogur, including **buses 1, 2,** and **28.** Buses leave every 30 minutes or so, the fare is 470ISK one-way, and it takes about 20 minutes by bus. Check www. straeto.is for more bus information.

HAFNARFJÖRÐUR

Hafnarfjörður is a picturesque fishing town that about 30,000 people call home. Attractions include a scenic harbor, pretty parks, and the famous Viking Village, a restaurant and hotel that plays host to numerous Viking-related events.

Sights
HAFNARFJÖRÐUR MUSEUM
Vesturgata 8, www.hafnarfjordur.is, 11am-5pm daily June 1-Aug. 31, 11am-5pm Sat.-Sun. rest of year, free
Hafnarfjörður Museum houses a collection of cultural artifacts and photographs that are significant to the town. The museum consists of six houses and nine exhibitions that showcase life in the town's early days. The six houses date from 1803 to 1906 and include the oldest house in the town, Sivertsen's House.

HAFNARBORG CENTER OF CULTURE AND FINE ART
Strandgata 34, tel. 354/555-0800, www.hafnarborg. is, noon-5pm Wed.-Mon., free
Hafnarborg Center of Culture and Fine Art consists of two galleries with rotating exhibitions ranging from contemporary art by modern Icelandic artists to works by some of the island's most celebrated artists of years past.

VIKING VILLAGE (Fjörukráin)
Strandgata 55, tel. 354/565-1213, www.vikingvillage.is
Viking Village is great fun for kids and adults alike. The closest thing Iceland has to a theme park, the Viking Village celebrates the island's history—with a sense of humor. It's kitschy, with lots of Viking horns, reproduced wood huts, and wooden furnishings. Guests can stay at the hotel, visit the gift shop, have a meal at the restaurant, or just check out the decor.

The Viking Village takes center stage every mid-June when the space hosts the **Viking Festival,** which takes place over five days. There are performances of jousts with participants in Viking costumes, food stands, metalwork demonstrations, and woolen goods and jewelry for sale.

Sports and Recreation
ÍSHESTAR
Sörlaskeið 26, tel. 354/555-7000, www.ishestar.is
This town is a lovely place to ride a horse. With its rolling landscape and picturesque views, it doesn't get much better than this in the greater Reykjavík area. Íshestar is a local company that offers an array of tours year-round. It provides transportation to the riding center from your accommodation and all gear needed to ride. A half-day tour starts at 11,500ISK.

SUÐURBÆJARLAUG
Hringbraut 77, tel. 354/565-3080, 6:30am-10pm Mon.-Thur., 6:30am-8pm Fri., 8am-6pm Sat., 8am-5pm Sun., 600ISK
Take a dip with the locals at the Suðurbæjarlaug pool, which has an outdoor pool with a waterslide, a steam bath, and a few hot tubs.

Food
SÚFISTINN
Strandgata 9, tel. 354/565-3740, 8:15am-11pm Mon.-Thur., 8am-11pm Fri., 10am-11pm Sat., 11am-11pm Sun., 800ISK
Súfistinn is a cozy café that sells stellar coffee drinks, fresh pastries, and light meals. Situated by the central downtown shopping area and performance hall, it's a perfect place to grab a blueberry muffin and latte or a soup or sandwich.

VIKING RESTAURANT
Strandagata 55, tel. 354/565-1213, www.fjorukrain. is, 2,800ISK
Viking Restaurant (Fjörugarðurinn) at the Viking Village is a restaurant that serves traditional Icelandic fare like lamb and

fish dishes in a fun, Viking-themed atmosphere. There are lots of wood furnishings and medieval accents displayed throughout the space. You can book a Viking performance in advance for groups of any size for a fee, which includes the guests being "kidnapped" from their bus, brought into a "cave" in the restaurant, served mead, escorted to dinner, and entertained with singing and music. The restaurant is open for dinner 6pm-10pm daily.

Accommodations
HÓTEL VIKING

Strandgata 55, tel. 354/565-1213, www.vikingvillage.

is, rooms from 16,000ISK

Hótel Viking at the Viking Village has 42 hotel rooms and 14 "Viking cottages" next to the hotel. All rooms and cottages include private bathrooms, comfortable beds, televisions, and stylish Viking accessories. The hotel features artworks from Iceland, Greenland, and the Faroe Islands. Guests have access to free Wi-Fi, free parking, and an on-site hot tub. Breakfast is included in the price.

Information and Services
TOURIST INFORMATION CENTER

Strandgata 6, tel. 354/585-5555, www.hafnarfjordur.

is, 8am-5pm Mon.-Fri. year-round, 10am-3pm

Sat.-Sun. June-Aug.

The tourist information center is situated in **Hafnarfjörður Town Hall.** You can arrange for transportation, buy tickets to local tours, and peruse brochures about the town's sights.

Getting There

Hafnarfjörður is just a 15-minute drive, 11 kilometers (7 miles) south of downtown **Reykjavík.** Take **Route 40** to get there.

City Bus 1 stops in town. Check www.straeto.is for bus schedules and information.

1: Viðey Island 2: Hafnarfjörður

Reykjanes Peninsula and the South

Itinerary Ideas 88
Reykjanes Peninsula . . . 90
The Golden Circle 99
The South Coast 108
Heimaey 130

South Iceland is the country's busiest tourist destination, but in many places it still feels untouched and exotic—a hiker's paradise.

Glaciers, mountains, and two active volcanoes (Katla and Hekla) beckon. A wide and diverse region, the South is home to well-known sights like Þingvellir National Park and the Geysir geothermal region, both on the popular Golden Circle tour, and lesser-known gems like Þórsmörk, an area with colorful mountains, waterfalls, canyons, and lava-shaped landscapes.

The terrain is rugged, even desert-like in some areas, while heather, moss, and lichen cover lava stones for miles. Hiking trails are well developed and the land mostly level, making for a relatively easy hiking

Highlights

Look for ★ to find recommended sights, activities, dining, and lodging.

★ **Blue Lagoon:** This gorgeous, geothermally heated spring heals the skin and soothes the body (page 95).

★ **Þingvellir National Park:** Appealing to both geology buffs and history enthusiasts, this park is home to where Europe and North America meet as well as the site where Iceland's first parliament gathered (page 99).

★ **Geysir:** Make the trip to see the Strokkur geyser shoot steam and boiling water up to 30 meters (98 feet), a natural phenomenon that occurs every 10 minutes or so (page 104).

★ **Gullfoss:** If you have time to see only one waterfall in Iceland, this should be it (page 106).

★ **Reykjadalur Hike:** This increasingly popular, relatively short hike gives you the chance to soak your feet in picturesque hot springs (page 110).

★ **Lava Centre:** Take a deep dive into Iceland's unique geology, from volcanoes to the constant small tremors that parts of the island experience (page 117).

★ **Hiking the Laugavegurinn Trail:** See vast glaciers, bubbling hot springs, and towering mountains on this 55-kilometer (34-mile), four-day hike, one of the most popular trails on the island (page 120).

★ **Fjaðrárgljúfur:** This long, narrow canyon is an extremely picturesque place to hike and take photos (page 128).

★ **Boat Tours off Heimaey:** From the tour offered by the new **Beluga Whale sanctuary** (page 130), to others offering views of rocky coastlines, bird cliffs, and ocean caves, the island of Heimaey is a lovely place to take a boat ride (page 130).

Reykjanes Peninsula and the South

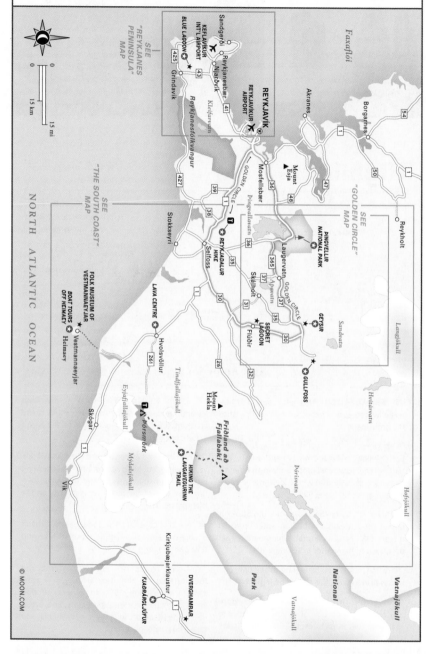

Faxaflói

SEE "REYKJANES PENINSULA" MAP

Sandgerði
KEFLAVÍKUR INTL AIRPORT
BLUE LAGOON
425
43
Reykjanesbær
Njarðvík
41
Grindavík
Kleifarvatn
Reykjanesfólkvangur

REYKJAVÍK
REYKJAVÍKUR AIRPORT

Akranes
Borgarnes
54
50
1
Reykholt

NORTH ATLANTIC OCEAN

427
39
Mosfellsbær
GOLDEN CIRCLE
Mount Esja
47
48
Þingvallavatn

SEE "THE SOUTH COAST" MAP

38
1
36
REYKJADALUR HIKE
Stokkseyri
Selfoss
35
Laugarvatn
365
ÞINGVELLIR NATIONAL PARK
SEE "GOLDEN CIRCLE" MAP

37
Skálholt
37
GOLDEN CIRCLE
GEYSIR
Sandvatn

LAVA CENTRE
1
30
31
SECRET LAGOON
Flúðir
35
30

Hvolsvöllur
26
32
GULLFOSS

FOLK MUSEUM OF VESTMANNAEYJAR
BOAT TOURS OFF HEIMAEY
Vestmannaeyjar
Heimaey

261
Tindfjallajökull
Mount Hekla

Friðland að Fjallabaki

Skógar
Eyjafjallajökull
Þórsmörk
HIKING THE LAUGAVEGURINN TRAIL

Mýrdalsjökull
Vík

Langjökull
Hvítárvatn
Hofsjökull

Þórisvatn

Kirkjubæjarklaustur
DVERGHAMRAR
FJAÐRÁRGLJÚFUR

Park
National
Vatnajökull

0   15 km
0   15 mi

© MOON.COM

locale. Trails are situated in picturesque areas with plenty of bird-watching opportunities in the summer, and the lack of trees means visitors have an uninterrupted view of the landscape.

Steeped in history, Þingvellir National Park is commonly referred to in Iceland as the site of the world's first democracy. It's said that a group of settlers met as a democratic legislature here close to a millennium ago. Geology buffs will be thrilled to visit the Mid-Atlantic Ridge, a fault line that lies in Þingvellir. Visitors can literally plant one foot on Europe's side and the other in North America. Outside of Reykjavík, Þingvellir is the most visited site in Iceland.

The South Coast is a scenic slice of Iceland not to be missed. Here you will find the romantic waterfalls Seljalandsfoss and Skógafoss, the vast black sand beach Reynisfjara, and the charming village of Vík. A gem of the South is a day trip to the Westman Islands, where you can go whale watching, explore a fascinating museum about the eruption on Heimaey in the 1970s, and pay a visit to a Beluga whale sanctuary.

Home to Iceland's only international airport, the Reykjanes Peninsula is one part of the country that visitors are sure to see. Reykjanes is also home to the famous heated waters of the Blue Lagoon, where you can soak away your jet lag.

PLANNING YOUR TIME

The dynamic Reykjanes Peninsula, **Golden Circle,** and Southern Coast region is defined by its vast lava fields, numerous hot springs, geothermal energy, and rugged terrain. Most tourists plan to visit at least two sites other than **Keflavík airport**—the **Mid-Atlantic Ridge** at **Þingvellir National Park** and the glorious **Blue Lagoon,** where you can soak in geothermally heated water.

If you are planning to spend one night in the Reykjanes Peninsula region, rather than just basing yourself out of nearby Reykjavík, base yourself in **Keflavík** or **Grindavík,** where there are several guesthouses and hotels, as well as the largest selection of restaurants and shops on the peninsula. From there, you are close to attractions such as the Blue Lagoon, **Garður lighthouses,** and the **Viking World** museum.

The south is home to the Golden Circle, arguably the most popular route on the island. It takes you to three must-see sites: the towering **Gullfoss waterfall,** Þingvellir National Park, and **Geysir.** The Golden Circle can be accomplished in one day, either by a bus tour or independently using a rental car. It makes the most sense to base yourself in the towns of **Selfoss** or **Hvolsvöllur** when traveling the Golden Circle, though it can also be done as a day trip out of Reykjavík. Meanwhile, the South Coast has black-sand beaches, waterfalls, and quaint villages like **Vík,** a good place to base yourself for extended exploration along the South Coast. The island of **Heimaey,** off the South Coast, is a wonderful place to explore as a day-trip. Here you hike, go whale watching, spot puffins (in the summer), and visit a Beluga whale sanctuary.

Plan to spend at least an afternoon on the Reykjanes Peninsula (likely, at the Blue Lagoon), one day for the Golden Circle, and at least one day exploring the South Coast.

REYKJANES PENINSULA AND THE SOUTH

Previous: Hekla is an active volcano; Reykjanes coastline; puffin on Westman Islands.

Itinerary Ideas

For maximum flexibility on this itinerary, you'll want your own **rental car.** Many people find themselves in the Reykjanes Peninsula on their way to or from Keflavík Airport; it would be possible to do Day 1 of this itinerary straight off your flight, but many people opt to head straight to the **Blue Lagoon** en route to Rekjavík, a more relaxed introduction to the island.

DAY 1: BLUE LAGOON AND REYKJANES PENINSULA

1 Start your day at **Keflavík's harbor** with an exciting early morning whale-watching tour to get a glimpse of Icelandic wildlife.

2 Drive 10 minutes south on Njarðarbraut, along the coast, to **Viking World** to take in some history.

3 Next, stop at the **Bridge Between Continents,** a 20-minute drive down Route 425, where you can get a close look at the mid-Atlantic ridge, a rift between two continental plates.

4 Enjoy a delicious seafood lunch at **Salthúsið,** 20 minutes east on Route 425.

5 Relax after your meal at the world-famous **Blue Lagoon,** just 10 minutes' drive north.

6 Finally, visit the **Krýsuvík** geothermal area, 30 minutes east on Route 427, where you can see bubbling mud pots and hot springs, before driving 40 minutes north on Route 42 to Rekjavík, where you'll stay for the night. (See Reykjavík chapter, page 30, for ideas on where to stay, go, and eat).

DAY 2: THE GOLDEN CIRCLE

1 From Reykjavík, embark on your Golden Circle tour, starting at **Þingvellir National Park.** Here, you can walk along a well-maintained path in the rift valley between the Eurasian and North American plates.

2 Drive to the Haukadalur geothermal area for a look at **Geysir,** the original geyser, and its spouting neighbor Strokkur.

3 Enjoy a break at the **Geysir Center,** grabbing lunch at their cafeteria.

4 Visit the roaring **Gullfoss** waterfall, watching the water thrash and tumble meters below.

5 Go for a dip at the geothermally heated **Secret Lagoon** in the village of Fluðir.

6 Stop by **Friðheimar** to check out the tomato greenhouses and taste one of the best Bloody Marys on the island.

7 Drive to Hvolsvöllur for the night, staying at **Midgard Base Camp** and having dinner there.

DAY 3: THE SOUTH COAST

1 Begin your morning with a 3-hour super jeep tour with **Midgard Adventure** in Hvolsvöllur, crossing rough terrain and seeing waterfalls and volcanoes.

2 Visit the **Lava Centre** in Hvolsvöllur to learn about Iceland's unique geology through interactive displays. Have lunch there before hitting the road to the quaint village of Vík.

Itinerary Ideas

DAY ONE

1 Keflavík's Harbor
2 Viking World
3 Bridge Between Continents
4 Gullfoss
5 Secret Lagoon
6 Blue Lagoon
7 Krýsuvík

DAY TWO

1 Þingvellir National Park
2 Geysir
3 Geysir Center
4 Gullfoss
5 Secret Lagoon
6 Friðheimar
7 Midgard Base Camp

DAY THREE

1 Midgard Adventure
2 Lava Centre
3 Dyrhólaey
4 Reynisfjara
5 True Adventure
6 Halldórskaffi

NORTH ATLANTIC OCEAN

Faxaflói

REYKJAVÍK

Mount Esja

Mosfellsbær

Þingvallavatn

Akranes

Borgarnes

Reykholt

Keflavík
Sandgerði
Njarðvík
Grindavík
Reykjanesfólkvangur
Kleifarvatn
Stokkseyri
Selfoss
Laugarvatn
Apavatn
Skálholt
Flúðir
Langjökull
Sandvatn

Hvolsvöllur
Vestmannaeyjar
Heimaey
Tindfjallajökull
Mount Hekla
Eyjafjallajökull
Skógar
Vík
Mýrdalsjökull
Þórsmörk
Friðland að Fjallabaki
Laugavegurinn Trail
Þórisvatn
Vatnajökull National Park
Kirkjubæjarklaustur
Vatnajökull

425
43
41
427
39
38
36
1
48
36
36
365
37
37
35
31
30
1
26
32
261
11
54
50
47
35

© MOON.COM

0 15 km
0 15 mi

3 Stop first at **Dyrhólaey** to see its unusual basalt columns.
4 Just a bit to the east are the black sand beaches of **Reynisfjara.**
5 Ride a thrilling zipline in Vík with **True Adventure** tours.
6 Finish a full day with a casual dinner at **Halldorskaffi.**

Reykjanes Peninsula

The Reykjanes Peninsula is home to a striking, dramatic landscape comprising lava fields, volcanic craters, geothermal waters and hot springs, and lava caves. The region is also a hotbed for outdoor activities, including horse riding, ATV riding, and bathing in hot springs.

REYKJANESBÆR (KEFLAVÍK AND NJARÐVÍK)

Reykjanesbær is where nearly every tourist's journey begins in Iceland, as it is home to the country's only international airport, Keflavík.

During World War II, British and American troops arrived in Iceland and built the country's first air base. Situated between the United States and continental Europe, Iceland's location served the Allies well; some may be surprised to learn that the last American troops left the island only in 2006.

While it may be tempting to get off the plane and straight on a bus to Reykjavík, Reykjanesbær, a municipality that includes the towns **Keflavík** and **Njarðvík,** is a great place to explore. The region's lava fields, majestic sea cliffs, and accessible hiking trails are worth a bit of your time to roam. Throw on some hiking boots and have your camera ready. This is also a good spot for birdwatching during the summer months, when you can see arctic terns and gannets.

Sights
REYKJANES ART MUSEUM
Tjarnargata 12, Keflavík, tel. 354/421-6700, www. listasafn.reykjanesbaer.is, noon-5pm Mon.-Fri., 1pm-5pm Sat.-Sun., 1,000ISK

This charming museum hosts exhibitions of local artists and gives a taste of the region's eclectic art scene. You can check out contemporary art as well as traditional paintings of the sweeping landscape, from its vast lava fields to the quaint houses along the sea.

REYKJANES MARITIME CENTER
Duusgata 2, Keflavík, tel. 354/421-6700, noon-5pm daily, 1,000ISK
The Reykjanes Maritime Center houses 100 model boats built by a retired local sailor, Grímur Karlsson. Models on display include masted schooners of the mid-19th century and steam-powered trawlers of the 20th century. Information is available on the types of boats and when they were used.

ICELANDIC MUSEUM OF ROCK 'N' ROLL
Hjallavegur 2, Keflavík, tel. 354/420-1030, www. rokksafn.is, 11am-6pm daily, 1,500ISK
The Icelandic Museum of Rock 'n' Roll is a perfect stop for those who love the music of Björk, Sigur Rós, Kaleo, and Of Monsters and Men, and are interested in learning about other rock and pop acts from Iceland. Visitors can listen to the music of local artists, see instruments, and check out costumes that have been worn by well-known local musicians, including one of Iceland's biggest pop stars, Páll Óskar. Guests can also learn about the histories of some of the island's most popular bands and singers. Interactive displays include a sound lab where you can have a karaoke-style singalong or play drums, guitar, or bass. A café and music shop are also on-site.

Reykjanes Peninsula

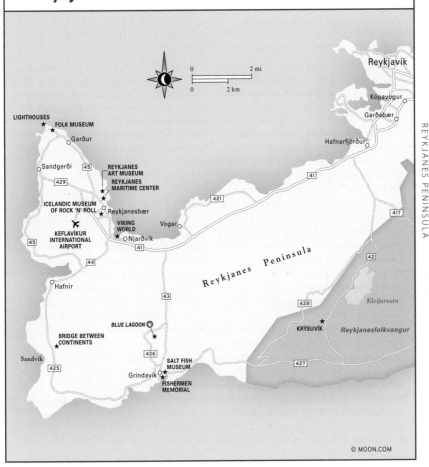

VIKING WORLD
(Vikingaheimar)

Vikingabraut 1, Njarðvík, tel. 354/894-2874, www.vikingworld.is, 7am-6pm daily, 1,500ISK

The Viking World museum is centered on the replica Viking ship *Íslendingur (Icelander)*, which was built in 2000 to sail from Iceland to Greenland in commemoration of Leifur Eiríksson's voyage to North America. The ship, which makes for a great photo op, is housed inside a grand building with huge windows overlooking the shore. Lifted slightly above the ground, the ship can be viewed from many angles; tables and chairs below allow you to spend time gazing at the boat with the ocean in the background. A video exhibit shows how Viking ships were constructed. Other exhibitions include information on the settlement of Iceland as well as Norse mythology. When the weather is pleasant, it's great to sit on the large grass field and enjoy a coffee from the café inside. For kids, there's a "settlement zoo" exhibit, which allows children to get up close and personal with baby lambs, calves, and birds.

Sports and Recreation
VATNAVERÖLD SWIMMING POOL
Sunnubraut 31, Keflavík, tel. 354/421-1500,
6:30am-8:30pm Mon.-Fri., 9am-6pm Sat.-Sun.,
900ISK
This pool in Keflavík is complete with hot tubs, heated pools, and a great swimming area for children. It's a wildly popular spot for locals and gives you a peek into an integral part of Icelandic society.

WHALE WATCHING REYKJANES
Grófin, tel. 354/779-8272,
www.whalewatchingreykjanes.is, 10,900ISK
Whale Iceland runs a tour from Keflavík Harbor. You'll have a chance to see dolphins and an array of whale species including minke, fin, orca, and humpback whales. The tours are three hours and operate on a large, 90-person boat. Tours run year-round and leave once a day at 1pm.

ANGLERS.IS
tel. 354/897-3443, www.anglers.is, 90,000ISK for
groups of 1-4, 145,000ISK for groups of 5-8
Fishing in Iceland not only requires the right equipment, but permits as well, and this tour company takes care of all the practicalities for you. Anglers offers an array of fishing day tours in the highlands, North Iceland, and along the Reykjanes Peninsula. The company's Reykjanes tour, just five minutes from Keflavik Airport, is for groups of 1-8 people, and you can catch haddock, cod, catfish, and mackerel. The tour lasts 3-4 hours.

Food
LANGBEST
Keilisbraut 771, Keflavík, tel. 354/421-4777,
www.langbest.is, 11am-10pm daily,
entrées from 1,790ISK
Situated in the heart of the town, Langbest serves up pizza, sandwiches, and fish and chips. It's a great place to stop for something quick and affordable.

KEF RESTAURANT & BAR
Vatnsnesvegur, Keflavík, tel. 354/420-7000, www.
kef.is, 11:30-11pm Sun.-Thur., 11:30am-11:30pm
Fri.-Sat., entrées from 3,500ISK
Housed in the Hótel Keflavík, KEF Restaurant & Bar is known for serving classic fish and meat dishes. Expect to see Icelandic cod, salmon, and lamb recipes on the menu. The chef focuses on sourcing local ingredients whenever possible. It opens for breakfast at 5am for early birds. During the winter, if the northern lights decide to make an appearance, the restaurant's glass façade allows expansive views of the lights dancing and flickering in the deep black sky.

KAFFI DUUS
Duusgata 10, Keflavík, tel. 354/421-7080, www.duus.
is, 11am-10pm daily, entrées from 3,800ISK
This lovely café is based in the Duus Museum, Reykjanesbær's arts and culture center. It has a casual atmosphere and attracts both locals and tourists. An impressive menu features creamy lobster soup, a popular starter, and main courses like pan-fried lobster, tandoori chicken, and vegetarian curry. The restaurant features spectacular harbor views, and the quality of food keeps people coming back.

LIBRARY BISTRO/BAR
Hafnargata 57, tel. 354/421-5220, www.librarybistro.
is, entrees from 2,690ISK, kitchen 11:30am-10pm
Mon.-Fri., 11am-10pm Sat.-Sun., bar 11am-11pm
Sun.-Thur. and 11am-midnight Fri.-Sat.
Library Bistro/Bar is the chic eatery at the Park Inn by Radisson hotel. The decor is modern and casual and the menu features sandwiches, salads, soups, burgers, and main courses like grilled leg of lamb and fried Bacalao. There are also several vegan options as well as a kids' menu for the little ones. On the bar side, they offer an impressive wine list as well as an array of author-inspired cocktails like Stephen King's Bloody Mary and Tolkein's Tanqueray Gimlet.

Accommodations
START HOSTEL
Lindarbraut 637, tel. 354/420-6050, www.

starthostel.is, rooms from 16,500ISK

Start Hostel offers a mix of doubles, quadruples, family rooms, and dorm beds. The rooms are clean but bare-bones, with just beds and a small table. Some rooms have private bathrooms, others share facilities, and there is a common room with a kitchen, luggage storage, free parking, and free Wi-Fi. Guests have access to laundry machines, and Keflavík International Airport is just an eight-minute drive away.

PARK INN BY RADISSON
Hafnargata 57, tel. 354/421-5222, www.

radissonhotels.com, rooms from 25,000ISK

Situated just 5 kilometers (3 miles) from Keflavik Airport, Park Inn by Radisson offers 81 rooms ranging from standard doubles to superior rooms to junior suites. Rooms are comfortable but sparsely decorated, with amenities including free Wi-Fi, kettles, and mounted flat-screen TVs. Park Inn has an on-site **restaurant**, a fitness center, luggage storage, and express check-out, as well as a free shuttle to and from the airport.

HÓTEL BERG
Bakkavegur 17, Keflavík, tel. 354/422-7922, www.

hotelberg.is, rooms from 26,550ISK

At Hótel Berg, modernized rooms are comfortable and have flat-screen televisions and free Wi-Fi. The boutique hotel, renovated in 2018, offers 36 rooms, free drop-off to Keflavik International Airport, a comfortable lounge area with a fireplace, and a rooftop pool. If you get one of the two loft suites during the winter months, you might catch a glimpse of the northern lights from the skylight.

HÓTEL KEILIR
Hafnargata 37, Keflavík, tel. 354/420-9800, www.

hotelkeilir.is, rooms from 29,000ISK

Keflavík's centrally located Hótel Keilir boasts modern, minimalist decor, average-sized rooms, and small bathrooms. A family suite is available that can comfortably sleep five people. This hotel is a good mid-range option and just a five-minute drive from the airport.

Information and Services
REYKJANESBÆR TOURIST OFFICE
Duusgata 2-8, tel. 354/420-3246, www.

visitreykjanes.is, noon-5pm daily

Reykjanesbær's tourist office offers a booking service for tours and has brochures on activities, restaurants, and sights in the region.

Getting There and Around
Reykjanesbær is 49 kilometers (30 miles) southwest from **Reykjavík**. By car, take **Route 41**, which is paved, to reach the region. It's about a 50-minute drive.

If you are coming from the **airport** and staying in Reykjanesbær, and don't have a car, be sure to contact your hotel or guesthouse to see if there is a shuttle to pick you up at the airport. If not, **taxis** are available at the airport.

Reykjanes has a **walkable** small downtown area, but a **rental car** is necessary to visit major attractions. There are tours for sights in Reykjanesbær, but if you want the freedom to roam, renting a car is essential. Reykjanesbær is about 3 kilometers (2 miles) from **Keflavik International Airport.**

GARÐUR
Garður is a placid seaside town on the northwest tip of Reykjanes and a great place to spend a couple of hours. Garður is best known for a pair of lighthouses. On sunny summer days, locals and tourists picnic by the lighthouses, basking in the sun and enjoying the serenity and scenery. The lighthouses are a great spot to catch a glimpse of the northern lights in the winter, as the location is away from the bright lights of downtown.

Sights
LIGHTHOUSES
Route 402

The highlights of Garður are the two lighthouses, each with unique charm. The older, more traditional red-striped lighthouse was built in 1847, while the newer square-designed one was built in 1944 in a more modern Nordic style. This is a popular destination for photos. Fishing boats can often be seen from shore, and there is rich birdlife in the region, ranging from hordes of gulls circling in the summer months to ravens dominating the skies in the winter. It's also common to see arctic terns and gannets in the summer. In the winter, the lighthouses appear against a backdrop of mist and mystery, and if you're lucky, you will see northern lights dancing in the night sky.

FOLK MUSEUM
(Byggðasafn Garðskaga)

Skagabraut 100, tel. 354/422-7220, www.svgardur.is, 9am-8pm daily Apr. 1-Oct. 31, open by appointment the rest of the year, free

The Folk Museum sits amid a rugged landscape with thriving birdlife. The quaint museum houses items that were essential for the livelihood of residents on both land and sea, including tools, fishing items, and maps. It offers a window into what life was like in past generations, reminding visitors that life in Iceland was not easy for early settlers. The museum also has an extensive collection of 60 functional engines provided by local resident Guðni Ingimundarson.

Food and Accommodations
THE OLD LIGHTHOUSE CAFÉ

Garðskagi, tel. 354/893-8909, noon-8:30pm daily June 1-Sept. 30, entrées from 1,900ISK

The Old Lighthouse Café, housed in an actual lighthouse, offers cakes, coffee, soft drinks, and light meals. It's a good place to grab a quick bite, and you can also go to the top of the lighthouse for a great view of the Reykjanes Peninsula, the lava fields, and, if you're lucky, maybe a whale in the distance.

GUESTHOUSE GARÐUR

Skagabraut 46, tel. 354/660-7894, www.guesthousegardur.is, apartments from 17,000ISK

This charming guesthouse has seven apartments ranging from studios to two bedrooms available year-round. Located close to the harbor, the apartments have private kitchens, bathrooms with showers, free Wi-Fi, and satellite TV. The friendly staff can help arrange local tours, including golfing, bird-watching, and fishing. The cozy guesthouse is just a 10-minute drive to Keflavík airport.

GARÐSKAGI CAMPGROUND

Skagabraut, tel. 354/422-7220, Mar. 1-Nov. 30, 1,400ISK

The Garðskagi campground is close to the two lighthouses in a quiet stretch of town. Campers have access to running water and toilets.

Getting There

Garður is 55 kilometers (34 miles) west of **Reykjavík**. By car, take **Route 41** to **Route 45.**

SOUTH OF REYKJANESBÆR
Bridge Between Continents

Road 425, GPS coordinates N63° 52′ 5.558″ W22° 40′ 31.588″

Travelers can visit a spot where the Mid-Atlantic Ridge crosses Iceland, the meeting point of the Eurasian and North American plates. The small footbridge is a symbolic site that connects the two land masses, and it offers visitors an impressive view of the ridge. You can reach the bridge from road 425.

Eldey Island

GPS coordinates N 63.8151, W 22.7033

Situated about 15 kilometers (9 miles) southwest from the southernmost tip of the Reykjanes Peninsula, Eldey Island is made up of sheer cliffs that jut out of the ocean and reach 77 meters (253 feet) high. Birdlife thrives on the island; Eldey has one of the biggest gannet bird colonies in the world. In recent years, an estimated 70,000 gannets have bred on the island from June to August. The best view of the island is from the hill where Reykjanes Lighthouse sits.

GRINDAVÍK

Grindavík is a placid fishing town steeped in fish trade history. Many of the same families have been trolling these waters for generations, and visitors can see fishers hauling their daily bounty of cod out of the harbor by day and dine on the local catch at night. The Grindavík area's greatest claim to fame, however, is the giant human-made geothermal expanse of the **Blue Lagoon.**

Sights

TOP EXPERIENCE

★ BLUE LAGOON
(Bláa Lónið)

Svartsengi, tel. 354/420-8800, www.bluelagoon.com, 8am-9pm daily Aug. 19-May 30, 7am-11pm daily May 31-June 27, and 7am-midnight daily June 28-Aug. 18, from 11,990ISK

Built on an 800-year-old lava field, the Blue Lagoon covers an area of 8,700 square meters (93,646 square feet) and draws visitors from around the world to soak in its gloriously milky-blue waters amid a dreamlike atmosphere. The heated water, which ranges between 37-39°C (98-102°F), is heavenly any time of year. Enjoying the steamy air while soaking during the summer is lovely, especially on sunny days. And in the winter, a visit here is eerie and wonderful; watching as snow falls from the jet-black December sky or as northern lights dance across it while lounging in the hot water is sublime.

The water isn't deep, about 1.5 meters (5 feet), and the bottom is covered with white silica mud, the result of a natural process of recondensation. It's common to see visitors cover their faces with the mud—it's great for your skin, and all guests receive a free silica mud mask with standard admission. The gift shop sells Blue Lagoon skin products that have ingredients ranging from silica mud to algae found in other parts of Iceland. At the **Lagoon Bar,** a swim-up bar in the main section of the lagoon, you can purchase drinks to be enjoyed while lounging in the waters. There are also two steam baths on the property, as well as a dry sauna and massage area, and spa treatments are available.

The **comfort package** fee is 11,990ISK for those over 14 years of age, and free for children 2-13. Children under the age of 2 are not allowed in the lagoon. Also included in the price of a ticket is a silica mud mask, the use of a towel, and your first drink of choice. The **premium package** (14,990ISK) includes

the Blue Lagoon

everything the comfort package offers, as well as slippers, a second mask of choice, use of a bathrobe, table reservation at **Lava Restaurant,** and sparkling wine if dining.

Because of the increase in tourism over the past several years, the Blue Lagoon now requires you to book a time slot ahead of your arrival, which you can do on its website. Reserve your time at least several weeks before your trip. Thousands of people visit the site every day, and it can get quite crowded during summer months. For the best chance of avoiding crowds, try to book early in the morning or late in the evening.

Many tours feature a visit to the Blue Lagoon, but if you're traveling independently, it makes sense to visit right after you fly in or before you head home, as it's very close to **Keflavík airport.** A rejuvenating soak is a great way to kick off your trip or end it on a relaxing note.

Driving from Reykjavík, the Blue Lagoon is about 48 kilometers (30 miles), roughly 45 minutes, away on paved roads; head southwest on Route 41 and turn left onto Route 43. From Keflavík International Airport, the Blue Lagoon is about 23 kilometers (14 miles) away; take Route 41 and turn right onto Route 43, and you'll arrive in approximately 20 minutes. If you're making your way to or from the airport, note that the Blue Lagoon offers luggage storage. Bus transfers via **Reykjavík Excursions** (tel. 354/580-5400, www.re.is) can be booked in conjunction with Blue Lagoon entrance tickets; the buses run between both Reykjavík and the Blue Lagoon and Keflavík International Airport and the Blue Lagoon. Buses are available from Reykjavík to the Blue Lagoon, every hour 7am-7pm year-round, with additional services seasonally. From KEF to the Blue Lagoon, there are seven daily departures year-round and added service during the high season.

SALTFISH MUSEUM
(Saltfisksetur)
Hafnargata 12A, tel. 354/420-1190,
9am-6pm daily, entrance 1,200ISK

The Saltfish Museum tells the story of Iceland's fish trade from 1770 to 1965, the period when saltfish was Iceland's top export. Photos, fishing equipment, and even a full-size fishing boat from the early 20th century are on display, explaining the economic and cultural importance of saltfish to Iceland. If you're curious about the region, would like to learn more about processing saltfish in the olden days, or would like to get a look at an old-school fishing boat, be sure to stop by.

FISHERMEN MEMORIAL
main garden near the Saltfish Museum

A sad part of Iceland's fishing history is the stories of men who went out to sea to never return. There's a moving memorial in downtown Grindavík showing a mother with her son and daughter waiting for their fisherman husband/father to return home from sea. It's a reminder that the fish used for consumption and trade has come at a high price for many families over the years. The memorial was created by sculptor Ragnar Kjartansson.

Sports and Recreation
4X4 ADVENTURES ICELAND
Tangasund 1, Grindavík,
tel. 354/857-3001,
www.4x4adventuresiceland.is, 13,900ISK

For those looking for a little adventure, 4x4 Adventures Iceland offers a number of ATV/quad bike tours that let you get off the beaten track. Its one-hour Panorama tour takes travelers around the Reykjanes Peninsula and near rocky lava formations, mountains, and even to a view over the Blue Lagoon. No experience is necessary for this year-round tour.

GRINDAVÍK SWIMMING POOL
Austurvegi 1, tel. 354/426-7555, www.grindavik.is,
6am-9pm Mon.-Fri., 9am-5pm Sat.-Sun., 950ISK

The Grindavík Swimming Pool is one of the best pools in South Iceland with its 25-meter (82-foot) pool, hot tubs, tanning beds, waterslide, children's pool, and fitness center.

Food

HJA HOLLU

Víkurbraut 62, tel. 354/896-5316, www.hjahollu.is,
8am-5pm Mon.-Fri., 11am-5pm Sat., entrées from
2,190ISK

This modern and casual eatery with a friendly atmosphere has a menu chock-full of healthy options like salads and vegan dishes. Guests can also choose from local cod, lobster pizza, steak sandwich, and vegetable soup.

★ SALTHÚSIÐ

Stamphólsvegur 9, tel. 354/426-9700, www.salthusid.
is, noon-10pm daily mid-May-mid-Sept., noon-9pm
mid-Sept.-mid-May, entrées from 3,300ISK

Salthúsið, or "the Salt House," is a favorite among local fishers, residents, and tourists. A lot of saltfish is on the quiet eatery's menu, but guests can also choose from lamb and chicken dishes, as well as burgers, sandwiches, and fish and chips. The garlic-roasted lobster with salad and garlic bread is delicious. If you have room, be sure to check out the decadent dessert menu, which includes items such as deep-fried bananas with vanilla ice cream and caramel sauce, and French chocolate cake with fresh cream.

MAX'S RESTAURANT

Grindavíkurvegi 1, tel. 354/426-8650, www.nli.is/
maxs, lunch noon-4pm daily, dinner 5:30pm-9:30pm,
entrées from 4,100ISK

Max's Restaurant is the in-house restaurant at the Northern Light Inn. The atmosphere is very much that of a hotel restaurant, with good service and not many surprises, but it charms with huge windows overlooking mountains and lava fields. The menu consists of classic Icelandic food like lamb fillet and fresh fish dishes.

★ BLUE LAGOON LAVA RESTAURANT

Svartsengi, tel. 354/420-8800, www.bluelagoon.
com, lunch 11:30am-2pm daily, dinner 5pm-9pm daily,
dinner entrées from 5,700ISK

The Blue Lagoon Lava Restaurant is very much a spa restaurant: ingredients are local, and the recipes are healthy. You will find fresh vegetables and fish as well as lean meats. The menu accommodates a host of dietary requirements. The atmosphere is minimalist chic with cool hues and modern accents. Casual clothing is allowed.

BLUE LAGOON MOSS RESTAURANT

Norðurljósavegur 11, tel. 354/420-8700, www.
bluelagoon.com, 6:30pm-11pm, meals from 13,500ISK

Moss Restaurant opened as part of the Retreat extension to the Blue Lagoon. The restaurant is elegant fine dining at its best, with unbeatable views of the volcanic landscape. The restaurant offers two five- and seven-course set menus from 13,500ISK a person. The first set menu includes fish and meat in the dishes, while the second is customized for vegan guests. The menus are seasonal and change often; contact the restaurant to find out what will be served. In addition to the two set menus, the restaurant also offers a chef's table, where the chef will create a seven-course meal (from 17,300ISK) based on the day's fresh catch and seasonal produce.

Accommodations

GUESTHOUSE BORG

Boragarhraun 2, tel. 354/895-8686, www.
guesthouseborg.com, rooms from 13,000ISK

Open year-round, Guesthouse Borg is a basic, no-frills guesthouse in the center of Grindavík and the best budget-friendly option in the area. The seven-room guesthouse has shared kitchen facilities, bathrooms, and washing machines, and is a five-minute drive from the Blue Lagoon. It's a clean and comfortable place to stay, but nothing to write home about.

GEO HOTEL GRINDAVÍK

Víkurbraut 58, tel. 354/421-4000, www.geohotel.is,
rooms from 19,000ISK

Geo Hotel Grindavík has double and family rooms, all with private bathroom facilities. The hotel's design includes a spacious social area for guests to relax in cozy surroundings.

Room walls are painted in muted colors, and there are wood floors and minimalist furniture. Shops and conveniences are nearby in the town center.

NORTHERN LIGHT INN

Grindavíkurvegi 1, tel. 354/426-8650, www.nli.is, doubles from 33,000ISK

The 32-room guesthouse Northern Light Inn offers cozy, bright, rooms with free Wi-Fi, satellite TV, and sweeping views. An in-house restaurant serves classic Icelandic fare with plenty of fish and lamb dishes, as well as a couple of vegetarian options. Its proximity to the Blue Lagoon is a big draw for tourists: It's just a 0.7-kilometer (0.4-mile) walk from the lagoon.

★ BLUE LAGOON SILICA HOTEL

Svartsengi, tel. 354/420-8806, www.bluelagoon.com, rooms from 68,000ISK

The Blue Lagoon Silica Hotel is a luxurious hotel connected to the Blue Lagoon. It has 35 bright and airy double rooms, each with private bathrooms and a terrace overlooking the surrounding lava fields. Silica offers luxury beds, modern decor, and beautiful views of the lagoon. Guests have access to a private lagoon open daily 9am-10pm.

Also at the Blue Lagoon, **The Retreat** (Norðurljósavegur 11, tel. 354/420-8700, www.bluelagoon.com, suites from 158,000ISK) opened in 2018 to target luxury travelers; suites start at a whopping 158,000ISK per night all the way up to 332,000ISK. The suites overlook The Retreat Lagoon, a body of water that has the same geothermally heated seawater as the Blue Lagoon, but for The Retreat guests only. Guests have access to private changing rooms, spa treatments at a hidden spa, and reservations for Moss Restaurant.

GRINDAVÍK'S CAMPSITE

Austurvegur 26, tel. 354/660-7323, mid-May-mid-Sept., 1,800ISK

The popular Grindavík's Campsite by the harbor accommodates tents, RVs, and campers, with access to hookups (electricity costs an extra 1,100ISK per night) and a dump station. There's a paved entrance and a large parking area, and the grassy field has beautiful mountain views. The campsite offers laundry facilities, a common eating area, and a playground with swings and a spider net.

Information and Services

The gas station **N1** and grocery chain **Netto** are situated downtown, on Víkurbraut.

GRINDAVÍK TOURIST INFORMATION CENTER

Duusgata 2-8, tel. 354/420-3246, 10am-5pm daily

The tourist information center is located in **Reykjane's maritime museum.**

Getting There

By car, Grindavík is 50 kilometers (30 miles) from **Reykjavík.** Drivers should take **Route 41** west to **Route 43** south, both paved roads. It's about a 50-minute drive.

EAST OF GRINDAVÍK
Krýsuvík

www.visitreykjanes.is

The Krýsuvík geothermal area, 35 kilometers (22 miles) south of Reykjavík, is popular among geology buffs and hikers. Gurgling mud pools bubble from the yellow, red, and orange clay-like earth, intertwined with dancing steam and hot springs. The many short walking paths allow you to feel lost in the outer space-like atmosphere. The region gives you a great sense of Iceland's raw, natural geothermal energy, which powers much of the island. Take some time to roam, but be sure to stay within the designated roped-off areas to avoid getting burned by spray and steam. Plan to spend 1-2 hours here.

Getting There

To get to the region, take **Route 42** south from **Reykjavík.** It's about a 40-minute drive on the paved road (36 kilometers/22 miles). From **Grindavik,** it is 30 kilometers (19 miles), about 27 minutes, on **Route 427.**

Self-Driving the Golden Circle

PLANNING YOUR TIME
In total, the Golden Circle is an approximately 300-kilometer (200-mile) paved circular route, leaving from and returning to Reykjavík. It's good to allocate **6-8 hours** if you're driving it yourself.

WHERE TO STAY
It makes the most sense to overnight in **Selfoss** or **Hvolsvöllur** if you do not plan to return to Reykjavík for the night.

THE ROUTES
With your rental car from Reykjavík, take **Route 1** to **Route 36** for Þingvellir. Continue on Route 36, then **Routes 365, 37,** and **35** to Geysir. From Geysir continue on Route 35 to Gullfoss before looping back toward Reykjavík, heading southwest on well-signed Routes 35 and 1.

The Golden Circle

TOP EXPERIENCE

If you ask an Icelander which tour you should take if you want a taste of Iceland outside of Reykjavík, he or she will most likely recommend the Golden Circle. Encompassing the three most visited sights in South Iceland, the Golden Circle gives you a slice of Icelandic history at Þingvellir, a view of Iceland's bubbling geothermal activity at Geysir, and a peek at a roaring, powerful waterfall at Gullfoss. The sights are classically Icelandic, and postcard-perfect in summer or winter. Because of the popularity of the sights, it's pretty easy to get there.

Tours
You can pre-book a tour through many tourism companies: **Troll Expeditions** (Fiskislóð 45G, tel. 354/519-5544, www.troll.is) offers a Golden Circle small group day tour from Reykjavík for 9,900ISK, including Gullfoss, Geysir, and Þingvellir, plus a stop at Kerið crater and a farm visit with free ice cream. If you have time for just one tour in south Iceland, the Golden Circle is highly recommended to learn about the history and geology of this island.

TOP EXPERIENCE

★ ÞINGVELLIR NATIONAL PARK
Route 36, 47 km / 30 mi (45 minutes) northwest of Reykjavík, free, parking 750ISK

The birth of Iceland as a nation happened at Þingvellir. Literally translated to "Parliament Plains," Þingvellir was the site of Iceland's first general assembly, which was said to have been established in the year 930, and was the meeting place of the Icelandic parliament until 1798. Many significant sights are at Þingvellir, including **Almannagjá** (All Man's Gorge) and **Lögberg** (Law Rock). Þingvellir was established as a national park in 1930.

Visitors also come to the area for its geological significance, as it is the site of a rift valley that marks the crest of the **Mid-Atlantic Ridge.** It's also home to Þingvallavatn, the largest natural lake on the island.

Sights
ÞINGVELLIR INTERPRETIVE CENTER
tel. 354/482-2660, www.thingvellir.is, 9am-8pm daily June-Aug., 9am-5pm Sept.-Apr., free

The Golden Circle

The Þingvellir Interpretive Center gives a great overview of the national park, its history, and its geological significance. Stop in to see the interactive display and then pick up hiking maps at the information center next door.

ALMANNAGJÁ

footpath from visitor's center leads to the gorge

The park's stony, moss-covered landscape is home to Almannagjá (All Man's Gorge), which is the tallest cliff face in the national park and the original backdrop to the Iceland's first parliament. This rock structure is considered the edge of the North American plate, which visitors can view up close. It's an impressive sight, so be sure you have your camera ready.

LÖGBERG

footpath from visitor's center

Lögberg (Law Rock) is where Icelandic democracy began. Iceland's Commonwealth period ran from 930-1262, and during that time,

The Birth of Iceland

Iceland's government dates back to the year 930, when the **Alþing** (parliament) was formed as an outdoor assembly just a few decades after settlement. Settlers came from Norway and settled along the coasts of the island. This makes it the oldest continuous parliament in history. The Alþing was formed by the island's most powerful chieftains and its main purpose was to decide on legislation. **The Law Council** (Lögrétta) was at the center of the assemblies and consisted of the chieftains and bishops. Legislation was passed on majority rule. Icelanders were invited to join the assemblies and lived in camps in Þingvellir during the meeting sessions; it was something of an annual family event. Sessions were held at Þingvellir until 1800, when the assembly was disbanded. A new high court was established in 1800 in Reykjavík and took over the functions of Alþingi. When parliament reconvened in 1844, meetings moved to Reykjavík.

While you're in Þingvellir, be sure to look out for the following landmarks, essential to the ancient annual gathering of Iceland's legislators:

- **Almannagjá** (All Man's Gorge): This was the location of Iceland's first parliament.

- **Lögberg** (Law Rock): From 930 to 1262, the Law Rock was the center of Alþing, where members gave speeches and held events.

- **Laugarvatn** (Bathing Waters): Historically, members of the Icelandic Parliament would bathe in these nearby springs, between Þingvellir and Geysir.

Still today, Þingvellir plays a role in Icelandic government, even if it's small: the farmhouse visible along the Öxará River is the summer residence of Iceland's prime minister.

the Law Rock was the center of the Alþing (parliament). Members of the Alþing gave speeches and held events at the rock, including confirming of the year's calendar and issuing legal rulings. A man known as the "law speaker," who was responsible for understanding all laws and required to memorize them, read the procedural laws aloud every summer standing on the rock.

ÖXARÁ RIVER

www.thingvellir.is/en

The Öxará (Axe) River flows over seemingly endless lava fields, emitting a haunting mist in the winter months. It's serene and eerie until it reaches Öxaráfoss, where the water tumbles and roars over the cliffs. At the river's edge are a church and farmhouse, the latter of which is the official summer residence of Iceland's prime minister. The church, **Þingvallakirkja** (9am-5pm daily mid-May-early Sept., free), is a charming wood structure built in traditional Icelandic design that dates from 1859. Visitors can go inside, take photos, and sit on a pew and reflect. The interior features a wooden pulpit and bells from earlier churches. There's a small cemetery behind the church where celebrated poets Einar Benediktsson and Jonasa Hallgrimsson are buried.

ÞINGVALLAVATN LAKE

www.thingvellir.is/en

Þingvallavatn is the largest natural lake in Iceland at 84 square kilometers (32 square miles) and partially lies within Þingvellir National Park. The rift valley lake is where the North American and Eurasian tectonic plates meet, and tourists can dive or snorkel in the Silfra fissure.

Hiking

Þingvellir is lovely for the casual hiker. Acres of flat lava fields make it an easy hiking spot, but be sure to watch for open rock fissures along the way; you could fall in. There are scores of walking paths and plenty of interesting rock formations and rugged terrain to see. You can get information about trails and the surrounding area at the **visitors center.**

SYÐSTA SÚLA

Distance: *13 km (8 mi) round-trip*
Hiking Time: *7 hours round-trip*
Information and maps: *www.south.is*
Trailhead: *left turn on route F-550*

If you're looking to scale some small mountains, check out Syðsta Súla, which reaches 1,085 meters (3,559 feet) in the northern region of the park and is the park's easiest peak to climb. The view from the top over the park is spectacular. Always be sure to check weather conditions before any hike, and make sure you have proper waterproof outer layers, sturdy footwear, a charged mobile phone, and drinking water. The ideal time to hike is the summer, as in the winter you will need proper snow gear.

Fishing and Watersports

Scuba diving or **snorkeling** in the naturally filtered, pure water of Þingvallavatn lake is sublime. Surveying the underwater basalt walls, multicolored algae, and sloping sands is magical and unique—you're able to snorkel or scuba in the **Silfa fissure,** the enormous crack between the Eurasian and North American continental plates. Don't even think about going in without a drysuit, as the water temperature hovers around 3°C (37°F). Diving is possible year-round, but there are rules to obey, so don't attempt to go without a guide.

Boats are not allowed on the lake, but **fishing permits** are sold at the information center, and they rent equipment too. Tourists have a chance of catching arctic char and brown trout. Be sure to obey the rules and pay for the permit. The fishing season at the lake runs May 1-September 30, and permits are about 8,000ISK.

DIVE ICELAND

Ásbúðartröð 17, Hafnarfjörður, tel. 354/699-3000, www.dive.is

Dive Iceland offers a Silfra diving tour for 29,990ISK. Travelers must be dry-suit certified to dive and must present their certification card. Snorkeling tours start at 15,990ISK.

Horseback Riding

Þingvellir is a popular spot for riding horses, with several trails that offer the chance to check out some of the more beautiful and geologically significant areas of the park.

REYKJAVÍK EXCURSIONS

tel. 354/580-5400, www.re.is, 20,399ISK

Reykjavík Excursions offers a year-round horse-riding day tour in Þingvellir.

Camping

There are no hotels within Þingvellir National Park. However, there are accommodations in nearby Laugarvatn and Selfoss. If you would like to stay within the park limits, your only option is camping at one of Þingvellir's five campgrounds, spread across two areas of the park: the **Leirar** section and the **Vatnskot** section. All campsites have access to toilets, electricity, and cooking facilities. The difference in the two sections is not access to amenities, but whether you want to camp close to the lake or stay near the information center. Both sections have great views and spacious fields. Campers must bring their own tents.

LEIRAR CAMPGROUND

GPS coordinates N 64°16'48.9426" W 21° 5'17.4444", www.tjalda.is, June 1-Sept. 30, 1,600ISK per person

The Leirar section is a five-minute walk from the Þingvellir information center. The Leirar campground is divided into four campsites: **Fagrabrekka, Syðri-Leirar, Hvannabrekka,** and **Nyrðri-Leirar.**

VATNSKOT CAMPGROUND

GPS coordinates N 64°14'40.9308" W 21° 5'22.0632", www.tjalda.is, June 1-Sept. 30, 1,600ISK per person

Meanwhile, the Vatnskot section, which is by Lake Þingvallavatn, is situated at an abandoned farm by the lake.

Information and Services
TOURIST INFORMATION CENTER
tel. 354/482-2660, www.thingvellir.is, 9am-10pm
daily May 15-Aug. 31, 9am-6pm daily Sept. 1-May 14
The tourist information center is close to the car park. Be advised that there is a service fee of 200ISK to use the **restrooms**. There is also a small **cafeteria** to purchase snacks and drinks.

Getting There and Around
Þingvellir is 46 kilometers (29 miles) northeast of **Reykjavík**. By car, it's about a 45-minute drive; take **Route 1** to **Route 36,** which will take you to the northern part of the park.

While there is no public transportation available to get to the park, a number of tours include a stop at **Þingvellir.** The park's attractions are all within a walkable distance, so plan to be **on foot.**

LAUGARVATN
Route 37, 32 km / 20 mi (30 min) from Þingvellir
Laugarvatn, or "Bathing Waters," is a lake situated between Þingvellir and the geothermal hot spot of Geysir. Historically, members of Iceland's parliament (Alþing) visited the springs due to their proximity to where parliament met at Þingvellir for hundreds of years. The lake's water temperature hovers around 40°C (104°F), making it a unique and warm swimming experience.

Sights
THE CAVE PEOPLE
Laugarvatnshellir, tel. 354/ 888-1922, www.
thecavepeople.is, 10am-6pm daily, 2,000ISK
A fascinating addition to the region, The Cave People offers a look at how Icelanders lived within the earth just 100 years ago. Here you can take a guided tour of two manmade caves that were inhabited by young Icelandic couples in the years 1910-1911 and 1918-1922. The residents had some horses, a cow, and a few sheep, and grew potatoes and harvested fresh berries. Tours are available every 30 minutes, and tickets can be purchased in advance online.

Pools and Hot Springs
LAUGARVATN FONTANA
Hverabraut 1, tel. 354/486-1400, www.fontana.is,
10am-10pm daily June 1-Aug. 31, 11am-10pm daily
Sept. 1-May 31, 3,800ISK adults, 2,000ISK children
13-16, free for children 12 and under
The Laugarvatn Fontana is worth a stop before or after you visit Geysir. The facility's sauna captures the steam just as it escapes from the earth. You can bask in the natural sauna and hot springs, enjoying the geothermal energy up close and personal. Towels, bathing suits, and bathrobes can be rented at the spa.

For an experience unique to the region, each day at 11:30am and 2:30pm there is a walk from the reception area to the on-site geothermal bakery (1,500ISK). Visitors can watch as the staff digs out rye bread that's been buried in the ground, left to bake naturally in the geothermally heated earth. You can try the bread, served hot from the ground with some butter—it's delicious! There is also a lunch buffet between noon-2pm daily for 2,900ISK and a dinner buffet between 6pm-9pm daily for 3,900ISK.

LAUGARVATN SWIMMING POOL
Hverabraut 2, tel. 354/486-1251, 10am-9pm
Mon.-Fri., 10am-6pm Sat.-Sun. June-mid-Aug.,
2pm-9pm Mon.-Thur., 4pm-7pm Fri., 1pm-6pm Sun.
mid-Aug.-May, 1,000ISK
Situated downtown, the Laugarvatn Swimming Pool is popular among locals, and it's a nice break from the summer tourist rush at the Fontana spa nearby. Head here if you would like a quiet spot to take a dip.

Shopping
GALLERI LAUGARVATN
Haholt 1, tel. 354/486-1016, www.gallerilaugarvatn.
is, 1pm-5pm daily
When not enjoying the soothing hot springs or the vistas, steal away for a few minutes at Galleri Laugarvatn, a charming little gallery that features local handicrafts, ranging from glass tea light holders to unique paper

crafts. There is also a **café** (sandwiches from 950ISK) and **guesthouse** (double room with shared bathroom from 14,000ISK) on site.

Food and Accommodations
RESTAURANT LINDIN
Lindarbraut 2, tel. 354/486-1262, www.laugarvatn.is, noon-10pm daily, entrées from 3,700ISK

At Restaurant Lindin, owner and head chef Baldur Öxdal Halldórsson has created an upscale, fine-dining experience in a town with fewer than 300 residents. Diners have a lot of choices, from Icelandic mainstays to more exotic fare, with dishes ranging from reindeer meat burgers and pan-fried arctic char to tender lamb fillets and smoked cod. The classic decor and friendly staff make this little restaurant a treasure.

LAUGARVATN YOUTH HOSTEL
Dalsel, tel. 354/486-1215, www.laugarvatnhostel.is, open Feb. 3-Nov. 27, private rooms from 12,000ISK, beds from 4,800ISK

One of the busiest hostels in South Iceland, Laugarvatn Youth Hostel can accommodate 140 people in single, double, and family rooms. Ten rooms have private bathroom facilities, while the rest share. Kitchen and laundry facilities are available, and the staff is very warm and helpful. There's also a big hot tub on the property.

HÓTEL EDDA ML LAUGARVATN
Skólatún, tel. 354/444-4810, www.hoteledda.is, mid-June-mid-Aug., rooms from 13,000ISK

Location is key for Hótel Edda ML Laugarvatn, as this 101-room hotel is a popular stop for those touring the Golden Circle. Rooms are basic and no-frills, with double beds, IKEA-style furniture, and crisp white bedding. Thirty-two rooms have private bathrooms, while the rest share facilities, and there is free Wi-Fi in common areas. Guests get a 10-percent discount for the geothermal steam baths at the nearby Fontana spa.

GOLDEN CIRCLE APARTMENTS
Laugarbraut, tel. 354/487-1212, www. goldencircleapartments.is, apartments from 19,500ISK

Golden Circle Apartments offers 25 apartments that are modern and perfect for families, with fully equipped kitchens, private bathrooms, a TV, free Wi-Fi, and free parking. Apartments are spacious, have new appliances, and are close to town attractions. They range from studios to three-bedroom family apartments.

EFSTIDALUR II
Bláskógabyggð, tel. 354/486-1186, www.efstidalur.is, rooms from 28,000ISK

Efstidalur II is a charming farmhouse bed-and-breakfast with an in-house restaurant, friendly staff, and horse rentals. Situated close to the Fontana spa, the B&B is also in proximity of the Golden Circle. On the farm, guests can meet dogs, cows, and horses, and can try fresh homemade ice cream.

Getting There
Laugarvatn is just 77 kilometers (48 miles) northeast from **Reykjavík**, a 1.25 hour drive, and is easily accessible by car and bus via **Route 36** to **Route 365**. If driving from **Þingvellir**, take **Routes 36** and **365** to **Route 37**. The 32-kilometer (10-mile) drive takes about 30 minutes.

★ GEYSIR
Route 35, 28 km / 17 mi (22 min) from Laugarvatn

Iceland's geysers are the most obvious demonstration of the island's natural geothermal energy, and historically, Geysir is the country's most famous example of the phenomenon—it's actually the source of the word "geyser." Geologists theorized that in the 13th century earthquakes stirred the underground workings of the natural hot springs here, causing them to gush, releasing pressure, steam, and water up to 20 meters (66 feet) into the air.

Visitors to the site today unfortunately aren't going to see the dormant Geysir erupt—it

1: Strokkur 2: Þingvellir National Park

hasn't blown since 2005. But don't fret; Geysir's nearby cousin, **Strokkur** (Churn), erupts every seven minutes or so. Crowds gather to watch the frequent eruptions, and the churning, gurgling pool of hot water turning out a rush of pressure from the clay-like earth is an impressive sight; be sure to have your camera ready. Please be careful and stay behind the ropes or you may get hit with hot spray.

Food and Accommodations
HÓTEL GEYSIR

Geysir, tel. 354/480-6800, www.hotelgeysir.is, rooms from 38,000ISK

You can't stay any closer to the geysers than at the Hótel Geysir. The newly opened property features 77 rooms and six suites just across the road from Geysir. Guests can also stay in chalets on the property that are essentially double rooms. The decor blends with the scenery in muted colors but modern scheme. Visitors have access to a spa, swimming pool, and hot tub. The in-house **restaurant** serves up delicious dishes ranging from fresh Icelandic cod to lamb and beef entrées.

Hótel Geysir also operates a campground 100 meters (300 feet) from the Geysir Area, with hot showers (500ISK), pool access, and a common barbecue area; you can pay for your campsite (1,800ISK) at the Geysir Shops just across from the campground. An additional 900ISK gives you access to electricity.

Information and Services
GEYSIR VISITORS CENTER

10am-10pm daily

After walking around the geothermal area, stop at the visitors center. It has a short multimedia exhibition about the geology of the region, a small **café** serving refreshments, and a **souvenir shop.**

GEYSIR CENTER

Biskupstungnabraut, tel. 354/519-6020, www. geysircenter.com, 9am-10pm daily June 1-Aug. 31, 9am-6pm Sept. 1-May 31

The Geysir Center is your one-stop shop for all your Geysir-related needs. There is a cafeteria that sells light meals and drinks, **bathrooms,** a large **gift shop,** and information and maps about attractions in the region.

Getting There

Geysir is about a 1.5-hour drive east from **Reykjavík.** You start out on **Route 1** and then take **Route 35,** which brings you directly to the site.

If following the **Golden Circle** route, continue from **Laugarvatn** on **Route 37** to **Route 35** for Geysir. The drive is just over 20 minutes.

★ GULLFOSS

Route 35, 10 km / 6 mi (10 min) from Geysir

The thundering, roaring waterfall of Gullfoss (Golden Falls) epitomizes the raw beauty of Iceland. Gullfoss tumbles into the Hvíta (White) River, which is a perfect name given the turbulent white water. There are three levels of water at the falls, ranging 11-21 meters (36-69 feet), meeting at a 70-meter (230-foot) gorge. If you get too close, expect to get soaked.

Because of Iceland's changing weather, you have a good chance to see a rainbow over the falls, making for a perfect snapshot of your visit. Plan to walk around the site, enjoying not only the wonder of the falls but also the beautiful surrounding landscape. In the summer, there are miles of lush green grass and frequent rainbows on sunny/rainy days. Be careful; it could be slippery.

No matter what time of year, there are scores of tour buses and independent drivers visiting the falls, and that's for a very good reason: It's gorgeous.

Food and Accommodations
GULLFOSS CAFÉ

tel. 354/486-6500, www.gullfoss.is, 9am-6pm daily, entrées from 1,800ISK

A short walk from the falls and parking area, Gullfoss Café (Gullfosskaffi) is the place to go when you're in the area. The Icelandic lamb meat soup on the menu is a winner, and a favorite among visitors, but sandwiches, cakes, and coffee are also available.

The Secret Lagoon

The **Secret Lagoon (Gamla Laugin)** (Hvamms-vegur, tel. 354/555-3351, www.secretlagoon.is, 10am-10pm June 1-Sept. 30, 11am-8pm Oct. 1-May 31, 3,000ISK adults, free for children 14 and under) has become a popular (and cheaper) alternative to the Blue Lagoon. It's located in **Fluðir,** a blip of a village with not much going on, but the Secret Lagoon brings tourists by the thousands while still offering a slightly more intimate, less touristy experience than the Blue Lagoon. The sur-roundings here are beautiful, with farmland and a geo-thermal area lush with moss covering lava stones and natural springs bubbling and steaming, just past the water's edge. You can rent towels and swimsuits here, and there is a café with drinks and snacks for sale.

Secret Lagoon

GETTING THERE

If following the conventional **Golden Circle** route from **Gullfoss** down Route 35 back to Route 1, you'll bypass the Secret Lagoon. But if you make a slightly larger circle, jumping off Route 35 and taking **Route 30** south instead, you'll pass right by Fluðir; it's about 38 kilometers (24 miles) south of Gullfoss, a 30-minute drive, and afterward you can connect from Route 30 back to Route 1 and Reykjavík.

HÓTEL GULLFOSS

Brattholt, tel. 354/486-8979, www.hotelgullfoss.is, rooms from 20,500ISK

Hótel Gullfoss is situated perfectly, just 3 ki-lometers (2 miles) from the falls in a remote area. The resort-like atmosphere is comfort-able and a great place to spend the night while touring the Golden Circle, which can be done in one day. Every room has a private bathroom and is classically furnished with comfortable beds. An in-house **restaurant** and hot tub out back make for a comfortable stay.

★ FRIÐHEIMAR

Bláskógabyggð, tel. 354/486-8894, www.fridheimar.is, noon-4pm daily

On Route 35 between Gullfoss and Selfoss, you might stop for lunch at Friðheimar, lo-cated in Reykholt, 30 kilometers (19 miles) south of Gullfoss, about a 30-minute drive. The farm is home to tomato greenhouses and a restaurant, as well as a horse-breeding

operation. It's an ideal place to have lunch: Tomatoes don't get any fresher in Iceland, and the menu takes advantage of this with items like tomato soup and creative Bloody Marys. Call ahead for lunch reservations. Groups of 10 or more can take a **tour** of the greenhouse with the owner or a staff member. Tours are offered year-round; email fridheimar@frid-heimar.is for more information.

Information and Services

Gullfoss's on-site **café** (tel. 354/486-6500, www.gullfoss.is, 9am-6pm daily) includes a **souvenir shop** and offers some brochures about the surrounding area.

Getting There

By car, Gullfoss is 115 kilometers (71 miles) northeast from **Reykjavík.** The drive takes about 1.5 hours on **Routes 1** and **35.**

Gullfoss is about 10 kilometers (6 miles) from **Geysir** on **Route 35,** a 10-minute drive.

The South Coast

If you're after hot springs and quirky museums, and you have some time to spend before or after you head to the Golden Circle, look no farther than the southern coast. Small towns like Hveragerði, Selfoss, and Vík have unique charm. Hveragerði is famed as the hot springs capital of Iceland. Selfoss is frequently used as a home base when exploring the Golden Circle, but it also has a couple of museums to check out. Vík boasts black-sand beaches. Outdoor activities like hiking, bird-watching, and jeep tours are popular in this region.

HVERAGERÐI

Some Icelanders affectionately call Hveragerði the "Capital of Hot Springs." It's just 30 minutes outside of Reykjavík, so tourists have no reason not to stop, especially as the town is on the way to the Golden Circle of Gullfoss, Geysir, and Þingvellir. Given its proximity to Reykjavík and its healing hot springs, the town is an all-year destination. After a visit to the springs, think about taking a peek at some of the local greenhouses populating the geothermal area. Tomatoes, cucumbers, and bell peppers are popular greenhouse-grown veggies in the region.

Sights
LÁ ART MUSEUM
(Listasafn Árnesinga)
Austurmork 21, tel. 354/483-1727, www.
listasafnarnesinga.is, noon-6pm daily May 1-Sept. 30,
limited hours during winter, free
The LÁ Art Museum offers several different exhibitions throughout the year, ranging from modern to traditional art from Icelandic artists local to the region. The museum also has a children's section, focusing on art for young visitors. It's a cute place to visit, especially if you are traveling with kids.

HVERAGERÐI BOTANICAL GARDEN
Breiðamörk, tel. 354/483-4000,
open 24/7, free
Located in the center of town, this is a favorite spot for locals and tourists to stroll and enjoy nature. Guests can find a lot of trees (a rarity in Iceland) and walk along the mighty river Varmá. When the weather is good, it's common to see locals chatting and walking the trails, and tourists taking photos of the surroundings. It's also a great spot for bird-watching in the summer.

HVERAGERÐI STONE AND GEOLOGY EXHIBITION
Breiðamörk 1b, tel. 354/847-3460, www.
mineralsoficeland.com, noon-6pm daily, free
This privately owned stone collection should not be missed by geology enthusiasts. Guests can see minerals, lava stones, crystals, and more. The owners are happy to chat about the collection, which goes back generations.

Pools and Hot Springs
HVERAGARÐURINN GEOTHERMAL PARK
Hveramörk 13, 9am-6pm Mon.-Sat.,
10am-4pm Sun., free
People flock to Hveragerði for one reason: hot springs. Whether they're under blue skies and sunshine or beset by rain, wind, and snow, the hot springs beckon visitors from around the world. The central geothermal area is in the center of town. The natural phenomenon is hypnotizing to watch, as water bubbles to the surface. It's a constant reminder that Iceland sits on a hotbed of natural geothermal energy. Follow the path between geysers and hot pools, and at the end of the walk, you can soak your feet in one of the hot springs.

The South Coast

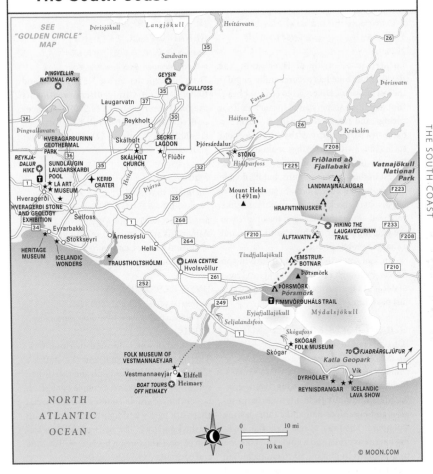

LAUGASKARÐ

Reykjamörk, tel. 354/483-4113, 6:45am-9:30pm Mon.-Fri., 9am-7pm Sat.-Sun., 920ISK

If hot springs aren't your bag, there's a lovely heated swimming pool downtown.

Hiking

HENGILL

Distance: *5 km (3 mi) round-trip*
Hiking Time: *3 hours round-trip*
Information and maps: *www.south.is*

Trailhead: *Parking area by the viewing platform overlooking Þingvallavatn*

Several trails between Hveragerði and Þingvallavatn lead up to Mount Hengill, which is 68 kilometers (42 miles) north of Hveragerði. The 803-meter (2,635-foot) mountain gives hikers a view of the vast volcanic landscape. Bring your camera and a good pair of boots. There are several active hot spots along the way, so be sure to stick to the trail.

★ REYKJADALUR

Distance: *7 km (4 mi) round-trip*
Hiking Time: *90 minutes round-trip*
Information and maps: *www.south.is*
Trailhead: *Parking lot, GPS N64.03309° W 21.21602*

Located just outside of Hveragerði, the Reykjadulur hike has become quite popular the last few years. Hikers get to enjoy the beautiful mountain scenery amid the bubbling hot springs, and are rewarded with the chance to bathe in a part of the river that blends ice cold spring water with hot springs, making for a relaxing soak to soothe your muscles. The hike is best in the summer months, but it's doable in the winter, if conditions are favorable. It is important to check weather conditions before you head out on the hike, and make sure you are wearing proper clothing, with water and a charged mobile phone.

You can reach the trailhead by driving on **Route 1** through Hveragerði to a gravel road that leads to the **parking lot.** The hike starts just past the car park.

Other Sports and Recreation
ICELAND ACTIVITIES
tel. 354/777-6263, www.icelandactivities.is, tours 17,900ISK per person

If you are interested in bicycling, Hveragerði-based Iceland Activities rents bikes in the region and organizes daily bike tours lasting 4-5 hours. The town is relatively flat, making for an easy ride, and a guide will take you to bike paths in and out of town, including to a geothermal area where you can see hot springs gurgle from the ground. You will get to boil eggs in one of the springs and you can taste rye bread that was baked in the hot earth. Tours and rentals are available year-round.

HVERAGERÐI GOLF COURSE
Gufudalur, tel. 354/483-5090, May-Aug., greens fees 4,500ISK

The Hveragerði Golf Course is a nine-hole course in a picturesque part of town, set against a backdrop of hot springs. It rents clubs and golf carts, and runs a café with light meals. Call ahead for a tee time.

NLFÍ HEALTH AND REHABILITATION CLINIC
Grænumörk 10, tel. 354/483-0300, www. heilsustofnun.is/en, 8am-4pm Mon.-Fri.

For a spa experience, the NLFÍ Health and Rehabilitation Clinic offers treatments ranging from mud baths (6,500ISK) to acupuncture (8,000ISK) to full-body massage (12,000ISK). Come to relax and pamper yourself.

Food
ALMAR BAKARI
Sunnumörk 2, tel. 354/483-1919, 7am-6pm daily, pastries from 700ISK

Almar Bakari is an ideal spot to grab some bread and pastries, and enjoy light meals like sandwiches, soups, and salads.

HVER RESTAURANT
Breiðamörk 1C, tel. 354/483-7000, www. hverrestaurant.is, 11:30am-10pm daily, entrées from 2,550ISK

Hver Restaurant is located in Hotel Örk. The restaurant is casual and the staff are friendly. The menu has lamb and fish dishes, soups, sandwiches, and a couple of vegetarian options. Sample courses include Arctic char with barley and lightly salted cod with mashed potatoes. The bar has a good selection of local and foreign beers as well as wine and cocktails.

Accommodations
HOTEL ORK
Breiðamörk 1, tel. 354/483-4775, www.hotelork.is, rooms from 31,000ISK

Hotel Ork offers 76 bright and airy standard rooms and nine superior rooms that are larger. The decor is dated with blue carpeting, but rooms are clean, with private bathrooms, a TV, mini refrigerator, complimentary tea and coffee, and free Wi-Fi. The hotel has an outdoor swimming pool, hot tubs, and a sauna. Breakfast is included in the price of the room.

★ FROST & FIRE HOTEL

Hverahvammur, tel. 354/483-4959, www.

frostandfire.is, rooms from 32,000ISK

The 17-room Frost & Fire Hotel is nestled in the heart of Hveragerði. Each room in the boutique hotel is adorned with works from local Icelandic artists and has private shower facilities and comfortable beds. Guests have access to a spa next to the river that offers treatments, hot tubs, and a swimming pool. The included breakfast is delicious.

HVERAGERÐI CAMPSITE

Reykjamork, tel. 354/483-4605, www.reykjamork-camping@simnet.is, mid-May-Sept., 1,750ISK

This campsite is just two minutes from the swimming pool. Visitors have access to a washing machine, dryer, toilets, and 220-volt electricity. There are about 80 spots on the large field, and the campsite accommodates tents, RVs, and campers. Electricity costs an extra 1,000ISK, and washing machines are 800ISK per wash.

Information and Services

SOUTH ICELAND REGIONAL INFORMATION CENTER

Sunnumörk 2-4, tel. 354/483-4601, www.south.is, 8:30am-6pm Mon.-Fri., 9am-4pm Sat., 9am-2pm Sun. June 1-Aug. 31, 8:30am-5pm Mon.-Fri., 9am-1pm Sat. Sept. 1-May 31

The South Iceland regional information center is right off Route 1 in Hveragerði.

Getting There

Hveragerði is 40 kilometers (25 miles) southeast of **Reykjavík.** The drive takes about 35 minutes on **Route 1.**

The **Strætó 51 bus** (tel. 354/540-2700, www.straeto.is) from Mjodd bus station in Reykjavík makes about 10 daily stops to Hveragerði year-round, stopping at the **Shell gas station** downtown. The bus ride is about 40 minutes and costs 1,410ISK.

SELFOSS

Located close to Gullfoss, Geysir, and Þingvellir, Selfoss is a service hub for South Iceland. Many visitors make a stop here to fill up their gas tanks, get a bite to eat, or rest their heads in one of the town's nice hotels or guesthouses. While the town's proximity to the Ring Road and sights in the countryside is a plus, Selfoss has a few attractions of its own that are worth checking out, too. History buffs will want to drop by the **Heritage Museum,** which features exhibitions of life in the town and the surrounding sights.

Sights
BOBBY FISCHER CENTER

Austurvegur 21, tel. 354/894-1275, www.fischersetur.is, 1pm-4pm and 7:30pm-9:30pm daily May 15-Sept. 15, or by appointment, 1,000ISK

The Bobby Fischer Center is located in a small white house in the heart of Selfoss. This may sound like an odd museum to find in Iceland, but Bobby Fischer, the famous chess player, lived in the town for a couple of years after applying for asylum in the country (after breaking international sanctions to play a chess match in Yugoslavia). The museum serves as the home of the local chess club, and you'll find Bobby Fischer memorabilia, mostly from his time in Iceland, on display. Bobby lived in Iceland from 2005 until his death in 2008.

KERIÐ CRATER

15 km (9 mi) north of Selfoss, 400ISK

The Kerið crater, which is just 15 kilometers (9 miles) north of Selfoss, is a cool place to stop and take a photo due to the sheer size of the crater lake. The collapsed scoria cone is 70 meters (230 feet) deep and is used for farming fish. There's a nice **path** along the rim (about a 30-minute walk) with good views; use caution and stay on the path.

SKÁLHOLT CHURCH

tel. 354/486-8870, www.skalholt.is, 9am-6pm daily; free

The site of the Skálholt church has great significance in Iceland's history and is a sacred site for many Icelanders. Gissur the White, a wealthy political figure, played an important role in the Christianization of Iceland and the growth of the early church. He built the first church in Iceland at Skálholt around the year 1000. His son, Ísleifur (1006-1080), chose Skálholt as the site of the first Episcopal see in Iceland, and the first bishopric was founded here in 1056 for southern Iceland.

In the 12th century, bishop Klængur Þorsteinsson built a great cathedral at Skálholt, and it served as a cultural center up to the Reformation in 1550. The last Catholic bishop of Iceland, Jón Arason, was executed at Skálholt in 1550, along with his two sons, because he opposed the Reformation forced upon Iceland by King Christian III of Denmark. A memorial stands at the site of the execution. Today, Skálholt is visited for the cathedral, the tomb of bishops, the museum, and the collection of ancient books on view in the tower. The church on the site today dates from 1963 and is a large, stark-white building with a dark top. The design is sharp, clean, and classically Nordic. In the summer months, there are cultural events and concerts open to the public.

There's a church service every Sunday at either 11am or 2pm, as well as evening prayers at 9am Mon.-Fri. and evening prayers at 6pm Mon.-Fri.

Skálholt is 39 kilometers (24 miles) northeast of Selfoss. The drive takes about 40 minutes on the paved **Route 35.**

Sports and Recreation
SÓLHESTAR

Borgargerdi, tel. 354/892-3066, www.solhestar.is

Sólhestar offers year-round horse tours ranging from one-hour rides for 9,000ISK to customized all-day tours for 24,000ISK.

Tours feature trails along scenic hot springs, volcanoes, remote beaches, and gorgeous waterfalls.

SUNDHÖLL SELFOSS

Bankavegur, tel. 354/480-1960, sundh@arborg. is, 6:30am-9:30pm Mon.-Fri., 9am-7pm Sat.-Sun., 1,000ISK

The Sundhöll Selfoss is a pool open year-round; towel and swimsuit rentals are available.

KIDJABERG GOLF COURSE

Kidjaberg, tel. 354/486-4495, 8am-10pm daily in summer, green fees 10,815ISK

The Kidjaberg Golf Course in Selfoss is an 18-hole facility near the Hvitá River with glorious views. A clubhouse and restaurant are on-site. Be sure to call ahead for a tee time, as this is a popular course among locals.

Food
KAFFI KRÚS

Austurvegur 7, tel. 354/482-1266, www.kaffikrus.is, 8:30am-11pm daily, entrees from 2,400ISK

Kaffi Krús is a favorite neighborhood joint that has something for everyone. Pizza is their specialty, but they also serve salads, soups, pasta dishes, burgers, and fish and chips, as well as lamb and fish entrees. You can't go wrong with their pizza, especially their duck pizza pie, with duck confit, mushrooms, red onions, chutney, sauce, and cheese topped off with truffle mayo.

★ KRISP RESTAURANT

Eyravegur 8, tel. 354/482-4099, www.krisp.is/en, noon-10pm daily, entrees from 2,890ISK

Opened in 2018, Krisp is a wonderful addition to Selfoss, with an inventive menu with a lot of surprises. You will find mainstays like burgers, cod, lamb, and salmon, but also Asian-influenced dishes like barbecue pork ribs with sesame seeds, steamed buns, butter-fried edamame, and wolfish skewers. Krisp also serves burritos and several vegan dishes.

1: the South Coast 2: Skálholt church

HAFIÐ BLÁA

Thorlákshöfn, tel. 354/483-1000, www.hafidblaa.is,
noon-9pm daily, entrées from 2,950ISK

Hafið Bláa, which translates to "the Blue Sea," is a seaside café where you can grab a quick coffee and cake or sit and enjoy a light meal and the beautiful view. The cream of mushroom soup is memorable. Lobster soup, arctic char, and salted cod are also on the menu.

RIVERSIDE RESTAURANT

Eyrarvegur 2, tel. 354/480-2500, www.hotelselfoss.
is, 7am-10pm daily, entrées from 3,400ISK

Riverside Restaurant is Hótel Selfoss's in-house restaurant. Guests are treated to fresh, local ingredients and eclectic recipes in an elegant atmosphere. The sesame fried salmon and bacon-covered monkfish are recommended. Vegetarian dishes are available.

Accommodations

SELFOSS HOSTEL

Austurvegur 28, tel. 354/660-6999, www.hostel.is,
private rooms from 12,500ISK, beds from 3,300ISK

One of the nicer hostels on the island, this 60-bed facility has spacious rooms, a common kitchen, small gym, and helpful staff. The hostel has a friendly atmosphere. Guests often meet up with fellow travelers and plan excursions together. Washing machines are available for use, and sheets are provided. A hot tub out back is a nice touch.

★ HÓTEL SELFOSS

Eyrarvegur 2, tel. 354/480-2500, www.selfosshotel.
is, rooms from 26,000ISK

Hótel Selfoss has the sort of stylish interior you'd expect in Reykjavík, so it comes as a delightful surprise in the countryside. The 99-room hotel has large rooms, including spacious bathrooms, and chic decor. Ten rooms are specifically designed for people with disabilities, and it is one of the most wheelchair-friendly hotels on the island. Business travelers are attracted to the hotel for its conference center, while those looking for luxury are thrilled about the in-house spa, which offers a number of treatments. The staff aims to please and are happy to chat and give recommendations about local sights.

★ TRAUSTHOLTSHÓLMI

tel. 354/699-4256, www.thh.is, yurt for two from
65,000ISK

Traustholtshólmi, located on a private island in the Þjórsá River, is a passion project of the island's owner, Hakón. This one-of-a-kind experience for travelers offers three Mongolian

Traustholtshólmi yurt

yurts that can sleep two adults and 1-2 children each. Hakón will collect you at a meeting place, which he will email to you, and you will be transported to the island in a 4-minute boat ride. The yurts are warm, comfortable, and pleasing to the eye, with bright doors and tasteful, rustic decor. Toilets and showers are close by. A stay on the island allows you to feel one with nature, soaking in the silence and tranquility.

Included in an overnight stay is a tour of the island by Hakón and his friendly sheepdog Skuggi, the chance to participate in catching and tasting wild salmon straight from the river, and a dinner of fresh fish and island-grown potatoes along with the tastiest rhubarb dessert. After a restful night, breakfast is served in the service yurt and you will have time to roam the island before being returned to the mainland. A truly unbeatable experience.

Information and Services
SELFOSS TOURIST INFORMATION CENTER
Austurvegur 2, tel. 354/480-1990, www.south.is, 8am-6pm Mon.-Fri., 10am-3pm Sat. June 1-Aug. 31, 8am-7pm Mon.-Fri., 10am-2pm Sat. Sept. 1-May 31

The tourist information center is a great place to pick up pamphlets, arrange tours, and ask questions of the staff.

Getting There
By car, Selfoss is off the familiar **Route 1,** 57 kilometers (35 miles) southeast from **Reykjavík.** The drive takes about 45 minutes.

If you're traveling by bus, the **Strætó 51 bus** (tel. 354/540-2700, www.straeto.is) leaves from bus station Mjodd in Reykjavík several times a day. The ride takes about one hour and costs 1,880ISK. Buses stop and pick up near the **main circle (Austurvegur)** downtown.

STOKKSEYRI
This small town was home to a thriving fishing industry, but today it's more of a tourist town with a couple of kitschy museums.

Sights
THE GHOST CENTRE
Hafnargata 9, tel. 354/483-1202, www. icelandicwonders.is, 1pm-6pm daily, 1,300ISK

This small, fun museum is dedicated to Iceland's most famous ghosts and their stories. During the tour, which takes about 40 minutes, you hear 24 ghost stories through a device and headphones that can be listened to in English, French, German, Russian, Japanese, or Icelandic. While you listen to the ghost stories, you look at displays about the various spirits. The phantoms include mountainside ghosts, ancient ghosts, ghosts in animal disguises, infant ghosts, and sea ghosts. The Ghost Bar is at the end of the tour, where you can order a drink and absorb everything you just took in. It's all in good fun, but it's not recommended for children under age 12.

ICELANDIC WONDERS
Hafnargata 9, tel. 354/483-1202, www. icelandicwonders.is, 1pm-6pm daily, 1,500ISK

Icelandic Wonders is next door to the Ghost Centre. Instead of ghosts, this exhibition focuses on Iceland's rich folklore, including elves, trolls, the Yule Lads (Iceland's version of Santa Claus), and northern lights. There's something for everyone at this charming museum, and it is much more child friendly than the Ghost Centre.

Food
★ FJÖRUBORÐIÐ
Eyrarbraut 3a, tel. 354/483-1550, www.fjorubordid. is/english, noon-9pm daily, entrees from 2,800ISK

If you are in the mood for seafood, this is your place. Fjöruborðið, which means seashore, specializes in tasty langoustines, from their langoustine soup, to langoustine tails sautéed in garlic and butter. The fish is fresh, tender, and full of flavor. If you aren't in the mood for seafood, don't fret, there is a beef carpaccio salad on offer as well as a vegetarian dish and roasted fillet of local lamb. For the kids, there are chicken nuggets with fries and a ham and cheese sandwich.

Getting There

Stokkseyri is 65 kilometers (40 miles) southeast of **Reykjavík** and accessible by **Route 1.** The drive takes about 55 minutes.

MOUNT HEKLA

Hekla's claim to fame is being the most active volcano in the country today (no easy feat, as there are currently 35 active volcanoes in Iceland). Hekla (Hood) should not be confused with nearby Eyjafjallajökull, which wreaked havoc on transatlantic air travel in 2010. Climbing 1,491 meters (4,891 feet), Hekla has erupted five times in the last hundred years and more than 20 times since Iceland was settled in the 10th century. Its last eruption was in 2000, and local scientists expect it to erupt in the near future. What makes Hekla somewhat unique is that it's a cone volcano, which is less common in Iceland than fissure volcanoes.

Sights
HEKLA CENTER

Leirubakki, tel. 354/487-8700, www.leirubakki.is, 10am-9pm daily May-Sept., 900ISK

The Hekla Center gives visitors a comprehensive look at one of the island's most active volcanoes. The exhibition emphasizes the influence of the volcano on the inhabited areas close to it, including Landsveit, Holt, and Rangárvellir. The center has special educational materials for children as well as tourist information in English. An on-site **café** offers light meals and coffee. It's an essential place to stop and read up on the region.

Hiking
HIKING HEKLA

Distance: *7 km (4 mi)*
Hiking Time: *8 hours round-trip*
Information and maps: *Hella Tourist Information Center (Thrudvangur 6, tel. 354/487-4800)*
Trailhead: *Parking lot at southeastern corner of the mountain*

Scaling Hekla should not be taken lightly. In four hours or so, you can reach the summit via a moderately challenging 7-kilometer (4-mile) trail. Along the way, you cross rough lava fields and see ice and snow as the peak gets nearer. At the top, the view is jaw-dropping. On clear days, you can see the Fjallabak mountains up to Vatnajökull glacier, Europe's largest glacier.

Now for some crucial safety tips. The ideal time to make the climb is in the **summer,** when it's not likely that you'll encounter a lot of snow at the top. Regardless of when you decide to climb, if you do intend to get to the top, you will need **glacier equipment.** All necessary equipment will be provided by guides on tours. **Arctic Adventures** (www. adventures.is) offer a hiking tour of Hekla. Always make sure to check weather conditions before you head out and let someone (such as the concierge of your hotel) know of your travel plans. Also check in with the **tourist information center** in Hella. Make sure you have an adequate amount of drinking water, appropriate clothing, and a charged mobile phone. Mount Hekla is an active volcano, so check with locals and consult www.safetravel.is before heading out on a hike.

Information and Services
HELLA TOURIST INFORMATION CENTER

Árhús, Rangárbökkum, tel. 354/487-5577

The Hella Tourist Information Center is located at Árhús. Here, visitors can book hiking, horse riding, and mountain biking tours, and obtain hiking maps.

Getting There

By car from **Reykjavík,** head southeast on **Route 1** and take unpaved **Route 26** toward the town of Hella. There is parking by the trailhead. The journey from Reykjavík is 93 kilometers (58 miles), which takes about 1.5 hours.

HVOLSVÖLLUR

Hvolsvöllur is a small town about 100 kilometers (62 miles) from Reykjavík, home to less than 2,000 people. Close to the Golden Circle route, and a growing interest in tourism, Hvolsvöllur houses a fascinating **Lava Centre** and the tourism company **Midgard,** which provides accommodation and tours right from Hvolsvöllur.

Sights
★ LAVA CENTRE
Austurvegur 14, tel. 354/415-5200, www.lavacentre.is, 9am-7pm daily, 3,950ISK
The Lava Centre is informative, fun, and extremely well done. The museum takes a deep dive into Iceland's unique geology, from volcanoes to the constant small tremors that parts of the island experience. There are interactive displays and an engaging film, and a lot of time was spent on capturing every detail about this volcanic island. This is highly recommended for adults and kids. There is a restaurant on site, **Katla Restaurant** (9am-8pm daily), and a gift shop.

Sports and Recreation
★ MIDGARD ADVENTURE
Dufþaksbraut 14, tel. 354/578-3180, www.midgardbasecamp.is
Hvolsvöllur-based Midgard has injected new life into the small town. The company offers a variety of day tours including a 10-14 hour hike along Fimmvörðuháls (39,000ISK), a bike and lava caving tour (25,000ISK), snowmobiling on Eyjafjallajökull volcano (26,900ISK), and an ice climbing and glacier walk (21,490ISK). Their popular Þórsmörk super jeep tour is highly recommended as you are driven about an hour from Hvolsvöllur into Þórsmörk, where you will see waterfalls and canyons, cross rivers, and get up close and personal with a glacier. The 6-8-hour tour costs 32,000ISK.

HVOLSVÖLLUR SWIMMING POOL
Vallarbraut, tel. 354/488-4295, 6am-9pm Mon.-Fri., 10am-7pm Sat.-Sun., 1,000ISK
Hvolsvöllur has a large outdoor swimming pool, with a slide for kids, as well as a gym, sauna, and hot pots.

Food and Accommodations
VALHALLA RESTAURANT & SAGA CENTER
Hliðarvegur 14, tel. 354/487-8781, 10am-11pm daily, entrees from 1,800ISK
Valhalla Restaurant is a family-friendly spot that offers casual food like hamburgers, smoked barbecue ribs, and pulled pork sandwiches. The menu is small and simple, centered around their charcoal grill. There is a veggie burger on the menu as well as a kids' burger. The restaurant has a Viking theme that is kitschy and fun. They even offer a place to practice your axe-throwing skills.

MIDGARD BASE CAMP
Dufþaksbraut 14, tel. 354/578-3180, www.midgardbasecamp.is, beds from 5,800ISK, private rooms from 24,900ISK
The same family that operates Midgard Adventure runs Midgard Base Camp, a relaxed, friendly hostel that offers dorm room accommodation as well as private rooms. Dorm rooms have design-forward bunk beds with a bedside light, charging sockets, and a privacy curtain, along with shared bathroom facilities. Private rooms can accommodate two travelers and have private bathrooms with a shower. All guests have access to a rooftop sauna and hot tub to relax in after a long day of adventure. There's a large common lounge area and an in-house **bar** and restaurant. The **restaurant** (breakfast 7am-11am, dinner 4pm-10pm, mains 2,600ISK) serves up options like a tasty lamb prime rib and local pan-fried salmon, as well as burgers, salads, and vegan dishes.

Getting There
By car from **Reykjavík,** head southeast on **Route 1** and take it to Hvolsvöllur. The journey from Reykjavík is 107 kilometers (67 miles), which takes about 1.5 hours.

ÞJÓRSÁRDALUR
Þjórsárdalur is a flat, lush valley near the Þjórsá River with a number of stunning waterfalls. The region has a lot of pumice because of the

numerous eruptions of Mount Hekla over the years, evidenced by **Stöng,** a reconstructed settlement-era farm that was completely buried by Hekla's eruption in the year 1104.

Sights
HÁIFOSS
Route 32

Háifoss, a beautiful waterfall near Mount Hekla, drops from a height of 122 meters (400 feet), making it the second-highest waterfall on the island. Set against the backdrop of the Þjórsá River, Háifoss is a wonderful place to stop and take photos. It is possible to **hike** to the waterfall from the farm Stöng, a moderate, six-hour, 18-kilometer (11-mile) round-trip hike, but there is a **parking lot** above the cascade, which makes it a car-friendly stop along the way to your next destination.

If you are planning to hike it, make sure you have proper footwear and adequate drinking water. From **Selfoss,** take **Route 1** for 14 kilometers (9 miles) to **Route 30;** follow Route 30 for 18 kilometers (11 miles) to **Route 32,** for another 43 kilometers (27 miles). All routes are paved.

HJÁLPARFOSS
from Route 32, drive about 20 minutes until you see a sign by the road that says Hjálparfoss.

Hjálparfoss is another gorgeous waterfall near Mount Hekla. While not particularly tall, the waterfall is special as it's where the Þórsa and Fossa rivers meet, and the falls are split in two. It is about 30 kilometers (19 miles) east of the village Flúðir and can be reached by a gravel road between **Route 30** to **Route 32** that winds through the Vikrar lava fields. From Route 32, drive about 20 minutes until you see a sign by the road that says Hjálparfoss.

STÖNG
tel. 354/488-7713, www.thjodveldisbaer.is/en, 10am-5pm daily June 1-Aug. 31, remainder of the year open by appointment, 1,000ISK, free for children up to 16

Stöng, a settlement-era farm, was completely buried by Hekla's eruption in the year 1104. A reconstructed 11th-century longhouse called Þjóðveldisbær was erected in this protected valley. For those looking to see a traditional "turf house" with grass on the roof, this is the place to go. The farm, as legend tells it, was the residence of Gaukur á Stöng from *Njál's Saga.* History buffs will want to make a stop, and visitors are welcome to go inside and take a look.

Sports and Recreation
ÞJÓRSÁRDALUR SWIMMING POOL
tel. 354/488-7002, 10am-9pm daily June-Aug., 950ISK

After erecting the local dam, the Búrfell hydroelectric station used its extra cement to build the open-air Þjórsárdalur Swimming Pool.

Getting There and Around
Þjórsárdalur is 118 kilometers (73 miles) east of **Reykjavík.** It's accessible by unpaved **Route 32;** a **four-wheel-drive** jeep is recommended to get around some choppy parts of the road. It is not recommended to venture out in a compact car, as the likelihood of getting stranded is high. The drive takes about 1.5 hours. Be sure to check weather forecasts before heading out on your journey.

ÞÓRSMÖRK AND LANDMANNALAUGAR
The spectacular Þórsmörk (Thor's Woods) region offers landscapes ranging from towering mountains to scores of glacial streams and miles of black sand. Þórsmörk is not an easy region to get to as there are river crossings and you need a vehicle that has a high enough clearance to cross. The region is dotted with waterfalls, canyons, lush vegetation, and vast open spaces. Making it here is no easy feat. Do not venture out in a compact car. Because of the **Krossá River,** this is a wet and turbulent ride that requires a jeep.

Nearby Landmannalaugar is a major hub for hikers, and for very good reason. There are several well-maintained trails throughout the region that range from day hikes to multiday treks. The landscape is one of wonder, with

---

1: Landmannalaugar 2: Þórsmörk

Hiking Laugavergurinn: Packing, Getting There, and Other Tips

For general information about the Laugavegurinn Trail, contact the Iceland Touring Association (Ferðafélag Íslands) (www.fi.is).

WHEN TO GO

The ideal months for this hike are June and July, but August is possible as well. The region is inaccessible the rest of the year due to snow levels and impassable roads, so if you want to attempt this hike, summer is your only option.

WHAT TO PACK

- Clothing: Waterproof pants, waterproof jacket, mid-layer, waterproof boots, gloves, hat, wool socks, sunglasses, gaiters, wool or synthetic base layers
- Gear: Sleeping bag, mattress, pillow, three-season tent, camping stove, lighter, gas, utensils, cooking pot, knives
- Food: All the food needed for duration of the journey, plus an extra emergency day, snacks, granola bars
- Personal hygiene: Toothbrush, toothpaste, toilet paper, sunscreen, towel
- Other necessities: Maps, GPS, water bottle, small first-aid kit

BEFORE YOU GO

Precaution is needed when hiking in the highlands. The region is remote, unforgiving, and there aren't conveniences like stores, or shelter. Therefore, before you head out, make sure you have informed someone of your plan; you can register your information at www.safetravel.is. It is imperative that you have the proper clothing and footwear, enough food and water, camping gear that can sustain fierce weather, or booked accommodation at mountain huts if you are not camping in designated campsites. Also, make sure you have maps and a charged mobile phone.

---

vast valleys, colorful rhyolite mountains, hot springs, and riverbanks. Landmannalaugar is a three-hour drive from Reykjavík and an F-road approved vehicle is necessary to drive in the highlands. From Reykjavík, you drive on Route 1 to Road 26, followed by the mountain roads F225, F208, and F224. While not an easy route, Landmannalaugar is not as challenging to reach as Þórsmörk.

The wildly popular Laugavegurinn hiking route from the Landmannalaugar region to the Þórsmörk area is a 55-kilometer (34-mile), four-day hike that attracts backpackers and hikers from around the world. If you're coming to Iceland to hike just one trail, this is the one. Its popularity stems from the variety of landscape along the way: bubbling hot springs, vast glaciers, beautiful mountains, stunning waterfalls, and roaring rivers.

TOP EXPERIENCE

★ Laugavegurinn Trail

DAY 1: LANDMANNALAUGAR TO HRAFNTINNUSKER

Distance: 12 km (7 mi)

Hiking Time: 4-5 hours

Trailhead: Landmannalaugar huts

The Landmannalaugar-Hrafntinnusker leg of the hike is considered moderately challenging. The trail goes through a rugged lava field, which makes this leg a bit more difficult, to the slopes of the volcano Brennisteinsalda. The landscape offers every color of the

GETTING THERE (AND GETTING BACK)

Starting in Landmannalaugar

From Reykjavík, Landmannalaugar is about 200 kilometers (124 miles). By rental car, drive on Route 1 to Route 30 to Route 26. Next, take Route 208 until you reach Landmannalaugar. The routes are signposted along the way. For those who wish to travel by bus, the company Trex (www.trex.is) operates buses for 17,300ISK round-trip. The trip from Reykjavík takes 4 hours and 15 minutes.

Starting in Þórsmörk

If starting the hike at Þórsmörk, it's important to note that it is not easy to reach, though it's worth the effort if you're looking for untouched and unspoiled land. There are significantly fewer visitors to Þórsmörk. You will need a jeep with high clearance to cross rivers to navigate these roads; do not attempt the trip in a compact car or city SUV. To reach Þórsmörk by car, drive on Route 1 to Route 249 to F-249.

Arranging Your Return Trip

There are buses that return to Reykjavík through Trex (www.trex.is) from both Landmannalaugar and Þórsmörk. One-way fares are 9,400ISK and tickets can be purchased online.

MOUNTAIN HUTS AND CAMPSITES

At night, hikers on the Laugavergurinn Trail rest their heads in mountain huts, which mark the starting and ending points of each leg of the trail. The huts are run by Volcano Huts (www.volcanohuts.com), and can sleep 2-16 people (beds start at 8,200ISK). They have running water, cooking facilities, a sauna, pool, and showers. it's required to call ahead for a spot in the mountain huts.

There are campsites that adjoin the mountain huts that are also operated by Volcano Huts. The facilities include a cooking area, toilets, and running water. It's always a good idea to call ahead for camping.

rainbow, from deep green moss to the bluest skies to yellow and red earth. After about four hours, you will reach a hot spring, Stórihver, which surges with activity, steam bubbling to the surface. The remainder of the trail to the Hrafntinnusker hut at Höskuldsskáli might be challenging depending on weather conditions, so be sure to monitor the forecast for snow and wind.

DAY 2: HRAFNTINNUSKER TO ÁLFTAVATN

Distance: *12 km (7 mi)*
Hiking Time: *5 hours*
Trailhead: *Hrafntinnusker hut*

The Hrafntinnusker-Álftavatn part of the trail is also moderately challenging, starting

out through a valley with some small gorges and dips in the land. If the weather is good, a climb up Mount Háskerðingur (1,032 meters/3,386 feet tall) will treat you to a spectacular view of the landscape and the road ahead. The trail continues through a region rich with mountains and glaciers. As you get closer to the Grashagakvísl River, the colors become more vibrant, with bright green moss and lichen alive along the riverbanks. It's a beautiful place to stop, take some pictures, and soak up the scenery.

DAY 3: ÁLFTAVATN TO EMSTRUR

Distance: *15 km (9 mi)*
Hiking Time: *7 hours*
Trailhead: *Bratthals ridge*

This moderately challenging trail starts out over the ridge Bratthåls, passes into the Hvanngil gorge, and crosses the Bratthålskvísl River by bridge. The landscape is vast and serene. As you continue on to the Kaldaklofskvísl River, there is a bridge for hikers. Past the bridge, you have two options as the trail splits. One branch leads east to Mælifellssandur, and the other path leads south to Emstrur. Most people opt for the southern trail to Emstrur because it's a bit more scenic, with mountain views and an interesting rocky landscape. Less than one kilometer (0.6 miles) from Kaldaklofskvísl from the southern trail, there's another river, Nyrðri Emstruá, where there is a bridge to cross.

DAY 4: EMSTRUR TO ÞÓRSMÖRK
Distance: 15 km (9 mi)
Hiking Time: 7 hours
Trailhead: Emstrur huts

The last leg of the hike, from Emstrur to Þórsmörk, starts out navigating the canyon of Syðri-Emstruá. The path down to the bridge is steep, so stay aware and be careful where you step while descending. Next, hikers come across the Almenningar region and will have to ford the Þröngá River. After wading through the river, it's a 30-minute walk to the Langidalur huts in Þórsmörk.

Getting There
Landmannalaugar is 193 kilometers (119 miles) southeast of Reykjavík. Take Route 1 to Route 26 to F225; the latter two roads are unpaved. It's about a 3.5-hour drive.

Þórsmörk is 157 kilometers (97.6 miles) southeast from Reykjavík. It's reachable by Jeep via Route 1 and Route 249. The drive takes about 3.5 hours.

By bus, Trex (tel. 354/587-6000, www.trex.is) has daily departures in the summer from Reykjavík to Þórsmörk (9,000ISK per person) and Reykjavík to Landmannalaugar (9,400ISK per person). Both rides take about 4 hours.

SELJALANDSFOSS
The mighty Seljalandsfoss is a highlight for many visitors to the South Coast. Tourists delight in the spray from the 40-meter (131-foot) falls, and rainbows are frequently seen here due to the changing weather and frequent rain showers. During the summer, the area around the falls is lush with bright green grass, a heavenly sight on bright days. What makes this waterfall unique in a land of spectacular waterfalls is that there's a path that lets you walk behind it. Those who do so are treated to a memorable view, but be prepared to get wet and be sure to wear appropriate footwear. Use caution during the winter, as it can be especially slippery.

Getting There
Seljalandsfoss is about 120 kilometers (76 miles) southeast of Reykjavík, about a 1.75-hour drive, and is right off Route 1.

EYJAFJALLAJÖKULL
Eyjafjallajökull became Iceland's most famous volcano after its eruption in 2010 halted air travel across Europe, stranding tens of thousands of people. For locals, it was a treat to hear foreign newscasters struggle to pronounce the name of the volcano on the nightly news. Clips were regularly shown on Icelandic TV. (For the record, it's pronounced EYE-ya-fyat-lah-YOH-kuht.)

Before Eyjafjallajökull made worldwide headlines, the volcano had been a popular destination to explore, and it remains so today, with a rugged and icy landscape. Never attempt to climb a glacier on your own. Eyjafjallajökull is completely covered by an ice cap; magma hitting the ice created the tremendous ash cloud during the eruption. The ice cap covers an area of about 100 square kilometers (39 square miles), which feeds several outlet glaciers. When people joke that "Iceland is green, and Greenland is icy," those who visit the Eyjafjallajökull region will think again. There is a lot of ice in Iceland. The ice cap is the island's fourth-largest glacier.

Eyjafjallajökull is a stratovolcano that ascends to 1,651 meters (5,417 feet) at its highest point. The volcano is fed by a magma chamber under the mountain, and it is part of a chain of volcanoes stretching across Iceland. Its nearest active neighbors are Katla to the north and Heimaey and Eldfell to the south. The volcano is thought to be related to Katla, in that eruptions of Eyjafjallajökull have generally been followed by eruptions of Katla. However, Katla did not erupt following Eyjafjallajökull's 2010 eruption. Scientists closely monitor the volcanoes' activity, measuring the size and frequency of the tremors.

Getting There

Eyjafjallajökull is on the Ring Road, **Route 1,** and is 140 kilometers (87 miles) east of **Reykjavík.** Buses do not stop near the volcano, so if you want to get up close and personal, you need access to a car.

SKÓGAR

Skógar is a tiny village of fewer than 40 people. The town suffered a major setback in the aftermath of the Eyjafjallajökull eruption, as it was covered in ash and life ground to a halt. The town has since recovered, and tourism to the region is back in full swing. The **Skógafoss** cascade is the main draw, but there is also a folk museum worth checking out.

Sights
SKÓGAFOSS

Skógafoss is an epic waterfall, one of the biggest in the country. It looms 25 meters (82 feet) high and has a drop-off of 60 meters (197 feet). According to Viking lore, a local settler buried a treasure chest in a cave behind the waterfall. It was said that locals discovered the chest years later, but it quickly disappeared before they could grasp it. Because of the amount of spray the waterfall produces, as well as the changing weather from sun to rain, it's common to see rainbows over the falls; be sure to have your camera ready. The waterfall is in town, near the southern Ring Road.

SKÓGAR FOLK MUSEUM (Skógasafn)

Austur-Eyjafjöllum, tel. 354/487-8845, www. skogasafn.is, 9am-6pm daily June 1-Aug. 31, 10am-5pm daily Sept. 1-May 31, 2,000ISK, children 12-17 1,200ISK, free for children under 12

Skógar Folk Museum is a charming initiative that started in 1949 at the behest of resident Þórður Tómasson, who curated the museum from its inception until his retirement in 2013, at the age of 92. The museum, which houses relics of the past, including tools, fishing equipment, and a fishing boat, does a great job of showing what life has been like in Skógar over the last several decades. A little coffee shop serves a great cup of coffee and delicious pastries.

Hiking the Fimmvörðuháls Trail

The trek through the Fimmvörðuháls pass from Skógar to **Þórsmörk** is one of the most popular hiking routes in the country. The trail takes hikers up from Skógar, along the **Skógá River** and its wondrous waterfalls, and up between the two enormous glaciers: **Eyjafjallajökull** and **Mýrdalsjökull.** There, hikers can see recently formed lava and craters. Heading down from the craters to the stunning Þórsmörk glacier valley, there are some amazing views over the highlands and the surrounding glaciers. The trek is only safely accessible from around **mid-June** to early **September.**

This is a demanding hike, with an elevation gain of over 1,000 meters (3,000 feet) and a total distance of about 25 kilometers (16 miles). It takes about 8-10 hours. Most tourists hike it in one day, but it can be done over two days as well. For those who want to take the **bus** back, check out www.trex.is for the timetable and rates. It's recommended that you start the hike at Skógar and end at Þórsmörk; starting at Skógar is more popular than starting in Þórsmörk because it's easier to get to. There are no facilities along the route, so be sure to have enough food and water, as well as proper gear. Good hiking boots and waterproof clothing are required, and having layers is strongly

recommended. You can encounter all types of weather, so be prepared.

Experienced independent hikers may opt to take a bus run by **Reykjavík Excursions** (tel. 354/580-5400, www.re.is) to Skógar, which leaves twice daily from Reykjavík June 1-August 31. The one-way fare is 7,500ISK. Upon completing the hike, travelers can take a Reykjavík Excursion bus back to Reykjavík from the Básar campsite, in the vicinity of Þórsmörk, for 8,500ISK.

DAY 1: SKÓGAR TO FIMMVÖRÐUSKÁLI HUT

Distance: 12 km (7 mi)

Hiking Time: 5-6 hours

Trailhead: Skógafoss waterfall; GPS coordinates N 63.37.320, W 19.27.093

The trek starts at the epic waterfall Skógafoss, where you'll want to spend some time exploring the area and admiring the thundering falls. The trail officially begins after climbing the makeshift stairs along the waterfall. You'll see a river ahead and a path, and you'll encounter myriad colors in the landscape, from lush greens in the first 7-8 kilometers (4-5 miles) to the muted grays and browns of the rugged, rocky terrain. Eyjafjallajökull and Mýrdalsjökull glaciers loom ahead as you make your way past gravelly ruts and fields of snow. Keep in mind that even in the summer, you will see snow. The Fimmvörðuskáli Hut, which is signposted and about 30-40 minutes west of the trail, is the halfway mark. The hut (tel. 354/562-1000, www.utivist.is, 6,500ISK) is open mid-June to August 31 and can accommodate 20 people. It has bathrooms, a gas stove, and kitchen accessories.

DAY 2: FIMMVÖRÐUSKÁLI HUT TO ÞÓRSMÖRK

Distance: 13 km (8 mi)

Hiking Time: 5-6 hours

Trailhead: Fimmvörðuskáli Hut

After a hopefully restful evening and soon after getting back on the trail, you'll make your way between the two glaciers—for many this is a highlight. Observe the smooth curves and jagged edges of the glaciers before getting ready to encounter snow as the elevation rises. The highest point is between the two mountains, Magni and Móði. Pressing ahead, you will encounter the site of the 2010 Eyjafjallajökull eruption and new lava fields created in its aftermath. The path continues through rocky plateaus before descending into valleys as you enter Þórsmörk.

Food and Accommodations
★ **HOTEL SKOGAR**

Skogum, tel. 354/487-4880, www.hotelskogar.is, rooms from 27,550ISK

Just a five-minute walk from Skógafoss waterfall, at the foot of Eyjafjallajökull, Hotel Skogar offers 12 rooms in a minimalist Nordic design. Rooms are bright and airy, with wood furniture and shockingly white bedding. It's clean, comfortable, and has a beautiful in-house restaurant in a killer location with stunning views. Breakfast is included, and guests have access to a sauna and outdoor hot tub. The **Hotel Skogar Restaurant** (breakfast 8am-10am daily year-round, lunch noon-3pm daily June-Aug., dinner 6pm-10pm daily year-round, entrées from 3,900ISK) offers a delicious selection of choice local meats and fish and other fresh ingredients.

Getting There

The tiny village of Skógar is 154 kilometers (96 miles) southeast of **Reykjavík** and is accessible by **Route 1**.

Some bus tours include Skógar in their itinerary. **Bus Travel Iceland** (tel. 354/511-2600, www.bustravel.is) offers a "Southern Iceland" 10-hour tour that includes Skógafoss and the village of Vík (13,990ISK).

VÍK

Vík, home to fewer than 400 people, has that small-town feel. The main tourist draws are the **Katla Geopark**—the region surrounding the mighty **Katla volcano**—and the area's hauntingly beautiful black-sand beaches.

1: eruption at Eyjafjallajökull 2: Skógafoss waterfall

Sights
ICELANDIC LAVA SHOW

Víkurbraut 5, tel. 354/823-7777, 10am-9pm daily, 4,900ISK adults, 2,900ISK children 2-12, free for children under 2

The Icelandic Lava Show is the only place in Iceland to see hot molten lava up close when there isn't a volcanic eruption. This show creates the conditions of an eruption, with molten lava seeping down a display. Guests get to see the lava, which reaches a temperature of 1,093°C (2,000°F), feel the staggering heat emitting from it, and hear the lava crackle and sizzle. This is a fun experience, and a winner for kids.

REYNISDRANGAR

Reynisdrangar is a cluster of striking basalt sea stacks that jut out from a sandy beach. The stacks sit under the mountain Reynisfjall just outside Vík. It's popular to climb on the stacks and take photos, then roam the black-sand beach, picking up stones and admiring the rock formations. Reynisdrangar is about 10 kilometers (6 miles) south of Vík and can be reached by Route 1 and Road 215, both paved roads.

REYNISFJARA

Reynisfjara, from which Reynisdrangar is visible, is probably the most famous black-sand beach in Iceland. The juxtaposition of the white waves crashing on the stark black sand and pebbles is beautiful, with towering basalt columns along the shore next to a small cave. As a popular sight in the south, there tends to be a lot of foot traffic in the area. Pay close attention to the warning signs in the parking lot, as there are sneaker waves that can drag you out to sea; there have been fatal accidents here in recent years. Reynisfjara is also about 10 kilometers (6 miles) south of Vík and can be reached by Route 1 and Road 215, both paved roads.

DYRHÓLAEY

Road 218

Dyrhólaey is a unique rock formation near Reynisfjara. The rock arch rises from the sea, peaking at 120 meters (394 feet), and offers views of the Reynisfjara black-sand beach, basalt columns, the ocean, and during the summer, seabirds, including puffins. You can drive to Dyrhólaey from Reynisfjara, which is about 20 kilometers (12 miles) west, taking paved Road 215 to paved Route 1 to unpaved Road 218. Visitors can walk to the arch from the small carpark.

Sports and Recreation
KATLA GEOPARK

www.katlageopark.com

Vík is the gateway to the Katla Geopark. Iceland's first geopark was designated in 2011 to protect the natural environment, promote local sustainable development, introduce local culture, and emphasize nature tourism. The name comes from one of the island's volcanoes, **Katla,** which is situated under the glacier **Mýrdalsjökull.** The geopark is 9,542 square kilometers (7,545 square miles), which is 9.3 percent of the total area of Iceland. Within the geopark are glaciers, volcanoes, mountains, rivers, waterfalls, and miles of lava fields. Visitors can enjoy hiking, caving, angling, horse riding, glacier walking, and ice climbing. The geopark is open year-round.

One of the best tours offered in the region is a three-hour jeep tour from **Katla Track** (tel. 354/849-4404, www.katlatrack.is), which takes you to see black-sand beaches, the Katla glacier, and Reynisdrangar. The tour is available year-round and costs 29,900ISK per person for a local guide and the jeep. Be sure to dress in warm, waterproof outer clothing, and good shoes.

TRUE ADVENTURE

Suðurvíkurvegur 5, tel. 354/698-8890, www.trueadventure.is, 14,900ISK, children ages 8-16 7,500ISK

Vík-based True Adventure runs a zipline tour in a region surrounded by sweeping valleys and waterfalls. You will start off with an easy hike through a canyon, followed by two zipline rides. The first zipline spans 235

1: puffin in Vík 2: the Reynisdrangar sea stacks

meters (771 feet), followed by a shorter zipline at 135 meters (443 feet). The guide will provide all the necessary equipment and will give you a safety briefing.

Food
★ HALLDORSKAFFI

Vikurbraut 28, tel. 354/487-1202, www.halldorskaffi. is, noon-9pm daily year-round, entrées from 2,790ISK

Halldorskaffi has it all for a tiny café. There are soups, sandwiches, pizza, hamburgers, and more upscale fish and lamb dishes. A children's menu offers chicken nuggets and hamburgers. The food is eclectic for a local café, and the owner is a big fan of garlic. The lamb sandwich with fresh, marinated meat in pepper sauce with a salad and french fries hits the spot.

SUÐUR-VÍK RESTAURANT AND CAFÉ

Suðurvikurvegur 1, tel. 354/487-1515, noon-10pm daily, entrées from 2,850ISK

Suður-Vík Restaurant and Café brings some much-needed food diversity to Vík. The menu is eclectic and includes some tasty Thai dishes that are perfectly spiced. The restaurant is situated in an old house on the top of a hill with amazing views of the landscape, including the sea and mountains.

STRONDIN PUB

Austurvegi 18, tel. 354/487-1230, www.strondin.is, 6pm-midnight Sun.-Thur., 6pm-1am Fri.-Sat., entrées from 2,990ISK

Strondin Pub is a cozy gastropub in the heart of Vík and a great place to stop for home-cooked comfort food. The small restaurant features wood furnishings and decor that conjures the atmosphere of a lodge, with a warm, friendly staff and a diverse menu. Guests can choose from pizzas, salads, and main courses like Icelandic cod stew, pan-fried Arctic char, and grilled lamb fillet.

Accommodations
ICELANDAIR HOTEL VIK

Klettsvegi 1-5, tel. 354/487-1480, www. icelandairhotels.com, rooms from 25,650ISK

Icelandair Hotel Vik is a 78-room hotel close to the major attractions in Vík. It's spacious and has contemporary decor with light colors and lots of windows. Economy, deluxe, and family rooms are available. The hotel also has a cozy bar, and a breakfast buffet is included in the rate.

HOTEL KATLA

Hofdabrekku, tel. 354/487-1208, www.keahotels.is, rooms from 30,000ISK

Hotel Katla offers 103 rooms that feel a bit dated, but they are large and great for a short stay. Guests have free access to an outdoor geothermal pool, sauna, and gym, as well as an in-house restaurant known for its buffets. The dinner buffet is offered in the summer from 6:30pm-9:30pm for 6,200ISK per person. Options include lamb, fish, chicken, turkey, pork, and vegetarian main courses as well as a salad bar, cold cuts, soup, fresh-baked bread, and an array of desserts.

Getting There

By car, Vík is 185 kilometers (115 miles) southeast of **Reykjavík** by **Route 1.** It's about a 2.5-hour drive.

KIRKJUBÆ-JARKLAUSTUR

Kirkjubæjarklaustur is a small village located between Vík and Höfn. The village, referred to as Klaustur by locals, is home to fewer than 150 people. Many tourists who struggle to find accommodations in Vík choose to stay here.

Sights
★ FJAÐRÁRGLJÚFUR

about 4 km (3 mi) from Route 1

Fjaðrárgljúfur is a large canyon that was a little-visited site until a couple of years ago when Canadian pop superstar Justin Bieber filmed a video there. Since then, tourism to the site has been on the rise. The canyon, which is believed to be formed during the last ice age, has been hollowed over millions of years by the Fjaðrá river, creating narrow walls. The canyon is about 2 kilometers (1.2

miles) long and about 100 meters (328 feet) deep, and visitors can walk on a foot path along the canyon's edge to admire the view and take photos. The contrasts are striking as the river weaves through towering rock formations that are lush in the summer months. Please be advised that it's important to stay on the path. The canyon is situated about 4 kilometers (2 miles) from Route 1. If you are driving toward the east, you will see a sign indicating Fjaðrárgljúfur is on the left, leading you to a parking lot.

DVERGHAMRAR

Route 1, GPS coordinates N63° 50' 56.404 W17° 51' 41.297", www.katlageopark.com

Just east of Kirkjubæjarklaustur, you can find Dverghamrar (Dwarf Cliffs), which is a small canyon that geologists believe was shaped during the last ice age. Higher sea levels would have hammered the canyon, creating the interesting jagged basalt columns. The cliffs can be found just off Route 1.

Sports and Recreation
KIRKJUBÆJARKLAUSTUR SWIMMING POOL

Kirkjubær, tel. 354/487-4656, 10am-8pm daily June 1-Sept. 30, 11am-8pm Mon.-Sat., 3pm-7pm Sun. Oct. 1-May 31, 900ISK

This popular outdoor swimming pool in the center of town has two hot tubs.

ICELAND BIKE FARM

Mörtunga 2, tel. 354/692-6131, www.icelandbikefarm. is, tours from 25,000ISK

Iceland Bike Farm is a family-run business that offers guided mountain bike tours on an array of tracks that pass canyons, waterfalls, and hills. Their single track full-day tour (25,000ISK), which is for advanced riders, starts with a super Jeep ride up the mountains before riding 15-25 kilometers (9-15 miles) over 4-6 hours. Iceland Bike Farm also offers multiday tours from July-Sept. for 100,000ISK.

Food and Accommodations
FOSSHOTEL NÚPAR

Núpar, tel. 354/517-3060, www.islandshotel.is, rooms from 26,500ISK

Fosshotel Núpar has 99 rooms, with some boasting a view of the glacier Vatnajökull. Rooms are clean, with private bathrooms, a simple desk, and a bedside table. There's an in-house **restaurant and bar** (11am-9pm daily, entrées from 3,000ISK), and breakfast is included in the price of the room.

HOTEL KLAUSTUR

Klausturvegur 6, tel. 354/487-4900, www. hotelklaustur.is, rooms from 28,000

Hotel Klaustur is a 57-room hotel just off the Ring Road, making this a convenient place to stay when exploring the South Coast. It offers twin and queen rooms as well as king junior suites. The rooms feel a little dated, with green carpeting and bright bed linens, but it's an adequate three-star hotel. The in-house restaurant offers a breakfast buffet every morning (7:30am-9:30am daily), and dinner (6:30pm-9pm daily). Main courses start at 2,650ISK and include grilled Arctic char, lamb fillet, and pasta dishes.

MAGMA HOTEL

Tunga, tel. 354/420-0800, www.magmahotel.is, rooms from 33,000ISK

Magma Hotel is a stylish addition to the area. The 14 self-contained cottage-style rooms are modern, chic, and heavy on Nordic design. Each room is tastefully decorated in muted colors with quality linens, wood furniture, and hardwood floors. All rooms have huge windows as well as a patio. Rooms range from doubles to family rooms and have a flat-screen TV with access to Netflix, Marshall speakers, free Wi-Fi, and a private bathroom.

Getting There

By car, Kirkjubæjarklaustur is about 250 kilometers (155 miles) southeast of **Reykjavík** on **Route 1,** an approximately three-hour drive.

Heimaey

The Westman Islands (Vestmannaeyjar) are chock-full of rocky ridges and bird-watching opportunities. Heimaey, the only inhabited island, is where all of the sights, restaurants, and museums are located. With fewer than 5,000 residents, it's an isolated community, surrounded by beauty. The other islands remain uninhabited but can be seen from the sea during a boat tour. In the summer months, Heimaey is a popular spot for puffin-watching.

SIGHTS
Eldfell
www.visitwestmanislands.com

Eldfell, which means "fire mountain" in Icelandic, is a volcanic cone that reaches 200 meters (656 feet) high. It was formed after the 1973 volcanic eruption on Heimaey, which came without warning and displaced more than 3,000 Icelanders. Ash from the eruption fell for weeks, destroying homes, livestock, and personal possessions. Most of Heimaey's residents left by boat, and thankfully there were no deaths.

Tourists can take a 30-minute **ferry** ride from **Landeyjaharbor** in the southern town of **Hvolsvöllur** to Heimaey to get a close look at Eldfell, which is possible to hike. Ferries (www.visitwestmanislands.com) depart seven times a day May-September (3,200ISK round-trip without a car).

Eldheimar
Gerðisbraut 10, tel. 354/488-2700, www.eldheimar. is, 9am-6pm daily, 2,400ISK, children 10-18 1,300ISK, free for children 9 and younger

Eldheimar is a fascinating interactive museum about Heimaey's 1973 volcanic eruption. It includes photos, surviving structures, and an overview of the volcanic geology of the region. Videos illustrate the force of the volcanic eruption and destruction left in its wake, and maps light up on the walls, pointing out volcanoes around the island.

★ Beluga Whale Sanctuary
Ægisgata, Vestmannaeyjabær, www. visitwestmanislands.com

The Westman Island's latest attraction is the arrival of Little Grey and Little White, two Beluga whales that were moved from China to Iceland in 2019. Sea Life Trust, a nonprofit, is behind the sanctuary, and guests can join a boat tour (8,500ISK) of the bay the whales now call home. The two-hour tour includes the boat tour and a stopover to the **visitor's center** and the **aquarium**. Tours run from July 1-Oct. 30.

Folk Museum of Vestmannaeyjar
Safnahúsinu við Ráðhúströð, tel. 354/488-0100, www.sagnheimar.is, 1,000ISK

The Folk Museum of Vestmannaeyjar contains an interesting group of permanent exhibits that include the 1973 volcanic eruption on Heimaey, the annual Vestmannaeyjar festival, which has been held every year since 1874, the role of women in the fishing station over the years, and an exhibit about the harbor area.

SPORTS AND RECREATION
★ Boat Tours
VIKING TOURS
tel. 354/488-4884, www.vikingtours.is, May 15-Sept. 15, 8,200ISK adults, 7,200ISK children 9-14 and seniors, free for children under 9

Viking Tours offers a lovely boat tour departing from Heimaey harbor daily at 11am. On the 1.5-hour tour, you'll see the rugged lava coastline, bird cliffs, and ocean caves. Near

---

1: Eldfell volcano **2:** Heimaey, one of the Westman Islands

its conclusion, you'll enter a cave along the harbor, where you'll listen to instrumental music that takes advantage of the cave's acoustics. It's a wonderful way to spend a couple of hours.

RIBSAFARI

Basaskersbryggja 6, tel. 354/661-1810, www.ribsafari. is, tours from 12,900ISK

From mid-May to mid-September you can take a thrilling ride on a RIB speedboat, zooming over waves off the shores of the Westman Islands. During the tour you get to explore sea caves that are only accessible by small boats, as well as spot seabirds like puffins, gannets, and fulmars. This is a great tour for adrenaline junkies who also want to see some nature by sea.

Bird-Watching

The island's puffin population is the main attraction for tens of thousands of visitors. Puffins are cute, charismatic, and classically Icelandic. Their bright orange feet, round bodies, and striped bills are irresistible to children and adults alike. Take a walk along the sea cliffs and spend some time with the adorable birds. Prime puffin-watching season is June-August.

Hiking

Heimaey has a little bit of everything. Because of its small size, it's impossible to get lost, but there are moments when you will feel completely isolated, and serene, if you choose to go on a hike. Many decide to roam the base of the Eldfell volcano, watch the personality-packed puffins in the summer, and stroll downtown. You won't find a plethora of arduous treks, but the island is an opportunity for casual strolls and prime picture-taking. There are about 12 kilometers (7 miles) of trails along the coast. You can find out more about the hikes at www.visitwestmanislands.com.

ELDFELL

Distance: *3 km (2 mi) round-trip*
Hiking Time: *2 hours*
Information and maps: *www.south.is*
Trailhead: *Path at the base*

Walking up Eldfell is a lovely way to spend a couple of hours in the Westman Islands. This is a rare opportunity to hike on a volcano that erupted less than 50 years ago. The earth is still warm enough in places to bake bread. The easy hike on the 220-meter (723-foot) high volcanic cone has a well-marked path from the trailhead to the top. You can walk to the trailhead from town and on clear days you have an outstanding view over the town.

Swimming
HEIMAEY SWIMMING POOL

Vestmannaeyjabær, 9am-9pm daily, 950ISK

The Heimaey Swimming Pool has a large indoor swimming pool, three hot tubs, a sauna, and a gym. There's a slide for children, and the pool is family friendly. It's open all year.

FOOD
GOTT

Bárustígur 11, tel. 354/481-3060, www.gott.is, 11:30am-9pm daily, entrees from 2,390ISK

GOTT is a bright eatery that uses fresh ingredients in creative ways. The menu features cod fillet with wild mushroom crust, handmade pasta with lobster, and a spicy chicken burger. There are also salads, soups, and more burgers on the menu.

★ SLIPPURINN

Strandvegur, tel. 354/481-1515, www.slippurinn.com, noon-2pm Wed.-Sun. and 5pm-10pm daily June 1-Aug. 31, entrées from 3,500ISK

If you want fine dining on the island, Slippurinn is your place. Only open during the summer months, the restaurant is a mix of modern and rustic, housed in an old machine warehouse near a shipyard. Local ingredients are featured in its scratch-made dishes. Guests will find divine seafood entrées like lobster soup, lemon sole, and a pan-fried fish of the day. Meat eaters can choose from lamb, beef, chicken, and even minke whale. Vegetarian options are limited.

ACCOMMODATIONS
ÁRNÝ GUESTHOUSE
Illugagata 7, tel. 354/481-2082,
www.arny.is,
rooms from 10,800ISK
Árný Guesthouse is a small guesthouse that favors wood decor and neutral tones. The beds and furniture are comfortable and homey, and guests have access to a shared kitchen and laundry facilities; bathrooms are also shared. A swimming pool is next to the guesthouse.

GUESTHOUSE HAMAR
Herjólfsgötu 4, tel. 354/659-3400,
www.guesthousehamar.is,
rooms from 23,900ISK
Guesthouse Hamar is a small, family-run guesthouse just 250 meters (820 feet) from the harbor. Rooms are spacious and have private bathrooms, and some rooms have a view of Eldfell volcano.

★ HOTEL VESTMANNAEYJAR
Vestmannabraut 28, tel. 354/481-2900,
www.hotelvestmannaeyjar.is,
rooms from 28,350ISK
Hotel Vestmannaeyjar offers 43 clean, small rooms with private bathrooms. The hotel has a restaurant and bar as well as a tour desk that can book excursions. There is also a spa on the lower floor that has hot tubs and a sauna, with massages and other treatments on offer. Breakfast is included in the price of the room.

INFORMATION AND SERVICES
HEIMAEY TOURIST INFORMATION CENTER
Bárustígur 2, tel. 354/482-3683, www.
vestmannaeyjar.is, 9am-6pm Mon.-Fri., 10am-4pm
Sat.-Sun. daily
The tourist information center is housed in the town's **Eymundsson bookshop** and is ground zero for pamphlets and booking tours.

GETTING THERE
By Air
HEIMAEY AIRPORT
tel. 354/481-3300
Heimaey Airport, which is roughly 3 kilometers (2 miles) from downtown Heimaey, hosts **Eagle Air** (tel. 354/562-4200, www. eagleair.is) with daily flights to and from Reykjavík. Flights are about 25 minutes and cost 16,000ISK each way.

By Ferry
Visitors can get to the island through the ferry **Herjólfur** (Básaskersbryggju, tel. 354/481-2800, www.herjolfur.is, 1,600ISK), which has frequent year-round service, daily May-September. Travelers can bring their cars on the ferry for an extra fee. The Herjólfur ferry departs from **Landeyjahöfn** in South Iceland, and the ferry ride is about 40 minutes. Landeyjahöfn is 137 kilometers (85 miles) southeast of **Reykjavík,** about 2 hours, accessible by **Route 1.**

GETTING AROUND
The island is **walkable** and bringing your rental car is not necessary, especially if you are taking tours. The restaurants, cafés, shops, and attractions are a short walk from where you disembark the ferry.

Snæfellsnes Peninsula and the Westfjords

Itinerary Ideas 137
Akranes and Inland 139
Snæfellsnes Peninsula. . 151
The Westfjords 164

A trip to West Iceland is ideal if you have limited time but want to see some of the countryside. Black-sand beaches, hot springs, quiet fishing towns, and a glacier accessible by foot await you, just 40 minutes up the West Coast from Reykjavík.

Perhaps the most beautiful park in Iceland, Snæfellsjökull National Park is the ultimate tourist treat. The glacier's ice-capped glory invites visitors to put on a pair of crampons and see it for themselves.

On the Snæfellsnes Peninsula, you can see the small fishing towns that serve as the backbone of the country, sustaining the island over the centuries. Without fish, there wouldn't be an Icelandic economy to speak of.

If you are in Iceland for an extended period of time, don't miss

Highlights

Look for ★ to find recommended sights, activities, dining, and lodging.

★ **West Iceland's Natural Pools:** Take some time in between sightseeing to bathe in two of West Iceland's newest warm pools, **Guðlaug** in Akranes (page 141) and **Krauma** near Húsafell (page 146).

★ **Settlement Center:** This museum in Borgarnes offers a crash course in the sagas and earliest days of Icelanders (page 143).

★ **Hiking in Húsafell:** Húsafell is a gem of a town in the West, with well-maintained hiking trails offering spectacular views of mountains and glaciers (page 148).

★ **Snæfellsjökull National Park:** Explore the giant glacier that was the setting for Jules Verne's *Journey to the Center of the Earth,* as well as lava-formed landscapes (page 151).

★ **Hiking the Westfjords Alps:** This gorgeous, moderate hike offers an uncrowded chance to explore the mountains (page 168).

★ **Bird-Watching at the Látrabjarg Cliffs:** Visit one of the best spots on the island to see puffins (page 172).

Snæfellsnes Peninsula and the Westfjords

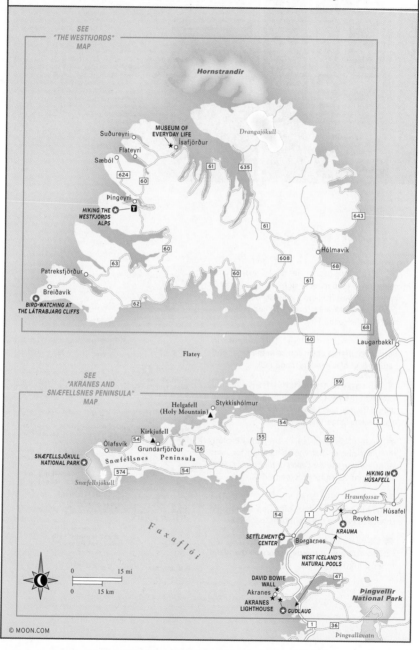

SEE
"THE WESTFJORDS"
MAP

Hornstrandir

Suðureyri

MUSEUM OF
EVERYDAY LIFE
Ísafjörður

Flateyri

Sæból

Drangajökull

624   60

Þingeyri

HIKING THE
WESTFJORDS
ALPS

61   635

61

643

60

63

608

Hólmavík

60

68

Patreksfjörður

60

61

Breiðavík

62

BIRD-WATCHING AT
THE LÁTRABJARG CLIFFS

68

60   Laugarbakki

Flatey

SEE
"AKRANES AND
SNÆFELLSNES PENINSULA"
MAP

59

Helgafell
(Holy Mountain)   Stykkishólmur

54

Kirkjufell

55   60

Ólafsvík   54

Grundarfjörður   56

SNÆFELLSJÖKULL
NATIONAL PARK   Snæfellsnes   Peninsula

574   54

HIKING IN
HÚSAFELL

Snæfellsjökull

Hraunfossar   Húsafel

54   Reykholt

1

KRAUMA

SETTLEMENT
CENTER   Borgarnes

F a x a f l ó i

WEST ICELAND'S
NATURAL POOLS

47

Þingvellir
National Park

DAVID BOWIE
WALL
Akranes

AKRANES
LIGHTHOUSE   GUDLAUG

1   36

Þingvallavatn

0   15 mi
0   15 km

© MOON.COM

the Westfjords, where you'll find steep cliffs with millions of nesting birds, well-maintained hiking paths, quirky museums, and some of the most striking beauty on the island.

PLANNING YOUR TIME

Tourism in the West is still growing, especially in the **Westfjords**. Independent travelers who **rent a car** for a day out of Reykjavík frequently make their way to **Akranes, Borgarnes,** and the **Snæfellsnes Peninsula,** which gives casual day-trippers a great taste of what the West has to offer,

including **mountains** and **charming fishing villages.** A trip farther northwest will treat you to pure beauty, along with everything from whale-watching excursions to quirky museums to mountain climbing.

A day is enough for a taste of the West Coast. To get a true sense of the western coast and the Westfjords, plan for at least **5-6 days,** with one day in Akranes/Borgarnes, two days in the Snæfellsnes Peninsula, and 2-3 days in the Westfjords. While buses stop at several towns, you need a car to see some choice spots in the Westfjords—**Hólmavík** and **Hornstrandir** in particular.

Itinerary Ideas

DAY 1: AKRANES AND BORGARNES

1 Head to **Guðlaug Natural Pool** in Akranes for a relaxing morning soak.

2 Walk along Langisandur beach followed by a walk around Akranes, stopping by the **David Bowie Wall** for some photos.

3 Visit **Café Kaja** for a delicious bowl of fish soup, or some avocado on toast, followed by a latte.

4 Stop by the **Akranes Lighthouse** for a chat with the lighthouse keeper before climbing to the top for panoramic views over the town, mountains, and ocean.

5 Make the 35-minute drive to Borgarnes and spend some time at the **Settlement Center** to learn about the founding of Iceland.

6 Grab a coffee and a tasty pastry at **Geirabakarí Kaffihus.** For a local treat, try a fresh *kleina* (an Icelandic donut). Take a drive around the town, stopping for photos along the waterfront, which is especially lovely on sunny days.

7 Have dinner at **La Colina;** the restaurant's scrumptious pizzas make it a favorite among locals.

TWO DAYS ON THE SNÆFELLSNES PENINSULA

Day 1

1 From Borgarnes, drive to the scenic Snæfellsnes peninsula, a region known as "Iceland in miniature" for its diverse landscapes. Start with a glacier hike on **Snæfellsjökull Glacier** with Arctic Adventures, getting up close and personal with the glacier made famous by Jules Verne in *Journey Into the Center of the Earth.*

Previous: Hraunfossar Waterfalls and the Hvita River in Húsafell; Little Free Library in Súðavík; the Langjökull Glacier.

Itinerary Ideas

AKRANES AND BORGARNES DAY ONE
1. Guðlaug Natural Pool
2. David Bowie Wall
3. Café Kaja
4. Akranes Lighthouse
5. Settlement Center
6. Geirabakari Kaffihus
7. La Colina

SNÆFELLSNES PENINSULA DAY ONE
1. Snæfellsjökull Glacier
2. Djúpalónssandur Beach
3. Hraun Restaurant
4. Laki Tours
5. Pakkhús Museum
6. Sker Restaurant

SNÆFELLSNES PENINSULA DAY TWO
1. Grundarfjörður Swimming Pool
2. Bjarnarhöfn Shark Museum
3. Narfeyrarstofa
4. Flatey Church
5. Sjávarpakkhúsið

© MOON.COM

2   Continue to **Djúpalónssandur Beach,** a black-sand beach dotted with lifting stones, which fishermen used in the old days to prove their strength.

3   Stop by **Hraun Restaurant** in Olafsvík for a hearty lunch. Their Icelandic meat soup really hits the spot.

4   Go for a whale-watching tour after lunch in Olafsvík with **Laki Tours** for a chance to spot killer whales.

5   Visit the **Pakkhús Museum** for a glimpse into the region's history, from the days of settlement to today.

6   Have dinner at **Sker Restaurant,** which is known for its enticing fish dishes, but also serves up a mean lamb steak.

Day 2

1   Start the morning as many locals do, by visiting a swimming pool. The **Grundafjörður Swimming Pool** is a lovely place to relax.

2   Get on the road and head to Stykkishólmur, arguably the prettiest town in Snæfellsnes. In Stykkishólmur, stop by the **Bjarnarhöfn Shark Museum** to learn about the region's long history of shark fishing.

3   Have lunch at **Narfeyarstofa** before heading to the ferry terminal to board the ship to Flatey, an island between Snæfellsnes and the Westfjords.

4   Spend the afternoon in Flatey walking along the one road, visiting **Flatey Church** and watching countless birds, before returning to Stykkishólmur.

5   Enjoy an elegant seafood dinner at **Sjávarpakkhúsið** before calling it a night.

Akranes and Inland

Charming little towns await travelers who pass through the Hvalfjarðargöng (Hvalfjörður Tunnel) from Reykjavík. Before heading to the Snæfellsnes Peninsula, spend some time exploring the region's small fishing villages.

AKRANES

Just a 40-minute drive from Reykjavík, Akranes is a popular detour for those looking to explore the West Coast. A town of 7,000 people, Akranes is a classic fishing village that also has deep industrial roots. It was once home to the country's only cement factory, and an aluminum smelter lies just outside the town. The town is peaceful and friendly, and it's home to a **lighthouse** open to the public; it offers spectacular views of Snæfellsnes on clear days.

Sights
AKRANES LIGHTHOUSE (Akranesviti)

Breið 2, 11am-6pm daily, 300ISK

This lighthouse is a delightful place to visit any time of year. Away from bright lights, tourists and townfolk flock to the site in winter to catch a glimpse of the northern lights dancing in the sky. In the summer, locals picnic outside the lighthouse, and when it is open, guests are invited in and can climb to the top. On clear days you can see the Snæfellsnes Peninsula and a spectacular view of Mount Akrafjall. Built in 1947, the lighthouse has been used in recent years to host concerts and art exhibitions. In 2013, the Icelandic band Amiina filmed a video here for a single off their album *The Lighthouse Project.*

Akranes and Snæfellsnes Peninsula

DJÚPALÓNSSANDUR BEACH

VATNSHELLIR CAVE

SNÆFELLSJÖKULL NATIONAL PARK

SNÆFELLSJÖKULL GLACIER

Hellnar

Hellissandur

Ólafsvík

MARITIME MUSEUM

SNÆFELLSJÖKULL NATIONAL PARK VISITORS CENTER

Grundarfjörður

GRUNDARFJÖRÐUR HERITAGE CENTRE

54

576

Snæfellsnes

Peninsula

56

55

BJARNARHÖFN SHARK MUSEUM

Stykkishólmur

Helgafell (Holy Mountain)

NORWEGIAN HOUSE

VOLCANO MUSEUM

54

Faxaflói

0   0

10 km   10 mi

AKRANES LIGHTHOUSE

AKRANES FOLK MUSEUM

Akranes

DAVID BOWIE WALL

51

GUÐLAUG

47

502

47

48

1

1

SETTLEMENT CENTER (LANDNÁMSSETUR)

Borgarnes

AGRICULTURAL MUSEUM OF ICELAND

539

54

54

60

50

DEILDARTUNGUHVER

KRAUMA

SNORRASTOFA

SNORRALAUG

Reykholt

50

50

ICELANDIC GOAT CENTER

1

60

Hvanneyri

Hraunfossar

Barnafoss

HIKING IN HÚSAFELL

Hvítá

Hallmundarhraun

Húsafell

© MOON.COM

AKRANES FOLK MUSEUM
(Safnasvæðið á Akranesi)

Garðarholt 3, tel. 354/431-5566, www.museum.is,
10am-5pm daily May 15-Sept 15., limited hours during
winter, 800ISK adults, 500ISK seniors, free for 18
and under

This folk museum is dedicated to exploring what Akranes was like in the days of settlement in the 10th century.

Outdoors, there are a few houses and boats that are key to the history of the town. One house, the red **Neðri-Sýrupartur,** was built in 1875, and it's considered the oldest wooden house in the town. Visitors can go inside the houses and explore. A wood building hosts the annual Nordic blacksmithing competition.

DAVID BOWIE WALL

Kirkjubraut 8

This new mural was painted in 2017, when two local David Bowie fans Bjorn Luðviksson and Halldor Lárusson were inspired to memorialize Bowie after his passing in 2016. The Akranes mural, which features several Bowie personas throughout the years, joins the likes of Bowie wall tributes in Jersey City, Seattle, London, and Warsaw.

Hiking

The mountain **Akrafjall** is the pride and joy of Akranes residents. Many locals have fond memories of foraging for gull eggs and playing on the mountain as children. The mountain can be reached by **Route 51** and is 11 kilometers (7 miles) east of town. It's known as a relatively easy climb, especially from the Akranes Water Works car park. There are two routes.

Glymur, Iceland's tallest waterfall, is a worthwhile detour before heading to Akranes from Reykjavík.

HAIHNUKUR

Distance: *6 km (4 mi) round-trip*
Hiking Time: *2.5 hours round-trip*
Information and maps: *www.west.is*
Trailhead: *the Akranes Water Works parking lot*
near the dam

A shorter climb takes you to the top of Haihnukur, which, at 555 meters (1,820 feet), has a nice view of the outskirts of town.

GEIRMUNDARTINDUR

Distance: *6.4 km (4 mi) round-trip*
Hiking Time: *5 hours round-trip*
Information and maps: *www.west.is*
Trailhead: *the Akranes Water Works parking lot near the dam*

If you're up for a longer climb, the highest peak is Geirmundartindur, at 643 meters (2,109 feet). The views from the top are breathtaking, especially on clear days when you can see Snæfellsjökull.

GLYMUR

Distance: *7.5 km (4.6 mi) round-trip*
Hiking Time: *3.5 hours round-trip*
Information and maps: *www.west.is*
Trailhead: *Parking lot along Botnsa river*

Glymur, which stands at 198 meters (650 feet), sits along the Botnsá river, with white water thrashing down the side of **Hvalfell mountain.** The hike up to the top of the waterfall is challenging, with uneven terrain and steep sections. But the view from the top, over Hvalfjörður, is worth it on a clear day. Make sure you have sturdy hiking boots and check the weather forecast before heading out.

Take paved **Road 47** to the parking area. You will see the hiking path marked by a large boulder that looks like an anvil.

Hot Springs and Pools
★ GUÐLAUG NATURAL POOL

Langisandur, gudlaug@akraneskaupstadur.is,
noon-8pm Mon.-Fri., 10am-6pm Sat., 10am-8pm Sun.
June-Aug., free

Guðlaug, which opened in 2019, is a heated natural pool situated along Akranes's sandy beach, **Langisandur.** The two-tier concrete structure is the perfect place to relax during a stop in the small town. The pool is free to enter, and the changing room is steps away. Hours are limited during the winter.

JADARSBAKKAR POOL

Innesvegur, tel. 354/433-1100, hkj@akranes.is,
6:15am-9pm Mon.-Fri., 9am-6pm Sat.-Sun., 620ISK
The Jadarsbakkar Pool is a splendid outdoor
pool with views of Mount Akrafjall. Take a
dip in the geothermally heated waters or soak
in one of the hot tubs.

Golf
GARÐAVÖLLUR

Garðar, tel. 354/431-2711, www.golficeland.org,
8am-6pm May 1-Sept. 30, 4,000-6,000ISK
This is a challenging 18-hole course with
beautiful scenery: Mount Akrafjall, sheep,
and horses in the background. Clubs and golf
carts are available to rent. Greens fees vary by
tee time, call ahead to book.

The club was recently renovated and now
includes a **restaurant** that serves burgers,
sandwiches, cakes, and pastries. Light meals
start at 2,400ISK.

Food
CAFÉ KAJA

Stillholt 23, tel. 354/840-1665, www.kajaorganic.
com, 9am-6pm Mon.-Fri., 10am-4pm Sat., noon-4pm
Sun.
Akranes's first and only organic café and market, Café Kaja offers sandwiches, cakes, juices,
and coffee drinks, plus a shop for local organic
produce. Kaja's fish soup is divine. The atmosphere is charming, with cozy furniture and
friendly staff.

LESBÓKIN CAFÉ

Kirkjubraut 2, tel. 354/864-1476, lesbokincafe@
gmail.com, 9am-6pm daily
In the heart of downtown Akranes, Lesbókin
Café serves up delicious cakes, soups, and
sandwiches. It's a casual eatery that's great for
a coffee beverage, light meal, or beer.

GAMLA KAUPFELAGID

Kirkjubraut 11, tel. 354/431-4343, www.
gamlakaupfelagid.com, 11:30am-9pm Mon.-Thur.,
11:30am-10pm Fri., noon-10pm Sat., 5pm-9pm Sun.,
entrées from 2,400ISK
Gamla Kaupfelagid is a cozy restaurant

situated downtown, close to the tourist office.
An eclectic menu ranges from fresh salads to
Indian-inspired naan bread sandwiches, and
the restaurant is not short on imagination.
Icelandic staples include lamb and fish dishes,
but hamburgers and tandoori oven-cooked
pizzas are on the menu as well.

★ GALITO RESTAURANT

Stilholt 16-18, tel. 354/430-6767, www.galito.
is, 11:30am-9pm Mon.-Wed., 11:30am-10pm Fri.,
noon-10pm Sat., 4pm-9pm Sun., entrées from
2,450ISK
Galito Restaurant is the most upscale restaurant in Akranes, but its prices are reasonable.
Diners can choose from traditional options
like shrimp soup and saltfish entrées, or hamburgers, pizza, sushi, and an array of sandwiches. The decor is modern and the staff is
friendly.

Accommodations
AKRANES HI HOSTEL

Sudurgata 32, tel. 354/868-3332, www.staywest.is,
rooms from 8,300ISK
This hostel offers single, double, triple, and
family rooms as well as dormitory-style accommodations. Rooms are clean, bright, and
cozy, and all have shared bathrooms. The
hostel also has two fully equipped kitchens,
a television lounge, free Wi-Fi, and laundry
facilities.

AKRA GUESTHOUSE

Skagabraut 4, tel. 354/587-3901, www.
akraguesthouse.com, rooms from 10,000ISK
Akra Guesthouse is a small, family-run guesthouse with countryside charm. The five rooms
are large and make you feel like you're staying
with grandparents. Akra features wood floors,
muted wallpaper, and a friendly staff. There's
a common dining room for guests as well as
an outdoor eating area and shared bathrooms.

GALLERY GUESTHOUSE

Merkigerdi 7, tel. 354/868-3332, www.stayakranes.is,
rooms from 10,000ISK
Gallery Guesthouse has doubles, triples, and

family rooms. The rooms are clean and simple and include towels, linens, a garden view, and access to a shared bathroom. Free parking is provided and guests can use a shared lounge with a TV.

TEIGUR GUESTHOUSE
Háteigur 1, tel. 354/431-2900, www.teigur-akranes. com, rooms from 12,000ISK
Teigur Guesthouse is a two-room guesthouse with the comforts of home. Guests have access to a full kitchen, washing machine, garden, and large terrace. A common living room has a TV, DVD player, and free Wi-Fi.

AKRANES GUESTHOUSE
Vogabraut 4, tel. 354/868-3332, www.stayakranes.is, rooms from 13,000ISK
Akranes Guesthouse offers dormitory accommodation in the summer (June-Aug.). During the winter, the property houses students from the local high school. The guesthouse is no-frills, with double beds or sleeping bag accommodations, but the staff are friendly and helpful. Guests have access to private bathrooms with a shower, as well as a small fridge and a stove.

Information and Services
AKRANES INFORMATION CENTER
Breið 2, 11am-6pm daily May 1-Sept. 15, 11am-5pm Tues.-Sat. Sept. 16-April 30
The Akranes Information Center is located in the Akranes Lighthouse. In addition to its regular hours, it's also open upon request for groups.

Getting There
Akranes is about a 40-minute, 48-kilometer (30 mile) drive from **Reykjavík** on paved **Route 51.**

Many people stop in Akranes before making the 39-kilometer (24-mile) journey to **Borgarnes,** which takes about 30 minutes.

The **Strætó 57 bus** (www.straeto.is, 940ISK) runs from the bus station Mjodd in Reykjavík to Akranes in a little over an hour.

BORGARNES

About a 75-minute drive from Reykjavík, Borgarnes is a picturesque town of about 2,000 people. Those traveling on the Ring Road will reach the town by Borgarfjarðarbrú, one of the longest bridges on the island, considered one of the country's largest architectural feats. Fans of the sagas will want to visit the town, as much of *Egil's Saga* takes place in the region. Film buffs may recognize Borgarnes from scenes in Ben Stiller's 2013 movie *The Secret Life of Walter Mitty.*

Sights
★ SETTLEMENT CENTER (Landnámssetur)
Brákarbraut 13-15, tel. 354/437-1600, www.landnam.is/eng, 10am-9pm daily, 2,500ISK adults, 1,900ISK students/seniors, free for children under 14
This is the place to get a crash course in the sagas and the earliest days of Icelanders during the settlement—including what everything on the newly discovered island was like, ranging from food to fashion. Interactive displays and replica dwellings are on exhibit. Audio guides are available in 10 languages. A gift shop sells everything from gourmet salts to woolen goods, and a restaurant serves up lamb, fish, and sandwiches.

AGRICULTURAL MUSEUM OF ICELAND (Landbúnaðarsafn Íslands)
Hvanneyri, tel. 354/844-7740, www. landbunadarsafn.is, 11am-5pm daily June-Aug., 1,200ISK
The Agricultural Museum of Iceland is dedicated to the farming history of Iceland during the 19th and 20th centuries. The museum holds an extensive collection of farm artifacts, including the first plows and other horse-driven equipment used in Iceland. The museum also has the first tractors imported to Iceland, as well as farming equipment of the present day.

BORGARNES MUSEUM
(Safnahús Borgarfjarðar)
Bjarnarbraut 4-6, tel. 354/433-7200, www.safnahus.
is, 1pm-6pm daily, 500ISK
This is a nice spot to spend a couple of hours, with two exhibitions: One features photography focusing on Iceland's 20th-century history, and the other is a collection of stuffed birds in a beautiful environment designed by the artist Snorri Freyr Hilmarsson. The museum is also home to the town's library and archives.

Sports and Recreation
BORGARNES SWIMMING POOL
Þorsteinsgata 1, tel. 354/433-7140, 6am-10pm
Mon.-Fri., 9am-6pm Sat.-Sun., 920ISK
The Borgarnes Swimming Pool is open year-round and has an outdoor swimming pool, a slide, hot tub, and gym.

BORGARNES GOLF CLUB
(Golfklúbbur Borgarness)
Hamar, tel. 354/437-1663, www.gbgolf.is, May-Sept.,
greens fees 10,000ISK
An 18-hole course situated on the property of Icelandair Hótel Hamar. The course, which is great for beginners, also has a driving range area and an 18-hole putting course. It's also easy to walk. Call ahead for a tee time.

Shopping
LJÓMALIND FARMERS MARKET
Brúartorg 4, tel. 354/437-1400, www.ljomalind.is,
11am-6pm daily
Ljómalind Farmers Market is a farmers market collective started by a group of 10 women in 2013. Situated on the main stretch of road in Borgarnes, the market sells fresh cream, eggs, jam, local meat, fresh produce, woolen goods, and souvenir trinkets. In the summer, you can find sunflowers and local tomatoes on offer.

Food
GEIRABAKARI KAFFIHUS
Digranesgata 6, tel. 354/437-1920, geirabak@
internet.is, 7am-5pm daily, pastries from 600ISK
Geirabakari Kaffihus offers light meals, including soups and sandwiches and an array of classic Icelandic cakes and pastries. The coffeehouse was used to film scenes from Ben Stiller's 2013 movie *The Secret Life of Walter Mitty*. Photos taken during filming are displayed throughout the space.

KAFFI KYRRÐ
Skúlagata 13, tel. 354/437-1878, www.blomasetrid.
is, 9am-9pm Mon.-Fri., 11am-7pm Sat.-Sun., pastries
from 800ISK
Kaffi Kyrrð is located inside Blómasetrið, a cute flower shop popular with locals. The café serves light meals like waffles, soups, and quiches, and well as coffee, tea, soft drinks, and beer.

LA COLINA
Hrafnaklettur 1b, tel. 354/437-0110, 5pm-9pm
Mon.-Fri., noon-9pm Sat.-Sun., entrées from 2,100ISK
La Colina opened its doors in 2016, and the warm and cozy pizzeria offers delicious pies. Pizzas range from a classic Margherita to creative pies with shrimp, tuna, and lobster.

★ SETTLEMENT CENTER RESTAURANT
Brákarbraut 13-15, tel. 354/437-1600, 10am-9pm
daily, entrées from 2,600ISK
The restaurant housed above the Settlement Center features a menu full of Icelandic staples like fish soup, mashed fish, and Icelandic meat soup. Burgers and sandwiches are on the menu as well, and there are vegetarian options and a kids' menu. For a quick snack, the freshly baked cakes are delicious. The restaurant serves a vegetarian lunch buffet on weekends for 2,400ISK, and is one of the best meals on Iceland's West Coast.

Accommodations
HÓTEL BORGARNES
Egilsgata 16, tel. 354/437-1119, www.hotelborgarnes.
is, rooms from 14,000ISK
This 75-room no-frills hotel is perfect for short stays. It offers small, comfortable rooms with private bathrooms, and an in-house

restaurant serves up a delicious breakfast buffet included in the price of the room.

BORGARNES HOSTEL

Borgarbraut 9-13, tel. 354/695-3366, www.
borgarneshostel.is, rooms from 14,800ISK, beds from
4,600ISK

Borgarnes Hostel offers 20 rooms ranging from singles to triples. It has private rooms with private bathroom, private rooms with shared bathroom, and dorm accommodation with shared bathroom options. The hostel is centrally located, just a quick walk from the harbor and Settlement Center. Guests have access to two fully equipped kitchens, laundry facilities, a computer room, free Wi-Fi, and a common living room.

ICELANDAIR HÓTEL HAMAR

Hamar, 310 Borgarnes, tel. 354/433-6600, www.
icelandairhotels.com/en/hotels/hamar, rooms from
21,000ISK

Icelandair Hótel Hamar was built on an 18-hole golf course and is in an especially scenic part of Borgarnes. Situated among waterfalls and lava fields, the 44-room hotel offers comfortable rooms with double beds and private bathrooms. There is an abundance of local art around the hotel, and it has a modern yet country atmosphere. The in-house restaurant is open 11am-10pm daily, serving everything from an Asian-inspired cod dish to lamb fillets.

B59 HOTEL

Borgarbraut 59, tel. 354/419-5959, www.b59hotel.is,
rooms from 22,500ISK

B59 Hotel, opened in 2018, is a sleek, modern addition to Borgarnes's hotel scene. Rooms are spacious, tastefully decorated in muted colors and high-quality linens, and feature flat-screen TVs, a mini fridge, free Wi-Fi, and organic Icelandic soaps in the bathrooms. The in-house spa, which is open to all guests for a small fee, has a sauna, hot tub, and indoor pool. Spa treatments are available by request. Breakfast is included in the price of the room.

ENSKU HÚSIN

Hótel við Langá, tel. 354/437-1826, www.enskuhusin.
is, rooms from 23,000ISK

This former fish lodge has been transformed into a guesthouse and space for special events. There are 11 bedrooms that each accommodate two people, with a mix of private and shared bathroom facilities. Rooms are no-frills, but are clean and comfortable, and the friendly staff make you feel at home. The hotel is located along the river Langá.

Information and Services
WEST ICELAND INFORMATION CENTER

Borgarbraut 58-60, tel. 354/437-2214, www.
westiceland.is, 9am-5pm daily

Located in the Hyrnutorg shopping center, the West Iceland Information Center has brochures, tour information, and a gift shop.

Getting There

Borgarnes is about a 75-kilometer (47-mile) drive north from **Reykjavík,** about 1.25 hours on **Route 1,** and 39 kilometers (24 miles) from **Akranes,** about 35 minutes on Route 1.

REYKHOLT

Reykholt is a placid, sleepy town about an hour from Borgarnes. Its laid-back, quiet atmosphere is part of the town's charm. A couple of sights are connected to Snorri Sturluson, one of the most famous and important figures in Icelandic literature. Snorri penned *Edda, Egil's Saga,* and *Heimskringla* before his death in 1241. Tourists might also want to take a look at **Deildartunguhver,** the largest hot spring in Europe, and explore the lava cave **Viðgelmir.**

Sights
ICELANDIC GOAT CENTER (Íslenska Geitin)

Haafell, tel. 354/845-2331, 1pm-6pm daily June
1-Aug. 31, 1,500ISK adults, 750ISK children 7-17, free
for children under 7

The Icelandic Goat Center was established

to protect and maintain the goat stock in Iceland—believe it or not, the Icelandic goat is an endangered species. Tourists are welcome to visit the grounds and meet the goats as well as other animals on the farm, including sheep, horses, and chickens. Workers at the center show an enormous amount of care for the animals. It's an especially great place to visit if you're traveling with children. The local food store sells many goat products, including sausages, cheeses, soaps, books, and handicrafts.

DEILDARTUNGUHVER

off Route 50, GPS coordinates N 64.6631, W 21.4112

Geology buffs will want to take a look at Deildartunguhver, which is considered Europe's most powerful hot spring. It provides 200 liters (52 gallons) per second of 100°C (212°F) water. Most of the water used for central heating in the towns of Akranes and Borgarnes is taken from Deildartunguhver. The hot-water pipeline to Akranes stretches 64 kilometers (40 miles), the longest in Iceland. The water is about 78-80°C (172-176°F) when it reaches the town. Be sure to keep your distance, as there is a chance of getting splashed if you get too close. Visitors will see water bubbling up and splashing against moss and rock.

SNORRASTOFA

GPS coordinates N 64.6648, W 21.2937, tel. 354/433-8000, www.snorrastofa.is, 10am-5pm daily May 1-Aug. 31, Mon.-Fri. Sept. 1-Apr. 30, 1,200ISK,

Snorrastofa is the cultural hub of Reykholt. It was established in 1995 as an independent research center to investigate and collect information on the medieval era in Iceland, with particular focus on the legendary saga writer and politician Snorri Sturluson, who lived in Reykholt until his death in 1241. The building also holds a tourist information center, an exhibition on Snorri Sturluson's sagas, and a public research library, and it hosts courses

and lectures. A gift shop sells books, CDs, and handicrafts.

SNORRALAUG

GPS coordinates N 64.664, W 21.2912, Route 518

Snorralaug, or "Snorri's Pool," is a geothermally heated pool preserved from Iceland's medieval period and is one of Reykholt's oldest structures. The hot tub was built with hand-hewn lava from the 10th century, cut and shaped to exact measurements. The hot water in the pool comes from the Skrifla hot spring through a canal. The site is open to the public, but visitors cannot enter the pool to bathe.

Sports and Recreation
THE CAVE

Fljotstunga, tel. 354/783-3600, www.thecave. is, 9am-6pm June-Aug., 10am-4pm Mar.-Oct., 10am-3pm Dec.-Feb., 6,500ISK, 3,500ISK for children 12-15, free for children 11 and under

Reykholt is home to the largest cave in Iceland, **Víðgelmir,** which is only accessible through a tour. The Cave can take you to explore the beautiful ice formations, including scores of stalactites and stalagmites. There is a walking path inside most of the cave, but there are uneven surfaces, so take care. Also, you will be provided a helmet with a headlight. The tour is 1.5 hours long.

★ KRAUMA

Deildartunguhver, tel. 354/555-6066, www.krauma. is, 3,950ISK adults, 2,000ISK children 13-16, free for children 12 and under

Adjacent to Europe's most powerful hot spring, Deildartunguhver, Krauma is a newly opened geothermal bath and spa, a welcome addition to West Iceland. Krauma has six baths at the facility, five of varying warm temperatures and one cold bath. Guests also have access to two steam baths and a relaxation room that contains comfortable lounge chairs, a roaring fireplace, and soothing music.

1: ship at the Akranes Folk Museum 2: Haafell goat
3: Snorralaug (Snorri's Pool)

Food and Accommodations

HVERINN RESTAURANT

Kleppjárnsreykir, tel. 354/571-4433, www.hverinn.is, 10am-9pm Sun.-Thurs. and 10am-11pm Fri.-Sat. May 1-Oct. 1, entrées from 1,800ISK

Hverinn Restaurant is a quaint farm-style restaurant serving up comfort food. It uses organic ingredients from its farm and local meats in each dish, ranging from soups and salads to lamb and fish dishes. Sandwiches, hamburgers, and pizza are also on the menu.

HÓTEL Á

Kirkjuból, tel. 354/435-1430, www.hotela.is, rooms from 21,000ISK

This former farmhouse was converted into a guesthouse with 22 double rooms and three family rooms. The decor is rustic and the staff friendly, and common rooms contribute to the laid-back vibe. Breakfast is included in the price of the room. The hotel also has an in-house **restaurant** (5pm-10pm daily) that offers meat (8,700ISK) and fish (7,700ISK) three-course dinners featuring local ingredients.

FOSSHOTEL REYKHOLT

Hálsasveitavegur, tel. 354/435-1260, www. islandshotel.is, rooms from 25,000ISK

Fosshotel Reykholt used to be the only hotel in the region. The 53-room property has dated furniture, and some rooms with carpeting, which is not common in Iceland. However, the dreary decor is made up for with free Wi-Fi, private bathrooms, free parking, and outdoor hot tubs. The included breakfast is adequate, but nothing to write home about.

Information and Services

Housed in the Snorrastofa complex, the **Reykholt Information Office** (tel. 354/433-8000, www.snorrastofa.is, 10am-5pm daily Mon.-Fri., May 1-Aug. 31, 10am-5pm Mon.-Fri., closed weekends Sept. 1-April 30) offers tourist brochures and art exhibitions and hosts occasional lectures and concerts. The GPS coordinates are N 64.6648, W 21.2937.

Getting There

Reykholt is 41 kilometers (25 miles) northeast of **Borgarnes** on **Route 518,** which is paved.

HÚSAFELL

Húsafell is a tiny village surrounded by glaciers, ample hiking opportunities, and miles of lava fields. Most tourists make a stop to camp, visit two beautiful waterfalls, **Hraunfossar** and **Barnafoss,** and check out some lava caves in nearby Reykholt or explore the **Langjökull** ice tunnel. Organized trips with a tour operator to Langjökull glacier are available from Húsafell throughout the year.

Sights

HRAUNFOSSAR

6.4 km (4 mi) west of Húsafell on Route 518, GPS coordinates N 64.7028, W 20.9777

Hraunfossar (Lava Waterfalls) is a series of waterfalls streaming over 900 meters (2,950 feet) out of a lava field. The lava flowed from an eruption from a volcano lying under the Langjökull glacier. The falls are beautiful to visit in any season, and rainbows are frequently seen near the falls on both rainy/sunny days. There is a parking area to the left of the falls, and it's a short walk to a platform overlooking Hraunfossar.

BARNAFOSS

GPS coordinates N 64.7015, W 20.9727

Two kilometers (1.2 miles) west of Húsafell on Route 518, Barnafoss (Children's Falls) is a stunning waterfall, wide with water rushing over a rocky landscape creating several cascades. It was named for children who disappeared from a nearby farm and drowned in the river, and lore has it that the mother of the disappeared children put a curse on the falls that people should not cross the river. Barnafoss shares the same parking area as Hraunfossar, and it is a short walk to the falls.

★ Hiking

Hikers have a number of options in Húsafell, ranging from easy walks to more challenging climbs. Before you set out, be sure to check the weather forecast, bring the proper gear and plenty of drinking water, and let people know your whereabouts. The prime hiking season is **June-August.**

MOUNT STRÚTUR

Distance: *2 k (1.2 mi) round-trip*
Hiking Time: *2 hours round-trip*
Information and maps: *www.west.is*
Trailhead: *Low hill north of Kalmanstunga*
While the climb to the summit of the 938-meter (3,077-feet) Mount Strútur, with an elevation gain of 469 meters (1,539 feet), isn't very difficult, it is quite long, several hours depending on the weather and your endurance. It is recommended you start from the low hill north of the farm **Kalmanstunga** and follow a signposted track that leads up the mountain. The payoff for reaching the top is a spectacular view of mountains and the Borgarfjörður fjord. Kalmanstunga is 17 kilometers (11 miles) north of Húsafell and can be reached by Route 518.

ODDAR

Distance: *4 km (2.5 mi) round-trip*
Hiking Time: *1.5 hours round-trip*
Information and maps: *www.husafell.is*
Trailhead: *Summerhouse settlement*
The summerhouse settlement (a collection of summerhouses) in the center of Húsafell is the starting point for wooded paths heading westward for an easy walk along **Oddar,** a group of brooks with diverse birdlife. From there it is just a short walk upriver to the meeting point of two rivers: the **Norðlingafljót** and **Hvítá.** Just below Hvítá is the waterfall **Hundavaðsfoss,** a great place to stop and marvel at the beauty. The route then leads southeast along the sands just past the waterfall to a path leading back to the summerhouse settlement. The walk is very easygoing.

Other Sports and Recreation
INTO THE GLACIER
Viðarhöfði 1, tel. 354/578-2550, www.intotheglacier.is, tours from 19,500ISK
For those looking for a little ice in Iceland,

Into the Glacier offers 3-4 hour tours to the world's largest human-made ice cave, **Langjökull.** A super truck picks up visitors close to **Hotel Húsafell** for a breathtaking journey across Langjökull to the tour company's base camp, which takes 25 minutes. The cave itself is an engineering feat where visitors are treated to views of crevices and the smooth ice walls. LED lighting embedded in the walls illuminates the ice nicely, and benches are scattered throughout the tunnel. Into the Glacier also offers a tour that combines the ice cave with a tour of the Golden Circle for 24,900ISK. It is not possible to explore the cave independently; you must book with the tour company.

HÚSAFELL SWIMMING POOL
Stórarjóður, tel. 354/435-1552, www.husafell.is, 10am-10pm daily June-Sept., 1pm-5pm Sat.-Sun. rest of year, 1,300ISK
The Húsafell Swimming Pool has two pools, two hot tubs, and a big waterslide for kids.

HÚSAFELL GOLF COURSE
GPS coordinates N 64.6991, W 20.8709, Stórarjóður, tel. 354/435-1552, www.husafell.is, 8am-6pm daily May-Sept., greens fees 4,000ISK
This nine-hole course is situated on a gorgeous patch of land overlooking mountains and lava fields. You must call ahead for a tee time.

Food and Accommodations
HRAUNFOSSAR RESTAURANT-CAFÉ
Hraunás 4, tel. 354/862-7957, www.hraunfossar.is, 10am-6pm daily, 2,000ISK
Located at the Lava Waterfalls, Hraunfossar Restaurant-Café has a good selection of light meals and snacks. Sit on the eatery's porch to enjoy coffee, cakes, ice cream, and sandwiches, along with a nice view.

★ HOTEL HÚSAFELL
Borgarbyggd, tel. 354/435-1551, www.hotelhusafell.com, rooms from 31,800ISK
This modern 48-room hotel opened in 2015.

The location is unbeatable, as it is nestled in a scenic spot with stunning views of the mountain landscape, close to lava caves and glaciers. Rooms feature comfortable beds, private bathrooms, and modern design accents, including wood furnishings and large windows. A breakfast buffet is included in the room price, and 24-hour room service is available. A pool and hot tubs are on-site, and the in-house **restaurant** (11:30am-10pm daily, entrées from 4,500ISK) is not to be missed. The menu features everything from tender lamb fillet to fresh fish.

HUSAFELL CAMPGROUND

tel. 354/435-1556, 1,500ISK

The Husafell Campground is an open campground surrounded by trees, which cuts down on the wind a bit. Caravans and tents are welcome, and the facilities include restrooms, showers, hot and cold water, and laundry machines. The site is a short distance to the swimming pool, golf course, and hiking trails.

Getting There

Húsafell is 25 kilometers (15.5 miles) east from **Reykholt** on **Route 518,** which is paved.

Snæfellsnes Peninsula

Snæfellsnes is considered the jewel of the western coast, in part because the region has a taste of everything: mountains, glacier walks on Snæfellsnesjökull, and whale-watching. Many locals refer to the area as "Iceland in miniature."

The western edge of the Snæfellsnes Peninsula is home to Snæfellsjökull National Park and small towns like Hellissandur, Ólafsvík, and Grundarfjörður. The Snæfellsjökull glacier, which lies on top of a volcano in the center of the national park, is the main event for many. You can book tours to walk on the glacier and explore some actual ice in Iceland. Charming fishing villages dot the peninsula and offer ample hiking routes and quirky museums.

PLANNING YOUR TIME

If you intend to add Snæfellsnes to your trip around the **Ring Road,** plan to spend some time here—at least **two full days.** The breathtaking landscape, with its long volcanic ridge spanning miles of rocky lava fields and towering mountains, demands more than a quick detour. The area is many Icelanders' favorite place on the island. Traveling to the region is not difficult, as there are numerous

tours going to Snæfellsnes, as well as **buses.** For a more leisurely visit, **rent a car.**

TOP EXPERIENCE

★ SNÆFELLSJÖKULL NATIONAL PARK

The Snæfellsjökull glacier became world famous after author Jules Verne described it as the starting point for the titular journey in *Journey to the Center of the Earth.* There is plenty to explore inside the park. Take some time, wear comfortable yet sturdy footwear, and bring your camera. Plan at least two days in the region.

Sights
ARNARSTAPI CLIFFS

Arnarstapavegur, off Route 547

The seaside cliffs in the small fishermen's town of Arnarstapi, at the gateway to Snæfellsjökull National Park, are spectacular, with basalt formations including holes and arches carved out by surf. The cliffs are a nesting ground for the artic tern, and you'll love taking photos with a huge stone statue of Bárður Snæfellsás with its back to the ocean not far from the parking lot. Easy paths weave through the cliffside area, making it a lovely place to spend 45 minutes or so.

1: Hraunfossar waterfalls 2: Hotel Húsafell

HELLNAR CLIFFS

Route 5730, off Route 547

Continuing just a few kilometers west down Route 547 from the Arnarstapi Cliffs, Hellnar is another small fishing village with beautiful seaside rock formations. A 4 km (2.5 mile) walking path connects the two cliff areas.

LÓNDRANGAR CLIFFS

parking area off Route 547

Yet another place to stop and have your breath taken away overlooking seaside cliffs, further west on Route 547 from Arnarstapi and Hellnar, in this case the basalt cliffs that are the vast remains of a crater eroded by the sea. Two stacks (the taller at 75 meters, the lower at 61 meters) are visible, home to puffins and fulmars in the summer.

SNÆFELLSJÖKULL GLACIER

near route 574

The Snæfellsjökull glacier lies on top of a volcano, situated in the center of the national park. The glacier's peak is 1,446 meters (4,774 feet), and it can be seen from Reykjavík on a clear day. The volcano is considered active, though the last eruption occurred 1,900 years ago. Travelers can explore the area around the glacier but should not venture onto the glacier without a guide as it can be dangerous. Plan to spend 1-2 hours here.

It's about 190 kilometers (118 miles) from **Reykjavík** to the Snæfellsjökull glacier; the drive takes about 2.5 hours. From Reykjavík, take **Route 1** north through the town of **Borgarnes** and then turn left onto **Route 54.** Head west on **Route 54** across the peninsula for about 98 kilometers (61 miles), connecting to **Route 574.** Continue west on **Route 574** for about 35 kilometers (22 miles). You'll find the road leading up to the volcano on the right-hand side, and signs are posted all the way up to a **parking lot.** Be sure to check the forecast before heading out and be advised that roads leading to the volcano are unpaved.

VATNSHELLIR LAVA CAVE

near Route 574

The Vatnshellir lava cave, opened to the public in 2011, is another highlight. Scientists believe the 200-meter (656-foot) long cave was created in an eruption 6,000-8,000 years ago. The cave has two main sections: the upper section, which showcases unique lava formations that are curved on the sides of the lava tube, while the lower part, which can be reached by a long and narrow but well-maintained staircase, takes tourists about 35 meters (115 feet) underground to a place hidden from the outside world for thousands of years.

The cave is accessible only through a guided tour from **Summit Guides** (tel. 354/787-0001, www.summitguides.is, 45-minute tours 3,750ISK adults, 3,000ISK students/seniors, 1,500ISK children 12-17, free for children 3-11). Tourists are required to have hiking boots, gloves, and warm clothing. The tour guide provides helmets and flashlights. The Vatnshellir cave is located in the southern end of the park, near Route 574.

DJÚPALÓNSSANDUR BEACH AND DRITVÍK COVE

near Route 574, GPS coordinates N 64.7493, W 23.9122

Djúpalónssandur beach, on the southwestern edge of the Snæfellsnes Peninsula, is one of the region's highlights. The vast beach is covered by small black stones that were shaped by the force of the tides and whipping of the wind. Visitors love to wander among the frozen lava landscapes and the interesting rock formations. Plan to spend an hour at the beach. A short, paved road through lava fields leads directly from **Route 574** to Djúpalónssandur beach.

From Djúpalónssandur, you can access Dritvík Cove via an easy hike. You'll see the remains of fishermen's huts in the cliffs above the beach.

1: Snæfellsjökull glacier 2: Djúpalónssandur beach

Hiking

Many Icelanders consider the hiking of Snæfellsnes unrivaled, calling the region their favorite place in the country. Why? Snæfellsnes has it all. There are mountains to climb, lava fields to explore, and glaciers to scale, all accessible by countless hiking trails with varying degrees of difficulty. Specific information on trails can be found at the park's visitors center.

Feel free to roam and take in the sights. Whether you head out alone, with a small group, or with a tour, always go out for a hike prepared: Check the weather forecast, bring proper gear and drinking water, and let people know your whereabouts.

RAUÐHÓLL

Distance: *2.3 km (1.4 mi) loop*
Hiking Time: *45 minutes*
Information and maps: *www.west.is*
Trailhead: *Unnumbered road off of Route 570*
Rauðhóll is a leisurely hike within the park, which takes hikers around a vast, jagged lava field and a treeless plain, giving unobstructed views of the glacier looming in the distance. The 2.3-kilometer (1.4-mile) loop hike is easy, on relatively flat ground, and takes about 45 minutes. The landscape is filled with moss and lichen-covered lava stones and lava tubes, where lava once flowed out of the volcano.

Coming from Hellissandur, you'll find the hiking path down an unnumbered road off of Route 570 (which is unpaved but no longer an F road); look for a sign that says "Eysteinsdalur Snæfellsjökull" and turn left. On the south side of the road is a signpost for the Rauðhóll trail, and red stakes along the path mark the way.

Tours

ARCTIC ADVENTURES

tel. 354/562-7000, www.adventures.is, Mar.-Oct., 40,000ISK
Snæfellsjökull, rising 1,446 meters (4,774 feet) from the western tip of the Snæfellsnes Peninsula, offers gorgeous views during a challenging trek, on which you can embark with a guided tour (this hike isn't recommended as an independent trek). The adventure starts and ends at the small fishing village of **Arnarstapi,** off **Route 54** down **Útnesvegur.** Arctic Adventures takes you to the **Jökulháls pass,** where you'll start your hike toward the summit of the glacier. The first part of the hike is over volcanic rock, but as you climb, the snow and ice increases, and crampons become necessary near the top. The hike is about 7-8 kilometers (4-5 miles), with a total elevation gain of 760 meters (2,500 feet), and it takes about 3-5 hours, depending on the conditions and weather.

Remember to bring warm outdoor clothing, a waterproof jacket and pants, a hat, and gloves. Good hiking shoes are essential on this tour. Waterproof outerwear and sturdy hiking shoes can be rented from the tour company with advance notice.

REYKJAVÍK EXCURSIONS

tel. 354/580-5400, www.re.is
If you're after other structured, guided tours, some companies offer excursions. Check out Reykjavík Excursions for a list, including a 12-hour **"Wonders of Snæfellsnes"** tour year-round from Reykjavík visiting **Snæfellsjökull** glacier, sandy beaches, craters, and fishing villages (16,999ISK adults, 8,499ISK children 12-15, free for children under 11).

Food and Accommodations

GUESTHOUSE LANGAHOLT

Ytri-Garðar Staðarsveit, tel. 354/435-6789, www. langaholt.is, rooms from 21,000ISK
Guesthouse Langaholt is a 20-room family-run guesthouse with spacious rooms, classic decor, free Wi-Fi, and a shared terrace. Amenities include an on-site restaurant, nearby golf course, plenty of free parking, and on-site camping facilities for budget travelers.

FOSSHOTEL HELLNAR

Brekkubær, tel. 354/435-6820, www.islandshotel.is, May-Oct., rooms from 35,000ISK
Fosshotel Hellnar is a beautiful 39-room

country hotel that takes pride in the small things. Guests can find fresh flowers throughout the hotel, a warm staff, and a splendid in-house restaurant. Each room has a private bathroom, comfortable bed, and television. The **restaurant** (8am-9pm daily, entrées from 2,600ISK), open for breakfast, lunch, and dinner in the summer, uses fresh, organic ingredients with lots of fish and meat options, along with options for vegetarians as well.

★ HÓTEL BÚÐIR

Búðir, tel. 354/435-6700, www.hotelbudir.is, rooms from 41,500ISK

Guests at Hótel Búðir are treated to a comfortable stay with spectacular views of the Snæfellsjökull glacier. The 20-room boutique hotel features clean and cozy rooms with private bathrooms. The hotel's top-notch breakfast is included in the price. It frequently hosts weddings and conferences. The **restaurant** (8am-9pm daily, entrées from 2,600ISK) features Icelandic staples like fresh cod and lamb dishes, but the chef likes to mix up the menu selections depending on the season. Expect shellfish on the menu. The food is fresh, elegant, and memorable. The hotel is 27 kilometers (17 miles) southeast of Ólafsvík on Route 54.

Information and Services
SNÆFELLSJÖKULL NATIONAL PARK VISITORS CENTER

Malarrif, tel. 354/436-6888, 10am-5pm daily mid-May-mid-Sept., 11am-4pm daily mid-Sept.-mid-May

The Snæfellsjökull National Park visitors center gives an overview of the history, flora, fauna, and geology of the park. The center also provides information on hiking paths and the wildlife that can be seen in the park.

Getting There

Snæfellsjökull National Park can be reached by **Route 574,** which spans the perimeter of the park along the coastline. A regular two-wheel-drive car will be fine on the unpaved road, but it's not feasible for cyclists.

The park is 197 kilometers (122 miles) from **Reykjavík**, about 3 hours taking **Route 1** to **Route 574.**

Tour companies such as **Reykjavík Excursions** (tel. 354/580-5400, www.re.is) include stops at Snæfellsjökull.

HELLISSANDUR

Hellissandur is a blink-and-you'll-miss it kind of town, but it's home to an interesting fishing museum that's worth a stop if that strikes your fancy.

Sights
HELLISSANDUR MARITIME MUSEUM (Sjómannagarður)

Útnesvegur, tel. 354/436-6961, 10am-5pm daily June 1-Sept. 30, 1,300ISK

Hellissandur Maritime Museum was established by the Council of Seamen of the towns of Hellissandur and neighboring Rif to preserve the history of fishers and fishing stations in the region. One-stroke engines, a fisherman's house (called Þorvaldarbúð), and Iceland's oldest preserved fishing boat, *Bliki,* are on display, showing the rich fishing history of the town. The well-curated museum is a must-see for those interested in fishing history.

INGJALDSHÓLSKIRKJA

Route 574, east of Hellissandur; tel. 354/436-6970

The other big draw in Hellissandur is Ingjaldshólskirkja, or Ingjaldshóls Church, which was, according to legend, the site where Italian explorer Christopher Columbus traveled in 1477 to meet with Icelanders. Columbus was interested in speaking with islanders whose ancestors had traveled to America. In the basement of the church is a mural of Columbus's meeting with the Icelanders. The church is a classic Icelandic structure built in 1903, and it has a white exterior and a red roof. However, the land has been a church site since the year 1317.

Hiking
EYSTEINSDALUR VALLEY HIKE
Distance: *20 km (12 mi) round-trip*
Hiking Time: *5 hours round-trip*
Information and maps: *Hellnar tourist information office, www.west.is*
Trailhead: *Unmarked gravel road between campground and Maritime Museum*

A great moderate, 5-hour round-trip day hike of around 20 kilometers (12 miles) total leads from Hellissandur village into the Eysteinsdalur valley. Hikers should take the unmarked gravel road between the Hellissandur campground and Hellissandur Maritime Museum, which leads toward **Snæfellsjökull.** The road becomes a hiking trail after about one kilometer (0.6 miles) and leads you to the **Prestahraun** lava field. Follow the trail to see a red scoria crater and rifts in lava and basalt rocks. The trail continues past waterfalls, the glacial river **Ljósulækir,** and breathtaking views of the glacier. Detailed hiking maps are available from the **tourist information office** in **Hellnar.**

Food and Accommodations
THE FREEZER HOSTEL
Hafnargata16, tel. 354/865-9432, www. thefreezerhostel.com, beds from 4,000ISK

The Freezer Hostel, located in Rif, several kilometers east of Hellissandur off Útnesvegur, is a former fish factory that's been converted into one of the coolest spots in the region. It's a hostel that offers dorm beds, a culture center, and an artist residency. The space is stripped down yet comfortable and serves as a social spot for tourists and locals alike. The Freezer hosts theater performances and concerts throughout the year. The owners of Freezer Hostel recently opened apartments for short-term rent for guests who would like a little more privacy. Apartments start at 22,600ISK.

HÓTEL HELLISSANDUR
Klettsbúð 9, tel. 354/430-8600, www. hotelhellissandur.is, rooms from 16,000ISK

Hótel Hellissandur is a 20-room hotel with standard double rooms featuring private bathrooms and free Wi-Fi. Rooms are big but sparsely decorated, and the in-house restaurant serves adequate meals.

Getting There
Hellissandur is 9 kilometers (6 miles) northwest of **Ólafsvík** and 35 kilometers (22 miles) north of **Hellnar.** By car, take **Route 574** to Hellissandur; this stretch is paved.

ÓLAFSVÍK
Ólafsvík is a charming fishing village situated on the western end of the Snæfellsnes Peninsula. The small town has approximately 1,100 residents, and is the main town of the Snæfellsbær municipality, which includes the villages of Hellissandur and Rif. Because of its proximity to the **Snæfellsjökull National Park,** Ólafsvík, which means "Olaf's bay," is often used as a base camp where travelers can get a bite to eat and gas up the car. Ólafsvík also might be the best whale-watching spot in West Iceland.

Sights
PAKKHÚS MUSEUM
12 Ólafsbraut, tel. 354/433-6929, www.snb.is, 9am-5pm daily June 5-Aug. 31, 800ISK

A former trading store built in 1844, the Pakkhús Museum is a national monument. The second and third floors house the Snæfellsbær regional museum, where guests can see items from as early as the days of Iceland's settlement, including fishing equipment and household goods. The museum gives insight into how Icelanders lived in this region of the island, managing on very little. On the ground floor, you'll find a general store and handicraft shop.

Sports and Recreation
ÓLAFSVÍK SWIMMING POOL
Ennisbraut 11, tel. 354/433-9910, 7:30am-9pm Mon.-Fri., 10am-5pm Sat.-Sun., 750ISK

The Ólafsvík Swimming Pool is popular among locals as well as tourists passing through. Amenities include an indoor swimming pool, hot tubs, and an outdoor area for catching some sun (when it's out).

LAKI TOURS

tel. 354/546-6808, www.lakitours.com, 2pm daily Apr.-Oct., 9,900ISK adults, 4,950ISK children 12-15, free for children under 11

Laki Tours operates three-hour whale-watching tours from Ólafsvík; if luck is on your side, you'll catch a glimpse of sperm whales or killer whales. This is the only area in Iceland where you can see them. Seeing these majestic creatures with the Snæfellsnes Peninsula behind them is breathtaking—the towering mountains, migrating birds, and looming glacier are gorgeous. If you strike out with killer or sperm whales, you also have a chance to spot minke, humpback, blue, and fin whales along with harbor porpoises and dolphins. Make sure you dress warmly and bring your camera!

Food

HRAUN RESTAURANT

Grundarbraut 2, www.hraunrestaurant.com, 11:30am-9pm Sun.-Thur., 11:30am-10pm Fri., entrees from 2,400ISK

Hraun is a neighborhood haunt worth a visit. The restaurant serves staples you would expect like Icelandic meat soup, lamb steaks, and pan-fried cod, but there are also some surprises on the menu. You can choose to partake in trout ceviche, Icelandic scallop tacos, duck salad, or tiger prawn skewers. There are also burgers, pizza, and fish and chips on offer.

★ SKER RESTAURANT

Ólafsbraut 19, tel. 354/436-6625, 11:30am-9pm daily, entrees from 2,700ISK

Sker opened in 2018 to rave reviews among locals. The casual eatery offers fish dishes like grilled salmon and smoked haddock, meat entrees including lamb steak, beef tenderloin, and burgers, and pizza and vegetarian options.

Accommodations

VIÐ HAFIÐ GUESTHOUSE

Ólafsbraut 55, tel. 354/436-1166, vid.hafid@hotmail.com, rooms from 15,000ISK

Við Hafið Guesthouse, close to the harbor and on the town's main street, has dorm beds as well as double, triple, and family rooms, all with shared bathroom facilities.

NÁTTSKJÓL HOMESTAY

Brautarholt 2, tel. 354/867-8807, rooms from 20,000ISK

Down a quiet street is the Náttskjól Homestay. It has family rooms with bunk beds and shared kitchen and bathroom facilities.

NORTH STAR HÓTEL ÓLAFSVÍK

Ólafsbraut 20, tel. 354/487-1212, www.olafsvik. northstar.is, rooms from 30,000ISK

North Star Hótel Ólafsvík offers 48 rooms in the center of town near the harbor. The rooms are large, bright, and comfortable. The decor is traditional and the staff is friendly. Most rooms have private bathrooms, and breakfast is included in the price. The hotel's **restaurant** (dinner 6pm-10pm, entrées from 2,500ISK) is the only option for fine dining in the town, but it stands up against competition. The menu features fresh, local ingredients, with an emphasis on fish, including cod, salmon, haddock, and langoustines. There are also meat dishes as well as a couple of vegetarian options.

Getting There

Ólafsvík is 26 kilometers (16 miles) west of **Grundarfjörður.** By car from Grundarfjörður, Ólafsvík is reachable by **Route 54** connecting to **Route 574,** both paved roads. Hellissandur is just 9 kilometers (6 miles) from Ólafsvík on Route 574.

GRUNDARFJÖRÐUR

Centrally located on the northern coast of the Snæfellsnes Peninsula, Grundarfjörður is situated in a spectacular mountain range that includes **Mount Kirkjufell,** which has a steep and treacherous-looking peak. Exploring the

town by foot is far and away the most popular activity for tourists. Those interested in spotting orcas have a great shot in Grundarfjörður, as the majestic whales are known to feast on herring off the shores of the town. The town has a few interesting museums and a lot of hiking opportunities.

Sights

GRUNDARFJÖRÐUR HERITAGE CENTER (Sögumiðstöðin)

Grundargata 35, tel. 354/438-1881, 9am-6pm daily May 16-Sept. 30, limited hours during winter, free

The Grundarfjörður Heritage Center is a quaint museum focusing on saga stories, the town's fishing history, and life during the settlement era in the 9th century. There are fishing boats and equipment on display as well as recreated dwellings and artifacts. A café and a tourist information center are on-site.

Sports and Recreation

LÁKI TOURS

Nesvegur 5, tel. 354/546-6808, www.lakitours.com, 9,900ISK

Láki Tours operates three-hour tours from Grundarfjördur (Dec. 15-Mar. 31) and from Ólafsvík (Apr. 1-Oct. 31). Guests have a good chance of spotting sperm whales and orcas in this region, as well as humpbacks, minke whales, dolphins, and porpoises.

KIRKJUFELL

Distance: *4 km (2.5 mi) round-trip*
Hiking Time: *4 hours round-trip*
Information and maps: *www.west.is*
Trailhead: *Parking lot on the side of the road opposite the mountain; arriving from the east, it will be on your left*

At the center of it all is Mount Kirkjufell, which looms 463 meters (1,519 feet) high. From a distance the mountain looks quite daunting, and it is a difficult climb, with the trickiest points near the top, as it gets

---

1: Mount Kirkjufell in Grundarfjörður
2: Stykkishólmur

quite steep. The hike is about four kilometers (2.5 miles) and takes about four hours round-trip. It's advisable to go during the summer months, but it's still important to check weather conditions and bring proper gear with you regardless of the time of year. If you arrive in winter and the weather is good, a walk along the base of the mountain is nice, but don't attempt a climb on your own as it can be very dangerous.

GRUNDARFJÖRÐUR SWIMMING POOL

Borgarbraut 19, tel. 354/430-8564, 7am-9pm Mon.-Fri., 10am-6pm Sat.-Sun. 900ISK

The Grundarfjörður Swimming Pool is a lovely local spot with a 16-meter (52-foot) outdoor pool, hot tubs, and a section for children.

Food

KAFFI EMIL

Grundagata 35, tel. 354/897-0124, 9am-6pm Mon.-Thur., 9am-5pm Fri.-Sun., entrées from 2,000ISK

Kaffi Emil is a family-run coffeehouse that serves light meals like soup and sandwiches as well as tasty cakes and coffee drinks. It's a cozy space with vintage furniture, books, and a friendly staff.

Accommodations

GRUNDARFJÖRÐUR HOSTEL

Hlíðarvegur 15, tel. 354/562-6533, www.hostel.is, rooms from 14,000ISK, beds from 5,000ISK

Grundarfjörður Hostel is in a cute countryside building that is painted bright red. In other words, you can't miss it. The staff are friendly and eager to give tips and help set up tours. Guests have access to a fully equipped kitchen, shared bathroom facilities, free Wi-Fi, and a common TV room.

GRUND GUESTHOUSE

Grund, tel. 354/840-6100, www.west.is, rooms from 14,000ISK

Grund Guesthouse is a small, seven-room guesthouse just 3 kilometers (2 miles) east from downtown Grundarfjörður. Guests have access to shared bathroom facilities, a washing machine, free Wi-Fi, and an outdoor grill.

KIRKJUFELL HOTEL

Nesvegur 8, tel. 354/438-6893, www.kirkjufellhotel.is, rooms from 19,000ISK

Kirkjufell Hotel offers 29 rooms, renovated in 2018, with glorious views of the Snæfellsnes Peninsula. The room decor is effortless and authentically Scandinavian. All rooms come with a private bathroom, free Wi-Fi, and access to a sauna and hot tub. The in-house **restaurant** (breakfast 7am-10am, dinner 5pm-9pm daily, entrées from 2,800ISK) is more than a hotel restaurant; it has a reputation among locals for delicious fish dishes. You will find fresh cod, salmon, and mackerel on the menu, but if you're not into fish, it offers lamb dishes as well as vegetarian options.

Information and Services
TOURIST INFORMATION CENTER

Grundargata 35, tel. 354/438-1881, www. grundarfjordur.is, 9am-6pm daily May 16-Sept. 30, 1pm-6pm daily Oct. 1-May 15

The tourist information center is housed in the **Grundarfjörður Heritage Center.**

Getting There

Grundarfjörður is 39 kilometers (24 miles) southeast from **Stykkishólmur** on paved **Route 54.** Grundarfjörður is 26 kilometers (16 miles) from **Ólafsvík** on Route 54.

STYKKISHÓLMUR

Stykkishólmur is a placid seaside town that hit it big when Ben Stiller decided to shoot crucial scenes of his 2013 film *The Secret Life of Walter Mitty* there. Since the movie's release, tourists have been flocking to the otherwise quiet town in droves. It's full of West Coast charm, with brightly colored houses and quaint guesthouses at the base of a mountain range.

Sights
NORWEGIAN HOUSE
(Norska Húsið)

Hafnargata 5, tel. 354/438-1640, www.norskahusid. is, 11am-5pm daily May-Aug., 2pm-5pm Tues.-Thurs. Sept.-Apr., 800ISK adults, free for 18 and under

The Norwegian House is the local museum of Snæfellsnes. Rotating exhibits focus on the fishing industry, the region's history, and art from regional artists. The building started out as the home of Árni Thorlacius, a 19th-century local trader, built in 1832, and was extraordinary at the time as the first two-story home on the island.

BJARNARHÖFN SHARK MUSEUM
(Bjarnarhöfn Hákarlasafnið)

Bjarnarhöfn, tel. 354/438-1581, www.bjarnarhofn.is, 9am-6pm daily, 1,200ISK

The Bjarnarhöfn Shark Museum is one of those interesting museums you won't see anywhere but Iceland. The museum is located on the farm of a family that has been shark fishing and processing shark meat for generations. The owners provide a guided tour of the museum, where you will see fishing boats and equipment used in shark fishing. Guests are then taken to the drying house, where you can witness the process of preserving shark meat. You can even take a taste if you dare. If you'd like to take some with you, shark meat (*hákarl*) and dried fish (*harðfiskur*) may be purchased at the museum.

VOLCANO MUSEUM
(Eldfjallasafn)

Aðalgata 6, tel. 354/433-8154, www.eldfjallasafn. is, 10am-5pm daily, 1,000ISK adults, free for 17 and under

The Volcano Museum showcases works of art, old and new, that depict volcanic eruptions, as well as artifacts and volcanic rocks. The museum is focused on volcanoes around the world, not just those in Iceland. If you would like an in-depth tour on the science behind volcanoes, the museum offers geology excursions on Mondays and Tuesdays, which take you to interesting locales along the Snæfellsnes Peninsula. Contact the museum for departures and price information.

HELGAFELL
Road 58
Helgafell, or Holy Mountain in English, stands at 73 meters (240 feet) and has a viewing dial at the top, for those who choose to walk up. The view offers panoramas over Breiðafjörður bay, which is lovely on a clear day. Like many mountains in Iceland, there is some folklore to be told. It is said that those that make the climb without looking back or speaking will be granted three wishes, as long as they tell no one else of the wishes and are facing east when making them.

Sports and Recreation
SEATOURS
Smidjustigur 3, tel. 354/433-2254, www.seatours.is, May-Sept., tours from 7,700ISK
Seatours runs a unique bird-watching tour by boat May-September. The two-hour tour leaves from Stykkishólmur harbor, and tourists have a chance to see white-tailed eagles, shags, puffins (in the summer), eider ducks, and fulmars. While scouting for birds, guests are treated to stunning views of Snæfellsnes, including cool basalt rock formations.

STYKKISHÓLMUR SWIMMING POOL
Borgarbraut 4, tel. 354/438-1150, 7am-10pm Mon.-Thur., 7am-7pm Fri., 10am-6pm Sat.-Sun.,950ISK
The Stykkishólmur Swimming Pool is an outdoor complex with a heated pool and hot tubs.

Food
SJÁVARPAKKHÚSIÐ
Sæbraut 2, tel. 354/438-1800, www.sjavarpakkhusid. is, noon-10pm daily, entrées from 2,800ISK
Sjávarpakkhúsið is a place for seafood lovers. The seafood is as fresh as it gets, with local mussels along with cod and a fish of the day. The restaurant is located directly above the

marina, and you can see the boats that the catch comes in on.

NARFEYRARSTOFA
Aðalgata 3, tel. 354/438-1119, www.narfeyrarstofa.is, noon-9pm daily, entrées from 3,250ISK
Narfeyrarstofa is an elegant restaurant serving Icelandic staples and savory comfort food. Guests can choose among Icelandic meat soup, cod fillet, salmon, and lamb dishes, among many other tasty choices. Minke whale steaks and guillemot are also on the menu, as are hamburgers and fried fish. The meat soup is divine.

Accommodations
HOLMUR FARM
Skulagata 4, tel. 354/899-9144, www.holmurinn.is, rooms from 14,000ISK
Holmur Farm is a seven-room guesthouse on a quiet street in Stykkishólmur, just past the main road. Rooms are small but modern and comfortable. Guests have access to a common kitchen and shared bathroom facilities with showers. Breakfast is included.

HOFÐAGATA GUESTHOUSE
Hofðagata 11, tel. 354/694-6569, www.hofdagata.is, rooms from 18,000ISK
Hofðagata Guesthouse is known as the oldest guesthouse in town. The concrete structure might not be much to look at from the outside, but inside it is warm and inviting. Rooms are decorated with great care, mixing warm hues with classic Scandinavian comfort. The four rooms include shared bathrooms, free Wi-Fi, and a hearty breakfast.

HÓTEL BREIÐAFJÖRÐUR
Aðalgata 8, tel. 354/438-1417, www. hotelbreidafjordur.is, rooms from 21,500ISK
The 11-room Hótel Breiðafjörður is a converted school that has been in business for more than 30 years. Rooms are sparsely decorated with a lot of wood throughout the house and vinyl flooring. The staff is accommodating, but the guesthouse is quite basic and not memorable.

FOSSHOTEL STYKKISHÓLMUR

Borgarbraut 8, tel. 354/430-2100, www.islandshotel.

is, rooms from 28,000ISK

Fosshotel Stykkishólmur is chic, stylish, and inviting. All 79 rooms have private bathrooms and large, comfortable beds. Guests have access to free Wi-Fi, free parking, an included breakfast buffet, and a hotel bar. The hotel **restaurant** (breakfast 7am-10am daily, dinner 6pm-10pm daily, entrées from 2,500ISK 800ISK) is delicious fine dining at its best. Located inside Fosshotel Stykkishólmur, it has a playful, eclectic menu featuring meat, fish, and vegetarian options using traditional, fresh, Icelandic ingredients.

Information and Services
TOURIST INFORMATION CENTER

Borgarbraut 4, tel. 354/433-8120, www.westiceland.

is, 10am-5pm daily

The tourist information center, located at the ferry terminal, provides brochures on local sights as well as places to see in the surrounding area.

Getting There

Stykkishólmur is approximately a two-hour drive from **Reykjavík,** traveling north along **Route 1** and then west along paved **Route 54,** 165 kilometers (103 miles) via the **Hvalfjörður** tunnel. Stykkishólmur is 37 kilometers (23 miles) from **Grundafjörður** on Route 54.

FLATEY

Flatey (Flat Island) is the largest of the western islands in **Breiðafjörður,** a bay that separates the Westfjords from the southern part of the country. It is reachable only by ferry. The small island, which is north of the Snæfellsnes Peninsula and about one kilometer wide (0.6 miles) and two kilometers (1.2 miles) long, is an ideal visit for those seeking a spot in Iceland that is as old world as it gets—as in, not much has changed on this island in centuries. The colorful wood houses and single

road evoke a simpler time, one that has not been overcrowded with industry.

Flatey is very much a seasonal destination, ideal for leisurely walks, bird-watching, and taking a break from some of the more popular attractions in the Westfjords. Icelanders who own a second home here make regular trips in the summer, and only a handful of people remain during the winter months. The main hotel-restaurant on the island is open for business only during the summer, so plan accordingly if you want to venture out to the island in the winter.

There are no addresses on the island, but don't worry about getting lost—there is just one dirt road.

Sights
FLATEY CHURCH

Eastern end of island

Flatey church, on the eastern end of the island, was erected in 1926. The exterior is classic minimalist Icelandic design, but the inside features works from Spanish painter Baltasar Samper, who captured scenes from the island in the 1960s. Baltasar is the father of renowned filmmaker Baltasar Kormakur, who directed movies like *101 Reykjavík* and *Everest* and the television show *Trapped.* Across from the church is a small cemetery that includes graves that are several hundred years old.

Bird-Watching

The island offers unspoiled nature at its best, with hordes of migrating birds coming to nest and few human souls occupying the island. Flatey is a good place to spot **puffins** that migrate to the island in the summer (June-Aug.), as well as other species, including **Arctic terns, gulls,** and **oystercatchers.** However, note that part of the island is restricted from mid-May to mid-July to protect nesting birds from outside interference. The best area to see birds is along the cliffs at the end of the very small island.

1: Flatey Church **2:** puffins **3:** Bladur Ferry to Flatey **4:** Flatey Island

Text inside image 3: EIMSKIP · STYKKISHÓLMUR - FLATEY - BRJÁNSLÆKUR · Sæ · BALDUR

Food and Accommodations
HÓTEL FLATEY
*tel. 354/555-7788, www.hotelflatey.is, June-Aug.,
rooms from 28,500ISK*

Hótel Flatey is housed in a traditional timber house, a type that is prevalent on the island. The rooms are small yet tastefully decorated in a classic Scandinavian style—wood furniture, quaint white linens, and lots of minimalist charm. Each of the rooms is named after a different bird species that inhabits the island. The staff are accommodating and the house is centrally located. This place is a winner. The in-house **restaurant** (9am-9pm daily in summer, entrées from 4,300ISK) is a favorite among tourists and locals, with a mouthwatering menu that includes lumpfish caviar, mussels, lamb fillets with blueberry salt, and a delicate pan-fried cod dish with lobster sauce. Breakfast costs 2,200ISK for guests not staying at the hotel.

KRÁKUVÖR
tel. 354/438-1451, 1,200ISK

The Flatey Krákuvör campsite is small and as basic as it gets. It's an open area with no shelter, and the weather can be unforgiving. Camping here isn't recommended unless you have top-notch equipment—including a waterproof tent that can withstand high winds.

Getting There
There is one way to get to Flatey—by **ferry**. The *Baldur* ferry is operated by **Seatours** (www.seatours.is, round-trip 7,840ISK) and departs from the harbor in **Stykkishólmur,** where you can buy round-trip tickets. In the summer there are two daily departures and it takes about 1.5 hours to reach the island. The schedule in the winter varies and is dependent on weather conditions. Be sure to check the website for up-to-date timetables.

The Westfjords

In a country full of beauty, the Westfjords may be the most lovely region of all. Endless coastlines, jaw-dropping cliffs, and gorgeous mountain landscapes await those who make the trip. Rent a car to explore the region because bus service is limited. For travelers looking for a shortcut, the Baldur ferry leaves from Stykkishólmur, taking 2.5 hours to get to Brjánslækur in the Westfjords.

Driving north from the West Coast, travelers will find that the Westfjords are the most sparsely populated inhabited area on the island, which is part of the region's charm. There is striking nature every which way you turn, from mountains, to empty beaches to winding roads where you may not encounter another car for hours.

ÍSAFJÖRÐUR
Ísafjörður is the unofficial capital of the Westfjords, but don't let that "title" fool you; it's just a tiny town of about 4,000 people. It's easy to feel isolated in Ísafjörður, but it's a feeling many tourists relish. Ísafjörður is a good base for exploring the Westfjords. The town itself is quaint, with a small downtown area with shops and restaurants, and picturesque surroundings, with a bustling harbor and mountains in the background. A short drive outside town, you'll find towering mountains, interesting rock formations, and more sheep than people.

Sights
WESTFJORDS HERITAGE MUSEUM (Byggðasafn Vestfjarða)
*Neðstakaupstað, tel. 354/896-3291,
www.westfjords.is, 9am-5pm daily May 15-Sept. 15,
1,200ISK*

The Westfjords Heritage Museum pays homage to the traditional methods of fishing, with equipment and fishing boats used in the old days on exhibit. The museum is housed in an 18th-century building that sets the tone for

The Westfjords

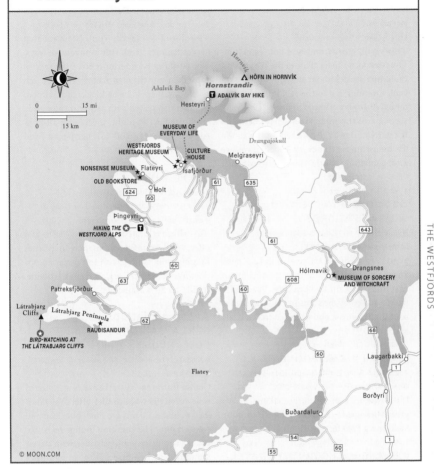

the exhibits. There are also ship models on display, informative documentaries on view, and a special exhibition on the processing of sun-dried salted fish and its significance to the town.

CULTURE HOUSE
(Gamla Sjúkrahúsið)

Eyrartún, tel. 354/450-8220, www.safnis.is, noon-6pm Mon.-Fri., 1pm-4pm Sat., free
Originally built in 1925 as the town's hospital, Ísafjörður's Culture House has morphed into Ísafjörður's library, with an art collection and photo archives that have a regional focus. The building itself is striking, with a white exterior and bright green roof. The interior is warm and cozy and a great place to hide out in for a couple of hours when the weather is particularly bad. There are several computers available for use with Internet connection for a small fee, and many treasures wait to be discovered in the archives.

MUSEUM OF EVERYDAY LIFE (Hversdagssafn)

Hafnarstræti 5, tel. 354/770-5503, www. everydaylife.is, 10am-5pm Mon.-Fri., 11am-2pm Sat. June 1- Sept. 30, closed in winter

This small, quirky museum houses exhibitions that focus on local life in the Westfjords, including stories about individuals that recently immigrated to the region, and an interactive display of shoes mounted on a wall, accompanied by headphones where guests can listen to stories by the owners of the shoes. This museum isn't for everyone, but if you are after something a little different, it's worth a visit.

Sports and Recreation
WILD WESTFJORDS

Hafnarstræti 9, tel. 354/456-3300, www. wildwestfjords.com, 11,900ISK

Wild Westfjords offers a year-round 2.5-hour kayak tour from Ísafjörður; it's perfect for an easy introduction to kayaking. Peacefully paddle and enjoy the stunning mountain surroundings, with a good chance to see birds and seals.

ÍSAFJÖRÐUR SWIMMING POOL

Austurvegur 9, tel. 354/456-3200, 10am-9pm Mon.-Fri., 10am-5pm Sat.-Sun., 850ISK

If the weather is particularly challenging, it's great to escape to the local indoor Ísafjörður Swimming Pool for a few hours.

ICELAND BACKCOUNTRY TRAVEL

Urdarvegur 27, tel. 354/861-2845, www.ibctravel.is

For those who would like to explore the rugged terrain of the Westfjords, local operator Iceland Backcountry Travel runs a year-round super-jeep tour from Ísafjörður. A two-hour tour (8,000ISK) takes you to Arnarnes, a cape on the outskirts of Ísafjörður, where it is possible to see **Drangajökull** glacier, the only glacier in the Westfjords; taking a tour is the only way to visit Drangajökull. The company also offers multiday sightseeing tours.

Food
★ TJORUHÚSIÐ

Nedstikaupstadur, tel. 354/456-4419, noon-2pm and 7pm-9pm daily June-Sept., entrées from 2,500ISK

Tjoruhúsið is a family-run restaurant that serves delicate, fresh fish in inventive ways. The rustic wood interior is cozy, the service top-notch, and the menu consists of the catch of the day. It could be haddock, cod, salmon, or other fish served with great care alongside fresh veggies. At night, there is an all-you-can-eat buffet for 6,000ISK per person, and it is well worth it.

VIÐ POLLINN

Silfurtorg 2, tel. 354/456-3360, www. isafjordurhotels.is, 11am-9pm daily June 1-Aug. 31, limited hours in the winter, entrées from 3,100ISK

Við Pollinn is located in Hótel Ísafjörður and offers locally sourced options including dishes ranging from lamb to fish to vegetarian options like nut steak. The grilled lamb is divine. A kids' menu is available.

Accommodations
GAMLA ÍSAFJÖRÐUR GUESTHOUSE

Mánagata 5, tel. 354/456-4111, www.isafjordurhotels. is, rooms from 11,500ISK

Gamla Ísafjörður Guesthouse is a standard nine-room guesthouse that offers the comforts of home. Rooms are small but clean and comfortable. The common lounge feels like you're visiting Icelandic relatives, with classic Scandinavian furniture and a reading corner with lots of books on the shelves. Guests have access to kitchen and laundry facilities.

HOTEL HORN

Austurvegur 2, tel. 354/456-4111, www. isafjordurhotels.is, rooms from 23,000ISK

Hotel Horn offers standard, deluxe, and family rooms year-round. All rooms have a private bathroom and free Wi-Fi, and family rooms also have a small kitchen. Rooms are tastefully decorated, and the lobby is bright and colorful. Breakfast is included in the rate of the room, and free parking is just outside the hotel.

HÓTEL ÍSAFJÖRÐUR

Silfurtogr 2, tel. 354/456-4111, www.hotelisafjordur. is, rooms from 25,000ISK

Hótel Ísafjörður is the nicest hotel in town, but you will pay for that stay. The 36-room hotel is decorated in standard Scandinavian simplicity and has private bathrooms, free Wi-Fi, free parking, and a staff that is happy to arrange tours and make recommendations. The hotel is centrally located, and all the main attractions are within walking distance.

Information and Services
TOURIST INFORMATION CENTER

Aðalstræti 7, tel. 354/456-5121, www.westfjords.is, 8am-6pm Mon.-Fri., 8am-3pm Sat.-Sun. June 1-Aug. 31; 10am-4pm Mon.-Fri. Sept. 1-May 31

The tourist information center offers many services, including the option to rent camping equipment and bicycles. Brochures on the region are available, and many tourists use the outpost as a place to join hiking groups.

Getting There

Ísafjörður is accessible by **Route 61,** which is paved. It's a little over 5 hours (456 kilometers/283 miles) from **Reykjavík.**

By plane, daily flights are available through **Air Iceland Connect** (www.airicelandconnect.is), which is operated at Reykjavík's domestic airport and Ísafjörður (tel. 354/570-3000). Depending on the weather, your 45-minute flight could be eventful due to wind conditions, but the view is amazing. A round-trip flight from Reykjavík is about 28,000ISK. Ísafjörður's very small airport is just a few minutes by car from town.

FLATEYRI

Flateyri was established as a trading post in 1792, and in the 19th century was a base of operations for whaling and shark-hunting. Most of the colorful houses on Flateyri's seafront street, **Hafnarstræti,** were built between 1880 and 1915. The town's fishing industry began to wane decades ago when a major fish company closed, and the town has since transformed itself to attract tourists in the summer months. Today, it's popular with sea anglers and kayak enthusiasts. A couple of museums and a stunning landscape of mountains and endless ocean make the tiny town a worthwhile stop when traveling through the Westfjords.

Sights
OLD BOOKSTORE
(Gamla Bókabúðin)

Hafnarstræti 3-5, tel. 354/865-6695, www. westfjords.is, 10am-5pm daily

Visitors to the Old Bookstore can have a look at an exhibition of the old living quarters of the merchant family who made their home in the building. It's a unique take on what life was like in the town a couple of centuries ago. The nondescript building also has an exhibition about dried fish, which was a big part of the town's history before Flateyri's fishing industry ground to a halt. Used books are sold by the kilo in the store, which also sells souvenirs and toys.

NONSENSE MUSEUM
(Dellusafnið)

Hafnarstræti 11, tel. 354/894-8836, 1pm-5pm daily June 1-Aug. 20, rest of year by appointment only, 1,000ISK, 12 and under free

The Nonsense Museum is one of those quirky museums that tend to pop up in the countryside of Iceland. This museum is a labor of love for the owner, and its wackiness is worth a visit. There's no rhyme or reason to the collections, but they are certainly fun and/or unexpected. For instance, there are more than 100 police hats on display, from forces around the world. There are also collections of ship models (including a huge replica of the *Titanic*), teaspoons and sugar packets, matchboxes, salt and pepper sets, and lighters. It's a fun place to peruse when the weather is bad, or if you have planned an extended stay in the region.

Sports and Recreation
ICELAND PRO FISHING
Hafnarstræti 9, tel. 354/456-6667,
www.icelandprofishing.com

Flateyri is a beautiful place to fish, with the chance to spot whales while angling for cod, haddock, and catfish. Iceland Pro Travel is a local tourism company that runs eight-day sea angling tours (295,000ISK) as well as day trips between April-September. Contact the company for detailed itineraries and prices.

FLATEYRI SWIMMING POOL
Tjarnagata, tel. 354/456-7738, 10am-8pm Mon.-Fri.,
11am-5pm Sat.-Sun., 850ISK

The Flateyri Swimming Pool is a central meeting place for locals, and tourists are more than welcome to take a dip and chat with the residents. The facility has a heated pool, hot tub, and sauna.

Food and Accommodations
VAGNINN
Hafnarstræti 19, tel. 354/456-7751, 4pm-11pm
Sun.-Thur., 4pm-3am Fri.-Sat., entrées from 2,200ISK

Vagninn is your best bet for a bite to eat when in Flateyri—otherwise you will have to settle for fast food at the local gas station. Even though Vagninn is the only game in town, it still goes out of its way to please diners. The food is exceptional, including classic Icelandic fish dishes, and other menu options range from sandwiches and soups to hamburgers. They also have a kids' menu. The atmosphere is fun and easygoing, with live music on the weekends.

SIMA HOSTEL & APARTMENTS
Ránargata 1, tel. 354/897-8700,
www.icelandwestfjords.com, May-Sept.,
rooms from 12,000ISK

Sima Hostel & Apartments offers rooms and apartments in the heart of Flateyri. Guests will find modern decor, luxury linens, and cozy common areas. Free Wi-Fi and free parking are available, and the property is close to local attractions.

HOLT INN
Holt, tel. 354/456-7611, www.holtinn.is, r
ooms from 26,000ISK

Holt Inn is a charming guesthouse, owned by a local couple that opened in 2018. There are 11 minimalist rooms with soothing blue colors and hardwood floors. The owners are warm, welcoming people and breakfast is included in the price of the room.

Getting There
Flateyri is about 20 kilometers (12 miles) west of **Ísafjörður** and can be reached via a paved stretch of **Route 60;** after about 12 kilometers (7 miles), turn right onto an unpaved but signposted road and follow it for about 7 kilometers (4 miles).

ÞINGEYRI

Þingeyri is a tiny village of fewer than 300 residents with scenic seaside views of the fjord **Dýrafjörður.** Tourism in the village isn't centered on museums or cultural exhibitions, but rather outdoor activities like hiking, swimming, and horse riding.

Hiking
★ WESTFJORDS ALPS HIKE
Distance: 25 km (16 mi) round-trip
Hiking Time: 5 hours round-trip
Information and maps: www.westfjords.is
Trailhead: Kaldbakur farm

From Þingeyri, you can hike into the Westfjords Alps, a striking mountain range with pointed peaks unlike the usual flat-topped variety. **Kaldbakur** peak is the tallest mountain in the Westfjords Alps at 998 meters (3,274 feet). This moderate out-and-back hike starts from Kaldbakur, a farm, which you can reach via **Route 60** and then **Route 622,** which you'll drive down for 13 kilometers (8 miles), turning left onto a gravel road where you'll be able to **park** your car. The trailhead is at the parking area, and you'll head west to climb **Helgafell.**

1: house in Flateyri 2: Dynjandi waterfall

This trail is in a stretch of Iceland that doesn't get a lot of tourist traffic; it's possible to be alone on it, which can be very appealing for some hikers. Several peaks, including Kaldbakur, are visible from the well-maintained trail, along with sweeping valleys and lush green vegetation. The highlight is reaching the top of Helgafell, where you'll catch views of the western Westfjords Alps. The round-trip hike takes about five hours, is about 25 kilometers (16 miles), and has an elevation gain of 549 meters (1,801 feet). Be sure to check the weather forecast before attempting the hike. Bring waterproof outer layers, hiking shoes, water, and a charged mobile phone.

DYNJANDI

Distance: 100 meters (328 feet) round-trip
Hiking Time: 30 minutes round-trip
Information and maps: www.westfjords.is
Trailhead: Parking lot

Dynjandi is likened to a bridal veil. The waterfall is 30 meters (98 feet) wide at its highest point and 60 meters (196 feet) wide at its lowest. It's the largest waterfall in the Westfjords, and visiting the chute makes for a beautiful little hike. From a parking area on Route 60, it's a 15-minute walk up to the base of the waterfall. Along the way you'll pass six other smaller falls, so plan on spending more time along the route for photo stops and to enjoy the surroundings.

Dynjandi is about 35 kilometers (22 miles) southeast of Þingeyri via an unpaved stretch of Route 60.

Other Sports and Recreation
SIMBAHÖLLIN

Fjarðargötu 5, tel. 354/869-5654, www.westfjords-horseriding.com

Simbahöllin offers horseback tours daily May 15-September 17. The two-hour tour (9,900ISK) takes travelers along the Sanda river, where you'll see lush vegetation along the calm riverbanks and take in stunning views of the Westfjords Alps. This is an easy tour, suitable for ages 6 and up.

ÞINGEYRI SWIMMING POOL

Þingeyraroddi, tel. 354/456-8375, 10am-9pm Mon.-Fri., 10am-5pm Sat.-Sun., 850ISK

The Þingeyri Swimming Pool is conveniently located right next to Þingeyri's campsite.

Food and Accommodations
SIMBAHÖLLIN

Fjarðargata 5, tel. 354/899-6659, www.simbahollin. is, 10am-6pm Sun.-Thur., 10am-10pm Fri.-Sat., light meals from 920ISK

Simbahöllin is a charming countryside café located in a 1915 building that served as a grocery store. The old-fashioned atmosphere is adorable, the cakes and pastries fresh, and the staff make you feel like family. The specialty is Belgian waffles with fresh rhubarb jam and cream. Your taste buds will thank you.

HOTEL SANDAFELL

7 Hafnarstræti, tel. 354/456-1600, www. hotelsandafell.com, rooms from 20,000ISK

Housed in the center of town, Hotel Sandafell offers 21 spacious rooms with free Wi-Fi and beautiful mountainous views. Some of the rooms have a private bathroom, and breakfast is included in the price of the room. There are six family rooms to accommodate larger traveling groups.

ÞINGEYRI CAMPGROUND

Þingeyraroddi, tel. 354/450-8470, 1,700ISK

The Þingeyri Campground is close to the swimming pool, so there's a lot of foot traffic in the area. It's a small campsite with an adequate cooking area, toilets, and room for tents and RVs. The campsite is in an open field with no shelter, but it has stunning views of the fjord. It's open mid-May to mid-September.

Information and Services
TOURIST INFORMATION CENTER

Hafnarstræti 5, tel. 354/891-6832, www.thingeyri.is, 10am-6pm Mon.-Fri., 11am-5pm Sat.-Sun. June 1-Sept. 1, limited winter hours

The tourist information center has brochures, suggestions for local tour operators, and Internet access.

Getting There

By car, Þingeyri is 49 kilometers (30 miles) southwest of Ísafjörður and is accessible via a paved stretch of Route 60.

PATREKSFJÖRÐUR

Patreksfjörður is the kind of sleepy fishing town you will come to love and expect as you travel along the Westfjords. Many travelers use the town as a base while heading out on excursions and day trips. Spend some time in Patreksfjörður if you're a sea angler or if you want to check out sights like the harbor area.

Sports and Recreation
PATREKSFJÖRÐUR SWIMMING POOL

Aðalstræti 55, tel. 354/456-1301, 8am-9:30pm Mon.-Fri., 10am-6pm Sat.-Sun., 1,000ISK

The town has one of the nicest swimming pools in the region. Patreksfjörður Swimming Pool is an outdoor pool with hot tubs, a steam bath, and an indoor gym.

WESTFJORDS ADVENTURES

Aðalstræti 62, tel. 354/456-5006, www. westfjordsadventures.com

The tour company Westfjords Adventures offers bird-watching tours by bicycle to see gorgeous landscapes and seabirds including puffins. The eight-hour "Bird Cliffs and Biking Tour" (36,800ISK pp) is available Tuesday-Saturday May 1-September 15. Tourists are advised to wear layers and comfortable footwear. The company also offers all-day jeep tours on rocky terrain for action junkies (35,700ISK) as well as a leisurely three-hour hike around town (4,900ISK), with a guide pointing out the major sights, including the scenic harbor area and fish market.

Food and Accommodations
STÚKUHÚSIÐ CAFÉ/RESTAURANT

Aðalstræti 50, tel. 354/456-1404, www.stukuhusid.is, 10:30am-10:30pm Mon.-Sat., noon-10pm Sun. June 1-Aug. 31, limited hours winter, entrées from 2,000ISK

Stúkuhúsið Café/Restaurant is a cute café situated just off the water. The eatery consists of a simple room with an outdoor deck for enjoying good summer weather. The menu includes cakes and pastries, along with soups and sandwiches. For dinner, you can choose between fresh fish of the day and a lamb fillet with roasted potatoes, vegetables, and pepper sauce. For starters, there's a choice of salmon or soup of the day.

STEKKABÓL GUESTHOUSE

Stekkar, tel. 354/864-9675, www.stekkabol.net, rooms from 21,500ISK

Stekkaból Guesthouse is a cute countryside guesthouse run by a husband and wife who aim to make you feel at home. The rooms are on the small side, but tidy, and free Wi-Fi is included. The guesthouse is in a picturesque spot on the fjord, making it a perfect spot to spend the night. Breakfast is available for an added cost of 1,700ISK per person.

HOTEL WEST

Aðalstræti 62, tel. 354/456-5020, www.hotelwest.is, rooms from 27,300ISK

Hotel West offers single, double, and superior rooms, all with private bathrooms. Rooms are clean and sparsely decorated, but many have views over the fjord. The hotel is close to the grocery store and pharmacy, and is a short drive from the Látrabjarg cliffs, where you can go puffin-watching.

★ FOSSHOTEL WESTFJORDS

Aðalstræti 100, tel. 354/456-2004, www. islandshotel.is, Apr.-Oct., rooms from 34,000ISK

Fosshotel Westfjords is one of the nicest outposts of Iceland's Fosshotel chain. The lobby and rooms have an earthy, natural feel with warm hues and lots of wood accents. The beds are quite comfortable. Rooms are larger than average and have free Wi-Fi, private bathrooms, and flat-screen TVs. Meals are served in the cozy in-house restaurant (6pm-10pm daily Apr.-Oct., entrées from 1,990ISK), which specializes in fish. Entrées are light and fresh, and the chefs have a classic sensibility. Expect cod, salmon, lobster, and other fish, as well as meat and a couple of vegetarian options.

Information and Services
TOURIST INFORMATION CENTER

Aðalstræti 62, tel. 354/456-5006, 10am-4pm

The tourist information center is in the Westfjords Adventures office in the center of town. You can book tours and pick up pamphlets and hiking maps for the region and access the Internet.

Getting There

Patreksfjörður is a 2.5-hour, 130-kilometer (81-mile) drive southwest of Þingeyri via an unpaved stretch of **Route 60** and unpaved **Route 62**. It is recommended to have a 4WD rental car.

LÁTRABJARG PENINSULA

The Látrabjarg Peninsula is in the northwest fjord region near Patreksfjörður and has dramatic sea cliffs and an abundance of bird species, making it a paradise for bird lovers. From June through August, the cliffs around the peninsula are home to numerous puffins, gulls, and kittiwakes.

Sports and Recreation
★ BIRD-WATCHING

Látrabjarg cliffs, short walk from parking area

Látrabjarg is one of the best bird-watching spots in West Iceland, as millions of seabirds gather to nest here each season. Puffins are a common sight in the summer months—you can see the adorable, bright-beaked birds May-August. You can also see fulmars, razorbills, and guillemots along the cliffs May-August.

The colossal rock formations of the **Látrabjarg cliffs** jut out of the earth at interesting angles, and the layered basalt forms intricate crevices that host nests. Trails allow you to access the cliffs by foot; stay on marked paths. Always be respectful of the area and be mindful where you step to avoid nests. The height of the cliffs is humbling, with some reaching up to 441 meters (1,447 feet). The cliffs offer some of the most scenic views on the peninsula.

If you trek the cliffs by foot, you will want to have a pair of binoculars on hand to get a closer look. It's best to park your vehicle at the end of **Route 612** and walk east toward the cliffs.

RAUÐISANDUR

Road 614

Rauðisandur is a secluded beach with golden-red sand and gorgeous views of the Látrabjarg area. Snæfellsjökull looms in the background. Take a walk along the shore and be on the lookout for seals bobbing in the water. **Route 614,** an unpaved road, takes you to the beach.

Food and Accommodations
HOTEL BREIÐAVÍK

Breiðavík/Látrabjarg, tel. 354/456-1575, www. breidavik.is, rooms from 22,600ISK

Hotel Breiðavík is just 12 kilometers (7 miles) away from the Látrabjarg cliffs and offers darling accommodations for your stay. Double rooms look a little dated, with bright carpet and old-fashioned linens, but the beds are comfortable, and some rooms with private bathrooms are available. All rooms have access to Wi-Fi, kitchen facilities, and a washing machine. The staff are warm and welcoming, and the breakfast is hearty. For budget travelers, there are sleeping bag rooms as well as camping, but be sure to call ahead for availability. The in-house **restaurant** (5pm-10pm daily, entrées from 2,500ISK) specializes in fish and lamb, but has other options. The salmon is fresh, seasoned perfectly, and highly recommended.

HÓTEL LÁTRABJARG

Fagrihvammur, tel. 354/456-1500, www.latrabjarg. com, rooms from 33,000ISK

Hótel Látrabjarg offers larger-than-average rooms with killer views from gigantic windows. Rooms are bright with standard beds (some are carpeted), and all rooms have simple furnishings ranging from two-seat couches to armchairs. Breakfast is included in the price of the room.

1: Látrabjarg cliffs 2: Hólmavík harbor

Getting There

You have one option to get to Látrabjarg: **Route 612**, which can be rough on your rental car because it's unpaved. Beware of steep drops and do not dream of exceeding the speed limit. Be safe. Látrabjarg is 59 kilometers (37 miles) southwest from Patreksfjörður.

HÓLMAVÍK

Hólmavík, while a small town, is the largest in the **Strandir** area, which makes up the easternmost tip of the Westfjords. It's a popular stop due to the unique **Museum of Sorcery and Witchcraft** and the cute **Sheep Farming Museum,** along with the beautiful coastline. Many travelers use the town as a base for exploring nearby villages.

Sights

MUSEUM OF SORCERY AND WITCHCRAFT (Galdrasafnið á Hólmavík)

Höfðargata 8-10, tel. 354/897-6525, www. galdrasyning.is, 9am-6pm daily, 950ISK adults, free for children under 15

The exhibits at the Museum of Sorcery and Witchcraft are truly unique. They tell the story of Iceland's infamous 17th-century witch hunts; this is the only museum on the island that gives a comprehensive overview of the period. The two-story facility also features wax figures, an audio tour, and information about spells and runes. The museum may be a little unnerving to children under the age of 12, as there are depictions of death and violence. If you still have an appetite, there's a gift shop and museum café that serves coffee and snacks.

SHEEP FARMING MUSEUM (Sauðfjársetur á Ströndum)

Sævangur, tel. 354/451-3324, www.strandir.is, 10am-6pm daily June-Aug., free

The Sheep Farming Museum is a region-specific museum that's great if you're traveling with children. The museum focuses on Icelandic sheep and sheep-farming methods

that have been employed in the Strandir region for centuries. A favorite among kids is feeding young sheep milk from a bottle while learning about the breed. There's also a souvenir shop and small café, where you can grab a coffee or cocoa and a snack.

Sports and Recreation

HÓLMAVÍK SWIMMING POOL

Jakobínutún, tel. 354/451-3560, 9am-9pm daily, 1,000ISK

The Hólmavík Swimming Pool is quiet and gets a bit of traffic in the summer because it's close to the campsite. There are a few hot tubs and a steam bath to enjoy as well.

HÓLMAVÍK GOLF CLUB

Hafnarbraut 18, tel. 354/892-4687, www.golf.is, greens fees 7,000ISK

Hólmavík Golf Club is a nine-hole course with sweeping views of the ocean, valleys, and mountains. Be sure to call ahead for a tee time. The facility is open year-round, but it's wise to confirm hours of operation because they're highly changeable.

Food and Accommodations

CAFÉ RIIS

Hafnarbraut 39, tel. 354/451-3567, 11:30am-9pm Sun.-Fri., 11:30am-3am Sat., entrées from 3,090ISK

Café Riis is the town's only place for a sit-down meal. The nondescript green building has a tourist-friendly menu ranging from traditional fish and lamb dishes to pizza, sandwiches, and snacks. On weekends, Café Riis serves as the town's main watering hole, where locals congregate to grab some drinks and let loose, especially late on Saturday nights.

FINNA HOTEL

Borgabraut 4, tel. 354/451-3136, www.finnahotel.is, rooms from 14,000ISK

Finna Hotel is a small guesthouse in a quaint yellow house on a quiet road in the center of town. Rooms are clean, smart, and furnished simply. If you have a choice, request a room on the second floor—those rooms underwent a recent renovation. Amenities include free

Wi-Fi, free parking, and shared bathrooms. Room rates with or without breakfast are available.

HÓTEL LAUGARHÓLL

Bjarnarfjörður, tel. 354/451-3380, www.laugarholl.is, rooms from 25,700ISK

Hótel Laugarhóll offers 17 rooms, 11 of which have private bathrooms. The rooms are bright and tidy, with Wi-Fi access and free parking. The hotel is in a large estate set within a rocky landscape. It's close to town, about 25 kilometers (16 miles) east of Hólmavík, but remote enough to maintain a countryside feel. The in-house **restaurant** (7am-9pm daily) offers a breakfast that's included in the room price, as well as a lunch and dinner menu. The dinner menu starts at 3,800ISK and offers a range of fish and lamb dishes to lighter items like soup, sandwiches, and vegetarian options.

HÓLMAVÍK CAMPGROUND

Jakobínutún, tel. 354/451-3111, 1,500ISK

The town has a centrally located, well-maintained campsite, Hólmavík Campground, that is close to the swimming pool. There are adequate cooking facilities and hot showers. Tents and RVs are welcome, with hookups available. The site is in an open field with no shelter, so be prepared for the elements if you're camping in a tent.

Information and Services
TOURIST INFORMATION OFFICE

Höfðagata 8, tel. 354/451-3111, www.holmavik.is, 9am-6pm daily

The tourist information office is in the center of town and offers Internet access, pamphlets about the region, and information on local tours and horse rentals.

Getting There

By car, Hólmavík is a popular stop on the Westfjords for travelers coming from Ísafjörður, as Ring Roaders tend to need gas by this point. **Route 61** is paved and connects Hólmavík, which is 223 kilometers (139 miles) southeast of Ísafjörður, to the **Ring Road**.

DRANGSNES AND GRÍMSEY ISLAND

Drangsnes is a small fishing village with fewer than 70 residents. It has an active harbor, a school, some summer houses, and a couple of popular **hot pots**. Boat tours leave from Drangsnes to Grímsey island, which is a prime spot for puffin-watching in the summer.

Birdwatching
GRÍMSEY TOURS

tel. 354/853-6520, www.westtours.is, 10,000ISK 13 and over, 5,000ISK children 4-12, free for children under 4

Just offshore from Drangsnes, the island of Grímsey is known for its **puffin colony** (about 80,000 nesting pairs) and a small lighthouse. No homes, buildings, or facilities are on the island—just birdlife and pristine nature. From Drangsnes, scheduled boat trips to the island take around 10 minutes, and tours last around four hours. Visitors spend their time independently exploring the small island, stopping by the lighthouse for photos, and observing puffins nesting on the cliffs. Tours depart twice a day daily at 9am and 1:30pm, weather permitting. Booking in advance via phone is recommended, but if there is space, walk-ups are taken. The fee can be paid at Malarhorn guesthouse.

Swimming
HOT POTS

Road 645

Drangsnes's three free hot pots are popular year-round with locals and visitors alike. They're great spots to relax and enjoy the scenery; from their location along the shoreline, you can see the harbor and Grímsey in the distance. They are visible from the road, Route 645, and there's a changing area across the street. Be sure to bring a towel.

DRANGSNES SWIMMING POOL

Grundargata 15, tel. 354/451-3201, sundlaug@ drangsnes.is, 10am-9pm Mon.-Thurs. and 10am-6pm Fri.-Sun. June 15-Aug. 30, 4pm-7pm Tues.-Wed. and Fri. and 3pm-5pm Sat.-Sun. Sept. 1-June 14, 850ISK

The Drangsnes Swimming Pool is a small outdoor pool with a hot tub that's popular with locals. It's located close to Malarhorn, the town's only guesthouse.

Food and Accommodations
MALARHORN

Grundargata 17, tel. 354/853-6520, www.malarhorn.is, rooms from 25,000ISK

Malarhorn is the only game in town in Drangsnes. The guesthouse has three buildings with singles, doubles, family rooms, luxury rooms, and self-catering cottages. There are common areas and a mix of shared and private bathrooms. Rooms are comfortable and sparsely decorated with simple wood furniture and bare walls. Guests have access to porches and gas barbecues. Malarhorn's **restaurant,** Malarkaffi, is open from dusk till dawn in the summer, and open by request the rest of the year. Soups, sandwiches, and burgers are on the menu for lunch, and dinner includes pan-fried cod, fish stew, grilled wolffish, and grilled lamb.

Getting There

The only way to get to Drangsnes is by car. From **Hólmavík,** head north on **Route 61** and then east on **Route 643** and south on **Route 645.** The trip is about 33 kilometers (21 miles) on the paved routes and takes 40 minutes.

HORNSTRANDIR NATURE RESERVE

The **Hornstrandir Peninsula** is the northernmost part of the Westfjords, and it is idyllically isolated. The Hornstrandir Nature Reserve, which was established in 1975, lies on the north edge of the peninsula. It's a perfect spot to explore by foot, enjoying hiking paths and observing the rich birdlife. Nature rules in this spot of the Westfjords—you won't find museums or cultural attractions, but who needs them when there are millions of seabirds and arctic fox sightings are common? It isn't just foreign travelers making their way to these parts, but also Icelanders in search of pure solitude and striking beauty.

On bird cliffs in the western end of the region, the subjects of postcard-perfect photos, you can see puffins, kittiwakes, fulmars, and guillemots. A long, sandy beach is the perfect place to roam while basking in the shadows of sharp mountains and the jagged landscape.

Travel to Hornstrandir is very much seasonal, with the high season being from the middle of June to the end of August. Because

Hornstrandir Nature Reserve

of its northern locale, the weather can be especially cold, even in the summer, and very wet.

Hiking

Be mindful that this stretch of land is fiercely protected; cars are banned within the reserve limits and fishing is strictly prohibited. Enjoy the land, but be respectful and obey the rules. The terrain could be treacherous depending on the weather, so it's not ideal for casual hikers, but rather for more experienced trekkers. Good maps are necessary and can be found online at www.galdrasyning.is. Because of its northern locale, the winds can be fierce and the rain plentiful. Make sure you are prepared with a good pair of boots, waterproof gear, and lots of layers because it can get really cold. Use common sense—there are streams that need to be crossed, sections can be slippery with ice, and portions where crampons are necessary. Visitors must bring their own tents if the plan is to camp overnight. Weatherproof equipment is necessary, as snow can be expected at any time of the year and storms can break with little warning. Thick fog often occurs in the region, and it's a good idea to have GPS with you.

If you are a novice hiker or would like the structure of an organized tour, **West Tours** (tel. 354/456-5111, www.westtours.is) offers packages and excursions throughout the year.

AÐALVÍK BAY HIKE

Distance: 12 km (7 mi) round-trip
Hiking Time: 8 hours round-trip
Information and maps: www.westfjords.is
The moderate hike between the small village of **Hesteyri** and **Aðalvík Bay** at the tip of Hornstrandir is the most popular option, and it's about an eight-hour hike at a leisurely pace, during which you can enjoy the cliffs, the rocky landscape, and unspoiled nature. It's about 12 kilometers (7 miles) round-trip with an elevation gain of about 300 meters (984 feet).

Accommodations
HÖFN IN HORNVÍK
GPS coordinates N 66.4232, W 22.4882
The campground Höfn in Hornvík (free) has basic camping facilities, including restrooms, a cooking area, and hot and cold water. Be respectful of the surroundings, dispose of your trash, and leave no trace. The campsite is in an open space with little shelter.

Getting There and Around
There are daily 45-minute flights from Reykjavík's domestic airport to **Ísafjörður** for 28,000ISK, and from Ísafjörður, you can catch a ferry operated by **Sjóferðir** (tel. 354/456-3879, www.sjoferdir.is) that stops at the ports Aðalvík, Hornvík, Grunnavík, and Hesteyri for 10,500ISK each way.

The easiest way to travel to the region is to book an **excursion,** as there are detailed logistics involved and it's best to have a local tour company handle them. There can be delays because of weather, and travelers can avoid headaches by booking a tour. Local tour companies include Ísafjörður-based **West Tours** (tel. 354/456-5111, www.westtours.is), **Arctic Adventures** (tel. 354/456-3322, www.adventures.is), and **Borea Adventures** (www.boreaadventures.com), also in Ísafjörður.

North Iceland

Itinerary Ideas 182
Húnaflói Area 184
Skagafjörður...........187
Tröllaskagi 192
Grímsey 199
Akureyri 203
Around Akureyri 213
Mývatn Region 215
Húsavík................222
Jökulsárgljúfur
    (Vatnajökull National
    Park—North) 227

There's a lot to explore in North Iceland, and

Akureyri is the center of it all.

Iceland's second most populous city, Akureyri has a thriving art scene, gorgeous gardens, and restaurants that rival Reykjavík's. The harbor serves as a port for large cruise ships, and visitors are treated to views of the country's highest peaks and longest fjord.

Akureyri is a perfect place to base yourself when exploring the North. The open terrain from Akureyri to Siglufjörður, the northernmost town in Iceland, treats visitors to traditional churches, wondrous waterfalls, and a dreamy seaside.

Farther west is Northwest Iceland. This region comprises sparsely populated farm country. In fact, depending on the time of year, you

Highlights

Look for ★ to find recommended sights, activities, dining, and lodging.

© MOON.COM

★ **Akureyri Botanical Gardens:** The northernmost botanical garden in the world has an eclectic collection of native and international flora (page 203).

★ **Goðafoss:** Witness the thundering Waterfall of the Gods, a spectacular sight any time of year (page 215).

★ **Mývatn Nature Baths:** Just try to resist taking a dip in the soothing, heated waters of Mývatn (page 215).

★ **Whale-Watching in Húsavík:** The unofficial whale-watching capital of Iceland offers a chance to view as many as 12 species of these gentle giants (page 223).

★ **Ásbyrgi:** This gigantic canyon features cool rock formations, looping walking paths, lush greenery, birds—and tons of photo opportunities (page 227).

★ **Dettifoss:** The largest waterfall on the island, and the most powerful in Europe, is 100 meters (328 feet) wide and 45 meters (148 feet) high (page 228).

North Iceland

GRETTISBÓL
ICELANDIC
SEAL CENTER
Laugarbakki
Hvammstangi
Vatnsnes
Pen.
HVÍTSERKUR
SELASIGLING
ÞINGEYRARKIRKJA
Hóf
Blönduós

Skagaströnd

TEXTILE
MUSEUM
TANNERY
VISITOR CENTER
Sauðárkrókur
SKAGAFJÖRÐUR
TRANSPORTATION
MUSEUM
1238: THE BATTLE OF ICELAND
SKAGAFJÖRÐUR
FOLK MUSEUM/
GLAUMBÆR
Varmahlíð
VÍÐIMÝRARKIRKJA

Drangey

Skagafjörður

Trö llaskagi

HERITAGE MUSEUM OF DALVÍK
Svarfaðardalur
Nature Reserve
Dalvík

Ólafsfjörður
Siglufjörður
FOLK MUSIC
CENTER
HERRING ERA
MUSEUM

Grímsey
GRÍMSEYJARKIRKJA
THE
LIGHTHOUSE

Grímseyjarsund

AKUREYRI BOTANICAL
GARDENS
Akureyri
LAUFÁS

Hrísey
Grenivík
Eyjafjörður

WHALE-
WATCHING
HÚSAVÍK
WHALE MUSEUM
Húsavík
GEOSEA
GEOTHERMAL
SEA BATHS
EXPLORATION
MUSEUM
HÚSAVÍKURKIRKJA
CULTURE HOUSE

Öxarfjörður
Kópasker

GOÐAFOSS
Laugar
Skjálfandafljót

MÝVATN NATURE
BATHS
MÝVATN
REGION
MAP
SEE

Jökulsárgljúfur
(Vatnajökull
National Park–
North)

DETTIFOSS
Hólmatungur
ÁSBYRGI
Jökulsá

Raufarhöfn

Þistilfjörður

Vatnajökull
National Park

SEE
"AKUREYRI"
MAP

Langanes

Vopnafjörður

Bakkafjörður

Lagarfljót

Vesturdalsá
Austari Jökulsá
Vestari Jökulsá
Blöndudalur
Langjökull
Hofsjökull

Húnaflói

Vatnsnes
Pen.

© MOON.COM

Arctic Coast Way

North Iceland's newest tourist route debuted in June 2019. The route spans 900 kilometers (560 miles) and has been dubbed the Arctic Coast Way. It leads travelers on a journey among 21 towns and villages close to the Arctic Circle. Nine days is recommended for this route, best traveled from the west in the town of **Hvammstangi** to the northeast in **Þórshöfn.** Along the way you will see spectacular landscapes of mountains, steep cliffs, charming fishing villages, glacial river deltas, and crossings to islands like **Grímsey** and **Hrísey.** For more information on the route, visit **www.arcticcoastway. is/en.**

Arctic Sea coast

may see more seals, birds, horses, and whales than people in areas like Húnaflói and Skagafjörður.

Heading from Akureyri toward eastern Iceland, stops include Krafla's steamy lava fields, Lake Mývatn's lush lands, and the majestic Dettifoss waterfall. In the summer, birders and geology buffs will want to stretch the drive out an extra couple of days.

From waterfalls and hiking trails to the best skiing on the island, the north has plenty to keep you busy.

PLANNING YOUR TIME

North Iceland is a huge chunk of land (for Iceland), but it's quite easy to split into manageable sections, using a major town as a home base and doing day trips from there. **Akureyri, Húsavík,** and **Mývatn** are the largest and most frequented destinations for tourists, with museums, outdoor activities, and historical sites to visit.

If you're traveling the **Ring Road,** Northwest Iceland would be your first destination after visiting the Westfjords. The northwest offers some of the most exquisite scenery on the island in its small towns and counties, including **Hvammstangi, Blönduós,** and **Skagafjörður.** Akureyri is a great base while visiting this area.

Akureyri rivals Reykjavík for the center of artistic life in Iceland. Plan to spend as much time as possible up here, with at least one day each in Mývatn and Húsavík and two days in Akureyri—three days if you want to include a trip to **Grímsey.**

When driving in the north, it's important to take the **weather** into consideration. Some roads are impassable in the **winter.** It's possible to see much of North Iceland by sticking to the Ring Road, which is the best-maintained road in the region. However, always be sure to check the road conditions and weather forecast before heading out in a car.

Previous: Siglufjörður; Dettifoss; Mývatn Nature Baths.

Itinerary Ideas

THREE DAYS IN THE NORTH

Day 1: Akureyri

1 Spend the morning exploring the center of town, strolling the harbor area and visiting the **Akureyri Botanical Gardens.**

2 Get a taste of the region's culture at the museum **Nonnahús.**

3 Go for a swim at one of the best swimming pools in the north, the **Akureyri swimming pool.**

4 Order a traditional lamb soup at **Kaffi Ilmir,** followed by some tasty local ice cream at Brynjar.

5 Get in your rental car and drive to the impressive waterfall **Dettifoss.**

6 After driving back to Akureyri, enjoy an elegant dinner at **Strikið,** opting for a lamb or fish entrée.

7 Spend the night at the modern and centrally located **Hotel Akureyri.**

Day 2: Whale-Watching in Húsavík

1 From Akureyri, drive to Húsavík on Route 1. Take a whale-watching tour from the harbor with **Gentle Giants.**

2 Have lunch by the harbor at **Salka Restaurant,** which serves up fantastic pizzas.

3 Walk along the harbor, photograph the Húsavík church, and make your way to the **Húsavík Whale Museum.**

4 Have a delicious seafood meal at the memorable **Naustið.**

5 Spend the night at the comfortable and central **Fosshotel Húsavík.**

Day 3: Hiking and Relaxing Around Mývatn

1 From Húsavík, make your way to the Mývatn area on Route 1. Before reaching Mývatn, make a small detour to the gigantic waterfall **Goðafoss.**

2 Drive to **Lake Mývatn** and soak in the scenery, which is lush in summer and snow-kissed in deep winter.

3 Have lunch at **Vogafjós Restaurant,** where you can visit the farm's cows and have a hearty meal.

4 Continue to **Dimmuborgir** and walk around the fascinating lava landscapes.

5 Drive to the Krafla caldera and explore the **Viti** explosion crater.

6 Soak in the soothing geothermal waters of the **Mývatn Nature Baths.**

7 Spend the night and have dinner at **Hotel Laxá.**

Itinerary Ideas

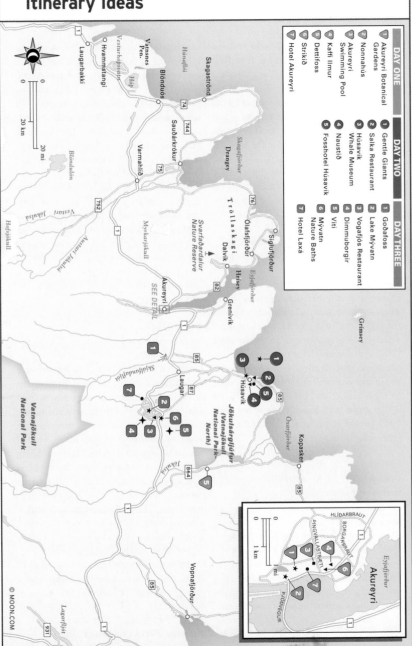

DAY ONE

1. Akureyri Botanical Gardens
2. Nonnahús
3. Akureyri Swimming Pool
4. Kaffi Ilmur
5. Dettifoss
6. Strikið
7. Hotel Akureyri

DAY TWO

1. Gentle Giants
2. Salka Restaurant
3. Húsavík Whale Museum
4. Naustið
5. Fosshotel Húsavík

DAY THREE

1. Goðafoss
2. Lake Mývatn
3. Vogafjós Restaurant
4. Dimmuborgir
5. Víti
6. Mývatn Nature Baths
7. Hotel Laxá

© MOON.COM

Húnaflói Area

Húnaflói is a large bay between the Strandir coast and the Skagaströnd region. It is about 50 kilometers (31 miles) wide and 100 kilometers (62 miles) long, with the small towns of Blönduós and Skagaströnd located on the bay's eastern side. The northwest is steeped in saga history, as legendary hero Grettir the Strong was said to have lived in the area, but most people travel to the Húnaflói area for the charming fishing villages and the opportunity to spot whales, seals, and birds. The region is lush in the summer, with a majestic coastline similar to the Westfjords.

VATNSNES PENINSULA

The Vatnsnes Peninsula is home to some of the best seal-watching opportunities in the north, and in the summer, you have a good chance of spotting harbor and gray seals, too. There's a museum with lovely exhibitions at the Icelandic Seal Center, which does research on local seal species. Hvammstangi is the largest town on the peninsula and the site of many tourist attractions. The Vatnsnes Peninsula juts out into Húnaflói, marked by jagged rocks and bobbing hills. Route 711, a gravel road accessible from the Ring Road, goes to Hvammstangi and around the peninsula.

Sights

ICELANDIC SEAL CENTER
(Selasetur Íslands)

Brekkugata 2, Hvammstangi, tel. 354/451-2345, www.selasetur.is, 10am-3pm Mon.-Fri. Oct. 1-Apr. 30, 9am-4pm daily May, 9am-7pm daily June 1-Aug. 31, 9am-4pm daily Sept., 1,100ISK adults, free for children under 12

The Icelandic Seal Center is as cute as it sounds, if you like seals. There is a serious research component to the facility, but the museum section captures these lovable, adorable creatures perfectly. Most of the exhibitions are geared toward children, and topics include the seals of the North Atlantic and the Arctic, the importance of seals in Icelandic culture and tradition, seal biology (with skeletons on display), and the evolution of seal hunting on the island. There are also documentaries on Icelandic seals in English. The main seals the center works with are harbor, harp, bearded, gray, hooded, and ringed seals. (There's also the odd walrus that comes ashore in Iceland from Greenland—the seal center is contacted in that event.) The staff has information on the best sites for seal-watching opportunities, and a small shop (hours variable; check website) sells souvenirs and light meals. For independent travelers, it is possible to go to the popular seal-watching spots without a tour guide, but the company **Selasigling** also offers seal watching tours from the Hyammstangi harbor.

GRETTISBÓL

Laugarbakki, tel. 354/451-0050, www.visithunathing.is/en

Grettisból, Grettir's Lair, is an outdoor area and cultural center dedicated to the great saga hero Grettir "the Strong" Ásmundsson from *Grettir's Saga.* One of the most infamous outlaws of the sagas, Grettir was born on the farm Bjarg, which is only 7 kilometers (4.3 miles) south of this cultural center. There is a Viking garden at Grettisból, and from the road you will see a big Viking sword sculpture. In the summer months (June-Aug.), a market in the house sells Viking-related wares, such as figurines, artwork, and woolen goods. The center is open year-round, and if you're a fan of the sagas, this should be on your itinerary.

An annual festival held at Grettisból in August is called **Grettistak;** locals have a strongman competition in the spirit of Grettir.

MERCHANT MUSEUM
(Bardúsa-Verslunarminjasafn)

Brekkugata 4, Hvammstangi, tel. 354/451-2747,

10am-6pm daily May 1-Oct. 20,
open rest of year by request, free

A small museum in Hvammstangi housed in the remains of an early-20th-century shop, The Merchant Museum today keeps all the old goods that were key to society in the town, such as fishing equipment, kitchen utensils, and other home goods. The museum also sells Icelandic-made handcrafts.

HVÍTSERKUR

Húnaflói Bay, GPS coordinates: N65° 36' 25.656"
W20° 37' 32.617

Hvítserkur is one of the most photographed sights in northwest Iceland. The stone structure, which stands 15 meters (49 feet) tall, is said to resemble a rhinoceros. The basalt rock stack juts out of Húnaflói Bay and serves as a nesting area for a variety of bird species including seagulls and fulmar. The best way to view Hvítserkur is along the eastern shore of the Vatnsnes Peninsula.

Seal-Watching
SELASIGLING

Höfðabraut 13, tel. 354/897-9900, 8,500ISK adults, 4,500ISK children 7-15, free for children 6 and under

This tour company offers 1.5-hour seal-watching tours from the Hvammstangi harbor, departing at 10am, 1pm, and 4pm daily from May 15- Sept. 30.

Entertainment and Events
THE GREAT SEAL COUNT
www.selasetur.is/en

The great seal count is an annual event every July or August in which locals and tourists volunteer their time to count seals during low tide four hours per day. The count takes place along Vatnsnes peninsula and the count is vital in determining the health of the seal population off the coasts of Iceland.

Food and Accommodations
SJAVARBORG RESTAURANT
Strandgata 1, tel. 354/451-3131, www.sjavarborg-restaurant.is, 11am-10pm daily, entrées from 2,550ISK

This popular eatery is located close to the town harbor. The building was originally a slaughterhouse, and then a freezing plant, before becoming the restaurant it is today. Its interior is a modern mix of concrete and wood with rustic driftwood accents. The menu is simple, with burgers, fish, and soup for lunch, and fish, steaks, burgers, sandwiches, pasta, and salads for dinner.

Hvítserkur in Húnaflói Bay

DÆLI GUESTHOUSE

Viðidalur, tel. 354/451-2566, www.daeli.is, rooms from 21,000ISK

Dæli Guesthouse has larger-than-average rooms, some wood-paneled, that are simple and smart. The 14 rooms have private bathrooms, TVs, and free Wi-Fi, and guests have access to a sauna, hot tub, mini golf, a playground, and a café. A kitchen is available to prepare meals, and guests have access to a barbecue grill.

HOTEL HVAMMSTANGI

Norðurbraut 1, tel. 354/855-1303, www.hotelhvammstangi.is, rooms from 26,000ISK

Hotel Hvammstangi is a guesthouse about 6 kilometers (3.7 miles) from the highway and in the middle of some great seal-watching spots. Rooms are small but neat and tastefully decorated. Each room has a private bathroom, there is a shared TV lounge with complimentary coffee and tea, and guests have access to free Wi-Fi. The town's public swimming pool, with hot tub and steam bath, is across the street from the hotel, and admission is free for guests.

★ GAUKSMÝRI LODGE

Þjóðvegur, tel. 354/451-2927, www.gauksmyri.com, rooms from 28,000ISK

This 25-room ranch is hands-down the area's best place to stay, especially if you love horses. Gauksmýri Lodge offers cozy, comfortable rooms with adorably appropriate horse-print bedding. The beds are comfortable, the decor is rustic cool, and the amenities are superb. Most rooms have private bathroom facilities, and all guests have access to free Wi-Fi and huge windows overlooking the gorgeous landscape. The owners are obviously horse enthusiasts (they also operate a horse-rental business). There are short guided horse tours and demonstrations showing the various gaits Iceland's horses are known for, and training and teaching facilities are on-site. Breakfast is included in the room price.

ÓSAR HOSTEL

Vatnsnesvegur, tel. 354/451-2678, www.hostel.is, beds from 12,780ISK, private rooms from 31,860ISK

Ósar Hostel is just 20 minutes from the Ring Road, making this a popular choice in the area for budget travelers making the trek around the island. Dorm rooms are adequate but nothing to write home about. It's open Feb. 1-Dec. 1.

Getting There

By car, Hvammstangi is 190 kilometers (118 miles) north of **Reykjavík** on **Route 1** and 200 kilometers (124 miles) west of **Akureyri**.

BLÖNDUÓS

Blönduós is a tiny town that was built around a bridge over the Blanda River (Blönduós means "mouth of the river Blanda" in Icelandic). Home to just a few shops, private homes, and guesthouses, the town is a small spot that has a few attractions. If you are traveling on the Ring Road and have some time, think about visiting the Textile Museum and the local church, which is steeped in history.

Sights

TEXTILE MUSEUM (Heimilisiðnaðarsafnið)

Árbraut 29, tel. 354/452-4067, www.textile.is, 10am-5pm daily June 1-Aug. 31, 1,200ISK adults, free for children under 16

This quaint museum is for fiber enthusiasts. On display are local crafts, Icelandic national costumes, looms of different sizes, and wonderful woolen products. The gift shop has a collection of cute wares, including wool for knitting projects and classically patterned Icelandic sweaters.

ÞINGEYRAKIRKJA

Austur-Húnavatnssýsla, tel. 354/895-4473, 10am-5pm daily June 1-Aug. 31, open by request rest of year, 500ISK

Þingeyrakirkja, Þingeyrar Church, offers one of the most beautiful panoramic views in all of North Iceland, overlooking Húnafjörður bay. Þingeyrakirkja was built out of stone in Romanesque style and was officially consecrated in 1877. The land surrounding the church was the site of Iceland's first monastery, which was founded in 1133. An important place from the time of early settlement, Þingeyrakirkja is mentioned in the saga literature as a regional assembly site. Next to the church is a large circular structure, which is believed to be a judgment circle; it is listed as a heritage site. In the summer, tourists can enter the church and have a look.

Horse Riding
GALSI HORSE RIDING
Arnargerði 33, tel. 354/692-0118, www.galsi.is
This small, family-run business offers tours for beginners and experienced riders. For an introduction to the Icelandic horse, Galsi offers a 20-minute lesson on how to properly saddle and sit on one. The course costs 3,500ISK per person. Galsi also offers an easy 1.5-hour ride in the scenic surroundings of Blönduós for 8,000ISK. Advanced riders can opt for a four-hour tour for 18,000ISK.

Food and Accommodations
B&S RESTAURANT
Nordurlandsvegur 4, tel. 354/453-5060, www.bogs. is, 11am-9pm daily, entrées from 1,890ISK
B&S Restaurant is housed in a bright orange building in the heart of town. The menu is full of comfort food like burgers, pizza, and sandwiches, as well as meat and fish dishes. The restaurant is also family friendly, with an extensive children's menu.

GLADHEIMAR COTTAGES
Brautarhvammi, tel. 354/820-1300, www.gladheimar. is, cottages from 27,000ISK
Gladheimar Cottages offers 20 self-contained cottages year-round that include private bathrooms, a patio, hot tub, barbecue grill, and proximity to the town's swimming pool. The cottages aren't luxurious, but they're clean, convenient, and won't break the bank for family accommodation.

HOTEL BLANDA
Aðalgata 6, 354/452-4205, www.hotelblanda.is, rooms from 27,000ISK
This family-run guesthouse is located in a quaint house in the heart of town. Hotel Blanda offers 19 rooms ranging from singles to family rooms. All rooms feature simple, modern decor with TVs and private bathrooms. Breakfast is included.

Getting There
Blönduós is 58 kilometers (36 miles), 45 minutes, northeast of **Hvammstangi** on **Route 1.**

Skagafjörður

With sloping mountains, a beautiful coastline, and chunks of glacial ice dotting the fjord, Skagafjörður's landscape is heavenly. Skagafjörður is often described as horse country, and that's very true. Horse farms and horse tour operators abound here—it's the only county in Iceland where horses outnumber humans.

Skagafjörður is just 40 kilometers (25 miles) long and 15 kilometers (9 miles) wide, with the towns of Sauðárkrókur and Varmahlíð the main areas for tourism. Here, farms reign supreme and all residents are involved in agriculture in one form or another. Tourism has picked up in recent years, and there are a few museums, some historical sites, and plenty of outdoor activities to keep visitors entertained.

VARMAHLÍÐ
Tourists don't typically travel to the town of Varmahlíð, but rather through it, as it's close to where **Route 1** passes through the area. There's a historic church to check out,

but those who stick around for a few hours usually have booked a river-rafting or horse tour. The town has defined itself as a place for **adventure activities** over the past few years.

Sights
VÍÐIMÝRARKIRKJA

GPS coordinates N 65.5389, W 19.4710, tel. 354/453-5095, 9am-6pm daily June-Aug., 1,000ISK

Just outside Varmahlíð lies Víðimýrarkirkja, one of the last remaining preserved **turf churches** in Iceland. Turf houses are representative of a very old building method. Víðimýri Church, which features a frame made from driftwood, was built in 1834 and has turf walls but timber gables both back and front. At the beginning of the 20th century, the church's fate was uncertain, but the National Museum of Iceland became responsible for its renovation and maintenance. The church still holds Sunday services at 11am, and tourists are welcome to attend.

Sports and Recreation
HESTASPORT

Vegamót, tel. 354/453-8383, www.riding.is, 1-hour tours 8,500ISK, 2-hour tours 12,000ISK

Skagafjörður is horse country. Hestasport offers riding tours year-round on scenic paths along the region. The staff clearly has a passion for horses, and guides are well informed, patient, and excited to take you to some hidden gems in the area. Options range from one-hour to full-day tours, and the staff has all the equipment you need for your excursion—helmets, rain clothes, and all other necessary gear.

BAKKAFLÖT RAFTING

560 Varmahlíð, tel. 354/453-8245, www.bakkaflot.is, 3-4-hour tour 14,500ISK

Bakkaflöt Rafting has been offering river-rafting tours for more than 30 years on the Austari Jökulsá river and the Vestari Jökulsá river, which are fed by the Hofsjökull glacier. Five levels of rafting classes range from easy to very demanding, based on an individual's

level of experience. Tours are available May-September.

Bakkaflöt is 37 kilometers (23 miles) from Sauðárkrókur, about 300 kilometers (186 miles) from Reykjavík, and about 100 kilometers (62 miles) from Akureyri. Once you arrive in Varmahlíð along **Route 1,** take **Route 752** and follow that for 10 kilometers (6.2 miles).

VARMAHLÍÐ SWIMMING POOL

560 Varmahlíð, tel. 354/455-6020, 10:30am-9pm Mon.-Fri., 10:30am-6pm Sat.-Sun. June-Aug., 9am-8pm Mon.-Thur., 8am-2pm Fri., 10am-3pm Sat. Sept.-May, 1,000ISK

The Varmahlíð Swimming Pool has two sections—one that is 12.5 by 25 meters (41 by 82 feet) for adults and a children's pool that's 12.5 by 8 (41 by 25) meters. The children's pool is extremely popular among local families, and the slide is a favorite with kids. For adults, there are hot tubs and a sauna in the sports hall that's connected to the pool area.

Food and Accommodations
HÓTEL VARMAHLÍÐ

tel. 354/453-8170, www.hotelvarmahlid.is, rooms from 28,000ISK

Located near Route 1, Hótel Varmahlíð is the only hotel in the area, and it's a lovely place to stay. The 19 rooms are cozy and modern, with private bathrooms, TVs, free Wi-Fi, and gorgeous photographs of the area by locals adorning the walls. It is a comfortable spot with hospitable employees and an in-house restaurant serving yummy dishes. A breakfast buffet is included in the price of the room, and lunch and dinner menus focus on local ingredients found in the region, such as lightly salted cod heads, horse fillets, and tasty rhubarb cobbler made from local farm products. The **restaurant** is open 7:30am-10pm daily, and entrées start at 3,800ISK.

Information and Services
TOURIST INFORMATION OFFICE

tel. 354/455-6161, www.visitskagafjordur.is, 1pm-7pm daily June 1 -Aug. 31, closed rest of year

In the center of the village, the Skagafjörður

tourist information office has pamphlets about the region, Internet access, maps, and the ability to book tours.

Getting There

Varmahlíð is 286 kilometers (178 miles) northeast of **Reykjavík** on **Route 1** and 93 kilometers (58 miles) west of **Akureyri** on Route 1.

SAUÐÁRKRÓKUR

Sauðárkrókur is Skagafjörður's largest town, but don't let that fool you—this is a village of fewer than 3,000 people. The name means "sheep's corner" in Icelandic, but that's a bit misleading, as this remains more of a fishing town than a sheep-farming town. To learn about the region, stop by the Skagafjörður Folk Museum.

Sights
SKAGAFJÖRÐUR FOLK MUSEUM (Byggðasafn Skagfirðinga)

GPS coordinates N 65.6104, W 19.5036, tel. 354/453-6173, www.glaumbaer.is, 10am-4pm Mon.-Fri. Apr. 1-May 19, 9am-6pm daily May 20-Sept. 20, 10am-4pm daily Sept. 21-Oct. 20, open by request rest of year, 1,700ISK adults, free for children under 17

The Skagafjörður Folk Museum is an extensive exhibition that includes 13 buildings, each of which had its own function, ranging from a kitchen to a sleeping room. According to the sagas, the first known inhabitants of the Glaumbær farm lived there in the 11th century.

The main event is the farmhouse, **Glaumbær**, which was built circa 1879. It was constructed from stones, turf, and timber, and the structure has been maintained incredibly well. The estate provided little rock suitable for building purposes, but there was plenty of good turf, so the walls of the farmhouse contain relatively little rock: builders made do with what they had.

Also on the museum grounds are two 19th-century timber houses, **Áshús** and **Gilsstofa,** that are typical of the homes built in the area at that time. Áshús contains exhibitions about the region and houses the museum's administrative offices. **Áskaffi** is a café housed in Áshús that serves traditional light Icelandic cuisine, including soup and sandwiches. In Gilsstofa, there are offices, an information center, and a souvenir shop.

The current iteration of **Glaumbær church** was built in 1926. Earlier churches at Glaumbær had been built of wood, and most of them were covered with turf for protection against the elements. However, the last wooden church was blown down in a storm. The church that currently stands is a more modern structure with a concrete base and wood over it.

The **Heritage House** showcases exhibitions that highlight four 20th-century tradesmen's workshops. Also on permanent display are objects from the private collections of novelist Guðrún from Lundur (1887-1975), composer Eyþór Stefánsson (1901-1999), and artist Jóhannes Geir Jónsson (1927-2003). Guðrún's books are still read widely today in Iceland, and Eyþór's songs are sung regularly around the country. Jóhannes Geir's paintings, on display, show saga scenes depicting life in the 13th century.

From the **Ring Road,** head north on **Route 75** to reach the Folk Museum.

SKAGAFJÖRÐUR TRANSPORTATION MUSEUM (Samgönguminjasafn Skagafjarðar)

Storagerdi, tel. 354/455-6161, www.visitskagafjordur.is, 11am-6pm daily mid-June-Aug., 800ISK

This is a great place to spend a little time inside if the weather is bad, admiring the large collection of classic vehicles under one roof. The makes and models of automobiles vary widely, and there's also some farm machinery on display dating back to the middle of the last century. Car fans will be pleased.

TANNERY VISITOR CENTER

Borgarmýri 5, tel. 354/512-8025, gestastofa@sutarinn.
is, 8am-4pm Mon.-Fri. and 8am-noon Sat.-Sun. May
15-Sept. 15, 11am-4pm Mon.-Fri. Sept. 16-May 14
Tannery Visitor Center is an interesting place for a stop. The center is the only tannery in Europe that focuses solely on fish leather, which is used for handbags, shoes, clothing, and a variety of high-end crafts. Here you can learn about the tannery process and purchase goods made from fish leather. **Tours** are available twice a day May-September and cost 500ISK.

1238: THE BATTLE OF ICELAND

Aðalgata 21, tel. 354/588-1238, www.1238.is,
8am-6pm daily, 2,700ISK adults, 1,900ISK children 6-12
The newly opened museum 1238: The Battle of Iceland uses virtual reality technology to transport guests back to the Viking age. The museum focuses on one of the most violent eras in Iceland's history, the Sturlung Era (1220-1264), when numerous battles took place. Virtual reality headsets make it seem like you are in the middle of it all.

Sports and Recreation
SAUÐÁRKRÓKUR SWIMMING POOL

Skagfirðingabraut, tel. 354/453-5226, 7am-9pm
Mon.-Fri., 10am-5pm Sat.-Sun. June-Aug.,
7am-8:30pm Mon.-Fri., 10am-4pm Sat.-Sun.
Sept.-May, 1,000ISK
The Sauðárkrókur Swimming Pool is a 25-meter (82-foot) outdoor pool with hot tubs, a sauna, and sun beds.

HLÍÐARENDI GOLF COURSE

Rte. 75, tel. 354/453-5075, www.gss.is, greens fees
4,500ISK
The Hliðarendi Golf Course is the longest nine-hole golf course in Iceland. It is located in picturesque country surroundings backdropped by mountains. Reserve a tee time in advance. The facility is open year-round, but call ahead for opening hours because they change frequently.

1: Siglufjörður harbor 2: Glaumbær

Food
HARD WOK CAFÉ

Aðalgata 8, tel. 354/453-5355, 11:45am-9:30pm
daily, entrées from 1,890ISK
Hard Wok Café is an interesting Asian/pizza fusion restaurant that seems out of place in a small town in Iceland, but it works. The food is surprising, with choices including fish and chips, stir-fry dishes, hamburgers, pizza, and Asian-inspired sandwiches. The restaurant is a favorite among locals.

KK RESTAURANT

Aðalgata 16, tel. 354/453-6299, www.kkrestaurant.is,
noon-10pm daily, entrées from 2,990ISK
KK Restaurant is in an attractive building on the main street of town that dates back to 1887. Today, it's a modern, comfortable restaurant that serves casual food like burgers and pizza, and appetizers like mozzarella sticks and onion rings. It also serves meat and fish dishes, including pan-fried Arctic char, roasted lobster tails, and lamb fillet. The dinner buffet (5,800ISK) is quite popular and features appetizers, pizza, and fish entrées.

Accommodations
MIKLIGARÐUR GUESTHOUSE

Kirkjutorg 3, tel. 354/453-6880, www.arctichotels.is,
rooms from 16,000ISK
This guesthouse does not get points for style—the decor is dated and the rooms are small and a bit sad—but the rooms are clean and the staff is accommodating. Guests have access to shared bathroom facilities, free Wi-Fi, and free parking, and a tasty breakfast is included in the room price.

HÓTEL MIKLIGARÐUR

Skagfirðingabraut 24, tel. 354/453-6330, www.
arctichotels.is, rooms from 26,000ISK
Hótel Mikligarður offers 65 small rooms with private bathrooms, and not much else. There aren't a lot of amenities, but the location is convenient and it makes for an adequate short stay. Free Wi-Fi is available, and breakfast is included.

NORTH ICELAND
SKAGAFJÖRÐUR

HÓTEL TINDASTÓLL

Lindargata 3, tel. 354/453-5002, www.arctichotels.is, rooms from 26,000ISK

Hótel Tindastóll occupies two adjacent buildings. The original, a green house with a traditional look, has the distinction of being the oldest hotel in Iceland. It opened in 1884 and has undergone a number of renovations. The rooms are cozy, tastefully decorated, and have the feeling of home. In 2012, the second building opened, and its rooms are spacious, bright, and modern with flat-screen TVs, free Wi-Fi, and private bathrooms. Breakfast is included.

Getting There

By car, take **Route 75,** which is paved, from the **Ring Road.** Sauðárkrókur is about 25 minutes or 25 kilometers (16 miles) north of **Varmahlíð.**

DRANGEY

Drangey is a small, rocky island, dotted with moss and grass, in the middle of Skagafjörður. Its steep cliffs jut almost 200 meters (656 feet) out of the sea. The island is home to pure natural beauty and thriving birdlife. Drangey is a favorite nesting spot for puffins and guillemots, along with razor-billed auks, ravens, gyrfalcons, and other seabirds.

Other than the secluded beauty and birdlife, Drangey is known for its inclusion in several sagas. Grettir Ásmundarson was said to have lived on the island for nearly three years with his brother Illugi. Grettir swam to Reykir (a farm) from Drangey to get equipment to make a fire, a pretty daring journey considering the water temperature.

Getting There

During the summer months you can reach the island by boat from the **Sauðárkrókur marina. Drangey Tours** (tel. 354/821-0090, www.drangey.net) operates daily boat trips (11am June-mid-Aug., 13,500ISK adults, 7,000ISK children 7-14, free for children 6 and under). The excursion takes about four hours, and it's a wonderful way to spend the day. Be sure to check the schedule, as it may change due to weather. It is not necessary to book in advance.

Tröllaskagi

Tröllaskagi (Troll Peninsula), which lies between the fjords Skagafjörður and Eyjafjörður, has a gorgeous mountainous landscape, with some peaks reaching more than 1,400 meters (4,594 feet) above sea level. Several deep valleys throughout the peninsula were created by glaciers and rivers. Tröllaskagi offers opportunities for outdoor activities, including hiking and whale-watching.

DALVÍK

Dalvík is a small fishing town perhaps best known to tourists as the gateway to **Grímsey** and **Hrísey** islands, as the ferry to those places departs from the **Dalvík harbor.** But it's also a great spot for hikers up for the challenge of navigating the hilly and mountainous landscape around the town. Every year in late June or early July, there is a **"hiking week"** in Dalvík, during which groups get together and hike with a guide.

Sights

SVARFAÐARDALUR NATURE RESERVE

Route 805

In a valley just west of town, the Svarfaðardalur Nature Reserve is about 8 square kilometers (3 square miles) of wetlands on the banks of the Svarfaðardalsá. The unspoiled environment is a perfect breeding ground for a number of bird species, including great northern divers and harlequin ducks. Be sure to watch where you walk to avoid nests. Wear rubber boots in wet weather.

HERITAGE MUSEUM OF DALVÍK
(Byggðasafnið Dalvík)

Hvoli við Karlsrauðatorg, tel. 354/460-4928, www.
dalvikurbyggd.is, 11am-6pm daily June 1-Aug 31.,
2pm-5pm Sat. Sept 1-Nov. 30 and Feb. 1-May 30,
adults 870ISK, seniors 540ISK

The Heritage Museum of Dalvík has an extensive collection of photographs and objects, including tools and home furnishings, that relate to the life and work of Dalvík's residents over the years. A natural history collection contains mounts of Icelandic mammals and birds, along with eggs, rocks, shells, and grass/moss. Other exhibits relate to renowned individuals that hail from the area, ranging from politicians to artists. The collection is vast and a bit quirky.

Sports and Recreation
THE BEER SPA
(Bjórböðin)

Ægisgata 31, tel. 354/414-2828, www.bjorbodin.is,
11am-9pm daily, 9,900ISK, couples bath 16,900ISK

The Beer Spa is an exciting development in North Iceland, owned and operated by local brewery Kaldi, which offers brewery tours daily (www.bruggsmidjan.is). The Beer Spa features seven spa tubs (maximum two people) made from kambala wood that are full of beer for a relaxing soak. Once you arrive at the facility, a staff member welcomes you, explains the soaking process, provides you with a towel, and shows you to the locker room.

After you secure your belongings and change into a bathing suit, you'll be shown to your bath in a private room. Guests have 25 minutes to soak in the beer bath, and then you head to a relaxation room for another 25 minutes. There are also two outside hot tubs requiring a separate entry fee (2,000ISK, 500ISK if you are taking a beer bath) that can hold 8-10 people. It's recommended you not shower for at least four hours afterward so your skin reaps the benefits of the therapeutic bath. It's also recommended you book your reservation in advance online.

At the 75-seat **restaurant** (entrées from 2,280ISK-390ISK), enjoy a meal or a beer

inside or, if the weather is nice, outside on a lovely patio that overlooks the mountainous landscape. It's a casual eatery with a friendly staff, and the menu includes nachos, french fries, sandwiches, and a soup of the day. The Kaldi Burger is the winner, topped with bacon, cheese, caramelized onions, and tomatoes. There's a kids' menu as well.

The Beer Spa is located about 12 kilometers (7 miles) southeast of Dalvík via **Routes 82** and **808**, both of which are paved.

ARCTIC SEA TOURS

tel. 354/771-7600, www.arcticseatours.is, daily,
9,900ISK per person

Arctic Sea Tours operates a three-hour whale-watching tour where you have a 98-percent chance of seeing whales or dolphins, according to the company. You might get to see white-beaked dolphins, minke whales, harbor porpoises, and, if you're lucky, a humpback whale or an enormous blue whale. At the end of the tour, you will have an opportunity to do some fishing, and the fresh catches (most likely cod) will be grilled back on land for all to enjoy. The tours leave from Dalvík harbor year-round.

DALVÍK SWIMMING POOL

Svarfaðarbraut 34, tel. 354/466-3233, 6:15am-8pm
Mon.-Fri., 9am-5pm Sat.-Sun., 900ISK

The Dalvík Swimming Pool is close to the town's campsite, so expect a crowd in the summer months. The facility has an outdoor pool, hot tubs, a children's pool, waterslide, sauna, and gym.

ARNARHOLT GOLF COURSE

Arnarholt Svarfaðardal, tel. 354/466-1204,
year-round, greens fees 5,000ISK

Just 7 kilometers (4.3 miles) outside Dalvík is the Arnarholt Golf Course, a nine-hole course said to have been built on a 9th-century burial ground. If that doesn't spook you away, you'll find a course that is well maintained, and carts, clubs, and equipment are available to rent. Be sure to call ahead for a tee time. An on-site **restaurant** is open 1pm-9pm daily.

Festivals and Events
HIKING WEEK
www.dalvikurbyggd.is, late June/early July
Dalvík is quite hilly, and locals love to hike. Every summer, locals and tourists gather for a "hiking week," which features nine different guided hikes over nine days on which hikers explore the mountains along Tröllaskagi. Hikes range between 2-10 hours and vary in difficulty from leisurely walks along the Dalvík harbor to steep mountain climbs. Pay in advance to join the hikes (check out their website for more information); shorter hikes cost 1,500ISK and longer hikes are 3,000ISK.

Food and Accommodations
GREGOR'S PUB
Goðabraut 3, tel. 354/847-8846, 6pm-10pm daily, entrées from 2,000ISK
Gregor's Pub offers a great casual dining experience ranging from soup to tender lamb fillets. The menu also includes hamburgers, sandwiches, and pizza. At night the place transforms into a bar where locals gather to grab a pint and catch up.

HOTEL DALVÍK
Skiðabraut 18, tel. 354/466-3395, www.fosshotel.is, rooms from 16,200ISK
Hotel Dalvík has 30 clean and average-sized rooms with standard beds, private bathrooms, and free Wi-Fi. The rooms have a bit of a 1980s feel to them, with red carpeting and gold accents. In addition to double rooms, Hotel Dalvík offers bungalos and a junior suite. An on-site restaurant serves breakfast (included in the price of the room), and guests have access to free parking.

YTRI-VÍK LODGE
Árskógsströnd, tel. 354/466-1982, www.sporttours.is, cottages from 30,000ISK
Ytri-Vík Lodge offers cottages that range from accommodations for two people up to a three-story house for a large group. The cottages are made from wood and have fully equipped kitchens, roomy sleeping spaces, and all the comforts of home. The cottages all have decks, which have glorious views of the sea with mountains looming in the background. It's a gorgeous scene to enjoy while sipping your morning coffee.

DALVÍK CAMPGROUND
Sundlaug Dalvíkur, tel. 354/460-4940, 1,700ISK
The Dalvík Campground is close to the town's swimming pool. The facility is pretty basic, with an adequate cooking area and warm showers. The campground, which accommodates tents and RVs (with hookups), is open June-August. In addition to the pool, there is a nice playground nearby, as well as a football pitch and a basketball court.

Information and Services
BERG MENNINGARHUS CULTURAL CENTER
Goðabraut, tel. 354/846-4908, info@dalvikurbyggd.is, 10am-5pm Mon.-Fri., 1pm-5pm Sat.
The tourist information center is based inside the Berg Menningarhus Cultural Center and offers Internet access, pamphlets about the region, maps, and information about local sights.

Getting There
BY CAR
Dalvík is 34 kilometers (21 miles) southeast of **Siglufjörður** on **Route 82,** which is paved; 18 kilometers (11 miles) south of **Ólafsfjörður** on Route 82; and 42 kilometers (26 miles) south of **Akureyri,** also on Route 82.

BY BOAT
The ferry **Sæfari** (www.saefari.is) provides daily trips from **Dalvík Harbor** to the islands of **Grímsey** (about 3.5 hours away) and **Hrísey** (a short 30 minutes away). Check the website for the latest timetable, as it tends to change.

HRÍSEY

Hrísey was established as a herring station and today is a major tourist draw. Known as the "pearl of Eyjafjörður," the island, which is 35 kilometers (22 miles) north of Akureyri, has a lot of appeal for **bird-watching** enthusiasts.

Hrísey is 7.5 kilometers (4.6 miles) long and 2.4 kilometers (1.4 miles) wide, and about 200 people call it home. Its population soars during the summer months when ferries full of tourists come to shore.

The attractions are minimal, but tractor rides on a hay wagon are quite popular, and there's a small exhibition on shark hunting. The **tractor rides** (tel. 354/695-0077, 1,300ISK, children are free) are about 40 minutes long and take visitors around the island. The main reason tourists come to Hrísey is for the nature, and it's wise to budget one full day for the island.

Sights
THE HOUSE OF SHARK-JÖRUNDUR (Jörundur Hus)
Norðurvegur 3, 354/695-0077, www.hrisey.net, 1pm-5pm daily June-Aug.
This small museum houses objects related to shark hunting. The house was owned and built by Jörundur Jónsson, called Shark-Jörundur, in 1885, using timber from Norwegian ships that had run ashore on Hrísey. In 1917 the house was moved down the hill to its current site, but a statue of Jörundur is erected where the house originally stood.

BIRD-WATCHING
About 40 bird species nest in Hrísey, and its populations thrive because hunting and egg collection are strictly prohibited and there are no predators (such as mice, mink, or foxes) on the island. Hrísey is known for having the densest population of ptarmigans in Iceland during the nesting season. The **southern part** of the island has the best bird-watching opportunities along the edges.

Festivals and Events
HRÍSEY FAMILY FESTIVAL
www.hrisey.is, July, free
A family festival is held on the island every year, on a weekend in July. The festivities include music, tractor rides around the island, food vendors, and a bonfire at night. For the kids, there's a playground, clowns, and sandcastle-building at the beach. The festival is free and open to everyone.

Food and Accommodations
Lodging options on the island are very limited. Many visitors opt to spend the day at Hrísey and sleep in Akureyri or Dalvík.

WAVE GUESTHOUSE
Austurvegi 9, www.waveguesthouse.com, rooms from 10,000ISK
If you would like to spend the night on Hrísey, Wave Guesthouse is your chance. The guesthouse has four rooms—three doubles and a single—and the warm hosts make you feel like you're staying with relatives. It's cozy, with comfy quilts in each room. Rooms are bright with simple IKEA furnishings, and guests have access to a common lounge, a shared kitchen, shared bathrooms, and a gas grill.

HRÍSEY CAMPGROUND
tel. 354/461-2255, June-Aug., 1,500ISK
The Hrísey Campground is small with adequate facilities. It's conveniently located next to the swimming pool. The campsite, which is in an open field, has showers, hot and cold water, and restrooms. The location in the center of town and close to the sea is lovely, but it can get quite chilly. Be sure to have appropriate gear for cold temperatures.

Information and Services
TOURIST INFORMATION OFFICE
Norðurvegur 3, tel. 354/695-0077, hrisey@hrisey. net, www.hrisey.is
The tourist information office is open daily June-August, and you can book tours, buy tickets for the ferry, and get maps and information about the island.

Getting There
The ferry **Sævar** (tel. 354/695-5544, www. hrisey.is) sails between the island and the nearby village of **Árskógssandur,** just a few kilometers east of Dalvík. Sævar sails nine times daily June 1-August 31, and a round-trip fare costs 3,000ISK for adults or 1,500ISK for

children 12-15. The ferry trip takes less than 30 minutes and is subject to weather conditions. Be sure to call ahead for current departure times, as they tend to change often due to stormy weather.

SIGLUFJÖRÐUR

Just a one-hour drive from Akureyri, secluded Siglufjörður is the northernmost town in all of Iceland. It's easy to fall in love with this beautiful harbor town. Siglufjörður's marina is home to much of the activity in the village, with bustling restaurants and a few town-specific museums focusing on the herring industry and the local music scene. For much of the year, the town of less than 2,000 is quiet, as it endures a sometimes-punishing winter with wind that feels like it's cutting right through you. That said, skiers are attracted to the region, and there are a couple of trails to enjoy. In the summer, however, the town comes alive with exhibitions, concerts, and packed coffeehouses and restaurants.

Sights

Buying a ticket to the Herring Era Museums also grants you entry into the **Folk Music Center;** the **Icelandic Poetry Center** (Túngötu 5, tel. 354/865-6543, noon-4pm daily), which houses numerous books of poetry and hosts events in Icelandic; and the **Old Slipway** (Snorragata 10, tel. 354/467-1604, 10am-6pm daily), a boatyard that includes an exhibition on the 200-year history of boatbuilding in the town.

HERRING ERA MUSEUM (Síldarminjasafn Íslands)
Snorragata 10, tel. 354/467-1604, www.sild.is, 10am-6pm daily June-Aug., 1pm-5pm daily May and Sept., by appointment rest of the year, 1,800ISK
The Herring Era Museum is one of the most well-presented museums in Iceland. Yes, it's educational and it's about fish, but it's anything but boring. The main exhibition is based in a large red building named Róaldsbrakki, a former Norwegian salting station that was built in 1907. Inside are interactive exhibits

of photographs and film clips showing how fish was processed and salted, which was the source of the town's livelihood for generations. There's a boat inside, along with a lot of fishing gear and equipment. It's clear that great care went into creating this museum. If you're in town, this is definitely worth a visit.

FOLK MUSIC CENTER (Þjóðlagasetrið Siglufjörður)
Norðurgata 1, tel. 354/467-2300, www.folkmusik.is, noon-6pm daily June-Aug., by request rest of year, 800ISK
The Folk Music Center is a charming two-floor museum set in what once was the private home of folklorist Reverend Bjarni Þorsteinsson (1861-1938). The museum showcases Bjarni's collection of classic Icelandic folk songs, along with interesting instruments, photographs, and film clips. You have the opportunity to listen to music that includes genres like hymns, the traditional chanting style called *rimur,* and nursery rhymes.

Festivals and Events
HERRING FESTIVAL
www.hatid.is, first weekend in August
The Herring Festival, which is held the first weekend in August, is a fun event for locals and tourists alike. Guests can enjoy music, theatrical performances, a huge herring buffet, and fireworks in the evening.

Sports and Recreation
SIGLUFJÖRÐUR SKIING CENTER
Tjarnargata 14, tel. 354/467-2120, 10am-4pm Mon. and Thur.-Sun., 3pm-7pm Tues.-Wed. in winter, 3,500ISK
Iceland is not known for skiing, but there are a few ski areas in the north, with the Siglufjörður Skiing Center being the best. Three lifts carry skiers up to the slopes, with the highest lift measuring 530 meters (1,728 feet) in length with a vertical rise of about 180

1: Dalvík **2:** The Beer Spa **3:** Herring Era Museum **4:** Restaurant Hannes Boy

meters (591 feet). The top of the lift is over 650 meters (2,133 feet). The scenery is breathtaking. All the equipment you need is available to rent, and there are instructors on-site. Snowboarding and cross-country skiing are also possible. It's typically open November-April, but that can change due to weather; be sure to call ahead.

SIGLUFJÖRÐUR SWIMMING POOL

Hvanneyrarbraut 52, tel. 354/467-1352, 6:30am-7pm Mon.-Fri., 10am-6pm Sat.-Sun., 800ISK

The Siglufjörður Swimming Pool is a delightful place to spend a couple of hours when the weather is frightful. You will find a lot of locals and their children enjoying the pool. The facility includes an indoor pool and a large hot tub outside.

Food

KAFFI RAUÐKA

Gránugata 19, tel. 354/467-1550, www.kaffiraudka.is, 11am-10pm daily, snacks from 800ISK

Kaffi Rauðka is hands down the town's best place to hang out in the summer. The outdoor seating area is filled with tourists and locals sipping coffee drinks or cocktails or enjoying light meals. Inside, the two levels are decorated in a rustic theme with lots of wood and loads of comfort. The bright red building is hard to miss, and it's owned and operated by the same folks who own Hannes Boy next door.

TORGIÐ

Aðalgata 32, tel. 354/467-2323, 5pm-9pm Sun.-Thur., 5pm-1am Fri.-Sat., entrées from 2,100ISK

Torgið is the best family-friendly option as well as the best place to grab a quick bite to eat before heading out to explore the surroundings. Tourist-friendly fare on the menu includes hamburgers, sandwiches, and pizza, as well as some seafood options.

HARBOR HOUSE CAFÉ

Gránugata 5b, tel. 354/659-1394, www.harborhouse. is, lunch noon-2pm, dinner 6pm-10pm daily, entrées from 2,490ISK

Harbor House Café is a small harborside café that sells light meals and coffee for lunch and delectable seafood dishes for dinner. The seafood soup with mussels, shrimp, and lobster is memorable. The café is small and cozy, and the staff is very friendly. You will see a local or two with their laptop and a cup of coffee or tourists curling up with a book to get out of the rain.

★ RESTAURANT HANNES BOY

Gránugata 23, tel. 354/461-7734, www.hannesboy.is, 11:30am-9pm daily, entrées from 2,690ISK

Restaurant Hannes Boy cannot be missed. Literally. It's a bright yellow structure on the harbor that doesn't give much of a hint to what's inside. The interior is chic with roomy wood tables, antique furnishings, and a menu that rivals restaurants in much larger cities. The small courses, using fresh ingredients including mackerel, herring, and cod, are a great way to start the meal, and the main courses are hard to choose from because they all sound so delicious. You can't go wrong with the catch of the day or the deep-fried pork belly with potatoes.

SEGULL 67 BRUGGHÚS

Vetrarbraut 8-10, tel. 354/863-2120, www.segull67.is

A newly opened family-owned microbrewery situated in the heart of Siglufjörður, Segull 67 Brugghús was established in a converted fish factory. The brewery offers tours that include a beer tasting for 2,500ISK per person. Call ahead for the tour schedule.

Accommodations

★ SIGLUNES GUESTHOUSE

Laekjargata 10, tel. 354/467-1222, www.hotelsiglunes. is, rooms from 18,000ISK

Siglunes Guesthouse is the hippest place to stay in the north, and it attracts a lot of young travelers. The interior is darling, with vintage wood furniture and cool rugs, art, and wallpaper. Ten rooms have private bathrooms. It's a mixture of vintage and retro furniture that works well. An old-fashioned piano and fireplace are in the lobby area, and it's a great place to relax after a day of exploring the sights. Rooms are larger than average, with comfy beds and an antique flavor to the decor. Breakfast is included in the room price, and the in-house restaurant and bar is quite popular.

THE HERRING HOUSE GUESTHOUSE

Hlíðarvegur 1, tel. 354/868-4200, www.theherringhouse.com, rooms from 22,000ISK

This charming guesthouse offers four rooms and is just a 2-minute walk to the center of town. The guesthouse has a lovely garden and a terrace with sweeping views of the mountainous scenery. Rooms are spacious with minimal decor, and there are shared bathroom facilities and free Wi-Fi during your stay.

SIGLÓ HÓTEL

Snorragata 3, tel. 354/461-7730, www.siglohotel.is, rooms from 40,000ISK

Sigló Hótel is a beautiful property along the harbor and close to major town attractions. Rooms, ranging from doubles to suites, are all bright and airy with private bathrooms. All rooms have a window seat overlooking the town, free Wi-Fi, a TV, and comfortable furniture. Breakfast is included in the price.

SIGLUFJÖRÐUR CAMPGROUND

Gránugötu 24, tel. 354/460-5600, mid-May-mid-Oct., 1,300ISK

The Siglufjörður Campground is near the center of town, close to the harbor and with beautiful mountain views. It has a cooking area and hot showers. The campsite is in an open field with little shelter and welcomes tent campers as well as RVs. The main museums and restaurants are all within walking distance. Electricity costs 1,100ISK and washing machines are available for 900ISK per wash.

Getting There

Getting to Siglufjörður is a trying exercise at times. From Akureyi, **Route 82** and **Route 76,** both paved, connect to Siglufjörður, if the weather is cooperating. This region can have heavy snowfall and it is always best to frequently check road conditions at www.road.is. The trip takes about 1 hour 15 minutes.

A **tunnel** links **Siglufjörður, Olafsfjörður,** and **Dalvík.** Driving through the one-lane, two-way tunnel can be heartstopping, with cars turning into pockets on the side to let the driver going the opposite way pass by. **Ólafsfjörður** is 17 kilometers (11 miles) southeast of Siglufjörður on Route 76.

Grímsey

About 40 kilometers (25 miles) off the coast of Iceland, Grímsey is a windswept and secluded island, about five square kilometers (3 square miles) in area, that is as striking in beauty as it is difficult to reach.

Just 100 people reside in Grímsey, and those who remain come from hardy stock, battling arctic temperatures and isolation. Fishers brave the elements, including frost and storms and waves that could reach 15 meters (49 feet) high. It's not an easy life.

Tourists come to explore the tiny island, bird-watch, and experience 24 hours of daylight in the height of the summer. Night does not reach Grímsey until late July, when the sun sets around midnight, only to rise a short time later. The island can be explored in one day.

SIGHTS
Grímseyjarkirkja

Center of town

Grímseyjarkirkja, the Grímsey Church, was built in 1867 from driftwood that washed ashore. The building was renovated and enlarged in 1932. The exterior is white with a reddish-brown roof. The highlight of the church is the altar painting, a copy of a

Crossing the Arctic Circle

Want to witness the **midnight sun?** That's when the sun remains above the horizon for a full 24 hours during the summer solstice on June 21. There's only one place you can experience this phenomenon in Iceland: where the Arctic Circle crosses the country's northernmost point, on Grímsey. (If you'd prefer nearly 24 hours of darkness, there's always **polar night,** on December 21.)

A small **symbolic bridge** crossing the Arctic Circle can be found at 66°33'N, north of Grímsey's airport terminal and next to Guesthouse Básar. Beside the bridge is a pole showing the distance to many well-known cities in the world, including London and New York.

Tourists who make the pilgrimage can buy evidence of their trip in the form of a **diploma** in the local gift store **Gallerí Sól** (Sólberg 611, tel. 354/467-3190, gullsol@visir.is), which is open Monday, Wednesday, and Friday during the summer months (June-Aug.). You can also reserve your diploma at Gallerí Sól by phone or email. Diplomas cost 1,000ISK. Those who come to Grímsey on a tour receive a diploma free of charge.

Leonardo da Vinci piece, that was done by a local artist in 1878.

The history of the church site is interesting; one of Iceland's early Catholic bishops, Jón Ögmundsson, consecrated a church on Grímsey in the 11th century, dedicated to St. Olaf, the patron saint of Norway. At the time, it was said that there should always be two priests at the church who should lead a daily mass (two a day on special occasions). Today a vicar from the mainland visits Grímsey to serve in the church approximately four times a year.

The Cliffs
East side of island

The cliffs on the east side of the island tower 60 to 100 meters (197 to 328 feet). In the old days, the basalt cliffs served as a major source of food, as locals collected eggs along the rifts. It was a tenuous task: a rope would be lowered 60 meters down from the edge of the cliff while the individual collected eggs. There was a great risk that the rope would break or a large rock could break off, hitting and killing the climber. Today, the egg collection practice is safer and more modern, but the cliffs are a reminder of the past and their importance to the island's sustenance. They're also interesting formations and serve as a great backdrop when photographing birds.

The Lighthouse
(southeast corner)

Bright yellow and close to the cliff's edge, Grímsey's lighthouse is one of the most significant buildings on the island. It was built in 1937 and is situated on the southeast corner of the island. It was originally operated manually with a gas lamp that had to be turned on and off by hand. Today, the lighthouse is automatic and still plays an important role in directing boat traffic along the coast. Although the lighthouse itself is closed to the public, it's a popular place for photos, capturing birdlife and the cliffs in the background.

FESTIVALS AND EVENTS

SUMMER SOLSTICE FESTIVAL
www.visitakureyri.is/en, June, free

The summer solstice brings nearly 24 hours of complete daylight to Iceland, and locals on Grímsey celebrate every June. The festival includes live music, markets, guided walks, a family scavenger hunt, and a seafood buffet. The festival is free, except for the seafood buffet, and is open to everyone.

GRÍMSEY DAY
www.grimsey.is, June

Grímsey Day is an annual festival that takes place at the beginning of June each year over three days. It focuses on old traditions from Grímsey, like collecting eggs from the cliffs, as well as enjoying seasonal local food, music, and art.

SPORTS AND RECREATION
Bird-Watching

Grímsey is one of the best spots in North Iceland for bird-watchers interested in seabirds. The high season for birding is from **April,** when birds migrate to the island to nest, to **August,** when birds depart the island for warmer weather. Bird-watchers will have a chance to see arctic terns, black-legged kittiwakes, northern fulmars, razorbills, common guillemots, black guillemots, and murres. You can also see white wagtails, northern wheatears, and snow buntings.

The main attractions, however, are the adorable **Atlantic puffins,** as Grímsey is home to one of the largest colonies in Iceland. The birds, with their bright beaks and big personalities, are a delight to watch nesting and gliding along the cliffs. Please be aware of eggs and be careful not to disturb nesting areas during the spring. Grímsey is a small island and the best birdwatching spots are the cliffs that line the island.

Swimming
GRÍMSEY ISLAND THERMAL POOL

tel. 354/461-3155, 8pm-9:30pm Mon.-Wed., 2pm-4pm Sat., 1,000ISK

The Grímsey Island Thermal Pool is situated near the airport and is a quiet spot to take a dip. You likely won't find crowds here, and the hours change often. For current hours, inquire at the tourist information office or at your guesthouse.

FOOD AND ACCOMMODATIONS
RESTAURANT KRIAN

Hafnargata 3, tel. 354/467-3112, www.grimsey.is, noon-midnight daily summer, entrées from 2,400ISK

Restaurant Krian is only open during the summer, but it will open to accommodate large groups (up to 50 people) on request. The menu focuses on local fare and is chock-full of fresh fish and meat from seabirds, like pan-fried puffin. Standard options include sandwiches and hamburgers.

GUESTHOUSE GULLSÓL

Sólbergi, 354/467-3190, www.gullsol.is, rooms from 13,000ISK

Guesthouse Gullsól offers four single rooms and two doubles in a charming wood house,

an Atlantic puffin colony on the cliffs of Grímsey

one of the oldest structures on the island. Rooms are small, but clean and neat, and it's the closest guesthouse to the main population area. Guests share bathroom facilities and have access to a fully equipped kitchen to prepare meals. It's open year-round.

GUESTHOUSE BÁSAR

tel. 354/467-3103, www.gistiheimilibasar.is, rooms from 20,000ISK

Guesthouse Básar, next to the small airport, is an eight-room guesthouse just steps from the Arctic Circle. Literally. Rooms are simple and neat, and amenities include a common TV lounge and a fully equipped kitchen. Breakfast is included, and lunch and dinner can be requested as well. The guesthouse is open year-round.

INFORMATION AND SERVICES

TOURIST INFORMATION CENTER

Hof concert hall, Akureyri, tel. 354/460-1199, www.visitakureyri.is

A few years ago, the towns of Grímsey, Hrísey, and Akureyri voted to become a municipality overseen by Akureyri. Tourist information and ferry fares schedules for all three towns can be found at the tourist information center at Hof concert hall by the harbor in Akureyri.

Safety

Weather can be your greatest enemy on the island, with unexpected wind gusts and horizontal rain. All children under the age of 14 must wear a life jacket when in the harbor area, whether they are playing, walking, or about to board a ferry. It is island law. The ferry staff provides life jackets at the harbor.

GETTING THERE
By Boat

Sæfari (tel. 354/458-8970, www.samskip.is) operates ferry service between **Dalvík** and Grímsey five times a week in the summer and three times a week in the winter. It takes about three hours each way, and the ferry holds 108 people. Book in advance in the summer months; tickets can be purchased at the **tourist information office** at Hof concert hall in Akureyri (tel. 354/450-1050, info@visitakureyri.is). A round-trip fare is 7,000ISK. Departure times from Dalvík in the summer are Monday, Tuesday, Wednesday, Friday, and Sunday at 9am; the ferry returns from Grímsey at 8pm. Check the website for up-to-date departure information. Schedules can vary due to weather.

By Air

The flight from **Akureyri** to Grímsey is one of the most beautiful 30-minute airplane rides you will ever take. The jaw-dropping views of the landscape make the trip feel a tad too short. The landing is not for the faint of heart, as the small plane has to land on a miniscule strip of grass on an island that looks like a rock in the middle of the ocean. During the summer (June-August), **Air Iceland Connect** (www.airicelandconnect.com) provides daily flights to Grímsey (the airport is within walking distance from town) from Akureyri (Urðargil 15) for about 40,000ISK round-trip. For current departure timetables and precise ticket prices, check Air Iceland's website. There are four flights a week September-May.

Akureyri

Akureyri is commonly referred to as Iceland's "second city," a moniker many of the town's 18,000 residents find amusing given its small size. Akureyri has its own personality, and it looks and feels quite different from Reykjavík, more low-key and relaxed than the capital city. There are gorgeous gardens to explore, charming museums, paddleboats littering the fjord in the summer months, and a booming art scene.

Akureyri has a tighter community than Reykjavík, and there is a lot of support for local artists. Painters, sculptors, and crafts-people occupy numerous private studios. The museums reflect the rich cultural landscape of the town, displaying varied works from some of the region's most important artists.

Akureyri also boasts delicious restaurants and first-rate hotels, and its concert hall, Hof, is a must-see for architecture enthusiasts. Akureyri is a perfect place to base yourself while exploring the Tröllskagi peninsula and Eyjafjörður, Iceland's longest fjord at 60 kilometers (37.2 miles).

Many tourists choose Akureyri as their home base when exploring the north, opting to spend nights in the town while booking day tours or putting some miles on their rental car to places like Húsavík and Mývatn.

Akureyri has gotten more traffic in recent years as a popular stop for cruise ships, and word is spreading about this charming, beautiful town. It's also surprisingly easy to get to. If you have the time, spend at least a couple of days here.

Akureyri

© MOON.COM

SIGHTS

★ Akureyri Botanical Gardens
(Lystigarður Akureyrar)

Eyrarlandsholt, tel. 354/462-7487, www.lystigardur. akureyri.is, 8am-10pm Mon.-Fri., 9am-10pm Sat.-Sun. June-Sept., free

The Akureyri Botanical Gardens are gorgeous and well kept; it's hard to find a better place in the city to take a stroll. The attraction is treasured by locals, and they're thrilled to share the beauty and tranquility with tourists. Known as one of the northernmost botanical gardens in the world, the public park opened in 1912, and flowers and plants made their debut in the park in 1957. Thousands of types of native and international flora can be found in the garden beds and nursery. While roaming the gardens during the summer, you'll see arctic poppy flowers, northern marsh violets, bilberry bushes, frog orchids, and hundreds of other species. The caretakers are always introducing new species to keep the collection fresh and eclectic. You'll also find walking paths, bridges, and a fountain in the gardens.

Akureyrarkirkja

Eyrarlandsvegur, tel. 354/462-7700, www. akureyrarkirkja.is, 10am-4pm Mon.-Sat., 4pm-7pm Sun. June 15-Aug. 15, free

The Akureyrarkirkja, the Akureyri Church, is in the center of the city, rising above it on a hill. The steep steps up to the grounds, with the church towering above, make for a great photo opportunity. The church was designed by state architect Guðjón Samúelsson, who delivered a design that is unique and Icelandic, with stark white walls, wood pews, and a lot of windows. While the outside is beautiful, the interior is exquisite, complete with a 3,200-pipe organ and a large central window that once belonged to Coventry Cathedral in England. The church, which was completed in 1940, is open to the public in the summer. The **Sunday service** is at 11am year-round, and tourists are more than welcome to join. Please note that the church is closed to tourists during funerals or other ceremonies.

Nonnahús

Aðalstræti 54, tel. 354/462-3555, www.nonni.is, 10am-5pm daily June 1-Sept. 1, 10am-5pm Thur.-Sun. Sept. 2-Oct. 1, closed rest of the year, 1,400ISK adults, free for children 17 and under

Nonnahús, or Nonni's House, is a museum in the childhood home of Jesuit priest and children's author Jón Sveinsson (1857-1944). The house gets its name from Jón's nickname, Nonni, and it's one of the oldest structures in the town. The house was built in 1850, and it looks like a nondescript black wooden house from the outside. Inside, however, you get a sense of the life and work of one of Akureyri's most treasured sons. On the ground floor, there is a collection of Jón's books, from about 40 different countries where his works were published. Upstairs, you can get a look at his bedroom and some personal artifacts. A little **gift shop** sells his books in various languages.

Center for Visual Arts (Sjónlistamiðstöðin)

Kaupvangsstræti 12, tel. 354/461-2610, www.listasafn. akureyri.is

The Center for Visual Arts comprises three art museums in three separate buildings. The first, the **Akureyri Art Museum (Listasafnið á Akureyri)** (10am-5pm daily May-Sept., noon-5pm daily Oct.-Apr., 1,500ISK), hosts exhibitions in a variety of media, including landscape and portrait paintings, sculpture, photography, and other visual arts. The exhibitions focus on contemporary art. New exhibitions are revealed every eight weeks or so. The second building is the gallery **Kettle House (Ketilhús),** which serves as a space for local concerts and meetings, as well as art- and design-related events. Exhibitions in Kettle House are by invitation only and can include everything from painting exhibitions to performance art. The third building, **Melting Pot (Deiglan),** across the street from the Akureyri Art Museum, is devoted to young artists, giving them a platform to express and show their work.

Museum of Icelandic Folk and Outsider Art (Safnasafnið)

Svalbarðsstrond, tel. 354/461-4066, www.folkart.is, 10am-5pm daily May 15-Aug. 31, 1,000ISK

For something a little different, try the Museum of Icelandic Folk and Outsider Art, one of those quirky museums that doesn't get the attention it deserves. The museum is the only institution on the island that collects and displays outsider art. It houses 5,000 works

1: the Akureyri Botanical Gardens **2:** Akureyri street **3:** Akureyrarkirkja

from local artists, as well as a library and research facility. You will find paintings, sculptures, drawings, models, books, dolls, tools, and toys. Every year there are about 15 new exhibitions on display, delighting locals and surprising tourists with art you won't see anywhere else on the island. The museum is 12 kilometers (7.5 miles) north of Akureyri on Route 1.

Friðbjarnarhús

Aðalstræti 46, tel. 354/863-4531, 1pm-5pm daily June-Sept., 2pm-4pm Sat. Oct.-May, 800ISK adults, free for children under 15

Friðbjarnarhús, Friðbjörn's House, holds an exhibition of 20th-century toys owned by Akureyri resident Guðbjörg Ringsted. The museum, in an old house built in 1856, is great for kids and kids at heart, with dolls, toy cars, models, and hundreds of other toys on display.

Aviation Museum
(Flugsafn Íslands)

Akureyri Airport, tel. 354/461-4400, www.flugsafn.is/en, 11am-5pm daily, 1,500ISK

The Aviation Museum is a small museum located at a hangar at the airport, dedicated to the planes and pilots who have flown the windy skies over Iceland. On display are a flying ambulance and Iceland's first gliders, as well as some relics from World War II, when U.S. and British troops occupied Iceland. There are lots of photographs and some accounts from pilots.

Akureyri Museum
(Minjasafnið á Akureyri)

Aðalstræti 58, tel. 354/462-4162, www.minjasafnid.is, 10am-5pm daily, 2,000ISK

The Akureyri Museum has historical exhibitions including displays that feature nautical maps, 19th-century photography, and artifacts from everyday life in the settlement era. The exhibits also detail the region's geological background and its role in saga stories. The museum grounds have a beautiful garden.

Akureyri Museum of Industry
(Iðnaðarsafnið á Akureyri)

Krókeyri, tel. 354/462-3600, www.idnadarsafnid.is, 10am-5pm daily June-mid-Sept., 2pm-4pm Sat. mid-Sept.-May, 1,500ISK

The Akureyri Museum of Industry displays relics from Iceland's industries, such as agriculture, fishing, and construction, throughout the years. Exhibitions include products, machinery, and photos of people hard at work in the region. It's a quaint museum with a passionate curator, but you can skip this if time is an issue.

Motorcycle Museum of Iceland
(Mótorhjólasafnið)

Krókeyri 2, tel. 354/866-3500, www.motorhjolasafn.is, noon-6pm daily June 1-Aug. 31, 3pm-7pm Sat. only Sept. 1-May 31, 1,000ISK adults, free for children 13 and under

A small museum founded in the memory of local biker Heidar Johannsson, this museum has about 50 bikes on display, as well as photographs, objects, and gear related to Iceland's 100-year history of motorbikes.

Into the Arctic
(Norðurslóð)

Strandgata 53, tel. 354/588-9050, www.nordurslod.is, 11am-6pm Mon.-Fri., 11am-5pm Sat.-Sun., 1,500ISK

Into the Arctic – Norðurslóð is a newly opened museum that showcases life in the Arctic, including the settlement era in Iceland, the wildlife of the frozen North, and Arctic exploration and aviation. The museum includes exhibitions ranging from videos to photos to important historical artefacts on display. It's a lovely addition to Akureyri's historical museums.

Christmas Garden
(Jólagarðurinn)

tel. 354/463-1433, 10am-6pm daily June-Aug., noon-6pm daily Sept.-Dec., 2pm-6pm daily Jan.-May, free

If you're a fan of Christmas, do not miss the Christmas Garden, just a 10-minute drive from downtown Akureyri. The bright red house, which resembles a gingerbread house, has an astounding number of Christmas decorations, ranging from traditional to Icelandic-themed wares featuring the Yule Lads (Christmas elves). You can pick up a locally made trinket and buy some Christmas-themed candy, or just enjoy the jolly atmosphere. A garden outside offers benches, local art, and a tiny place to buy waffles and coffee. It's a cute space.

The Christmas Garden is about 10 kilometers (6 miles) south of downtown Akureyri on **Route 821.**

SPORTS AND RECREATION

Fishing

ICELAND FISHING GUIDE

tel. 354/660-1642, www.icelandfishingguide.com, tours 40,000ISK

Iceland Fishing Guide provides guided fishing tours to lakes and rivers around Akureyri. You'll have a chance at reeling in salmon, trout, and arctic char, among other fish. The tours, available April-September, are suitable for beginners as well as experienced anglers, and you can choose from day tours or longer trips. The licenses needed for the tour are arranged in advance.

Hiking

While Akureyri is known as more of an urban playground, similar to Reykjavík, there are some hiking opportunities on the outskirts of town, namely around **Eyjafjarðardalur,** a wide valley surrounding the Eyjafjarðará River. To get information on trails and pick up maps, visit the **tourist information center** at Hof. Most hikes are moderate in difficulty.

Ice-Skating

SKAUTAHOLLIN

Naustavegi 1, tel. 354/461-2440, www.sasport.is, 1pm-4pm and 7pm-9pm Fri., 1pm-5pm Sat., 1pm-4pm Sun. Sept.-May, 900ISK

Skautahollin is a delightful skating hall chock-full of local families. If the weather is bad outside, visit the hall, rent a pair of skates, and join the fun.

Skiing

HLÍÐARFJALL

tel. 354/462-2280, www.hlidarfjall.is, day pass 5,000ISK adults, 1,500ISK children 6-17

The Hlíðarfjall ski area is just a few minutes outside of town and offers more than a dozen well-kept trails. If you're dying to ski on a glacier, this is your chance. Bear in mind that the trails are 1,000 meters (3,280 feet) at the highest, so don't expect major vertical drops. A shuttle bus can pick you up at the tourist information office for 1,500ISK round-trip if you don't have a rental car. Other activities include snowboarding and cross-country skiing. You can rent all the equipment you need at the ski area. The season is November-April. Check the website for hours, as they tend to change due to weather.

Swimming

AKUREYRI SWIMMING POOL

Þingvallastræti, tel. 354/461-4455, 6:45am-9pm Mon.-Fri., 8am-9pm Sat., 8am-7:30pm Sun., 1,000ISK

If you're going to visit one swimming pool in North Iceland, the Akureyri Swimming Pool should be it. The fantastic facilities include two outdoor pools, children's pools and play areas, waterslides, a sauna, and a steam room. The pool is in the center of town and well-maintained, drawing both locals and tourists. Rain or shine, this is a great spot to relax and spend some time.

Golf

AKUREYRI GOLF COURSE

Jadar, tel. 354/462-2974, greens fees 6,000ISK

Akureyri Golf Course is a wildly popular 18-hole facility that has the distinction of being the northernmost course in the world. The par-71 course loops around broad ridges and is quite scenic, with towering mountains in the background. Club and gear rentals are available on-site. Be sure to call ahead for a tee time. The course also plays host to the Arctic Open, held during the summer solstice. It's open year-round, but call ahead for opening hours because the schedule is changeable.

Tours
SAGA TRAVEL
Kaupvangsstræti 4, tel. 354/558-8888, www. sagatravel.is,

Saga Travel is an Akureyri-based company that offers day tours from Akureyri and Mývatn, including horse-riding, lava cave visits, super-jeep tours, sightseeing by bus, and hiking excursions. Day tours start from 19,900ISK.

NONNI TRAVEL
Brekkugata 5, tel. 354/461-1841, www.nonnitravel.is

Another Akureyri-based tour company is Nonni Travel, which offers day tours in North Iceland to sites like Goðafoss, Dettifoss, Grímsey, and Lake Mývatn. Day tours start at 11,000ISK.

ENTERTAINMENT AND EVENTS
HOF
Strandgata 12, tel. 354/450-1000, www. menningarhus.is

Hof is the striking building by the harbor that is home to Akureyri's big concert performances, including rock concerts, symphonies, and everything in between. Hof, which opened in 2010, also houses the restaurant 1862 Nordic Bistro and the main tourist information office. Even if you're not going to attend a concert, or pick up brochures at the tourist office, architecture buffs will want to visit this building for its unique round concrete design. The interior is amazing, with modern curved wood accents intertwined with metal. It's open 8am-10pm daily, or later when there is a performance.

AK-EXTREME
www.akx.is

Dedicated to winter extreme sports, AK-Extreme is an annual snowboard and music festival held in Akureyri over four days in mid-April. There's skiing, snowboarding, live music, and lots of fun.

FOOD
Icelandic
KAFFI ILMUR
Hafnarstræti, tel. 354/571-6444, www.kaffiilmur.is, daily 8am-11pm, entrées from 2,490ISK

Kaffi Ilmur is a delightful little café off the main street in town. You'll find soups, sandwiches, salads, snacks, and fresh pastries, along with a great cup of coffee. Situated in a two-story house perched on a small hill, it's a lovely, quiet spot to have a light meal in the heart of downtown Akureyri. The lunch buffet is very popular with locals and costs 2,290ISK. The buffet includes hot dishes, a salad bar, soup of the day, and fresh homemade bread. Kaffi Ilmur is especially great to visit during the summer when the large patio is filled with people enjoying meals and drinks, overlooking the town.

★ 1862 NORDIC BISTRO
Strandgata 12, tel. 354/466-1862, www.1862.is, 11:30am-9pm Mon.-Sat., 11am-9pm Sun. summer, 11:30am-6pm Mon.-Sat., 11am-6pm Sun. winter, entrées from 3,950ISK

1862 Nordic Bistro is housed in Hof, the main concert hall in Akureyri right next to the harbor, and the views from the restaurant's huge windows are stunning—you'll see the town, harbor, and mountains in the distance. If you're visiting during the winter and the forecast is favorable, it would be a lovely spot to view the northern lights. The restaurant is known for its brunch buffet, which features Icelandic delicacies including traditional fish gratin, smoked lamb, and marinated herring. There are also Danish-style open-face sandwiches with a variety of toppings.

Seafood
RUB 23
Kaupvangsstræti 6, tel. 354/462-2223, www.rub23. is, 11:30am-10pm Mon.-Fri., 5:30pm-10pm Sat.-Sun., entrées from 4,990ISK

Rub 23 is your best bet if you're looking for

fresh and eclectic fish dishes. The restaurant, which also serves scrumptious sushi, specializes in cod, arctic char, blue ling, and salmon with a choice of "rubs," including citrus rosemary, Indian, sweet mango chili, Texas barbecue, and Asian fusion, among others. Meat dishes include lamb, chicken, beef, and minke whale with your choice of rub. Dinner for two, with drinks, can be pricey, but if you want a taste, the lunch menu (available on weekdays from 11am-2pm) is glorious as well.

Casual
BERLÍN AKUREYRI
Skipagata 4, tel. 354/772-5061, 8am-6pm daily, entrees from 1,350ISK
A recent addition to the Akureyri food scene, Berlín Akureyri fills an important gap in town: brunch. The coffee shop offers breakfast, brunch, and lunch daily. A favorite among locals, you will find classics like bacon and eggs, pancakes and waffles, plus smoothies, salads, and a vegan burger.

ICELANDIC HAMBURGER FACTORY (ÍSLENSKA HAMBORGARAFABRIKKAN)
Hafnarstræti 87-89, tel. 354/460-2000, www.fabrikkan.is, 11:30am-10pm Sun.-Thur., 11:30am-11pm Fri.-Sat., 2,499ISK
Icelandic Hamburger Factory (Íslenska Hamborgarafabrikkan) is the best spot to grab a hamburger in Akureyri. The family-friendly joint offers 120-gram hamburgers on a square bun, ranging from traditional beef burgers to more exotic whale-meat burgers. There's something for every meat eater here. The "surf and turf burger" is a sight to behold, with a beef patty, tiger prawns, Japanese seaweed, cheese, red onions, lettuce, tomatoes, and a garlic-cheese sauce. Other combinations include a barbecue burger, a lamb burger, and a Mexican-inspired salsa burger.

GREIFINN RESTAURANT
Gléragata 20, tel. 354/460-1600, www.greifinn.is, 11:30am-10pm daily, entrées from 2,590ISK
Greifinn Restaurant feels like the Icelandic version of TGI Friday's. There are mozzarella sticks, hamburgers, nachos, soups, sandwiches, burritos, and even pizza. It's casual, family friendly, and quick, with no surprises.

STRIKIÐ
Skipagata 14, tel. 354/462-7100, www.strikid.is, 11:30am-10pm Mon.-Thur., 11:30am-11pm Fri.-Sat., 5pm-10pm Sun., entrées from 2,990ISK
Strikið does a nice job with lamb and fish dishes, some more traditional, others with a Middle Eastern and Italian flair. The restaurant occupies one of the highest buildings in Akureyri, allowing fantastic views of the town. There's a lovely four-course menu (7,490ISK) available that incorporates fresh, local ingredients including fish and meat. If you're after some fine dining that doesn't break the bank (by Iceland standards), this is a good option.

BAUTINN
Hafnarstræti 92, tel. 354/462-1818, www.bautinn.is, 11am-9pm Sun.-Thur., 11am-10pm Fri.-Sat., entrées from 3,290ISK
Bautinn is a typical casual eatery with plenty of tourist-friendly fare. You will find hamburgers, pasta, pizza, sandwiches, and soup on the menu, as well as more traditional Icelandic cuisine such as lamb, horse, whale, and beef steaks and an array of fish dishes. This is a popular place for locals as well as large tourist groups. The service is friendly and accommodating.

Asian
INDIAN CURRY HUT
Hafnarstræti 100b, tel. 354/461-4242, www.curryhut.is, 11:30am-1:30pm and 5:30pm-9pm Mon.-Fri., 5:30pm-9pm Sat.-Sun., entrées from 1,895ISK
Indian Curry Hut is a surprisingly wonderful Indian takeaway restaurant housed in a small shack-like structure on the main street. Don't be fooled, though; this is a great spot to get a tasty, affordable meal. The food is fantastic, with cooks specializing in perfectly spiced chicken and lamb dishes.

KRUA SIAM

Strandgata 13, tel. 354/466-3800, www.kruasiam.
is, 11:30am-1:30pm and 5pm-9:30pm Mon.-Fri.,
5pm-9:30pm Sat.-Sun., entrées from 2,110ISK
Krua Siam has all the main dishes you'd expect at a Thai restaurant, without many surprises. The mainstays are here, including spring rolls, pad thai, and beef and curry with coconut milk. The lamb and fish are fresh, local, and divine.

Mediterranean

BRYGGJAN

Strandgata 49, tel. 354/440-6600, www.bryggjan.
is, 11:30am-9pm Sun.-Thur., 11:30am-10pm Fri.-Sat.,
entrées from 2,550ISK
Bryggjan is known for its perfect pizzas in just about any combination of ingredients you could imagine. You can go the traditional route with a ham and pepperoni pizza, or more exotic with a shrimp, tuna, onion, and tomato pie. If you're not up for pizza, there are soups, sandwiches, and starters, such as mozzarella sticks and nachos.

Cafés

TE OG KAFFI

Hafnarstræti 91-93, tel. 354/540-2180, www.
teogkaffi.is, 9am-10pm daily
Te og Kaffi is a popular coffee chain housed in the front of the Eymundsson bookstore on the main street. There's a decent selection of teas, coffee drinks, and fresh pastries on offer from this popular chain shop. You'll see locals perusing magazines while sipping on lattes.

BLÁA KANNAN CAFÉ

Hafnarstræti 96, tel. 354/461-4600,
8:30am-11:30pm daily summer, 9am-11:30pm
Mon.-Fri., 10am-11:30pm Sat.-Sun. winter, 1,800ISK
Bláa Kannan Café is a charming café housed in a bright blue building on the main street, one of the oldest structures in the city. The interior is quaint and cozy, and the friendly staff serves freshly baked bread, pastries, soups, and sandwiches. The café tends to get crowded during lunchtime, when fresh soup

is served with bread and butter. During the summer, locals and tourists sip drinks and soak up the sun at the outdoor tables. The central location and simple, good food make this place a winner.

KAFFI KÚ

Garður farm, tel. 354/867-3826, www.kaffiku.is,
11am-6pm Mon.-Fri., noon-6pm Sat.-Sun., 2,000ISK
Kaffi Kú (Café Cow) is a fun experience for everyone from solo travelers to families. The café is housed in a cowshed, and guests can order light meals, coffee, and cakes while overlooking the cows from a glass partition. It's located on a farm just 10 kilometers (6 miles) south of Akureyri, about a 10-minute drive via Routes 1 and 829.

Ice Cream

BRYNJA

Aðalstræti 3, tel. 354/462-4478, noon-11pm daily,
from 400ISK
Ice cream is serious business in Iceland, and the holy grail is Brynja. Icelanders are known to enjoy ice cream in any type of weather, and Brynja has been supplying locals with delicious creamy concoctions since 1942. In the summer, it's common to see a line outside the shop. In short, the ice cream is fantastic. Try a scoop or two.

BARS AND NIGHTLIFE

GÖTUBARINN

Hafnarstræti 96, tel. 354/462-4747, 5pm-1am
Sun.-Thur., 5pm-4am Fri.-Sat.
Götubarinn is a wildly popular bar that has a great selection of beers and wines. It's situated in the city center in a nondescript green building, but the inside is warm, friendly, and crowded.

GRÆNI HATTURINN

Hafnarstræti 96, tel. 354/461-4646, 8pm-3am
Fri.-Sat.
Græni Hatturinn, which means "The Green Hat," is a centrally located bar that features live music and DJs. The crowd tends to be on the younger side, and it can get very loud

and very crowded on weekends. The opening hours vary depending on special events, but it's usually open 8pm-3am Friday-Saturday. Check local listings for concerts and events during the week.

ACCOMMODATIONS
Under 10,000ISK
HÓTEL EDDA AKUREYRI
Þórunnarstræti, tel. 354/444-4900, www.hoteledda.is, mid-June-mid-Aug., rooms from 10,000ISK

Hótel Edda Akureyri offers 204 rooms during the summer. The rest of the year, the hotel serves as accommodations for university students. For hotel guests, the digs are comfortable, with private bathrooms for 132 of the rooms (the rest have shared facilities), free Wi-Fi, and clean, minimalist decor. The rooms with private bathrooms are large with comfortable beds. The remaining no-frills rooms are small but clean and comfortable. A breakfast buffet is also available (2,450ISK adults, 1,225ISK children 6-12, free for children 5 and under).

THÓRUNNARSTRÆTI CAMPING
Hafnarstræti 49, tel. 354/462-3379, May.-Sept., 1,600ISK

There are two main campsites in town. The first, Thórunnarstræti Camping, is in an ideal location right next to the town's swimming pool and a stone's throw from shops, restaurants, and museums. The facilities are good, with hot showers and a decent cooking area. Electricity is available for 1,000ISK and washing machines for 500ISK per wash. Tent and RV campers are welcome.

HAMRAR CAMPING
Kjarnaskógur, tel. 354/461-2264, May.-Sept., 1,600ISK

The second campsite, Hamrar Camping, is a little outside the city center, but it's larger and slightly less crowded. The facilities are similar, with hot showers and an adequate cooking area, and both tent and RV campers are welcome. Hookups are available.

10,000-20,000 ISK
AKUREYRI BACKPACKERS
Hafnarstræti 98, tel. 354/571-9050, www. akureyribackpackers.com, dorm room from 4,900ISK, private rooms from 16,500ISK

Akureyri Backpackers caters to the 20-something traveler looking for a fun atmosphere and a clean place to stay. Rooms range from privates to dormitory-style accommodations. However, tourists tend to stay here for the facilities and the opportunity to meet fellow travelers. The hostel's bar tends to get packed, and its restaurant frequented by young guests. Tourist information services are top-notch; there's a desk for booking tours, buying bus and flight tickets, and renting cars. A common cooking area allows you to prepare your own meals, and laundry facilities are available. Recommended for young travelers.

HÓTEL NORÐURLAND
Geislagata 7, tel. 354/462-2600, www.keahotels.is, rooms from 20,000ISK

Hótel Norðurland is a 41-room hotel owned by the same folks as the nearby Hótel Kea. It's a more simple and affordable option, and the decor is dated, but the location is good, the staff are friendly, and the rooms are clean and adequate. All rooms have private bathrooms, free Wi-Fi, and satellite television. Breakfast is included in the room price.

Over 20,000 ISK
★ ICELANDAIR HÓTEL AKUREYRI
Þingvallastræti 23, tel. 354/518-1000, www. icelandairhotels.com, rooms from 21,000ISK

Icelandair Hótel Akureyri is one of Icelandair Hótels' latest additions and one of the loveliest hotels in the north. The 99-room hotel is beautiful, with art and design accents touching every corner of the property. The lobby is rustic and Nordic chic with sheep and reindeer skins adorning gorgeous wood furniture. Rooms range from standard twins to family rooms and suites, and the clientele ranges from business travelers in town for a night to families staying multiple days. The hotel restaurant also doesn't disappoint; fresh and local ingredients go beyond traditional lamb and fish dishes. Breakfast is included in the room price.

HÓTEL AKUREYRI

Hafnarstræti 67, tel. 354/462-5600, www. hotelakureyri.is, rooms from 25,000ISK

Hótel Akureyri is a posh boutique hotel close to the city center. The exterior looks quaint and old-fashioned, but the inside reveals modern and tastefully decorated rooms with standard beds, private bathrooms, free Wi-Fi, and free parking. For an extra fee, you can request a room with a beautiful ocean view. A standard breakfast buffet is included in the room price.

HÓTEL KEA

Hafnarstræti 87-89, tel. 354/460-2000, www. keahotels.is, rooms from 28,000ISK

Hótel Kea has modern amenities and first-class service. The 104-room hotel, which is a stone's throw from the Akureyri Church, features an elegant interior. Spacious rooms offer hardwood floors, big, comfortable beds, free Wi-Fi, satellite television, and private bathrooms. Some of the luxury stems from 24-hour room service and same-day dry-cleaning services. The hotel restaurant serves a hearty breakfast that's included in the room price.

INFORMATION AND SERVICES

TOURIST INFORMATION OFFICE

Strandgata 12, tel. 354/450-1050, www.visitakureyri. is, 8am-6:30pm daily June 1-Sept. 20, 8am-4pm daily Sept. 21-May 31

The tourist information office is based in Akureyri's main concert hall, Hof, by the harbor. It has pamphlets on tours and seasonal events, along with a gift shop that sells unique Icelandic wares. Just a few steps from the information center is the restaurant 1862 Nordic Bistro.

Medical Services

If you have a medical emergency, dial 112 for help.

AKUREYRI HOSPITAL

Eyrarlandsvegi, tel. 354/463-0100, www.sak.is

Akureyri Hospital is North Iceland's largest hospital. The hospital provides general and specialized health care services and emergency care.

AKUREYRI PHARMACY (AKUREYRARAPÓTEK)

Kaupangur, tel. 354/460-9999, www. akureyrarapotek.is, 9am-6pm Mon.-Fri., 10am-4pm Sat., noon-4pm Sun.

Akureyri Pharmacy (Akureyrarapótek) is close to the swimming pool and camping area.

GETTING THERE
By Air
AKUREYRI AIRPORT

(Urðargil 15, tel. 354/424-4000)

Akureyri Airport sits at the base of Eyjafjörður, just 3 kilometers (1.8 miles) from the city center, and is a quite small commuter airport. Air Iceland Connect operates daily flights from **Reykjavík City Airport,** which take about 45 minutes. The flight offers spectacular views of the landscape when the weather is clear. Check flight schedules and book tickets at **Air Iceland Connect** (tel. 354/460-7000, www.airicelandconnect.com, starts at 15,000ISK each way).

Taxis to the airport can be hired at **Hof,** along the harbor, or arranged by your hotel or guesthouse. It's a 30-minute walk or a 5-minute drive from downtown. Taxis are available at the airport.

By Car

By car, Akureyri is 391 kilometers (243 miles) from **Reykjavík** on **Route 1.** In good weather, it will take you about five hours. Always check weather and road conditions at www.road.is before setting out on your road trip.

Parking in Akureyri is considered a sport by some. If you are a local with a personal parking space, you're in the clear. Tourists, however, must be mindful of where they park and how long they have left the car. To deal with the limited parking spaces, the town has instituted a system where you must retrieve a small cardboard clock that has movable hands from the tourist information center or local gas stations. Before you leave your car in a designated parking area, move the hands of the clock to show the current time and display it clearly on the dashboard. Most spaces allow for two-hour parking, but make sure. Also, parking attendants closely monitor the clocks, and if you are past the time, or the attendant cannot see the clock, you will be issued a fine of 15,000ISK.

By Bus

The **Strætó** 57 bus (www.straeto.is) leaves **Mjodd bus station** in **Reykjavík** a few times a week, reaching downtown Akureyri in about eight hours for 10,340ISK. Check the website for details.

By Boat

Arriving to Akureyri by sea is becoming more common, as cruise ships are increasingly adding Akureyri as a port of call. Most cruise ships dock at **Strandgata,** a few steps from downtown Akureyri.

GETTING AROUND
By Bus

Akureyri is small and walkable, but if you want to hop on a local town bus, they are free of charge. The **yellow buses** run 6:25am-11pm on weekdays and noon-6pm on weekends and holidays. The schedule can be obtained from your hotel or guesthouse or from www.straeto.is.

By Taxi

BSO (Strandgata, tel. 354/461-1010, www.bso. is) is the only cab company in Akureyri, and it provides service 24 hours a day. It's possible to get taxis that can take up to eight people, as well as special cars for people with disabilities. Akureyri is a small town, but expect to pay 2,000ISK-3,000ISK for a short ride.

Around Akureyri

LAUFÁS

tel. 354/463-3196, www.visitakureyri.is, 9am-5pm daily June 1-Aug. 31, 1,200ISK

Laufás is an ancient farm estate that gives a peek inside what life was like in the region as far back as the settlement era, complete with turf-covered houses that you can enter. The farm is even mentioned in historical records soon after the settlement of Iceland (874-930). The church on the property was built in 1865 and contains a pulpit dating from 1698, and the rectory dates from 1853. There have been numerous churches built, and then rebuilt, at the site over the centuries. It's a lovely place to spend a couple of hours, soak in the scenery, and reflect on what farm living looked like in the 19th century. There's a café in the service center, along with a small souvenir shop.

The farm is 30 kilometers (19 miles) north of Akureyri and can be reached by **Route 83.**

HIKING MOUNT KALDBAKUR

Distance: *2.2 km (1.4 mi) round-trip*
Hiking Time: *1 hour round-trip*
Information and Maps: *www.visitakureyri.is*
Trailhead: *Several routes up the mountain, see map at tourist information office*

Fewer than 400 people call **Grenivík** home, but the small, close-knit village is a popular place to stop to take some photos of the stunning fjord and mountainous landscape or to climb **Mount Kaldbakur,** which stands at 1,167 meters (3,829 feet). Hikers rave about the view from the top, where on clear days you can get a glimpse of Hrísey Island. For hiking routes, stop by the **tourist information office** at Hof by the harbor in Akureyri (tel. 354/460-1199, www. visitakureyri.is).

Kaldbakur Tours (tel. 354/837-3770, www.kaldbaksferdir.com) offers snowcat

and sledding tours January-May, starting at 7,500ISK.

Grenivík is 38 kilometers (23 miles) north of **Akureyri** via **Route 83.**

★ GOÐAFOSS

In a country full of spectacular waterfalls, what sets Goðafoss apart is the sheer width of the tumbling falls. White water surges over the rim, thundering down and crashing into rocks and water. The water of the Skjálfandafljót River falls from a height of 12 meters (40 feet) over a width of 30 meters (98 feet). It's quite a show. Plan to spend some time here, walking along the perimeter, snapping photos, and taking in the beauty.

Goðafoss, which means "waterfall of the gods," derives its name from Iceland's long history with Christianity. In AD 1000, lawyer Þorgeir Þorkelsson made Christianity the official religion of Iceland. After his conversion, Þorgeir threw his statues of the Norse gods into the waterfall. The name Goðafoss was born.

Food and Accommodations
GOÐAFOSS HOTEL AT FOSSHÓLL
tel. 354/464-3108, www.godafoss.is, mid-May-mid-Sept., rooms from 27,000ISK
Goðafoss Hotel at Fosshóll is a newly renovated hotel just 500 meters (1,640 feet) from Goðafoss. The charming yellow house offers 21 rooms, including singles, doubles, and triples. Rooms are simple, bright, and cozy, with standard beds. Some rooms have private bathrooms, and guests have access to free Wi-Fi and free parking. It's also near a gas station and a grocery store, which is a plus. Book early, as rooms tend to sell out.

Getting There
Goðafoss is located just off **Route 1,** 50 kilometers east of **Akureyri** and 49 kilometers (30 miles) west of **Reykjahlíð.** It's 46 kilometers (29 miles) from **Húsavík** via **Route 85** and then **Route 845.**

Mývatn Region

Mývatn is one of the most popular tourist destinations in the northeast. Visitors are lured by gorgeous hiking trails, rich birdlife, activities along Lake Mývatn, and the soothing Mývatn Nature Baths. The region has been shaped over time by punishing volcanic eruptions. It's a place to soak in the rugged landscape, with its vast lava fields, gigantic craters, soaring mountains, and, of course, the 36.5-square-kilometer (14.1-square-mile) lake that is home to scores of bird and fish species.

The Mývatn region is perfect for independent travelers who prefer to roam on their own time. Jump into a rental car and discover everything from the charming town of Reykjahlíð, on the northeastern shore of Lake Mývatn, to roaring waterfalls, volcanic craters, and black lava rock pillars. Alternatively, tours in the region include bird-watching, whale-watching, and jeep tours.

SIGHTS
★ Mývatn Nature Baths
(Jarðböðin)
tel. 354/464-4411, www.myvatnnaturebaths.is, 9am-midnight daily May 15-Sept. 30, noon-10pm daily Oct. 1-May 14, Jan. 1-Apr. 30 4,500ISK, May 1-Sept. 30 5,300ISK, Oct 1.-Dec. 31 4,500ISK
Despite obvious comparisons to the Blue Lagoon, the Mývatn Nature Baths, 3 kilometers (1.9 miles) east of Reykjahlíð, have their own unique personality and atmosphere. There's more room to wade and fewer people in the locker rooms, and the steam baths are far from full.

1: Laufás 2: Goðafoss waterfall

Mývatn Region

The bathing experience is heavenly, soothing your skin and relaxing every inch of your body. The views of the landscape are striking, with the volcanic crater of Hverfjall and the edge of Lake Mývatn in the background.

The milky-blue water, which stands at 36°C (96.8°F), comes from the National Power Company's borehole in Bjarnaflag. The water temperature reaches a scorching 130°C (266°F) when it arrives to the basin next to the lagoon, but it cools significantly before filtering into the glorious man-made hot spring.

Overall, the basin and lagoon hold about 2.5 million liters (660,000 gallons) of water.

The bottom of the lagoon is covered by gravel and sand, and it contains a large amount of minerals. Because of its chemical composition, vegetation and bacteria are not a problem. There is some sulfur in the water, which is beneficial for skin problems such as eczema and psoriasis, as well as respiratory issues. However, it's not a good idea to wear silver or brass jewelry in the water, as the pieces can be damaged by the sulfur.

Café Kvika (11am-9pm daily June-Aug., noon-8pm daily Sept.-May, snacks from 600ISK) serves light, healthy meals overlooking the lagoon including soup, sandwiches, pastries, and a salad bar. Beer and wine are available for purchase, and you're allowed to bring drinks to the lagoon, provided you have a wristband.

From Akureyri, the Nature Baths are about 87 kilometers (54 miles) east on the **Ring Road,** about 1.15 hours.

Dimmuborgir

Route 87

Dimmuborgir, which means "dark cities" or "dark castles," comprises interesting rock formations jutting out of the ground, resembling a fort guarding an ancient city. The black lava pillars were born from a collapsed lava tube created by a large volcanic eruption more than 2,000 years ago. Scientists say that lava pooled over a small lake in the region, and as it crossed wet land the water started to boil; the vapor emitting from the lava then formed pillars, some of which reach several meters in height. There's a popular photo opportunity in the structure known as Kirkjan (the Church), which is a curved lava tube resembling a steeple. While it's tempting to scale many of the structures, climbing is strictly prohibited.

To get there, head south from **Húsavík,** turning onto **Route 87;** keep straight once you reach the first junction at Lake Mývatn and then follow it around the eastern edge. It is about a 45-minute drive from Húsavík.

Hverfjall

GPS coordinates N 65.6061, W 16.8751, car park 15 km (9 mi) east of Mývatn off of Route 848

Hverfjall (or Hverfell, depending on which Icelander you ask) is the largest tephra crater in the Mývatn region. Tephra craters are created from volcanic debris. The crater is striking because it's almost a perfect circle, and considering its size, 140 meters (5,511 feet) deep and 1 kilometer (0.6 miles) across, it's quite impressive. Scientists have said that the crater was formed after repeated eruptions over 2,500 years ago. There are two walking paths around the rim, one on the north side and one on the south, and it takes about 15 minutes to climb. It gives you a good view of the landscape.

Take **Route 1** to get to Hverfjall. It's 15 kilometers (9 miles) east of **Mývatn** off of **Route 848,** about a 20-minute drive.

Krafla

car park is 24 km (15 mi) northeast of Mývatn off of Route 1

The Krafla lava fields are home to **Víti** (Hell), one of the best-known craters in Iceland. Víti is huge, about 300 meters (984 feet) in diameter, exposing interesting formations that resulted from lava flows and hydrologic forces. The crater was formed during a massive volcanic eruption in 1724. The eruption continued for five years, and Víti's bubbling cauldron of mud boiled for more than a century after that. The area is another reminder of how active this island has been, and continues to be, with spectacular eruptions continually reshaping of land. Today you can visit this region to get a glimpse of the crater, hike around the area, and take in the very-much-alive hot springs and mud pools.

Krafla is 24 kilometers (15 miles) northeast of Mývatn off of Route 1, about a 25-minute drive. Víti is situated near Krafla, and a paved road leads up to it from Route 1. The **car park** area is right next to the rim; you should allow at least an hour walking around the rim.

Námaskarð

15 km (9 mi) northeast of Lake Mývatn on Route 1

Námaskarð is a big draw for tourists because of its sheer otherworldly atmosphere. The yellow and brown colors of the clay, along with the gray mud pools, make it look like a movie scene from another planet. A short path loops around the region; be sure to stay on it for safety reasons, as the mud pools can reach temperatures of 100°C (212°F). The area is secluded and the smell of sulfur can be a bit much for some, but it's worth a visit.

The Mysterious *Marimo* of Mývatn

A rare form of algae is disappearing from Lake Mývatn. The algae, called *marimo* (which means "water plant ball" in Japanese), is a round spongy moss that collects on the bottom of lakes. It exists only in this part of Iceland and parts of Japan, Scotland, and Estonia.

Iceland's *marimo* can be found in water that is about 2 meters (7 feet) deep, and they grow at most to 12 centimeters (5 inches) in diameter. The *marimo* in Mývatn was discovered in 1978. You can see the moss gently roll back and forth in the waves. The lake balls are a curiosity, as they can grow only in very specific conditions with the right amount of sediment, certain light conditions, and lake current. Perhaps most curious, for non-scientists, is the Icelandic translation: Lake balls are called *kúluskítur*, which means "ball of shit" in Icelandic. The numbers of *marimo* have been declining, and scientists are unsure why.

Námaskarð is 15 kilometers (9 miles) northeast of **Lake Mývatn** on **Route 1.**

Sigurgeir's Bird Museum
Fuglasafn Sigurgeirs

GPS coordinates N 65.6288, W 16.9951, Ytri-Neslond, tel. 354/464-4477, www.fuglasafn.is, noon-5pm daily mid-late May, 9am-6pm daily June-late Aug., noon-5pm daily late Aug.-Oct., 2pm-4pm daily Nov.-mid-May, 1,500ISK adults, 800ISK children 7-14, free for children 6 and under

Sigurgeir's Bird Museum is Iceland's largest privately owned mounted bird collection. It is at the farm Ytri-Neslond near Lake Mývatn. The museum features about 180 species of birds and more than 300 birds in total, ranging from goldeneye ducks to puffins. The birds are in glass displays, and they are labeled with information about the species. An on-site café serves coffee and snacks. Binoculars are available to use for bird-watching outside the museum. The museum was created in honor of Mývatn resident Sigurgeir Stefansson, who had a passion for birds and died tragically in an accident in 1999 at the age of 37.

Take **Route 1** to reach the bird museum, which is on the north side of the lake.

SPORTS AND RECREATION
Bird-Watching

All of Iceland has been established as a

bird-watchers' paradise, but Mývatn gets particular props for hosting a few species not found in much of the island, namely the duck species—gadwall, shoveler, and common scoter. In the bay of **Neslandavík,** you can see large flocks of greater scaup, Eurasian wigeon, and tufted duck species, as well as common pochard and ring-necked ducks. The **Laxa River** is a popular spot for locals to bring binoculars and a pair of boots to walk along the perimeter in search of harlequin ducks. Other waterbirds that are common to the area include the red-breasted merganser, whooper swan, and great northern diver. Short-eared owls are seen rarely. Keep your eyes peeled.

The best season for bird-watching is from the beginning of May to the middle of August, as that's the high nesting season, but some species, such as geese, remain in the autumn. Remember that the lake is a protected area, and some regions are off-limits to cars. Stop by the **tourist information office** in Reykjahlíð (Hraunvegi 8, tel. 354/464-4390, www.visitmyvatn.is) for maps and tips on where to catch certain species, and always remember to be careful of nests.

Hiking and Biking
HIKE AND BIKE

tel. 354/899-4845, www.hikeandbike.is

Hike and Bike is a Mývatn-based tourism company that offers a range of tours April-September, including three- to four-hour day tours and overnight tours that allow you to explore the region by mountain bike, by foot, or both. The company provides all the gear you need, and there are tours available for all levels of experience. A popular tour is the "Bike and Bath," which is about 4-5 hours and costs 13,500ISK per person (an extra 5,000ISK for pick-up at hotel in Mývatn). A guide takes you by mountain bike to sites including an old steam bath, the fissure of Grjotagja, ancient bathing caves, and ultimately the Mývatn Nature Baths for an hour of soaking in the milky-blue, geothermally heated water.

Jeep Tours
SEL HÓTEL MÝVATN
tel. 354/464-4164, www.myvatn.is/en, tours 23,000ISK per person

Sel Hótel Mývatn offers action-packed super-jeep tours year-round. They range from riding on mountain tracks in the summer to navigating on top of fresh winter snow. Tours take you to the rock formations of Dimmuborgir, the crater at Hverfjall, and some hidden places that the local tour guide knows well. It's a great option to get out and explore nature with an experienced guide who has all the safety equipment needed to handle any difficult weather conditions. Tours are about three hours.

Swimming
MÝVATN SWIMMING POOL
GPS coordinates N 65.6431, W 16.8932, Mývatnssveit, tel. 354/464-4225, 8am-8pm Mon.-Fri., 10am-7pm Sat.-Sun., 900ISK,

If you aren't up for a dip in the Mývatn Nature Baths but want to swim, the Mývatn Swimming Pool is just outside Reykjahlíð.

FOOD
GAMLI BISTRO (GAMLI BAERINN)
Mývatnssveit, tel. 354/464-4170, www.myvatnhotel. is, 10am-11pm daily, entrées from 1,900ISK

This cozy countryside café offers soups, sandwiches, burgers, coffee, and cakes. Its Icelandic meat soup is hearty and hits the spot.

KAFFI BORGIR
tel. 354/464-1144, www.kaffiborgir.is, 10am-9:30pm daily, entrées from 2,450ISK

Kaffi Borgir is conveniently situated near the Mývatn Nature Baths and Dimmuborgir, which means this place can get crowded in the summer months. It's a cafeteria-style café that serves hot meals like lamb or fish, coffee, and pastries. It's good for a quick bite to eat.

SEL MÝVATN RESTAURANT
Skútustaðir, Mývatn, tel. 354/464-4164, www. myvatn.is, noon-2pm and 6pm-9pm daily summer, 6pm-9pm daily winter, entrées from 2,590ISK

Sel Mývatn Restaurant, at Sel Hótel Mývatn, is your best bet for a traditional Icelandic dinner buffet featuring island delicacies, such as smoked trout and marinated salmon, and more exotic dishes, such as shark, blood pudding, smoked lamb, liver pudding, and sheep's head jelly. But if you're not after something so exotic, don't fret, because there are plenty of fish and lamb dishes on the menu.

VOGAFJÓS RESTAURANT
Vogar, tel. 354/464-4303, www.vogafjos.is, 11am-10pm daily summer, 10am-9:30pm daily winter, dinner entrées from 4,150ISK

This is a cute and quirky eatery based in a dairy barn on a family farm. While enjoying your meal of sandwiches, salads, or hot food, you can watch dairy cows get milked from the other side of a glass partition (milkings are at 7am and 6pm). Many of the ingredients are locally sourced, including the beef; the hamburger you order will literally be farm-to-table. And try the fresh mozzarella. The entire experience is worthwhile, from the cows to the quality food to the beautiful landscapes you see from the café's huge windows.

ACCOMMODATIONS
Under 10,000ISK
There are a couple of camping opportunities around Mývatn, but it's important to note that they become quite full during the summer months.

BJARG

tel. 354/464-4240, May-Sept., 1,700ISK

The Bjarg campsite is situated perfectly, right next to the lakeshore of Lake Mývatn near Reykjahlíð. It's close to shops, the tourist information office, and excellent hiking trails. The facilities are top-notch, with laundry facilities, a cooking area to prepare meals, hot showers, and a place to rent bicycles. It's in an open field with no shelter. Tents and RVs are welcome.

HLÍÐ

tel. 354/464-4103, www.myvatnaccommodations. is, 2,000ISK

Hlíð is a campsite that includes cottages for rent. The camping section is on the northern shore of Lake Mývatn, and it's a short five-minute walk to the grocery store and tourist information office. It's in an open field with no shelter, in a pretty space close to the lake. It has an adequate cooking area, warm showers, and an area for tents and caravans. There are laundry facilities on-site. Two-bedroom cottages cost 40,000ISK per night and are available June-early September.

10,000-30,000ISK
VOGAFJOS GUESTHOUSE

Vogafjós Vegur, Mývatn, tel. 354/464-4303, www. vogafjos.is, rooms from 26,000ISK

Vogafjós Guesthouse has been owned and operated by the same family for more than a century. With spectacular views of mountains and lava fields, the guesthouse offers 26 rooms. All have private bathrooms, and breakfast is included.

DIMMUBORGIR GUESTHOUSE

Geiteyjarströnd 1, Mývatn, tel. 354/464-4210, www. dimmuborgir.is, rooms from 26,000ISK

Dimmuborgir Guesthouse offers eight double rooms with private bathrooms, as well as nine cottages. Rooms are bright and clean with simple furnishings and free Wi-Fi. A living room has a television. Cottages are roomy and wood-paneled, and half have private bathrooms. The owners are warm and friendly

and have a long tradition of smoking trout in a nearby smokehouse that they love to show guests. Breakfast is included.

★ HOTEL LAXÁ

Olnbogaás, tel. 354/464-1900, www.hotellaxa.is, rooms from 26,690ISK

Hotel Laxá is a stylish addition to Myvatn. The 80-room hotel is modern, convenient to the major attractions in the region, and gets high points for service. During the winter months, guests can request northern lights "wake-up calls" if the natural phenomenon makes an appearance. Rooms are spacious, with large windows, wood furnishings, and modern accents. There is also an in-house restaurant and bistro bar for lighter fare.

HÓTEL GÍGUR-KEA HOTELS

Skútustaðir, tel. 354/464-4455, www.keahotels.is, rooms from 27,000ISK, mid-May-Sept.

Hótel Gígur-Kea Hotels is in a dynamite location near the southern shore of Lake Mývatn. The 37 rooms, mostly doubles, have private bathrooms, free Wi-Fi, free parking, and an in-house restaurant. The hotel feels a bit dated, especially the restaurant, but it's clean, centrally located, and a convenient place to spend a couple of nights. The staff is friendly, and breakfast is included in the room price.

ICELANDAIR HOTEL MÝVATN

Kísilvegur, Reykjahlíð, tel. 354/444-4000, www. icelandairhotels.com, rooms from 27,000ISK

Icelandair Hotel Mýatn is a smart and modern hotel that opened in summer 2018, with 59 spacious rooms, killer views, and accommodating staff. Rooms have big comfy beds and huge windows overlooking gorgeous scenery. The hotel **restaurant** serves up a delicious breakfast that is included in the room price. And the dinner menu has all the lamb and fish dishes you'd expect.

FOSSHOTEL MÝVATN

Grímsstaðir, tel. 354/453-0000, www.fosshotel.is, rooms from 30,000ISK

Fosshotel Mývatn opened its doors in July

2017, adding 92 rooms to the popular region. The exterior blends into the surrounding nature thanks to its turf roof, muted colors, and wood design. Rooms are bright and spacious, with modern furnishings and wood floors. Options range from standard doubles to suites with access to an outdoor hot tub. Breakfast is included in the rate of the room.

Over 30,000ISK

SEL HÓTEL MÝVATN

Skútustaðir, Mývatn, tel. 354/464-4164, www. myvatn.is, rooms from 39,900ISK

Sel Hótel Mývatn is halfway between modern and quaint. The hotel's exterior is a gray block structure that looks fairly new, while the rooms boast vintage furniture, dainty linens, and all the comforts of home. The in-house restaurant does a fantastic Icelandic dinner buffet.

INFORMATION AND SERVICES

TOURIST INFORMATION CENTER

Hraunvegi 8, Reykjahlíð, tel. 354/464-4390, www. visitmyvatn.is, 9am-4pm daily May, 7:30am-6pm daily June-Aug., 9am-4pm daily Sept., 9am-noon Mon.-Fri. Oct.-Apr.

Mývatn's tourist information center offers Internet access, pamphlets about the region, and the chance to book tours in the area.

GETTING THERE

It's best to have a **car** to explore the region or to book a **tour** from **Akureyri.**

By car, Lake Mývatn is 92 kilometers (57 miles) east of Akureyri on **Route 1.** The town of **Reykjahlíð** connects to paved **Route 848,** which follows Lake Mývatn's northern edge. The lake's perimeter is about 40 kilometers (25 miles).

Húsavík

Húsavík has transformed itself from a placid small town with little appeal to the outside world to a must-see destination for tourists interested in some of the best **whale-watching** opportunities on the island. Húsavík is home to fewer than 3,000 full-time residents, but in the summer the numbers spike dramatically as Icelanders from other towns, tourists coming in on bus tours, and independent travelers converge on Húsavík's harbor. The main draw for tourists is, of course, whale-watching tours, but the charm of the small town, with its tasty restaurants and classic Icelandic hospitality, makes this a destination to consider even if you're not up for a boat tour.

SIGHTS

Húsavík Whale Museum
(Hvalasafnið á Húsavík)

Hafnarstétt 1, tel. 354/414-2800, www. whalemuseum.is, 8:30am-6:30pm daily June-Aug., 9am-6pm daily May and Sept., 10am-4pm daily Oct., 10am-4pm Mon.-Fri. Nov.-Apr., 2,000ISK adults, 500ISK children, family price (2 adults, 1-5 children) 4,200ISK

The Húsavík Whale Museum is a comprehensive museum on Iceland's most famous marine mammals. The exhibits have been developed and maintained with great care, and the curator clearly has a passion for whales. The museum, which is housed in a huge building that used to be a slaughterhouse, provides information on the whale species that inhabit the waters off Iceland's coasts as well as whale ecology and conservation. There are 10 different whale skeletons to check out, as well as a sperm whale jawbone that is the size of a car. It's incredible to stand next to it. Short films available in English teach about whales, and a library has a large selection of marine books. If you visit only one museum in Húsavík, this should be it.

Exploration Museum
(Könnunarsögusafnið)

Héðisbraut 3, tel. 354/848-7600, www.

explorationmuseum.com, 11am-4pm May 1-Sept. 30, open by request rest of year, pay what you wish

The Exploration Museum is a great spot to see something a little different in Iceland. The museum focuses on various types of exploration, from Vikings coming to Iceland to Americans landing on the moon. Maps and photographs are on display, and documentaries about Apollo astronauts training in Húsavík before missions are available in English. It may not sound like it makes sense, but the exhibits work, doing a nice job of tying Viking captains, arctic explorers, and astronauts together.

Culture House at Húsavík
(Safnahúsið á Húsavík)

Stóragarði 17, tel. 354/464-1860, www.husmus.is, 10am-6pm daily June-Aug., 10am-4pm Mon.-Fri. Sept.-May, 1,000ISK

The Culture House at Húsavík features two fantastic exhibitions that provide a window into life in Húsavík over the ages. The first exhibit has a maritime theme and includes a number of boats, many of which were built in Húsavík. Other displays include fishing equipment, tools used for seal and shark hunting, and photos and documentaries in English. The second exhibit focuses on daily life and natural history in the region. Here you can view homemade objects and crafts and learn about subsistence farming. Regional archives and a library are on-site.

Geosea Geothermal Sea Baths

Vitaslóð 1, tel. 354/464-1210, www.geosea.is/en, 10am-midnight daily May 1-Sept. 30 and noon-10pm daily Oct. 1-Apr. 30, 4,300ISK adults, 1,800ISK children 16 and younger

Húsavík's newest swimming facility is the GeoSea Geothermal Sea Baths. The new baths, located along the coast of Húsavík, harness naturally heated geothermal water from Húsavikurhöfði and bathers enjoy the water at a temperature of 38-39°C (102-104°F). The concrete structure has a curvy shape, and an inner ledge allows guests to sit comfortably in the water. There is a restaurant on-site that serves soups, sandwiches, pastries, and juices as well as beer and wine.

Húsavíkurkirkja

9am-11am and 3pm-5pm daily June-Aug., free

Located close to the harbor, the Húsavíkurkirkja is one of the most significant landmarks in the town. Built in 1907, the Húsavík Church stands 26 meters (85 feet) high and has a white exterior with reddish-brown trim and a dark green steeple/roof. The interior features strong wood beams, beautiful windows, and red-cushioned pews. Icelandic state architect Rögnvaldur Ólafsson designed the church, and all of the wood used to construct it was imported from Norway. The painting behind the altar is revered by town locals. Icelandic artist Sveinn Thórarinsson was commissioned to portray the resurrection of Lazarus for the church. His work incorporated Iceland's landscape, including the mountains and mist of Dettifoss.

SPORTS AND RECREATION
★ Whale-Watching

If you leave Húsavík without getting on a whale-watching boat to view the gentle giants up close, you're missing out. The main whale-watching season runs from the middle of May to the end of October, but the high season is June and July. That time frame is your best chance to see as many as 12 species of whales, with the most common being minke and humpback whales. If you're lucky, you'll spot fin whales, orcas, and blue whales. You can always count on sighting dolphins, as they love to hang out close to the bay. Many of the guides are passionate about whales and love sharing stories about up-close-and-personal encounters.

Three main companies offer whale-watching tours. Each company operates boats of different sizes and all have stellar reputations for ethical environmental practices. The tours are about three hours and depart daily.

- **Gentle Giants** (tel. 354/464-1500, www. gentlegiants.is, 10,400ISK adults, 4,400ISK children 7-15, free for children 6 and under), April 1-November 30

- **North Sailing** (tel. 354/464-7272, www. northsailing.is, 10,500ISK adults, 3,500ISK children 7-15, free for children 6 and under), March 1-October 14

- **Salka** (tel. 354/464-3999, www.salkawhale-watching.is, 9,950ISK adults, 4,200ISK children 7-15, free for children 6 and under), mid-May-mid-September

Bring your camera, plus a pair of binoculars if you're inclined, and dress warmly, even in the summer. The tours do venture out into the open ocean and sea conditions vary according to the weather; it can get very wet and windy. Bring a hat, gloves, scarf, and layers, including a waterproof layer.

Swimming
HÚSAVÍK SWIMMING POOL
Héðinsbraut, tel. 354/464-1144, 6:45am-9pm Mon.-Fri., 10am-6pm Sat.-Sun., 800ISK
The Húsavík Swimming Pool is close to the campsite, which means it can get pretty crowded. Besides the pool, a couple of hot tubs also draw a crowd.

FOOD
GAMLÍ BAUKUR
Hafnarstett 9, tel. 354/464-2442, www.gamlibaukur.is, 9am-9pm daily, entrées from 2,700ISK
Gamlí Baukur is a unique restaurant built from driftwood found along the coastline of Húsavík. The rustic vibe continues inside, with large tables and photos of the town's fishing history adorning the walls. The food is hearty, and the fish and lamb dishes hit the spot. The meat soup is also divine. The casual ambience of the restaurant carries over to

the evening, when it transforms into a concert venue for local and visiting Icelandic acts. The combination of good music and good beer is hard to beat.

SALKA RESTAURANT
Garðarsbraut 4, tel. 354/464-2551, 11:30am-10pm daily, entrées from 2,800ISK
Salka Restaurant is a harborside eatery that is owned by a whale-watching company. The food is good but predictable, though the pizzas are quite nice. There are also soups, sandwiches, hamburgers, and fish and lamb dishes on the menu. The restaurant is proudly whale friendly, so whale meat is not an option.

★ NAUSTIÐ
Naustagarður 2, tel. 354/464-1520, noon-10pm daily, entrées from 2,800ISK
Naustið is known for its seafood. The restaurant uses fresh ingredients and local fish including cod, salmon, and blue ling. An outdoor eating area is delightful in good weather, and local musicians often play concerts. The interior is rustic, with wood-paneled walls and seafaring-related artwork.

ACCOMMODATIONS
Under 10,000ISK
HÚSAVÍK CAMPGROUND
Héðinsbraut, tel. 354/845-0705, May 15-Sept. 30, 1,750ISK
The Húsavík Campground regularly receives kudos. It's a well-maintained, large, and efficient facility that is wildly popular in June and July. The kitchen area is great and the showers are steaming hot. The campground, which is close to the center of town, is situated in an open field with no shelter. Tents and RVs are welcome.

10,000-30,000ISK
HÚSAVÍK GUESTHOUSE
Laugarbrekka 16, tel. 354/463-3399, www. husavikguesthouse.is, rooms from 17,000ISK
Húsavík Guesthouse is a family-run

1: a whale in Húsavík **2:** Húsavíkurkirkja **3:** Húsavík harbor guesthouse with options ranging from singles to family rooms. The atmosphere looks and feels very much like you're staying in a comfortable, well-loved home. There's art on the walls, jam-packed bookshelves with everything from novels to travel guides, and comfortable guest rooms. Guests share bathroom facilities, and breakfast is included.

FOSSHOTEL HÚSAVÍK
Ketilsbraut 22, tel. 354/464-1220,
www.islandshotel.is, rooms from 18,000ISK
Fosshotel Húsavík is a 70-room hotel, with 44 standard rooms and 26 superior rooms with king-sized beds, satellite TV, and private bathrooms. The hotel is decorated in nautical accents, and superior rooms have a fun and fresh whale theme to the decor. The hotel's bar is appropriately called Moby Dick, and the restaurant, Terian, serves fresh fish and other traditional Icelandic cuisine. Guests have access to free Wi-Fi and free parking, and breakfast is included.

ÁRBÓL GUESTHOUSE
Ásgarðsvegur 2, tel. 354/464-2220,
www.arbol.is, rooms from 24,000ISK
Árból Guesthouse is a quaint guesthouse close to the center of town. Some of the rooms have the look of a wood-paneled hunting lodge, while others look like you're staying at your grandmother's house. The rooms (singles, doubles, triples, and family rooms) are clean and comfortable and a bit larger than average. All rooms share bathroom facilities, and breakfast is included.

Over 30,000ISK
HÚSAVÍK CAPE HOTEL
Laugarbrekka 26, tel. 354/463-3399, www.
husavikhotel.com, rooms from 35,500ISK
Húsavík Cape Hotel is housed in a historic 1950 building that was owned by the Húsavík Fishing Company. In 2012 it was transformed into a smart and rustic hotel, complete with standard beds, hardwood floors, and simple furnishings. Guests have access to free Wi-Fi, and breakfast is included.

INFORMATION AND SERVICES
TOURIST INFORMATION OFFICE
Hafnarstett 1, tel. 354/464-4300, www.visithusavik.
is, 10am-4pm daily June-Sept.
The tourist information office is close to the harbor and offers Internet access, pamphlets about the region, and tour bookings.

GETTING THERE
By Car
By car, Húsavík is 90 kilometers (56 miles) northeast of **Akureyri** via paved **Route 85,** and it's 56 kilometers (35 miles) north of **Mývatn** on **Route 87,** which is also paved.

By Air
HÚSAVIK AIRPORT
10 km (6 mi) southwest of town, tel. 354/424-4000
Húsavík Airport is 10 kilometers (6 miles) south of the center of Húsavík. **Eagle Air** (tel. 354/562-4200, www.eagleair.is) offers 10 flights a week from **Reykjavík.** It's about a 45-minute flight and costs about 25,000ISK each way.

Jökulsárgljúfur (Vatnajökull National Park—North)

Jökulsárgljúfur National Park was established in 1973 and became part of Vatnajökull National Park in 2008, forming the largest national park in Europe. Jökulsárgljúfur is the northern division of Vatnajökull National Park. Within it are some of North Iceland's most visited sites, including Dettifoss and Ásbyrgi. Several well-maintained hiking trails travel along the perimeter of waterfalls, rivers, and canyons. Many tourists stop at Dettifoss to photograph the powerful waterfall, but the park has other treasures that are worthy of a longer visit; the mountainous landscape is breathtaking. Try to spend at least one day in this area.

Note that hikers must register with the park office at Ásbyrgi before they set out on their journey. Safety first.

SIGHTS
★ Ásbyrgi
Route 85

Ásbyrgi (Shelter of the Gods) is an enormous canyon full of interesting rock formations, lush grass, well-maintained walking paths, thriving birdlife, and several bodies of water, including rivers and waterfalls. The horseshoe-shaped canyon measures roughly 3.5 kilometers (2.2 miles) in length and 1.1 kilometers (0.7 miles) across.

Scientists have said that Ásbyrgi was most likely formed by glacial flooding of the Jökulsá á Fjöllum River after the last ice age, and additional flooding some 3,000 years ago. However, Icelandic folklore has a different explanation for the unique shape of the canyon. The canyon has been nicknamed Sleipnir's Footprint, as folklorists have said that the canyon was formed when Odin's eight-legged horse, Sleipnir, touched one of its feet to the ground, creating the depressions. Folklore also stipulates that the canyon is the central meeting point of the *huldufólk* (hidden people) who live among the cliffs.

Tourists make the trek to Ásbyrgi to take in the steep rock formations and enjoy a **hike**. In some spots hikers have to be careful in navigating the rocks. Be sure to wear proper footwear and take caution over any slippery-looking patches. One easy hike, which is about one kilometer (0.6 miles) and takes 30-60 minutes, starts at the **car park** at Ásbyrgi and leads to a platform at a small pond named **Botnstjörn**. Along the way are lots of trees, shrubbery, and rock formations. A lovely view over the pond takes in ducks and other birds and offers vistas of the western side of the canyon.

Ásbyrgi is 65 kilometers (40 miles) south of **Húsavík**. To reach the **visitors center** (Gljúfrastofa, tel. 354/470-7100) in Ásbyrgi from Húsavík, take paved **Route 85.**

Hólmatungur
Route 85

Hólmatungur is an area on the western side of the canyon of the glacial **Jökulsá river** that has breathtaking basalt column formations, along with choppy streams and the wondrous waterfall **Rettarfoss**. It's a beautiful spot that offers scenic views and wonderful photo ops.

To reach Hólmatungur from **Ásbyrgi** and **Route 85,** head south on **Route 862,** which is on the west side of the **Jökulsá.** Route 862 is a gravel road between Route 85 and **Dettifoss.** (Heading south of Dettifoss to Route 1, the road is paved.) Hólmantungur lies along this unpaved stretch. The gravel road is passable for normal vehicles, but it's closed during wintertime and does not open until late **May** or early **June.**

★ Dettifoss
Route 862

Dettifoss, which means "tumble falls," is the largest waterfall on the island, and the most powerful in Europe, with an average flow of 200 cubic meters of water per second. During an especially rainy day, the flow can reach 500 cubic meters per second. This force is not because of the fall's height, but its width. Spanning 100 meters (329 feet) wide and 45 meters (148 feet) high, Dettifoss is gigantic. The grayish color of the water comes from sand and rocks that get picked up along the way.

Because of the waterfall's size and sheer beauty, plan to spend at least a couple of hours here to take it all in. There are several viewing platforms. This is an open, slippery spot with lots of steps and minimal guardrails; be careful. If you're visiting on a windy day, expect to get hit with spray—but that's part of the fun, to really experience the falls. It's also common to see a rainbow or two depending on the weather.

Tour companies include Dettifoss as part of the **"Diamond Circle,"** a popular route around the Mývatn region and Húsavík, based in Akureyri. For a day tour, check out **Reykjavík Excursions** (tel. 354/580-5400, www.re.is).

Dettifoss is 28 kilometers (17 miles) south of **Ásbyrgi.** From Ásbyrgi and **Route 85,** head south on **Route 862** on the west side of the river **Jökulsá.** Route 862 is a gravel road between Route 85 and Dettifoss. (Heading south of Dettifoss to **Route 1,** the road is paved.) The gravel road is passable for normal vehicles, but it's closed during wintertime and does not open until late **May** or early **June.**

ACCOMMODATIONS
ÁSBYRGI CAMPGROUND
tel. 354/470-7100, 1,900ISK

You won't find any hotels or guesthouses within the park limits; the only option for overnight guests is the Ásbyrgi campground. The site, which is situated in an open field, is open from mid-May through September and allows for 350 tents as well as caravans (with hookups). There are adequate cooking facilities, hot showers, and a small shop that sells some food and hiking gear. Bring all the food, water, and supplies you need with you.

Dettifoss

Visiting Vatnajökull National Park

Vatnajökull National Park (www.vatnajokulsthjodgardur.is), which was named a UNESCO World Heritage site in 2019, is huge, covering 13 percent of the island and 13,700 square kilometers (5,290 square miles), and is the largest national park in western Europe.

Jökulsárgljúfur National Park and Skaftafell National Park were combined with Vatnajökull glacier in 2008 to form Vatnajökull National Park. Jökulsárgljúfur and Skaftafell are now considered the northern and southern divisions of the park.

Vatnajökull National Park has several visitors centers; some of the main ones are listed here.

- Jökulsárgljúfur visitors center (671 Kópasker, Ásbyrgi, tel. 354/465-2195, www.ust.is, 11am-3pm daily) is the best gateway to the northern part of the park and blockbuster sights like the Ásbyrgi canyon and Dettifoss.

- Snæfellsstofa visitors center (701 Egilsstaðir, Skriðuklaustur, tel. 354/470-0840, 9am-3pm daily June 1-Aug. 31, 10am-4pm daily Sept., open by request in winter) serves as a gateway to the eastern part of the park and Mount Snæfell (page 244).

- Skaftafell visitors center (Skaftafellsvegur, 785 Öræfi, tel. 354/478-1627, www.vatnajokulsthjodgardur.is, 10am-6pm daily Jan.-Feb., 9am-6pm daily Mar.-May, 8am-7pm daily June-Aug., 9am-6pm daily Sept.-Oct., 10am-6pm daily Nov.-Dec.) serves as both a national park office and visitors center near the southern entrance to the park.

There are no roads in the national park except for the tracks leading up to private farms. Wardens operate in the park, assisted by park rangers during the summer months (June-Aug.). Visitors are encouraged to seek information and advice from park staff, who can teach visitors about the area and find out its history, ecology, and geology. There are a variety of hikes throughout the park and everyone should be able to find a suitable outing.

INFORMATION AND SERVICES
TOURIST INFORMATION CENTER
671 Kópasker, tel. 354/465-2195, www.ust.is, 11am-3pm daily

The national park's tourist information center is based at Ásbyrgi and open year-round.

GETTING THERE AND AROUND

It's best to have a car to explore the park. Keep in mind that while Jökulsárgljúfur is open year-round, the roads beyond Ásbyrgi, including Route 862, are closed during wintertime and do not open until late May or early June.

If you don't have a car, a tour could be a great option. Akureyri-based SBA (tel. 354/550-0700, www.sba.is) offers a Dettifoss Grand Tour (22,500ISK) from mid-June to mid-September. The tour departs from the Reykjahlíð information center and takes you from Mývatn to Dettifoss, Ásbyrgi, Húsavík, and back to Mývatn.

East Iceland and the Eastfjords

Itinerary Ideas 233
Vopnafjörður 235
Fljótsdalur Valley.......238
The Eastfjords..........244
The Vatnajökull Region .259

East Iceland is where you find some actual "ice," including Vatnajökull glacier, a giant white spot on the map that is truly breathtaking in person. You can drive or hike right up to the glacier's edge in Skaftafell.

In the summer, it can be crowded with fellow travelers, but there are plenty of detours to take to avoid the hordes. Lacking infrastructure and people, the East is one of the most remote part of the island, and travel can be difficult in winter.

One of the least visited destinations in Iceland is one you should keep on your radar: the Eastfjords. If you're looking for remote, unspoiled beauty, it's here. The Ring Road weaves through the fjords, where you will see gorgeous mountains, charming fishing villages, and

Highlights

Look for ★ to find recommended sights, activities, dining, and lodging.

© MOON.COM

★ **Mount Snæfell:** It's only a moderate hike to the top of Iceland's highest mountain, where views span from the highlands to Vatnajökull and all the way out to sea (page 242).

★ **Hiking in Seyðisfjörður:** This tiny town of fewer than 1,000 residents offers a variety of hiking gems for hikers of all levels (page 248).

★ **Vatnajökull Glacier:** Covering about 8 percent of the country, this is the biggest glacier in Europe—and under the ice cap are still-active volcanoes (page 263).

★ **Jökulsárlón:** At the Glacier Lagoon, the deepest lake in Iceland, huge blocks of ice constantly break off a glacier and float on the surface (page 263).

★ **Skaftafell (Vatnajökull National Park—South):** One of East Iceland's most beautiful places has striking white glaciers set against a backdrop of green fields and black sands (page 264).

East Iceland and the Eastfjords

SKAFTAFELL (VATNAJÖKULL NATIONAL PARK-SOUTH)

Skaftafell

Svínafell

Nónhamar

DIAMOND BEACH

JÖKULSÁRLÓN

VATNAJÖKULL GLACIER

Vatnajökull

Vatnajökull National Park

SEE "VATNAJÖKULL REGION" MAP

Höfn

Lónsöræfi

Háálón

Kreppa

Jökulsá á Fjöllum

Brandarjökull

MOUNT SNÆFELL
▲ 1833m

Jökulsá í Kelduá

Fljótsdal

SEE "FLJÓTSDALUR VALLEY" MAP

Papey

Djúpivogur

Berufjörður

95

SEE "EASTFJORDS" MAP

Hengifoss

Lagarfljót

Jökulsá á Brú

931

Hallormsstaður

1

85

Egilsstaðir

Hof

93

Fardagafoss

95³

94

Seyðisfjörður

HIKING IN SEYÐISFJÖRÐUR

917

Vopnafjörður

85

26

1

NORTH ATLANTIC OCEAN

Borgarfjörður Eystri

0   15 km
0   15 mi

© MOON.COM

thriving wildlife. It's not easy to get around the region (you need a car), but it's worth the costs and trouble.

The East is also home to one of the most active volcanic areas on the island, and Vatnajökull National Park deserves at least one day of its own. Navigating the glacier (with a guide and proper equipment) is one of those unforgettable, bucket-list excursions.

East Iceland is often overlooked, but has some of the most pristine, untouched nature in Iceland. If you can spare a couple of days, spend some time hiking and photographing the Eastfjords. Even during the high season, there's a good chance you won't bump into many other tourists. The East can be your own private treasure.

PLANNING YOUR TIME

East Iceland is not conducive to tight schedules, as weather can be unpredictable and winds punishing. It's best to visit in the late spring, summer, or early autumn. Winter travel to and around the area is challenging. The wind and snow can make travel difficult at best, dangerous at worst. Monitor weather conditions closely and check to see if roads have been closed.

The Ring Road (Route 1) takes you through the East, and most people choose either Egilsstaðir or Seyðisfjörður as a base. Both towns are complete with guesthouses, restaurants, bus stations, and airports. Some guesthouses and restaurants operate only June-August. Seyðisfjörður is the best option for an extended stay in the Eastfjords.

The East is a paradise for hikers as there are numerous places to roam and experience the pristine nature of the region with few fellow travelers nearby. The East is sparsely populated and many tourists drive past the region to get from Höfn to Mývatn. Dedicate three days to enjoy the natural wonders such as Jökulsárlón and Svartifoss and to also have some time to hike.

Itinerary Ideas

THREE DAYS IN EAST ICELAND

Day 1: Scenic Skaftafell and Vatnajökull National Park

Pack a lunch today, as restaurant options are scarce and you have an active day.

1 First, visit Skaftafellsstofa Visitor Center for maps and an orientation of the region.

2 From the visitors center, you can take a quick, mile-long hike to Svartifoss waterfall and photograph the unique basalt columns surrounding the falls.

3 Call ahead to Icelandic Mountain Guides to arrange for a glacier hike on the Svínafellsjökull glacier tongue.

4 After a busy day of hiking, have dinner and spend the night at Hotel Skaftafel.

Day 2: Exploring Jökulsárlón and Höfn

1 Start the day with a drive to Fjallsárlón, a small glacier lagoon, where you can walk along the calm shore and take photos.

Previous: Seyðisfjörður; Glacier lagoon in Vatnajokull National Park; Arctic tern.

Itinerary Ideas

DAY ONE

1 Skaftafellsstofa Visitor Center
2 Svartifoss
3 Svínafellsjökull
4 Hotel Skaftafell

DAY TWO

1 Fjallsárlón
2 Diamond Beach
3 Jökulsárlón Glacier Lagoon Café
4 Jökulsárlón
5 Humarhöfnin
6 Hótel Höfn

DAY THREE

1 Djúpivogur Swimming Pool
2 Havarí
3 Lagarfljót
4 Hallormsstaður
5 Sláturhúsið
6 Icelandair Hótel Hérað

2 Get back in your car for a 10-minute drive to the **Diamond Beach,** where polished pieces of ice lay atop the rich black sands, resembling diamonds.

3 Have lunch at the **Jökulsárlón Glacier Lagoon café** before walking along the shore, admiring the icebergs.

4 Take a guided boat tour on **Jökulsárlón** with Glacier Lagoon to get up close to the mammoth icebergs bobbing in the lagoon.

5 Drive to Höfn and explore the harbor area before having dinner at **Humarhofnin.**

6 Spend the night at **Hotel Höfn.**

Day 3: The Charming Eastfjords

1 Make your way farther east to the beautiful town of Djúpivogur and explore the harbor area before relaxing at the **Djúpivogur swimming pool.**

2 Drive to the organic farm and café **Havarí** for lunch.

3 Continue north to walk along **Lagarfljót,** Iceland's own Loch Ness.

4 Roam around the largest forested area in Iceland, **Hallormsstaður.**

5 Drive to Egilsstaðir and visit **Sláturhúsið,** a cultural center with art exhibitions.

6 Have dinner and spend the night at **Icelandair Hotel Herað.**

Vopnafjörður

Vopnafjörður (Weapon Fjord) is full of picturesque mountains, pure waterfalls, and historic farms. It's one of the best spots to get a glimpse of orcas. It's pretty, steeped in medieval history, and home to gorgeous wildlife.

The history of the town, also called Vopnafjörður, dates back 1,100 years. The bay was first settled by Viking seafarers from Norway. Foreign merchants frequently sailed to Vopnafjörður in the early modern age, and a settlement gradually formed on the peninsula where the village of Vopnafjörður now stands. It became one of Iceland's major commercial harbors in the 18th and 19th centuries. In the last half century, the fishing industry has grown considerably, and is today the largest business sector in the area.

The town has also had an impact on literature: *Independent People,* the epic Icelandic novel by Nobel Prize winner Halldór Laxness, was said to have been inspired by life in the highlands around Vopnafjörður.

SIGHTS
Bustarfell
off Rte. 85 about 20 km (12 mi) south of Vopnafjörður, tel. 354/471-2211, www. visitvopnafjordur.com, 10am-5pm daily June 1-Sept. 20, 1,200ISK

The old farm of Bustarfell is one of the best-preserved of the traditional Icelandic turf houses. The museum offers a great opportunity to see how people's ways of living have changed through the centuries. The foundations of the current house are from 1770, but the house has undergone alterations over the years. The rooms are authentically furnished in the style of centuries past. The museum covers life from the 18th century to the mid-20th century. The **café** is a good spot to enjoy coffee, light meals, and yummy pastries as well as exhibitions from local artists.

East Iceland Emigration Center
(Vesturfaramiðstöð Austurlands)

Kaupvangur 2, tel. 354/473-1200, www. visitvopnafjordur.com, 10am-5pm Mon., Thur. and Sat. June 1-Sept 20., 10am-5pm Mon. and Thur. Sept. 21-May 31, free

The East Iceland Emigration Center is dedicated to the period of 1875-1914, when many residents emigrated from the region after the great Askja eruption of 1875 displaced hundreds. The center is focused on the history of the region and renewing contact with emigrants' descendants. There are documents and photos on display.

Múlastofa Cultural Center

Hafnarbyggð 4a, tel. 354/473-1331, www.east.is, 10am-10pm daily June 1-Aug. 25, closed rest of the year, 600ISK

Múlastofa is a small exhibition dedicated to local brothers Jón Múli Árnason and Jónas Árnason. The brothers, who were writers, singers, and musicians, grew up in Vopnafjörður, and their father managed the general store between 1917-1924. On display are photographs, videos, and interactive exhibits where guests can listen to the brothers speak, sing, and perform plays.

Fuglabjarganes

Strandhafnarvegur, off Route 85

Fuglabjarganes is a prominent cliff that juts out on the northern coast of the town. You can get a good look at it from a marked walking path from the unpaved **Strandhafnarvegur road,** which is along the **Fugla River.** The scenery is beautiful, with white sand beaches, stone walls, towering cliffs, and impressive rock caverns and pillars.

SPORTS AND RECREATION
Bird-Watching

Vopnafjörður is a bird-watcher's dream. You can see a mix of seabirds, waterfowl, waders, passerines, and raptors. A couple of the best spots to see birds are the **Tangi Peninsula**

north of Vopnafjörður, which is a beautiful and remote place to watch seabirds, and the area around the **Nypslon estuary,** which provides habitat for various duck species. The region can be reached by **Route 85** and is signposted.

Fishing

There are several fishing opportunities, through tours, within a few minutes' drive of Vopnafjörður.

HOFSA RIVER

92 km (57 mi) from Égilsstaðir via Route 917

The Hofsa River is just a 15-minute drive east from Vopnafjörður, and the stretch of the river open to angling encompasses 30 kilometers (19 miles) in a wide valley. Salmon season runs **July 1-September 20.** Permits are needed and must be secured in advance. For details on permits, visit the region's website (www.vopnafjordur.com/activities/angling).

SELA RIVER

100 km (62 mi) from Egilsstaðir via Route 917

The Sela River is a 10-minute drive north from Vopnafjörður and has long been one of the most popular of Icelandic salmon rivers. Fishing is fly only, and the river has a catch-and-release system in place. **Guides**, like Anglers (www.anglers.is), are available.

VESTURDALSA RIVER

92 km (57 mi) from Égilsstaðir via Route 917

The Vesturdalsa River is a 15-minute drive south from Vopnafjörður. It originates from the runoff of **Lake Arnarvatn** in the highlands above Vopnafjörður, flows 34 kilometers (21 miles) to the lowlands, and empties into **Nypslon estuary.** The fishing area reaches 27 kilometers (17 miles) up to a waterfall not accessible to salmon. A catch-and-release policy is in effect.

Hiking

Vopnafjörður offers several hiking routes that vary from easy to challenging. Beginners will find a wide range of mapped routes and marked trails that offer scenic views of the whole of Vopnafjörður—the bay, the Tangi Peninsula, inland areas, and mountains. For maps and detailed trail information, visit the tourist information center (Hafnarbyggd 4a, tel. 354/473-1331, www.vopnafjordur.com), and always be sure to check the weather forecast and report your itinerary.

GLJUFURSA RIVER HIKE

Distance: 6 km (34 mi) round-trip
Hiking Time: 3 hours round-trip
Information and Maps: Vopnafjörður Tourist Information Center
Trailhead: Small walking path from parking lot off Route 917

An easy route that is popular among locals is around Drangsnes Peninsula to the towering waterfalls at the Gljufursa River. The out-and-back hike is accessible via Routes 85 and 917, about 3 kilometers (2 miles) south of town.

KROSSAVIK MOUNTAIN HIKE

Distance: 2.2 km (1.4 mi) round-trip
Hiking Time: 1 hour round-trip
Information and Maps: Vopnafjörður Tourist Information Center
Trailhead: Walking path from Route 917

More experienced hikers looking for a challenging trail should hike to the top of Krossavik mountain, which reaches 1,080 meters (3,543 feet). The mountain stands opposite the village on the other side of the bay, and the trailhead is accessible via Route 917.

Swimming
SELÁRLAUG

3.5 km (7.2 mi) from Rte. 85, tel. 354/473-1499, noon-10pm daily May 1-Aug. 31, 2pm-7pm Tue.-Fri., noon-4pm Sat.-Sun. Sept. 1-Apr. 30, 700ISK

The local swimming pool is called Selárlaug, where you will find locals taking a dip and socializing with friends and family. The facility has a large sun deck, patio chairs, and hot pots.

FOOD
CAFE HJALEIGAN

tel. 354/471-2211, www.bustarfell.is, 10am-5pm daily June 1-Sept. 15, snacks from 800ISK

Cafe Hjaleigan is the café at Bustarfell museum off Rte. 85, about 20 kilometers (12 miles) south from Vopnafjörður. It serves coffee, soft drinks, and light meals such as sandwiches, as well as pastries.

OLLASJOPPA

Kolbeinsgata 35, tel. 354/473-1803, 10am-10pm daily, entrées from 1,800ISK

Ollasjoppa is a tiny café that offers quick fare including pizza, hamburgers, sandwiches, and pitas, along with hot dishes with lamb, fish, and chicken.

ACCOMMODATIONS
SIREKSSTADIR FARM COTTAGES

Sireksstadir, tel. 354/473-1458, www.sireksstadir.is, rooms from 14,000ISK

Sireksstadir Farm Cottages offers two cottages for families or groups that can accommodate 4-6 people, as well as seven double guest rooms. The cottages are cozy and have a large deck and a barbecue grill. Guests are invited to observe farm activities, and the rooms are available year-round. The staff are friendly, welcoming, and inclusive.

HOTEL TANGI

Hafnarbyggd 17, tel. 354/473-1203, www.hoteltangi.com, rooms from 15,000ISK

Hotel Tangi is a standard countryside hotel with 17 rooms, a restaurant, and a bar. The exterior of the block building isn't much to look at, but the inside is comfortable, with standard beds and IKEA-like furniture. There are single and double rooms, some with shared bathroom facilities.

SYÐRI-VÍK

tel. 354/473-1199, www.heyiceland.is, May 1-Nov 1., rooms from 18,000ISK

Syðri-Vík is a six-room guesthouse based on a working farm. Guests have access to a fully equipped kitchen, common dining and living rooms, and shared bathroom and laundry facilities. The owners are very friendly, and it's a lot of fun to stay in such an active farm. The owners also rent out two summer cottages for families or large groups. Syðri-Vík is 8 kilometers (5 miles) from the village of Vopnafjörður, located near Route 85.

INFORMATION AND SERVICES

VOPNAFJÖRÐUR TOURIST INFORMATION OFFICE

Hafnarbyggd 4a, tel. 354/473-1331, www.vopnafjordur. is, 10am-5pm Mon.-Fri., noon-4pm Sat.-Sun.

The main tourist information office is housed in a huge yellow building in the center of town. It has brochures and maps about the region, as well as a small food store to stock up on essentials if you're staying at a self-catering guesthouse or farm.

GETTING THERE

By Car

By car, the paved Route 85 connects Vopnafjörður with Bakkafjörður, a small fishing village 34 kilometers (21 miles) south of Vopnafjörður. Route 1, in the south, connects to Egilsstaðir (75 minutes). For the most scenic route, take unpaved Route 917 over the mountains. Vopnafjörður is 212 kilometers (132 miles) from Akureyri, about 2.5 hours on Route 1.

By Plane

VOPNAFJÖRÐUR AIRPORT

tel. 354/424-4000

There are flights from the northern town of Akureyri to Vopnafjörður Airport, which is situated at the bottom of the fjord. Daily flights are about 45 minutes. One-way flights cost about 7,000ISK.

Fljótsdalur Valley

Fljótsdalur Valley encompasses the towns of Egilsstaðir and Fellabær, which form the largest urban center in East Iceland. The region supports a strong rural community that stretches from Biskupsháls in the west and Héraðsflói, a bay in the north, to the mountain ranges surrounding the central eastern fjords in the East and Vatnajökull and Öxi in the south. While Egilsstaðir is the largest town in the region, nature takes center stage in the valley: The region is home to Mount Snæfell, the highest mountain in Iceland.

EGILSSTAÐIR

Egilsstaðir is considered the unofficial capital of East Iceland, but it still has fewer than 3,000 residents. The quaint town earned its name based on a reference to the nearby farm Egil's stead, which appears in saga stories. The community developed and grew after Iceland gained independence from Denmark in 1944. That said, the town today remains

sparsely populated, but the harbor welcomes thousands of visitors who come to Iceland via ferry from mainland Europe.

Sights

EAST ICELAND HERITAGE MUSEUM (Minjasafn Austurlands)

Laufskógar 1, tel. 354/471-1412, www.minjasafn.is, 10am-6pm daily June 1-Aug. 31, 11am-4pm Tue.-Fri. Sept.1-May 31, 1,200ISK adults, free for 17 and under

The East Iceland Heritage Museum showcases how life was lived in the region over the last 200 years. The main exhibition features objects including clothing, food, and tools, as well as items used for hunting, crafts, food production, and hobbies. You can also enter a room of a 19th-century farmhouse that was moved from the countryside into the museum. The display depicts a small bedroom/living room, with sparse furnishings. It's an interesting view into what life was like in this remote part of Iceland—a hardscrabble, difficult existence.

Fljótsdalur Valley

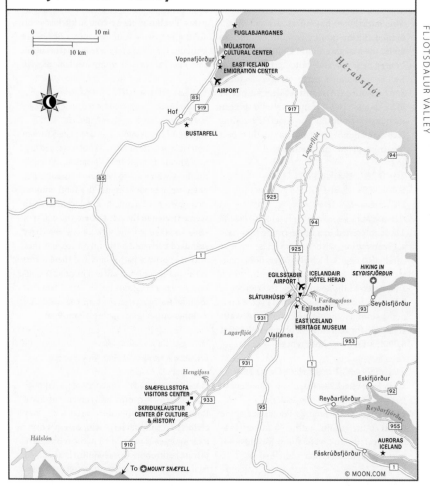

SKRIÐUKLAUSTUR CENTER OF CULTURE & HISTORY

Skriðuklaustur, tel. 354/471-2990, www. skriduklaustur.is, 10am-6pm daily June 1-Aug. 31, 11am-5pm May and Sept., noon-4pm Apr., open by request Oct.-Mar., 1,100ISK, free for children under 16

The Skriðuklaustur Center of Culture & History is an impressive historical site that includes the ruins of a 16th-century monastery as well as the home of the celebrated novelist Gunnar Gunnarsson, the author of *Af Borgslægtens Historie (Guest the One-Eyed)*, the first Icelandic book made into a movie. Gunnar's home was built in 1939 and was donated to the state by the writer in 1948. You can view photographs and objects that belonged to Gunnar Gunnarsson, and the building also serves as a cultural center where various events and exhibitions are held throughout the year.

SLÁTURHÚSIÐ

Kaupvangur 7, tel. 354/471-1479, www.slaturhusid.is,
10am-4pm Mon.-Fri., free

The Sláturhúsið has injected some much-needed culture into Egilsstaðir. Founded in 2006, the Slaughterhouse Culture Center is home to theater and dance productions as well as workshops, performances, lectures, and exhibitions. An artist residency available to locals and visitors provides studio space in exchange for tuition. The concrete building is cold and nondescript, but one might expect that from an old slaughterhouse.

Sports and Recreation

SANDFELLSSKÓGUR HORSEBACK RIDING

17 km south of Egilsstaðir on Rte. 1, tel. 354/471-2420

Those interested in a horse-riding tour have a great option with the travel service at Sandfellsskógur, which also offers horse rentals. Beautiful trails wind through the forest and traverse hills and valleys. You can rent a horse for 1-4 hours, and there's even a midnight summer tour. Horse tours are available June through mid-September and cost 8,000ISK for a one-hour rental.

EGILSSTAÐIR SWIMMING POOL

Tjarnarbraut 26, tel. 354/470-0777, 6:30am-8:30pm
Mon.-Fri., 10am-6pm Sat.-Sun., 1,000ISK

The Egilsstaðir Swimming Pool is one of the nicest in the region, with a 50-meter (164-foot) heated pool, waterslides for kids, hot tubs, and a fitness center.

EKKJUFELL GOLF COURSE

Fellabær, tel. 354/894-0604, greens fees 2,500ISK

The Ekkjufell Golf Course is the sole course in the town. It's open year-round and is frequented by locals, so be sure to call ahead for a tee time.

Food and Accommodations

HÚSEY

Hróastunga, tel. 354/471-3010, husey@simnet.is,
beds 5,300ISK, 2-person private room 11,100ISK

Húsey is a 20-bed youth hostel that was converted from an old farmhouse. It's in an isolated part of the village, and there are great opportunities to spot seals and hike remote paths. The hostel has a common kitchen available for preparing your own meals. Sheets are available for a fee, and there is a barbecue on site. There are private rooms available as well.

HÓTEL EDDA EGILSSTAÐIR

Tjarnarbraut 25, tel. 354/444-4880, www.hoteledda.
is, June-mid-Aug., rooms from 20,000ISK

Hótel Edda Egilsstaðir is an adequate 52-room hotel just outside of town. What it lacks in luxury is made up for with the location, especially for those who want to be close to nature. The hotel is close to a 25-meter (82-foot) outdoor swimming pool, a nine-hole golf course, and a scenic stretch in the fjord where you can spot seals and take woodland walks. Rooms have standard beds and basic furniture, but they also have private bathrooms and there is free Wi-Fi in the common areas. The hotel restaurant serves a breakfast buffet 7am-10am that includes waffles, fresh fruit, and oatmeal, and a dinner buffet is available 6:30pm-9pm.

HÓTEL EYVINDARÁ

Eyvindará 2, tel. 354/471-1200, www.eyvindara.is,
rooms from 23,200ISK

Hótel Eyvindará is a ranch-style guesthouse that offers 28 rooms and seven cottages. Rooms are tastefully decorated with cozy country accents and large windows that overlook a gorgeous view. Most of the rooms have private bathrooms, but a handful have shared facilities. The hotel's restaurant serves breakfast daily, and dinner is available late May through early September. The dinner menu emphasizes fish and lamb dishes but has a few vegetarian options.

LAKE HOTEL EGILSSTAÐIR

Egilsstöðum 1-2, tel. 354/471-1114, www.lakehotel.is,
rooms from 31,000ISK

Lake Hotel Egilsstaðir is a comfortable 50-room guesthouse with a country farmhouse theme. Rooms are large and range from singles to triples. While all have wooden floors,

Iceland's Loch Ness Monster

Scotland has the Loch Ness monster, and Iceland has **Lagarfljótsormur,** a huge worm-like monster said to call **Lagarfljót** home. People have reported spotting the monster inside the freshwater, glacier-fed lake, which is about 30 kilometers (19 miles) long, as well as outside the body of water. It is said to have many humps and slither in a slow fashion. The tale is part of Icelandic folklore, and locals have a sense of humor about "sightings." If you do happen to see the monster, make sure you report it to the local **heritage museum** in Egilsstaðir.

a TV, and free Wi-Fi, some rooms also boast sweeping mountain views. There is also an in-house restaurant and a spa.

★ ICELANDAIR HÓTEL HERAÐ

Miðvangur 5-7, tel. 354/471-1500, www. icelandairhotels.is, rooms from 34,000ISK
Icelandair Hótel Heraðir is the town's most upscale lodging option. The 60-room hotel, which is huge for the location, is chic, modern, and has that classic Nordic style you'd expect to see in Reykjavík. But this is an Icelandair Hótel, so the sleek interior and rooms are to be expected. The decor is heavy on wood, with gorgeous hardwood floors throughout the building, classic Scandinavian wood furnishings, and even modern wood art. The restaurant (11:30am-9:30pm daily, entrées from 4,000ISK) has the most upscale dining you'll find in the town, and the chefs don't disappoint, serving dishes with fresh ingredients you'd expect, like fish and lamb, but includes some surprises as well, like a reindeer steak. From September to the end of May, the restaurant offers a delicious brunch on Sundays from 11:30am-2pm for 3,800ISK.

EGILSSTAÐIR CAMPSITE

Kaupvangur 10, tel. 354/471-2320, June-Aug. 31, 2,000ISK per adult, free for children under 12
The Egilsstaðir Campsite can be quite busy in the summer. The campsite is close to town, and amenities include hot showers and adequate cooking facilities. There are areas for tents and RVs with hookups. The campsite is situated in an open field with trees along the perimeter. You must pay at the tourist information center.

Information and Services

TOURIST INFORMATION CENTER

Kaupvangur 17, tel. 354/470-0750, www.east.is, 8am-10pm daily June-Aug., 9am-6pm Mon.-Fri., noon-4pm Sat.-Sun. Sept.-May
Egilsstaðir's tourist information center is the largest and most comprehensive in the region, and one of the largest in the country. You will find hiking maps, basic travel supplies, a café and souvenir shop, Internet access, and a booking center for an array of tours. The site is also home to the bus station and the local campsite.

Getting There

By car, **Route 1** connects Egilsstaðir with the North Iceland town **Akureyri,** which is 3.5 hours and 266 kilometers (165 miles) away. Egilsstaðir is 128 kilometers (79.5 miles) from **Vopnafjörður,** about 1.5 hours.

EGILSSTAÐIR AIRPORT

tel. 354/424-4040
Egilsstaðir Airport is in the heart of town, and there are daily flights by **Air Iceland Connect** (www.airicelandconnect.com) from Reykjavík's domestic airport. Flights take about one hour and cost around 17,000ISK each way.

AROUND EGILSSTAÐIR

Egilsstaðir is situated along a beautiful glacial lake called **Lagarfljót** that stretches 35 kilometers (21.7 miles) long and offers numerous opportunities for hiking and outdoor recreation.

Hallormsstaður

20-minute drive on Route 931
You've probably noticed that trees are a rare sight in Iceland. Hallormsstaður has the distinction of being the largest forest in the country, though it would be considered small by other standards. It stretches along Lagarfljót and a small cove; it's beautiful to roam among native birch trees that have survived inclement weather and found a way to thrive. There are also scores of imported species, including willow and rowan.

Hallormsstaður is 23 kilometers (14 miles) southwest of Egilsstaðir on **Route 1** and **Route 931,** which is unpaved, about a 20-minute drive.

Hengifoss

Car park off of Route 931
After roaming Iceland's largest forest, take a walk to the opposite side of the lake and look at the towering 120-meter (394-foot) waterfall Hengifoss. The landscape reveals a layer of basalt above ancient tree trunks. Have your camera ready.

Hengifoss is 34 kilometers (21 miles) from Egilsstaðir on **Route 931,** a gravel road. For a close look you can stop at the designated **car park** off of Route 931 and walk uphill about 2.5 kilometers (1.6 miles) to the waterfall.

Fardagafoss

Road 93
Fardagafoss is a waterfall that weaves up the Fjardarheiði mountain, flowing over a rocky ridge. It's about 5 kilometers (3 miles) from Egilsstaðir on **road 93.** There is a small parking lot, and the waterfall is a short walk from the road.

★ MOUNT SNÆFELL

Distance: *8 km (5 mi) round-trip*
Hiking Time: *12 hours round-trip*
Information and Maps: *Snæfellsstofa Visitors Center*
Trailhead: *Snæfellsskáli Mountain Hut, GPS N 64.8042, W 15.6418*
Mount Snæfell (Snow Mountain) is the highest mountain, excluding glaciers, in Iceland. Despite towering 1,833 meters (6,013 feet), it's fairly easy to scale. The dormant volcano offers spectacular views over the highlands, down Fljótsdalur valley, and of Vatnajökull glacier. You can see rivers, canyons, and valleys—and you may even catch a glimpse of a reindeer herd. Climbing doesn't get better.

A well-kept trail begins at the base of the mountain and continues to the top. Hiking groups start at the mountain hut **Snæfellsskáli.**

The moderate hike is about 8 kilometers (5 miles) and takes about 8-9 hours. The top of the mountain is snowcapped all year long. Bring good boots and waterproof gear, alert people of your travel plans, and monitor the weather closely. If conditions are not good, do not attempt a climb.

HIKING FROM MOUNT SNÆFELL TO LÓNSÖRÆFI

Distance: *55 km (34 mi)*
Hiking Time: *4 days*
Information and Maps: *Snæfellsstofa Visitors Center*
Trailhead: *Snæfellsskáli Mountain Hut, GPS N 64.8042, W 15.6418, tel. 354/575-8400*
Lónsöræfi is an isolated wildlife preserve in a raw part of the East, with birds outnumbering humans by the thousands. Bird enthusiasts looking for a glimpse of whimbrels will love Lónsöræfi. The brown and white waders with curved bills can be seen year-round.

The landscape is striking but unforgiving, with strong winds and remnants of sub-glacial eruptions of the past. It's a beautiful patch of land, but be sure to monitor the weather closely before you head out for a hike, and keep in mind that there are not a lot of guesthouses or eateries nearby. You will feel like you're on your own, because in much of the area, you are.

The trek from Mount Snæfell to Lónsöræfi is growing in popularity. The landscape is rocky and angular, with sweeping hills and

1: Hengifoss 2: Lagarfljót lake 3: Mount Snæfell

vast valleys. Colors are muted, and the atmosphere is serene. Along the trek, hikers see glaciers, waterfalls, and cliffs. The hike, which starts at the **Snæfellsskáli mountain hut,** is about 55 kilometers (34 miles) and takes four days, with 6-8 hours of walking per day. The maximum elevation is 250 meters (870 feet). It's challenging and for experienced hikers only—recent years have seen many search-and-rescue operations deployed in this isolated region in the name of stranded hikers. As such, it's strongly recommended you explore the region as part of a **tour.**

The only road into the Lónsöræfi reserve is the **F980,** a rough gravel road off of Route 1 that ends after 25 kilometers (16 miles) at Illikambur. As it's only drivable for super jeeps (which are huge and outfitted for rugged terrain) and experienced drivers, please do not attempt to take a compact car or SUV on the trip. There is a river crossing along the way, and you will get stuck.

ICELANDIC MOUNTAIN GUIDES
tel. 354/587-9999, www.mountainguides.is
Icelandic Mountain Guides offers a fully guided tour, departing from Reykjavík with air transfers, an experienced guide, food for four days, and mountain hut accommodation for 154,000ISK. Departures are in July and August. Make sure you have proper gear like waterproof clothing for rain and wind.

Accommodations
SNÆFELLSSKÁLI MOUNTAIN HUT
tel. 354/575-8400, 6,000ISK
The mountain hut offers basic amenities including beds, bathrooms, and cooking facilities. The whole area is open only in the summer.

Information and Services
SNÆFELLSSTOFA VISITORS CENTER
Skriðuklaustur, tel. 354/470-0840, 9am-3pm daily June 1-Aug. 31, 10am-4pm daily Sept., open by request in winter
The Snæfellsstofa visitors center is the information center for the east area of Vatnajökull National Park. The visitors center houses a fascinating exhibition on the area, the glacier, and local flora and fauna. Snæfell is one of the most visited destinations within the national park, and the center gives you a preview into the vast region. The center's souvenir shop focuses on local products, including woolen goods and food products.

Getting There
To get to the base, take unpaved **Route 910** to **Route F909.** The journey from Egilsstaðir takes about 1.5 hours and is 93 kilometers (58 miles). Getting here requires a rugged **four-wheel drive,** as the roads are at best challenging and at worst treacherous. Don't try to make it in a compact rental car or you'll wind up stranded.

The Eastfjords

The Eastfjords are some of the most remote and unspoiled parts of Iceland. In all, there are 14 fjords, each with its own charm and tiny population. There are waterfalls among small fishing villages, and unique museums lure tourists off the Ring Road. If you're on an extended trip to Iceland, you should make time to explore this wonderful land where wildlife greatly outnumbers humans.

BORGARFJÖRÐUR EYSTRI
This fjord is a prime destination for hiking, as there are numerous well-maintained trails, gorgeous mountains, and deserted bays. The big draw is the spectacular scenery that you don't have to share with hordes of tourists, unlike in other parts of the country.

Sights
KJARVALSSTOFA
Fjarðarborg, tel. 354/472-9950, www.dyrfjoll.
is, noon-6pm daily June-Aug., open by request
Sept.-May, 1,00ISK

Kjarvalsstofa is a small museum dedicated to the work of celebrated artist Jóhannes Kjarval (1885-1972), who is known for his haunting landscape paintings as well as works that depict saga stories and Iceland's folklore.

The Eastfjords

ÁLFABORG
Route 94, GPS N 65.3119, W 13.4832

Álfaborg, or "fjord of Borg," is a 30-meter (98-foot) rocky hill known in folklore as the home of the queen of Iceland's hidden people. Many locals are amused by this history and happily relay stories of elves that have been passed down through the years. Álfaborg is a legally protected natural site, and a fun "elf rock" to photograph and climb upon. It can be found off of Route 94, a few kilometers south of town.

Bird-Watching

Birdlife thrives in the area. About 8,000 pairs of puffins nest every summer in Borgarfjörður Eystri from mid-April to mid-August. Other common bird species nesting there are fulmars, kittiwakes, and eider ducks. An observation platform at the marina connects to a small islet that puffins love, giving you a close-up view from about two meters away. The region is a photographer's dream; the birds are plentiful and the scenery breathtaking. The marina in the center of the village is the best place to spot puffins and kittiwakes.

Hiking

Borgarfjörður Eystri is home to numerous well-maintained hiking trails and has earned the nickname "Paradise of the Hiker." There are 27 day routes in the region where hikers can see black-sand beaches, towering mountains, ancient farm ruins, and colorful hills and valleys. The region is also known for its exceptional hiking facilities, including lodges and restrooms at certain points. A hiking map is for sale at local tourism businesses as well as the information center in Egilsstaðir. The hikes vary in degree of difficulty and length, so be sure to consult the maps closely.

Food and Accommodations
ÁLFACAFÉ
Iðngarðar, tel. 354/472-9884, alfacafe@simnet.is,
noon-9pm daily mid-May-mid-Sept., limited hours
mid-Sept.-mid-May, entrées from 2,200ISK

Álfacafé is a charming café that serves delicious fish soup, salted cod snacks, and fresh pastries and breads.

BLÁBJÖRG GUESTHOUSE

Gamla Frystihusið, tel. 354/846-0085, www. blabjorg.com, rooms from 20,000ISK

Blábjörg Guesthouse offers 11 rooms in an unexpected building: a renovated fish processing factory. Rooms are bright and cozy, and six rooms have beautiful seaside views. Amenities include a common kitchen and dining room, shared bathroom facilities, and free Wi-Fi throughout the building. The ground floor features a spa and wellness center with hot tubs and saunas.

ALFHEIMAR GUESTHOUSE

Brekkubær, tel. 354/861-3677, www.alfheimar.com, rooms from 23,00ISK

Alfheimar Guesthouse is a remote 32-room guesthouse situated near a puffin colony. The hosts, a husband and wife, are inviting, making you feel like you're staying with friends. Rooms are spacious and have the comforts of home. The free Wi-Fi is surprisingly strong for the region, and the in-house **restaurant** (7am-8pm daily, entrées from 2,800ISK) has some delicious options. A breakfast buffet is included in the price of the room.

Getting There

Borgarfjörður Eystri is 70 kilometers (43 miles) north of **Egilsstaðir**. **Route 94**, a paved road, connects to Egilsstaðir, which is about an hour away from the fjord.

SEYÐISFJÖRÐUR

Seyðisfjörður gets a lot of traffic for a tiny town of fewer than 1,000 residents. This is due to the harbor, which acts as the main ferry terminal for passengers to and from continental Europe. You may be arriving as a point of necessity, but the darling town has lots of reasons to stay a couple of days and explore.

Sights

BLAA KIRKJAN

Hafnargata 44, tel. 354/470-2308, www.blaakirkjan.is

The Blaa Kirkjan, or Blue Church, is a quaint wooden structure built in 1922 that hosts a series of concerts during the summer months. Genres range from classical music to choral to jazz. Concerts are held in July and August and cost 2,800ISK. Check the website for the summer schedule. If you like traditional churches, be sure to check it out, but if you're not seeing a concert here, you can skip it.

TECHNICAL MUSEUM OF EAST ICELAND (Tækniminjasafn Austurlands)

Hafnargata 44, tel. 354/472-1696, www.seydisfjordur.org, 11am-5pm Mon.-Fri., 1,000ISK, free for children under 17

The Technical Museum of East Iceland is home to the first telegraph station in Iceland, along with exhibitions that depict technical innovations from 1880 to 1950. There are tools on display, a letterpress machine and type, and equipment used in the fishing industry. It's an unexpected museum due to the remote surroundings, and it's worth the trip. A couple of exhibitions are geared toward children.

TVÍSÖNGUR

walking path from Hafnargata 47

Tvísöngur is a "sound sculpture" by German artist Lukas Kühne that is situated on a mountainside in Seyðisfjörður. The concrete structure consists of five interconnected domes of different sizes ranging 2-4 meters (7-14 feet). Each dome has its own unique resonance that corresponds to a tone in the Icelandic musical tradition of five-tone harmony, and the dome works as a natural amplifier to that tone. Guests can experience an acoustic sensation that can be explored and experimented with. The site's remoteness and serenity offer a perfect setting for playing music or

---

1: horses grazing in the Eastfjords 2: the Blaa Kirkjan

1

2

singing—alone, in harmony, or even for an audience.

Tvísöngur is accessed by a gravel walking path that starts across from the Brimberg Fish Factory (Hafnargata 47). It takes 15-20 minutes and is a moderately difficult walk. Make sure you have good shoes.

SKAFTFELL CENTER FOR VISUAL ART (Myndlistarmiðstöð Austurlands)

Öldugata 14, tel. 354/472-1632, www.skaftfell.is, noon-6pm daily, free

The Skaftfell Center for Visual Art works hard to bring contemporary art exhibitions to a predominantly rural area—and it succeeds. The center hosts exhibitions by local and visiting artists as well as a permanent exhibition of contemporary art featuring Icelandic and international artists. You can take a private tour for 2,500ISK (maximum five guests).

DVERGASTEINN

Vesturgata 12

Dvergasteinn, or Dwarf Boulder, was once the site of a church, with the namesake boulder behind it. The church moved, but the boulder remained, and folklore enthusiasts say the stone is inhabited by dwarves, or "hidden people."

★ Hiking

Seyðisfjörður has quite a few trails to choose from, ranging from easy to more challenging. Hiking maps are available at the town's tourist information center.

VESTDALSEYRI NATURE RESERVE HIKE

Distance: *4 km (2 mi) round-trip*
Hiking Time: *2.5 hours round-trip*
Information and Maps: *Seyðisfjörður Tourist Information Center*
Trailhead: *Vestdalseyri entrance off of road 951*
The Vestdalseyri Nature Reserve, about one kilometer north of town, is a valley known for its many waterfalls and rich birdlife. It's a beautiful place to roam and take in

the mountain scenery. It contains an easy hike that is one of the most popular trails in Seyðisfjörður. You can start at the Vestdalseyri entrance and follow the trail. After passing a few glorious waterfalls, you will arrive at a small lake, Vestdalsvatn, which remains frozen most of the year.

SKALANES NATURE RESERVE HIKE

Distance: *9 km (6 mi) round-trip*
Hiking Time: *2.5 hours round-trip*
Information and Maps: *Seyðisfjörður Tourist Information Center*
Trailhead: *Parking area by the Austdalsa River*
For an easy lowland hike, start from the parking area by the Austdalsa River and head to the nature reserve Skalanes, where there is a guesthouse and museum. This hike includes views of the gorgeous Skalanesbjarg bird cliffs, where you can see nesting eider ducks May-July. Please be mindful of nests and eggs and be careful where you step along the way.

AFRETTADALUR VALLEY HIKE

Distance: *17 km (11 mi) round-trip*
Hiking Time: *8 hours round-trip*
Information and Maps: *Seyðisfjörður Tourist Information Center*
Trailhead: *Austdalsa parking lot*
A more challenging trail starts from Skalanes and goes up along the edge of the cliffs to the Skollaskard pass, which is steep. You continue on into a valley, Afrettadalur. The landscape is breathtaking, but be careful to monitor weather conditions. The hike has an elevation gain of 643 meters (2,109 feet).

BRIMNES HIKE

Distance: *5.5 km (3.4 mi) round-trip*
Hiking Time: *2 hours round-trip*
Information and Maps: *Seyðisfjörður Tourist Information Center*
Trailhead: *Selsstadir farm, which is signposted, about 10 km (6 mi) from the center of town*
The hike through Brimnes is another gem of a trek. Brimnes is on the north shore of

Seyðisfjörður and was for centuries one of the major fishing villages in East Iceland. Start at the Selsstadir farm, which is signposted, 10 kilometers (6 miles) from the center of town, where you'll find ruins of old buildings and a small orange lighthouse. A walk out to Brimnes in good weather with good visibility is memorable. Be sure to have your camera ready. This is a moderately difficult hike.

BREKKA SETTLEMENT HIKE

Distance: 24 km (15 mi) round-trip
Hiking Time: 14 hours round-trip
Information and Maps: Seyðisfjörður Tourist Information Center
Trailhead: Austdalsa parking area, 17 km (11 mi) east of Seyðisfjörður

Experienced climbers with endurance should check out the historical trail that leads from the Austdalsa parking area and up past the abandoned farmstead Austdalur. It's extremely important to follow the trail posts down into the Brekkugja opening, as well as to be careful when crossing the snowbanks above it, before continuing down the Brekkudalur valley to the Brekka settlement, a historic village. The highest elevation reached is 781 meters (2,562 feet), and the trail has some steep climbs. This is typically done as a long day hike in the summer, strictly in June-August while monitoring weather conditions.

Other Sports and Recreation
SEA ANGLING SEYÐISFJÖRÐUR

at the marina, tel. 354/471-3060, 30,000ISK for 1 hour

Sea Angling Seyðisfjörður is a company operated by local fisherman Haraldur Arnason, who will take you out to fish, observe bird settlements, and enjoy the open sea. You can have your catch prepared at Hótel Aldan's restaurant for a fee. The tour is available all year but is dependent on the weather conditions. Call for the schedule and rates, as they vary depending on the time of year.

STAFDALUR SKI AREA

tel. 354/898-2798, www.stafdalur.is, Dec.-May, lift tickets 1,500ISK Mon.-Fri., 2,600ISK Sat.-Sun.

The Stafdalur Ski Area is 9 kilometers (6 mi) southwest from Seyðisfjörður and has a 1,000-meter (3,280-foot) ski lift, as well as a lift for children. Cross-country skiing and snowmobiling are possible from the ski area; there is excellent access for snowmobiles from the ski area to magnificent mountains, deserted fjords, and the famous Dyrfjoll mountains.

SUNDHÖLL SEYÐISFJARÐAR SWIMMING POOL

Suðurgata 5, tel. 354/472-1414, 7am-11am and 3pm-8pm Mon.-Fri., 1pm-4pm Sat., 950ISK

The town swimming pool, Sundhöll Seyðisfjarðar, is small, but it's frequented by locals and their children. If the weather is bad, a dip in one of the hot tubs is divine.

Food
SKAFTFELL BISTRO

Austurvegur 42, tel. 354/472-1633, www.skaftfell.is, noon-10pm daily, entrées from 2,000ISK

Skaftfell Bistro is a cool spot to grab a bite to eat. It's decorated with works by the artist Dieter Roth, and has shelves of art books to check out while you dine. Sandwiches, pizza, pastries, and soup are on offer.

KAFFI LÁRA EL GRILLO BAR

Norðugata 3, tel. 354/472-1703, www.elgrillobar. com, 11:30am-1:30am Mon.-Thur., 11:30am-3:30am Fri.-Sat., 12:30pm-1:30am Sun., entrees from 2,600ISK

Kaffi Lára El Grillo Bar is a relaxed café in town where you can have a cup of coffee, watch a football game, and dine outside when the weather is nice. You can buy coffee, cakes, soups, sandwiches, and other light meals. At night, the place turns into the local bar, and locals gather to drink a few pints and listen to music.

Accommodations
HAFALDAN SEYÐISFJÖRÐUR HOSTEL

Suðurgata 8, tel. 354/611-4410,
www.hafaldan.is, rooms from 13,000ISK

Hafaldan Seyðisfjörður Hostel offers rooms in two buildings. Halfaldan Harbor Hostel is on the north side of the fjord, just two minutes from the town center, offering twin, double, and four-bed rooms, all with shared bathroom and kitchen facilities. The second location, Hafaldan Hospital Hostel, occupies a historic former hospital building. It offers private double rooms as well as double, twin, and dormitory rooms with shared facilities. In both locations, the dining and living rooms are lively and great places to meet fellow travelers. Rooms aren't pretty, but they are clean and adequate. The guests tend to be young budget travelers.

HÓTEL SNÆFELL

Austurvegur 3, tel. 354/472-1277,
www.hotelaldan.com, rooms from 20,000ISK

Hótel Snæfell is operated by the same owners as Hótel Aldan. This guesthouse is based in a large three-story wooden house and offers 12 rooms. The rooms are bright and spacious and feature comfortable beds, but they lack the charm of rooms at Hótel Aldan. Guests have access to free Wi-Fi, a private bathroom with a shower, a small television, and laundry service. Breakfast is included.

POST-HOSTEL

Hafnargata 4, tel. 354/898-6242,
www.posthostel.is, 23,320ISK

Newly opened in 2019, Post-Hostel offers double and family rooms in the heart of Seyðisfjörður. Rooms are bare bones with beds and a little table, but they are large and clean. Guests have access to shared bathroom facilities, a communal kitchen, laundry room, and garden.

★ HÓTEL ALDAN

Norðurgata 2, tel. 354/472-1277, www.hotelaldan.is,
rooms from 28,000ISK

Hótel Aldan is an adorable guesthouse that features seven double rooms and two triples with vintage furniture, antique lamps, and modern amenities, including Wi-Fi, minibars, private bathrooms with showers, TV and DVD players, and laundry service. Rooms are tasteful, charming, and Icelandic chic, with wood furnishings, muted colors, and minimalist design. Breakfast is included in the room rate, and the hotel is open year-round.

SEYÐISFJÖRÐUR CAMPSITE

Ranargata 5, tel. 354/472-1521, May 1-Sept. 30,
1,600ISK per adult, free for children under 14

You have the option to camp close to the town center at the Seyðisfjörður Campsite, in a facility that has showers, hot and cold running water, and shared kitchen facilities. There's also a free Internet connection. The campsite accommodates tents and RVs, and hookups are available. Washing machines are available for 700ISK, tumble dryers for 700ISK, and showers for 100ISK per 2 minutes.

Information and Services
SEYÐISFJÖRÐUR TOURIST INFORMATION CENTER

Ferjuleira 1, tel. 354/472-1551, 9am-5pm Mon.-Fri.
May 1-Sept. 30, Mon.-Fri. 12:30pm-4pm Oct. 1-Apr.
30

The tourist information center is at the ferry terminal by the harbor. You can find brochures about the region, ferry timetables and rates, hiking maps, road maps, and stamps. There's also free Wi-Fi, and a small café serves coffee, soft drinks, and snacks.

Getting There

Seyðisfjörður is 27 kilometers (17 miles) east of **Egilsstaðir**, the nearest hub. By car, **Route 93,** which is paved, is your only option to get to Seyðisfjörður.

Smyril Line (tel. 298/345900, www.smyrilline.com) operates a ferry from **Denmark** to the **Faroe Islands** to Iceland, with weekly departures from Hirtshals, Denmark. The trip from Denmark to Iceland is approximately 47 hours and costs about 237,000ISK round trip for two people with a vehicle. For more information, check the rates and schedule online.

REYÐARFJÖRÐUR

Reyðarfjörður's population hovers around 1,000, and locals are amused by the attention their tiny town has been getting of late. The longest and widest of the eastern fjords, Reyðarfjörður has the charm you'd expect from a small town, with quaint accommodations and scenic mountain walks.

Sights
ICELANDIC WARTIME MUSEUM
Spitalakampur, tel. 354/470-9063, 1pm-5pm daily June 1-Aug. 31, rest of year by request, 1,000ISK

A war museum may seem odd in one of the most peaceful countries in the world. Iceland has never had its own military, but British and American troops were based in Iceland for decades leading up to and following World War II. This museum is dedicated to the days when Allied troops were stationed in the region. See photos, models, weapons, uniforms, and information on how troops passed their time here.

Hiking

Reyðarfjörður is the perfect town for taking leisurely strolls. The lovely slopes above the village include a short trail beginning along the southern part of the **Búðará River** that makes for a nice walk. Above the residential area, you will find delightful areas to explore. Grab hiking maps in the **Reyðarfjörður tourist information office** (Heiðarvegur 37, tel. 354/470-9000, 1pm-5pm daily June-Aug.).

Food and Accommodations
HJÁ MARLÍN GUESTHOUSE
Vallargerdi 9, tel. 354/474-1220, www.bakkagerdi. net, rooms from 13,000ISK

Hjá Marlín Guesthouse is a cozy guesthouse that features singles, doubles, and dorm accommodations. Rooms are small and no-frills, but some rooms have private bathrooms. Guests have access to a fully equipped kitchen, TV lounge, sauna, and laundry facilities. The **restaurant** (5pm-8pm daily, entrées

from 2,600ISK) serves lots of lamb dishes as well as fresh seafood, including lobster, scallops, cod, and salmon.

TÆRGESEN GUESTHOUSE
Buðargata 4, tel. 354/470-5555, www.taergesen. com, rooms from 24,000ISK

Tærgesen Guesthouse is an old-fashioned guesthouse that features rooms with standard beds, free Wi-Fi, and wood furnishings. Some rooms have spectacular views of the landscape. The in-house **restaurant** (5pm-10pm daily, entrées from 3,790ISK) offers classic Icelandic cuisine, such as smoked leg of lamb and salted cod, but also tourist-friendly fare like hamburgers, nachos, and pizza.

HOTEL AUSTUR
Búðareyri 6, tel. 354/474-1600, rooms from 28,000ISK

Hotel Austur looks and feels like a hunting lodge with dim lighting, lots of wood furnishings, and a remote location. Rooms are average-sized and sparsely decorated, and Wi-Fi is available. It's close to a host of activities, including horse riding, golf, skiing, and fishing. The room price includes a breakfast buffet, and the **restaurant** (6pm-10pm daily, entrées from 2,800ISK) serves classic Icelandic food for dinner with lots of fish and lamb on the menu.

Getting There

Reyðarfjörður is 58 kilometers (36 miles) south of **Seyðisfjörður** on **Route 92,** the only way to the town. Be sure to check the weather forecast before you head out as the road, though paved, can be challenging—even dangerous—during wet weather.

ESKIFJÖRÐUR

Eskifjörður is a small, single-road village that was established as a base of operations for Norwegian fishermen. Today, it's a quiet town of about 1,000 residents with a couple of guesthouses that draw tourists in the summer months. A few scenic hiking paths offer splendid views of the landscape and local birdlife.

Sights

EAST ICELAND MARITIME MUSEUM
(Sjóminjasafn Austurlands)

Strandgata 39b, tel. 354/470-9063,
1pm-5pm daily June 1-Aug. 31,
open by request Sept.-May, 1,000ISK

The East Iceland Maritime Museum pays tribute to the town's rich fishing history with exhibits of items relating to fishing and seafaring, as well as artifacts of local trade, industry, and medicine from times past. The collection is housed in a black wooden building that was built in 1816, called Gamlabúð.

Hiking

MOUNT HOLMATINDUR

Distance: *10 km (6 mi) round-trip*
Hiking Time: *8 hours round-trip*
Information and Maps: *www.east.is*
Trailhead: *signpost 3.5 km (2.2 mi) east of town, off of route 92*

Mount Holmatindur, which stands 985 meters (3,231 feet) high, towers over the fjord opposite the town. Locals take great pride in the peak. The trek to the top, which has fantastic views of the East, can be challenging, but those who make it can sign a logbook declaring their achievement. Because the trailhead is situated near paved Route 92 just 3.5 kilometers (2.2 miles) east from the center of town, it's quite easy to get to the mountain. The 10-kilometer (6-mile) round-trip is moderately difficult and takes about eight hours total to hike. Check the weather forecast before you head out, bring the proper gear, and alert your hotel of your plans.

Other Sports and Recreation

ESKIFJÖRÐUR SWIMMING POOL

tel. 354/476-1218, 6am-9pm Mon.-Fri., 10am-6pm Sat.-Sun. June-Aug., 6am-8pm Mon.-Fri., 1pm-6pm Sat.-Sun. Apr.-May and Sept.-Oct., 650ISK, 200ISK for children 6-17

The Eskifjörður Swimming Pool features an outdoor 25-meter (83-foot) pool, a children's pool with three waterslides, and two hot tubs, a sauna, and a fitness center.

BYGGÐARHOLT GOLF COURSE

Strandgata 71a, tel. 354/892-4622, year-round, greens fees 3,000ISK

The Byggðarholt golf course is a nine-hole course with yardage markers, a putting green, chipping green, and practice bunker area.

ODDSSKARÐ SKI REGION

tel. 354/476-1465, www.oddskard.is, 2pm-10pm Mon.-Fri., 10am-4pm Sat.-Sun. during winter

Oddsskarð is the largest skiing region in East Iceland, with three lifts, a ski lodge for 40 people, and tracks for cross-country skiing. Skis and snowboards are available to rent.

Food and Accommodations

MJOEYRI GUESTHOUSE

Strandgata 120, tel. 354/477-1247, www.mjoeyri.is, rooms from 21,000ISK, cottages from 35,900ISK

Mjoeyri Guesthouse offers two types of accommodations: standard rooms at the guesthouse and five self-catering cottages. Cottages are equipped with a kitchen, dining room, one bedroom, and a balcony with a beautiful view of the landscape. Rooms are no-frills with standard beds and basic furnishings. The owners are friendly and accommodating. A breakfast buffet costs 2,100ISK per person.

HOTEL APARTMENTS
IN ESKIFJÖRÐUR

Strandgata 26, tel. 354/892-8657, www.hotelibudir. net, apartments from 22,000ISK

Hotel Apartments in Eskifjörður has four self-catering apartments for rent. The apartments are 60 square meters (646 square feet), with one bedroom (two beds, extra beds and mattresses available), a living room with a dining area, a fully equipped kitchen, a laundry room, and a bathroom. The apartments have all the comforts of home, including free Wi-Fi. The location is perfect, in the center of town and close to the harbor.

HOTEL ESKIFJÖRÐUR

Strandgata 47, tel. 354/476-0099, www. hoteleskifjordur.is, 24,500ISK

Hotel Eskifjörður is a new hotel situated in the

center of town that offers spacious rooms with impressive views of the Holmatindur mountains. Rooms are tidy with minimalist decor and the front desk can arrange a number of activities in the area, including horse riding, boating, hiking, and history tours.

Getting There

Eskifjörður is 73 kilometers (45 miles) south of **Seyðisfjörður** on **Route 92.** Be sure to check the weather forecast before you head out; the road, though paved, can be challenging—even dangerous—during wet weather.

NESKAUPSTAÐUR

Fifty years ago, Neskaupstaður was only accessible by sea, making it the most remote and untouched spot in the Eastfjords. However, a tunnel was built that connected the town with Eskifjörður via paved **Route 92.** There still isn't a lot to do here, but there is a trio of museums to visit if you want to make a quick stop before continuing on the Ring Road.

Sights
MUSEUM HOUSE
(Safnahúsið)

Miðstræti 1, tel. 354/470-9063, www.fjardabyggd.is, 1pm-5pm daily June 1-Aug. 31, 1,000ISK

The Museum House (Safnahúsið) is home to three museums. The **Museum of Natural History** will be a winner if you're traveling with children, as a special exhibition allows them to touch different animals. There are also displays of Icelandic mammals, birds, insects, and shellfish, as well as exhibitions on stones and flora found in East Iceland. The **Josafat Hinriksson Maritime Museum** showcases relics relating to ironwork, fishing, boatbuilding, and the way in which people lived in East Iceland in the old days. The town's art museum, the **Tryggvi Olafsson Art Collection,** is dedicated to the works of local artist Tryggvi, who was born in the town in 1940. He is one of East Iceland's most revered contemporary artists. Tryggvi's bright, colorful paintings mix abstract art with wildlife and landscape themes.

RAUÐUBJÖRG LOOKOUT POINT
Route 92

Rauðubjörg, which means "red cliffs," is a great example of the varied landscape of East Iceland. While the cliffs are predominantly red, you can see hues ranging from brown to white, and it's a striking sight against the bright blue sea. You'll find a lookout point where you can safely pull off the road just south of Neskaupstaður via paved Route 92.

Food and Accommodations
NESBÆR KAFFIHÚS

Egilsbraut 5, tel. 354/477-1115, 9am-6pm Mon.-Sat., 1pm-5pm Sun., entrées from 1,990ISK

Located in the center of town, Nesbær Kaffihús is a cozy coffeehouse popular among locals and tourists for lunch. The menu features crepes, sandwiches, salads, and soup.

HILDIBRAND HOTEL

Hafnarbraut 2, tel. 354/477-1950, www. hildibrandhotel.com, rooms from 21,000ISK, apartments from 35,000ISK

Hildibrand Hotel is a guesthouse offering nine double rooms and 15 self-catering apartments. While the guesthouse rooms are a little on the Spartan side, the apartments are spacious, with full-size kitchens, large sofas, flat-screen TVs, and ocean views.

Getting There

Neskaupstaður is 72 kilometers (45 miles) southeast of **Egilsstaðir** on **Route 92.** Check the weather forecast before you head out, as the road, though paved, can be challenging—even dangerous—during wet weather.

FÁSKRÚÐSFJÖRÐUR

Fáskrúðsfjörður is a small village of fewer than 500 people nestled on a long fjord of the same name. It's the most "French" part of Iceland. The village was originally a base for more than 5,000 French fishermen who came every year to fish the Icelandic waters. Some settled here in the late 19th century. The village had a hospital, chapel, and cemetery that were built by the Frenchmen, and both the buildings and the history remain, as the streets of Fáskrúðsfjörður are marked in both Icelandic and French.

Sights

FRENCH FISHERMEN IN ICELAND

Hafnargata 12, tel. 354/475-1170, 10am-6pm daily June 1-Aug. 31, 1,000ISK

A museum aptly named French Fishermen in Iceland does a great job of describing the history of the town and the importance of the impact of the French, and it even has a delightful and popular little café that sells coffee, cakes, and light meals.

AURORAS ICELAND

Hafnargata 7, tel. 354/783-9500, www.auroras.is, 12:30pm-5pm daily June 15-Aug. 15, open by request rest of the year, 1,000ISK

Auroras Iceland is an unexpected treat in this small village. The gallery offers a photo exhibition of northern lights that were captured above the fjord. Guests can see large photos of the natural phenomenon along with time-lapse videos of northern lights dancing and flickering in the sky.

Festivals and Events

FRENCH DAYS

www.east.is, July

If you visit during the last weekend in July, you can join in with the French Days festival, which celebrates the town's history with French-inspired food and flags.

Food and Accommodations

CAFÉ SUMARLÍNA

Búðavegur 59, tel. 354/475-1575, www.sumarlina.is, 11am-10pm daily, entrées from 2,650ISK

Café Sumarlína occupies a cute white house in the center of town. The atmosphere is warm and inviting, and the staff is the same. The menu features pizzas, burgers, lamb and fish entrées, and quite a few French-inspired dishes, like crepes and baguette sandwiches.

FOSSHOTEL EASTFJORDS

Hafnargata 11-14, tel. 354/470-4070, www. islandshotel.is rooms from 24,500ISK

Fosshotel Eastfjords is a 47-room hotel with French-inspired decor, paying homage to the history of the town. It offers standard, superior, single, and triple rooms with hardwood floors, muted wallpaper, quality linens, and simple furniture. It has an in-house **bar and restaurant** (6:30am-9pm daily, dinner entrées from 3,700ISK), free parking, and free Wi-Fi. Breakfast is included in the price of the room.

Getting There

Fáskrúðsfjörður is 50 kilometers (31 miles) south of **Egilsstaðir** on **Route 92.** Be sure to check the weather forecast before you head out because the road, though paved, can be challenging and dangerous during wet weather.

STÖÐVARFJÖRÐUR

Stöðvarfjörður is another minuscule village in the Eastfjords that has strikingly beautiful nature to explore, including rocky terrain, mountains, and a gorgeous shoreline.

Sights

PETRA'S STONE & MINERAL COLLECTION

(Steinasafn Petru Stöðvarfirði)

Fjarðarbraut 21, tel. 354/475-8834, www. steinapetra.is, 9am-6pm daily May 1-Sept. 30, closed Oct. 1-Apr 30. and Feb.-Apr., 1,500ISK, free for children 13 and under

Petra's Stone & Mineral Collection is a stunning private collection of more than 1,000 stones that are cut and polished, revealing crystals and other beautiful facets. The owner started amassing stones in 1976, and the collection includes lava, crystals, basalt, pearls, granite, opals, and amethysts.

SAXA

Route 96

Saxa, a sea geyser, is an interesting natural phenomenon where the waves crash into a rocky crevice and shoot high into the air, creating water "eruptions." The name Saxa is derived from the kelp and seaweed that are *saxað* (chopped) inside the crevices and then hurled into the air with the waves. The sea geyser is a cool sight and unique to the area.

Food and Accommodations
SAXA GUESTHOUSE

Fjarðarbraut 41, tel. 354/511-3055, saxa@saxa.is, rooms from 12,000ISK

SAXA Guesthouse is close to the harbor in the heart of the town. Its 14 rooms are bright and minimalist. A common lounge has a TV and a terrace to enjoy in good weather. Breakfast is included. The in-house café (7am-9pm daily, entrées from 2,700ISK) is open for breakfast, lunch, and dinner and offers soups, salads, sandwiches, and lamb and fish meals.

Getting There

Stöðvarfjörður is 73 kilometers (45 miles) southeast of **Egilsstaðir** on **Route 92.** Be sure to check the weather forecast before you head out; the road, though paved, can be dangerous during wet weather.

BREIÐDALSVÍK

Breiðdalsvík is a blip of a town with fewer than 200 residents. There's not much going on here, but a couple of guesthouses serve those who need a break from the Ring Road.

Food and Accommodations
THE OLD GENERAL STORE

Sólvellir 25, tel. 354/475-6670, www.breiddalsvik.is, 7am-9pm daily

The Old General Store is a quaint café and shop that retains the charm of its history. Built in 1956, it has its original wood shelves and displays some old product tins of brands that were popular in Iceland during the 1950s and 1960s. It's also a great spot to grab a cup of coffee and slice of cake or pick up some necessities for your journey.

HÓTEL BLÁFELL

Solvellir 14, tel. 354/475-6770, www.breiddalsvik.is, rooms from 19,000ISK

Hótel Bláfell is a darling 34-room country hotel offering singles, doubles, and family rooms that range from simple modern decor to wood-paneled, rustic chic. All rooms have private bathrooms, free Wi-Fi, and standard beds. The hotel also has a sauna, lounge with fireplace, and library with interesting books and even board games. The **restaurant** (7am-9pm daily, entrées from 3,750ISK) does a nice take on classic fish and lamb dishes, but the menu doesn't have any surprises.

HÓTEL STAÐARBORG

tel. 354/475-6760, www.stadarborg.is, rooms from 23,000ISK

Hótel Staðarborg offers 30 rooms ranging from singles with shared bathrooms to family rooms. Rooms are small but adequate, with minimal furnishings. There's a hot tub out back, but that's where the amenities end. The **restaurant** (6pm-9pm daily) is a bit pricey, as it costs 3,000ISK for breakfast and almost 6,000ISK for a meat or fish dinner. The hotel is located on Route 1, about 7 kilometers (4 miles) from Breiðdalsvík. It's a fine spot to spend a night while navigating the Ring Road, but you'll pay quite a bit.

EYJAR FISHING LODGE

Eyjar, tel. 354/567-5204, rooms from 28,000ISK

Eyjar Fishing Lodge has the look and feel of an authentic fishing lodge, with some luxury amenities. Its eight rooms come with heated floors and free Wi-Fi, and are decorated with lots of wood and fish-inspired art. The lodge also has a common lounge, hot tub, and sauna.

Getting There

Breiðdalsvík is 83 kilometers (52 miles) southeast of **Egilsstaðir.** Check the weather forecast before you head out because wet weather could make the road challenging—even dangerous.

DJÚPIVOGUR

Djúpivogur, a town of fewer than 500 people, has a history of fishing and trading dating to 1589. A picturesque landscape is the backdrop to countless hiking trails, which are free to roam and explore. The 1,069-meter (3,507-foot) Mount Búlandstindur looms over the town, dominating the terrain. A few museums are aimed at tourists looking to spend time indoors.

Sights
LANGABÚÐ

*Búð 1, tel. 354/478-8220, www.langabud.
is, 11am-6pm daily May 15-Sept. 15, open by
appointment mid-Sept.-mid-May, 500ISK*

Langabúð is the oldest building in the town, dating back to 1790, and it houses a heritage museum as well as an exhibition dedicated to a local sculptor. The folk museum contains an eclectic collection of pieces integral to the town's history, including fishing equipment such as whale harpoons as well as antique parts that belonged to early wagons. The collection may seem like there isn't a strong theme, but that's part of the charm, a mishmash of town history. As for the art portion of the building, artist Ríkarður Jónsson (1888-1974) was known as the founder of a national folk-art movement in Iceland. Classic themes of work and family are depicted in his portraiture and wood sculpture, and the museum houses many of his wood carvings and the tools he used in his work.

BIRD AND MINERAL MUSEUM
(Fuglavefur Djupavogs)

*Bakka 1, tel. 354/478-89288, www.djupivogur.is,
10am-6pm daily in summer, open by appointment in
winter, 500ISK*

The Bird and Mineral Museum holds about 130 species of stuffed birds, along with nests and eggs. There are also photos and books about birdlife and Icelandic minerals. The focus may seem random, but the curators have taken great care to unify the bird and mineral collections under one roof.

Hiking and Bird-Watching
BULANDSNES PENINSULA HIKE

Hiking the serene and well-kept trails around the flat Bulandsnes Peninsula is a must for bird-watchers. Most of the birds nesting in Iceland can be seen on or around Bulandsnes during the migration period in the summer, with the places of greatest interest being the lakes Breidivogur and Fyluvogur. In this area, you can see tufted ducks and pintails, as well as less common species like red-throated divers and black-tailed godwits.

Two different routes begin and end at the cairn Bondavarða east of Djúpivogur. The longer route is about 10 kilometers (6 miles), a moderate four-hour hike, and the shorter one is easier and approximately 5 kilometers (3 miles), which takes about two hours.

If you opt for the shorter route, you must turn on Ulfseyjarsund (a fork) and continue to the airstrip, then continue to the lakes Breidivogur and Fyluvogur and back to where you started.

If you choose the longer route, you have to turn near Ulfseyjarsund, go to the airstrip, and from there hike to Ulfsey beach. At the southwest tip of Ulfsey, there is a sign, and from there you can choose whether to view Ulfsey, Hvaley, or Sandey, a trio of islets that are now connected to the mainland. Then you go back the same way from the sign in Ulfsey, to the airstrip and then to the lakes Breidivogur and Fyluvogur and back to Bondavarða.

Hot Springs and Pools
DJÚPIVOGUR SWIMMING POOL

*Varða 6, tel. 354/478-8999, 7am-8:30pm Mon.-Fri.,
10am-6pm Sat.-Sun, 650ISK*

On a rainy day, the Djúpivogur Swimming Pool is a great option. In the winter, you will see locals and their children taking a dip in the heated pool or one of the hot tubs, but the summer sees a lot of tourist traffic.

1: Mount Holmatindur 2: Langabúð

Food and Accommodations

LANGABÚÐ

Búð 1, tel. 354/478-8220, 10am-6pm daily May 15-Sept. 15, snacks from 800ISK

Langabúð is a tiny café that serves pastries, coffee, and light meals that hit the spot. The cakes are hard to resist, and the ingredients for the soups and sandwiches are local and fresh.

BERUNES HOSTEL

Berufjörður, tel. 354/869-7227, www.berunes.is, Apr. 16-Oct 31., rooms from 14,500ISK

Berunes Hostel is a charming converted farmhouse just outside of Djúpivogur. The hostel offers rooms that accommodate 1-4 people as well as five self-contained cottages that can house 2-5 people. Rooms are small but comfortable, and some of them remind you of a guesthouse out of the 1970s. Berunes serves meals in a building next to the hostel. **Gestastofa Café** serves breakfast year-round (7am-10am daily), and a three-course dinner is served in July and August (6pm-9pm daily).

★ HÓTEL FRAMTÍÐ

Vogalandi 4, tel. 354/478-8887, www.hotelframtid. com, rooms from 34,900ISK

Hótel Framtíð is the place to go if you want to stay in town. This is the only close option. The 42-room hotel has wood-paneled rooms that remind you of a hunting lodge, standard beds, and simple furnishings. Its **Framtíð Restaurant** (call ahead because opening hours vary, entrées from 3,860ISK) features entrées including baked fish with white butter sauce, chicken breast with salad and potatoes, and lamb fillets with fresh vegetables and potatoes. Desserts are scrumptious, including whipped *skyr* with cream and mixed berries and apple cake with fresh cream. Group menus are available for parties of 10 or more.

HAVARÍ

Karlsstaðir, tel. 354/663-5520, www.havari.is

Havarí is an organic farm, hostel, café, and music venue operated by Svavar Eysteinsson, of the band Prins Póló, and his wife Berglind Häsler. The couple serves up their own vegan sausages as well as soup, cakes, sandwiches, and waffles at the café (8am-9pm daily). The hostel offers double and family rooms as well as dorm accommodations; hostel accommodations start from 6,000ISK and rooms start from 13,000ISK. In the summer, the farm hosts concerts from some of the most popular musicians and bands in the country. Havarí is 42 kilometers (26 miles) north of Djúpivogur on Route 1.

DJÚPIVOGUR CAMPGROUND

tel. 354/478-8887, May 1-Sept. 30, 1,750ISK per person

The Djúpivogur Campground is conveniently situated close to Hótel Framtíð, which is where you pay the camping fees. At the height of the summer season (July), the site is littered with vans and campers, but it can feel like a little community and it's fun to meet fellow travelers. The facilities are decent, with an indoor cooking area and steaming-hot showers (300ISK). The campground is in an open field, and there is room for tents and RVs, with hookups available. Electricity is available for 850ISK and washing machines for 1,050 per 100 minutes.

Information and Services

TOURIST INFORMATION CENTER

Bakka 3, tel. 354/478-8204, www.djupivogur. is, 9am-5pm Mon.-Fri., noon-4pm Sat.-Sun. May 15-Sept. 15

The tourist information center offers hiking maps, brochures about the region, and Internet access.

Getting There

Djúpivogur is 86 kilometers (53 miles) south of **Egilsstaðir** on Route 1.

The Vatnajökull Region

In the Vatnajökull region, Iceland earns its "fire and ice" reputation. You'll see the glacier descend into black sands and hot streams erupt from frozen banks of ice.

The region is easy to access, as there are frequent flights and buses between Reykjavík and Höfn. For flights, check out **Eagle Air** (www.eagleair.is), and for buses, try **Strætó** (www.straeto.is) and **Reykjavík Excursions** (www.re.is). Höfn is the best gateway to the region and the perfect town in which to base yourself.

HÖFN

Höfn, which means harbor, is the gateway to Vatnajökull glacier, and guesthouses and cafés accommodate the growing number of tourists to the region. There are roughly 2,000 residents of Höfn, which makes it quite a sleepy town, but it comes alive in the summer, when legions of tourists from around the world gear up to scale the glacier. The town has a few small museums, including a spectacular one dedicated to the looming Vatnajökull.

Sights
FOLK MUSEUM
(Gamlabúð)
Heppuvegur 1, tel. 354/470-8330, 9am-5pm daily Oct. 1-Apr. 30, 9am-6pm daily May 1-May 31, 9am-7pm daily June 1-Aug. 31, 9am-6pm daily Sept. 1-Sept. 30, free

The Folk Museum has a small collection of artifacts that shows what life was like in one of the most isolated parts of the country from the 19th century on. You will find objects related to the old ways of farming, including antique tractors and cars. The museum is small, and free, but don't feel bad if you miss it.

HORNAFJÖRÐUR ART MUSEUM
(Listasafn Hornafjarðar)
Hafnarbraut 27, tel. 354/470-8000, 9am-4pm Mon.-Fri., 11am-4pm Sat.-Sun. May-Sept., 9am-4pm Mon.-Fri. and by request rest of year, free

The Hornafjörður Art Museum displays the work of celebrated local artist Svavar Gudnason, who had a strong connection to his hometown of Höfn and the Vatnajökull region. Svavar was born in Höfn in 1909 and spent his youth there before moving to Reykjavík in 1928. He had been introduced to landscape painting at an early age, and his work depicts the natural surroundings in southeast Iceland, portraying the sea, glaciers, lakes, and mountains. In the winter months, works from other artists are displayed alongside those of Svavar.

Bird-Watching
Bird-watchers must head to **Ósland**, a conservation area in the south of Höfn that was once an island but is now connected to the mainland (you can reach it by walking from the harbor in Höfn). Arctic terns are a common sight during their nesting season, which takes place early in the summer, and there are walking trails along the perimeter of a pond they frequent.

Located on the hill **Óslandshæð** is a memorial to fishermen lost at sea and an information board about the surrounding natural area, including details on the flora and fauna.

Other Sports and Recreation
HÖFN SWIMMING POOL
Víkurbraut 9, tel. 354/470-8477, 6:45am-9pm Mon.-Fri., 10am-7pm Sat.-Sun. mid-May-Sept., 6:45am-9pm Mon.-Fri., 10am-5pm Sat.-Sun. Oct.-mid-May, 950ISK

The Vatnajökull Region

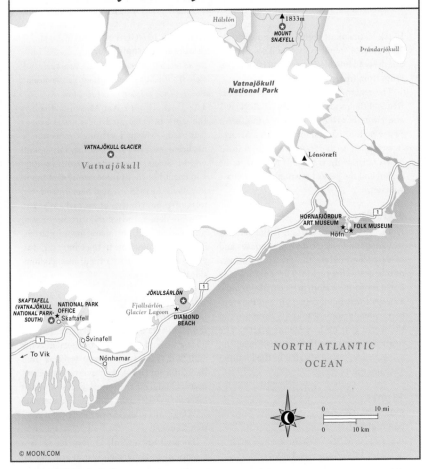

Hálslón
▲1833m
⊕
MOUNT
SNÆFELL

Þrándarjökull

Vatnajökull
National Park

VATNAJÖKULL GLACIER
⊕
Vatnajökull

▲ Lónsöræfi

HORNAFJÖRÐUR
ART MUSEUM ★ ○ FOLK MUSEUM
Höfn ★ ○ 1

JÖKULSÁRLÓN
⊕ 1
Fjallsárlón
Glacier Lagoon ★
DIAMOND
BEACH

SKAFTAFELL
(VATNAJÖKULL NATIONAL PARK
NATIONAL PARK- OFFICE
SOUTH) ⊕ ○ Skaftafell

1
← To Vik ○ Svínafell
Nónhamar ○

NORTH ATLANTIC
OCEAN

0   10 mi
0   10 km

© MOON.COM

The local Höfn Swimming Pool isn't as spectacular as some of the other pools in the region, but it's a nice spot for a dip when taking a break from hiking and touring.

SILFURNESVÖLLUR

Dalbraut, tel. 354/478-2197, greens fees 4,000ISK
The Silfurnesvöllur golf course is on the outskirts of Höfn. It is a well-kept nine-hole course open year-round that stretches along the shore with a breathtaking view over Vatnajökull glacier and its mountain ridge.

Food
★ HUMARHOFNIN

Hafnarbraut 4, tel. 354/478-1200, www.
humarhofnin.is, langoustine entrées from 5,900ISK,
other entrées from 2,900ISK
Humarhofnin is a quaint but can't-miss restaurant for those who want a taste of fresh Icelandic lobster; it focuses on local langoustines. Located close to the harbor where the daily catch comes in, guests are treated to some of the freshest food on the island. If you're traveling with a non-seafood eater,

there are some other options on the menu, including Icelandic lamb and veggie courses.

PAKKHÚS RESTAURANT

Krosseyjarvegi 3, tel. 354/478-2280, www.pakkhus.is, entrees from 3,100ISK

Pakkhús is a lovely restaurant that overlooks the Höfn harbor, next to the tourist information center. The fresh langoustines are to die for, but there are many options for those that don't enjoy seafood, including lamb, beef, pork, and duck entrees. There is also a vegetarian option.

Accommodations

NÝIBÆR GUESTHOUSE

Hafnarbraut 8, tel. 354/478-1736, www.hostel.is, rooms from 24,000ISK

Nýibær Guesthouse is in a pretty location, just a two-minute walk to the harbor. Rooms are small but brightly decorated, and guests have access to free Wi-Fi and free parking. Bathrooms are shared, and guests can use a common coffee area. Breakfast is included.

MILK FACTORY GUESTHOUSE

Dalbraut 2, tel. 354/478-8900, www.milkfactory.is, 24,000ISK

The Milk Factory is a newly renovated guesthouse that overlooks Vatnajökull glacier and is close to attractions including Jökulsárlón and Skaftafell. The 17 rooms are spacious and modern, yet minimalistic in decor, and include private bathrooms, flat-screen TVs, and free Wi-Fi. Doubles and family rooms are available.

HÓTEL HÖFN

Víkurbraut 20, tel. 354/478-1240, www.hotelhofn.is, rooms from 26,000ISK

Hótel Höfn is a 68-room hotel that looks and feels like a chain hotel designed for business travelers. The rooms are sparsely furnished with standard beds, hardwood floors, flat-screen TVs, and free Wi-Fi. The in-house restaurant serves classic Icelandic cuisine ranging from fresh fish to lamb dishes. There are a couple of vegetarian options. The

restaurant (6pm-10pm daily, 3,990ISK) has an eclectic menu. There are a few dishes serving lobster caught by local fishermen, and you can't go wrong with any—though the chili-and-garlic-roasted lobster tails in particular are divine. Other menu options include "tapas for two," featuring cod, lamb, beef, and shrimp options; pizza; vegetarian entrées; and pasta.

HÓTEL EDDA HÖFN

Ranarslod 3, tel. 354/444-4850, www.hoteledda.is, mid-May-Sept 30., rooms from 28,000ISK

Hótel Edda Höfn is a chain hotel offering 36 rooms that are spacious and bright, but devoid of character. But the amenities are good, and each room has a private bathroom. Guests have access to free Wi-Fi and parking, and a yummy breakfast buffet is available for 2,450ISK per person, 1,225 for children 6-12 and free for children five and under.

FOSSHOTEL VATNAJÖKULL

Lindarbakki, tel. 354/478-2555, www.islandshotel. is, 38,000ISK

Fosshotel Vatnajökull is a new 66-room hotel that offers doubles, suites, and family rooms. Overlooking Vatnajökull glacier and the surrounding mountain scenery, the view is unbeatable in southeast Iceland. Rooms are large and tastefully decorated in contemporary design, and include a private bathroom, flat-screen TV, free Wi-Fi, a coffee maker, and small refrigerator. The in-house restaurant is open for lunch and dinner, and breakfast is included in the price of the room.

HÖFN CAMPGROUND

Hafnarbraut 52, tel. 354/478-1606, Apr. 15- Sept. 30, 2,000ISK per person

The Höfn Campground is one of the nicer ones in the region and gets quite a bit of traffic when it's open in summer. Campers have access to steaming-hot showers and a nice cooking area, along with washing machines and the Internet. The site accommodates tents and RVs, with hookups available.

Information and Services

TOURIST INFORMATION CENTER

Heppuvegur 1, tel. 354/470-8330, www.
visitvatnajokull.is, 9am-6pm daily May 1-Sept. 30,
9am-5pm daily Oct 1.-Apr.30

The tourist information center has tourist brochures about the region and hiking maps as well as Internet access and booking information for day tours.

Getting There

Höfn is on **Route 1,** 187 kilometers (116 miles) south of **Egilsstaðir** and 451 kilometers (280 miles) east of **Reykjavík.**

Eagle Air (tel. 354/562-4200, www.eagleair.is) operates daily flights from Reykjavík for around 26,000ISK each way. The flight takes about one hour. The airport is about 5 kilometers (3 miles) north of town.

★ VATNAJÖKULL GLACIER

Vatnajökull (Water Glacier) is a cool spot to visit—quite literally, as it's Iceland's remaining piece of the last ice age. Vatnajökull features miles of white, pure ice, intertwined with blue and smoky hues in interesting shapes formed by compression. It's a wide-open space, sitting on top of active volcanoes. You will experience whipping winds, sky-high elevations, and cold temperatures.

Vatnajökull has the distinction of being the largest glacier in Europe and the third largest in the world (after glaciers in Greenland and Antarctica). It spans 8,805 square kilometers (3,400 square miles), which covers about 8 percent of the country, and the average thickness is 400 meters (1,312 feet).

Of the volcanoes, the most active are the systems near **Mount Grímsfjall** (1,719 meters/5,640 feet), and at **Grímsvötn** (1,725 meters/5,659 feet). **Mount Barðarbunga** (2,009 meters/6,591 feet) awakened in 2014 and is another volcanic fissure. **Mount Kverkfjöll** (1,929 meters/6,329 feet) and **Mount**

Hvannadalshnjúkur (2,110 meters/6,923 feet) also lie beneath the glacier.

Vatnajökull's vast, rugged terrain is a large draw for hikers and climbers from around the world, but be sure you come prepared. Bring the necessary gear, monitor weather conditions, and alert people of your whereabouts.

Tours

You can explore the glacier on a tour or with a private guide.

VATNAJÖKULL TRAVEL

Bugðuleira 2, Höfn, tel. 354/894-1616, www.
vatnajokull.is

If you'd like to explore the glacier by snowmobile and jeep, Vatnajökull Travel offers tours all year. An 11-hour tour includes pickup at your hotel, jeep and snowmobile rides, and a boat ride on Jökulsárlón, which features large pieces of glacial ice that languish offshore. It's a spectacular sight. It's a fantastic way to spend the day and explore the region. The tour costs 50,000ISK.

ATLANTSFLUG

Skaftafell Airport, tel. 354/854-4105, www.
flightseeing.is

Atlantsflug offers flights May-September from Skaftafell Airport, its private airport near Vatnajökull National Park, to various locations around Vatnajökull glacier, including Grímsvötn (volcano), Katla (volcano), Eyjafjallajökull (volcano), Langisjór (lake), Laki (crater), and Lakagigar (crater). You'll get a spectacular aerial view of volcanoes, mountains, glaciers, lakes, and rivers. Flight tours start at 54,100ISK for 45 minutes. There is a minimum of two passengers per flight.

TOP EXPERIENCE

★ JÖKULSÁRLÓN

Jökulsárlón (Glacier Lagoon) is a spectacular sight that begs to be photographed. Chunks of ice are scattered about, walls of ice jut from the sea, and icebergs of various sizes float on the water. Huge blocks of ice

---

1: Höfn 2: Höfn harbor 3: lobster dinner in Höfn
4: Vatnajökull Glacier

constantly break off the Breiðamerkurjökull glacier into the lagoon, which, though not very wide, is up to 250 meters (821 feet) deep—the deepest lake in Iceland—and then slowly move toward a river mouth and the Atlantic Ocean.

Jökulsárlón is a popular destination throughout the year, but it's quite crowded during the height of the summer season (July-Aug.). Even without a tour, plan to spend a couple of hours here to wander around and take in the beauty.

Diamond Beach
off Route 1

You can also venture to the river mouth and nearby **Diamond Beach.** Chunks of ice sometimes wash ashore, and are scattered about like giant diamonds against a backdrop of black sand. The scene is spectacular any time of year, but truly magical when the sun is shining.

Tours
GLACIER LAGOON
Jökulsárlón Ehf, tel. 354/478-2222, www.icelagoon.is, 10am-5pm daily in May, 9am-7pm daily June-Sept., 10am-5pm daily Oct., 5,800ISK

If you'd like a closer look at the icebergs, Glacier Lagoon offers tours on amphibious boats May-October. During the excursion, you sail among the huge icebergs, get to taste the 1,000-year-old ice, and, if you're lucky, see seals bobbing in the lagoon. The tour lasts about 40 minutes and includes an English-speaking guide who explains the geology of the lagoon. Tours are weather-dependent, so be sure to call ahead. Zodiac boat tours are available for 9,990ISK.

Getting There
Jökulsárlón is close to **Route 1,** 80 kilometers (50 miles) west of **Höfn** and 377 kilometers (234 miles) east of **Reykjavík,** about 5 hours.

★ SKAFTAFELL (VATNAJÖKULL NATIONAL PARK-SOUTH)

Skaftafell is one of East Iceland's most beautiful places, where visitors are treated to striking white glaciers against a backdrop of green fields and black sands. Skaftafell and Jökulsárgljúfur National Parks, along with Vatnajökull glacier, combined in 2008 to become Vatnajökull National Park. Skaftafell is the southern division of the park. For more information on the park, see page 229.

A common draw for many tourists is the black-sand beaches, which are a result of glaciers grinding down the bedrock. They're particularly striking on clear days with the snowcapped mountains and blue skies in the background. Much of the black sand is carried to the sea by glacial rivers, the waves and winds shaping the sand into complex formations. In the westernmost part of the Vatnajökull region is 1,000-square-kilometer (386-square-mile) **Skeiðarársandur,** which is the largest black glacier sand area in the world. It can be accessed by Route 1.

Tours
Tourism companies offer everything from ice walks to jeep tours.

ICELANDIC MOUNTAIN GUIDES
tel. 354/587-9999, www.mountainguides.is

Icelandic Mountain Guides offers a year-round guided walking tour on the **Svínafellsjökull** glacier tongue in Skaftafell. The two-hour tour costs 10,500ISK.

Waterfalls
HUNDAFOSS
1.5 km (0.9 mi) uphill from the visitor's center, on the way to Svartifoss

Hundafoss (Hound Falls) was named after the

1: Jökulsárlón, Glacier Lagoon 2: Svartifoss waterfall, Skaftafell National Park

Glacial Floods

When Grímsvötn volcano erupted underneath Vatnajökull in 1996, the world watched in fascination as lava flowed from fissures and ash launched thousands of feet into the air. But another phenomenon captured the attention of millions—*jökulhlaup,* which is Icelandic for glacial floods. A glacial flood occurs when water dammed by a sub-glacial lake is released, triggered by volcanic eruptions. Glacial lakes can hold millions to hundreds of millions of cubic meters of water and can wreak havoc on surrounding areas when released.

Locals still talk about the 1996 eruption, and you have a chance to relive it through a film shown at the **Skaftafell visitors center.**

many dogs that were swept over the edge during floods. Be prepared to take a lot of pictures here. The falls are gorgeous in all seasons. In the summer, the rocky terrain behind the falls is surrounded by beautiful greenery. The drop is steep and the roar is soothing.

ÞJÓFAFOSS
viewing point 4 km (2 mi) northwest from Route 26
Þjófafoss (Thieves' Falls) is a smaller waterfall set against a backdrop of lava fields.

SVARTIFOSS
about 1.5 km (0.9 mi) from the Skaftafell visitor's center
Ahead is the more spectacular Svartifoss (Black Falls) waterfall, where thundering white water cascades over striking black basalt rock columns. Svartifoss cannot be seen from the road, but it is just 1.5 kilometers (0.9 miles) from the **Skaftafell visitors center,** and the trail is clearly marked. The **hike** is easy, and it may be a surprise that you're going uphill; the view from above will alert you. The hike is about 90 minutes round-trip at a leisurely pace.

You can either return the same way or cross the river by Svartifoss and return from there. That route gives you a closer look at Þjófafoss.

Hiking
NÚPSSTAÐARSKÓGAR TO SKAFTAFELL HIKE
Distance: *60 km (37 mi)*
Hiking Time: *5 days*

Information and Maps: *www.east.is*
Trailhead: *bottom of the valley of Núpsstaðarskógar*
Hiking from Núpsstaðarskógar, a valley rich with birch trees and rivers, to Skaftafell is an ideal five-day backpack that gives you a great slice of the beautiful east. The hike is a challenging one, clocking in at 60 kilometers (38 miles), and reaching an altitude of 800 meters (2,625 feet) with an ascent of 450 meters (1,475 feet). Most people start the hike at the bottom of the valley of Núpsstaðarskógar, and average 6-7 hours of walking a day. Along the way, hikers are rewarded with numerous waterfalls, steep canyons, a glacier lagoon, towering mountains, and a glorious birch forest. The hike is strenuous and only safe in the summer, but it's worth it.

For those interested, **Icelandic Mountain Guides** (tel. 354/587-9999, www.mountain-guides.is) offers a guided trek in July and August for 150,000ISK. The tour includes an experienced guide, transportation from and to Reykjavík, food for five days, and camping gear.

Food and Accommodations
Bringing your own food is your best option here. Your only close option is the restaurant at **Hótel Skaftafell.**

HOF 1 HOTEL
Austurhus, tel. 354/478-2260, www.hof1.is, rooms from 24,000ISK
Hof 1 Hotel offers 37 rooms and a few self-catered cottages. The ranch-style countryside

hotel has spacious, surprisingly modern rooms, a friendly staff, and a great breakfast buffet included in the room price. The hotel is about a 15-minute drive from Skaftafell.

HÓTEL SKAFTAFELL

Skaftafelli 2 Freysnesi, tel. 354/478-1945, www. hotelskaftafell.is, rooms from 29,000ISK

Hótel Skaftafell is a 63-room hotel that looks a bit rustic, but it's comfortable and close to the national park. Rooms are standard with private bathrooms and classic countryside decor. A standard breakfast is included. The restaurant (8am-9pm daily, 3,000ISK) serves breakfast, lunch, and dinner, including traditional lamb and fish dishes as well as a few vegetarian options. The huge banquet room tends to fill up with busloads of tourists.

SKAFTAFELL CAMPGROUND

tel. 354/470-8300, open year-round, 1,750ISK per night adults, 1,000ISK children 13-16, free for children under 12

If you want to stay inside the park, the Skaftafell Campground is your only option. The campground is next to the entrance gate to the park; vehicle entry is allowed 7:30am-11pm. Visitors should register prior to camping. The facilities are great, but keep in mind that there is a distance between the facilities and where you set up camp. The campground offers hot showers and bathrooms (bring flip-flops; it can get pretty dirty during the height of camping season). Visitors can stock up on food and basic supplies at the visitors center, but it is advisable to bring what you need with you. The visitors center is also where you pay the camping fees. The open field accommodates about 400 tents, and there is a section for RVs with the option to pay for electricity.

Information and Services

NATIONAL PARK OFFICE

Skaftafellsvegur, tel. 354/478-1627, www. vatnajokulsthjodgardur.is, 10am-6pm daily Jan.-Feb., 9am-6pm daily Mar.-May, 8am-7pm daily June-Aug., 9am-6pm daily Sept.-Oct., 10am-6pm daily Nov.-Dec.

The national park office, which is near the entrance to the park, also serves as the visitors center. Here, you will find information, maps, and someone on hand to answer all your questions about the history and geology of the region.

Getting There

Skaftafell is on the **Ring Road,** Route 1, about 330 kilometers (205 miles) east of **Reykjavík** and 130 kilometers (81 miles) west of **Höfn.**

The Highlands

Route F26
  (Sprengisandur)......272
Route F35 (Kjölur)......277

Dramatic and wild, Iceland's uninhabited interior is home to an otherworldly landscape that must be seen to be believed.

It's cut by endless wind and marked by vast expanses of ice and desert. This is the most distinctive and unforgiving landscape on the island, complete with lava fields and volcanoes. The country's largest glaciers—Vatnajökull, Langjökull, and Hofsjökull—form the region's backdrop.

The isolation seems romantic to some, especially travelers seeking a relatively tourist-free area. But the highlands are not for those seeking lush greenery and gorgeous ocean views in the background. Largely devoid of plant life, the highlands are essentially a desert, dry but starkly

Highlights

Look for ★ to find recommended sights, activities, dining, and lodging.

© MOON.COM

★ **Ódáðahraun:** See unusual lava and sand formations shaped by eruptions on the largest lava field in Iceland—which is actually considered an arctic desert (page 272).

★ **Laugafell:** This popular geothermal hot spot is a desert oasis in an isolated stretch of the highlands (page 272).

★ **Hiking Mount Askja:** A can't-miss adventure, hiking this volcano offers sensational views (page 274).

★ **Langjökull Glacier:** Iceland's second-largest glacier, this mammoth ice cap beckons (page 277).

★ **Hveravellir Nature Reserve:** Soak in a hot spring and camp overnight in one of Europe's last great wilderness spots (page 277).

The Highlands

Laugarbakki

Vesturhópsvatn

1

37

F338

35

Langjökull

LANGJÖKULL GLACIER

Heiðarvatn

Sandvatn

KJÖLUR

F35

To Selfoss

HRAUNEYJAR

Kvíslon

Þórisvatn

F26

HVERAVELLIR NATURE RESERVE

Hveradalir

KJÖLUR

Blöndulón

F35

F733

F35

To Varmahlíð

752

KASTALI

Mt. Loðmundur

Kerlingarfjöll

Mt. Snækollur

Hofsjökull

1

Eyjafjarðardalur

Austari Jökulsá

SPRENGISANDUR

F26

NÝIDALUR

LAUGAFELL

ÓDÁÐAHRAUN

Ódáðahraun

F821

To Akureyri

F26

To Goðafoss and Laugar

Skjálfandafljót

SPRENGISANDUR

Vatnajökull

Mt. Trölladyngja

Vatnajökull National Park

Víti

MOUNT ASKJA

HIKING

F910

Kverkfjöll

To Hrossaborg

F88

0

15 km

0

15 mi

© MOON.COM

beautiful. If you are an avid hiker, informed and prepared, and looking to explore something different in Iceland, this destination may be for you.

PLANNING YOUR TIME

Planning a trip to the highlands depends very much on what you want to see and do. For a peek at the interior without the burden of driving, take a **day tour** to see glaciers, volcanoes, and the landscape. Most companies offering tours to the highlands are based in Reykjavík. Other travelers like to plan **multiday hikes** throughout the interior. If you are keen on a lengthy hike, be sure to plan thoroughly, bring adequate gear and supplies, and take proper safety precautions.

Travelers have far fewer choices for accommodations (mainly huts) and food, and they must stay abreast of the weather forecast throughout the day, as the weather can change quickly. Be prepared for anything in the highlands, and make sure to book your accommodations ahead of time.

SAFETY

Navigating the highlands should not be taken lightly. The roads are rough, the wind punishing, and the weather can be unpredictable—it can snow any day of the year. Pay close attention to road closures, and if a road calls for a **super jeep** (a huge jeep with gigantic tires outfitted to handle rough terrain), heed the warning. If you attempt the ride in a smaller car or city SUV, you will likely damage your rental vehicle. The best plan is to discuss your itinerary with the rental company and see if a super jeep is necessary. Do not guess; a mistake will be costly. Also, be sure to **fill up your tank** before heading out, because there are no full-service gas stations in the highlands.

If you are planning a **hike,** be sure to wear **appropriate windproof clothing,** bring an adequate amount of **water** and **food,** and alert people of your trip itinerary. You can, and should, **register your trip** at www. safetravel.is. Bring maps, a **GPS device,** and a **compass,** and know where all the **emergency huts** are located on your route. Be prepared for anything, and don't underestimate Iceland's weather; always check for **weather alerts** before setting off on any hike. If you find yourself in an emergency, dial the **emergency number 112.**

GETTING AROUND

The highlands are a seasonal destination, and that season is short. Snow could fall any day of the year. If you are planning a trip in the summer, you may still face road closures due to a late snowfall or possible volcanic activity. Roads to the interior are typically only open **mid-June-August,** but check for closures before you head out. For up-to-date conditions, visit the **Icelandic Road and Coastal Administration** website at www. road.is.

When it comes to **car rentals,** don't skimp on your vehicle choice if you are planning to drive to the region. You're required to drive an **F-road-approved four-wheel-drive vehicle** in the highlands, which have many unpaved, rough roads and other challenges. Many different insurance options are offered on car rentals, and be mindful that driving the Ring Road is very different from driving in the highlands, where there can be sandstorms and wind damage, so pick the right insurance for the region you plan to travel to. Fill up with gas before you leave and take gas cans.

TOURS

Don't want to worry about renting a car and navigating the highlands on your own? These tour companies offer everything from day trips to multiday tours.

Previous: the volcanic landscape of the highlands; flowers growing in Askja's lava field; a super jeep at Langjökull Glacier.

ARCTIC ADVENTURES
tel. 354/562-7000, www.adventures.is

Arctic Adventures is a Reykjavík-based company that operates an October-April three-day tour where you start off by exploring the Golden Circle (Þingvellir National Park, Geysir, and Gullfoss) and then continue to the rugged landscapes of Kerlingarfjöll. The tour (129,990ISK) includes hiking, sightseeing, snowmobiling, and bathing in geothermal pools. Guests are picked up in Reykjavík. The tour also includes a northern lights hunt and a snowshoeing excursion.

ICELANDIC MOUNTAIN GUIDES
tel. 354/587-9999, www.mountainguides.is

Icelandic Mountain Guides runs a nine-day tour in July and August that hits all the hot spots in the highlands. Super jeeps will take you through the Kjölur and Sprengisandur routes, where you will see the Vatnajökull glacier, the Askja volcano, and the geothermal mountains of Kerlingarfjöll and Landmannalaugar. The package will run you 351,000ISK. Guests are picked up in Reykjavík.

Route F26 (Sprengisandur)

Black lava, gigantic boulders, and towering mountains await you along Sprengisandur. Tourists travel to this region to check out what is essentially an arctic desert. It's dry and barren, with its water trapped in the glaciers. Iceland's summer is warm enough for significant melting.

SIGHTS
Trölladyngja
Route F910, GPS coordinates N 64.8931, W 17.2547

Trölladyngja (Troll's Volcano) is the largest shield volcano, a domed volcano that is comprised of fluid lava flows, in the country and connects the Grímsvötn and Bárðarbunga central volcanoes. Mount Trölladyngja (1,468 meters/4,816 feet) is still active and only viewable from the road. It's 10 kilometers (6 miles) in diameter with a 100-meter (328-feet) crater on top. Lava flowed from it in all directions, especially to the north and west. The Gæsavötn Route F910 passes through the north of it.

★ Ódáðahraun
Route F88

Ódáðahraun (Crime Lava Field) is not only the largest lava field in Iceland, it's the largest desert in Europe, spanning more than 6,000 square kilometers (2,317 square miles).

Black, brown, and gray colors dominate the landscape. Visitors to the area will see endless sand, vast expanses of lava, and interesting geological formations caused by volcanic activity over the centuries. The lava shapes range from flat and smooth to rough and jagged. The region garnered its name, "crime lava," based on lore that numerous criminals hid out in the area trying to elude the authorities. The wind blows strongly, and there always seems to be a chill in the air. The isolation can be overwhelming—it's an eerie place to visit, though great for roaming and taking photos. Route F88 takes you to Ódáðahraun.

★ Laugafell
Route F821, GPS coordinates N 65.0278, W 18.3319

Laugafell (Bath Mountain) is situated near the northeast of the **Hofsjökull glacier,** about 20 kilometers (12 miles) southwest from the end of the **Eyjafjarðardalur valley.** It's a special place in the vast barren stretch of the highlands, with the spectacular 879-meter (2,883-foot) mountain adjacent to a geothermal hot spot. Two **hot springs** (free) open to visitors are in the northwestern portion of the mountain, and patches of grass and plants among the bubbling pools make it a desert oasis. It is important to have a good map for this region to find the hot springs and trails. Three

Bárðarbunga Blows!

Holuhraun eruption

Iceland's most recent volcanic eruption began in August 2014 in the **Bárðarbunga volcanic system** and ended a few months later. After a swarm of thousands of earthquakes over several weeks, the eruption began, emitting huge volumes of sulfur dioxide, impacting air quality in parts of Iceland, especially the East. The so-called fissure eruption occurred in the **Holuhraun** lava field, which is northeast of the Bárðarbunga caldera. Lava fountains shot several meters into the air from the crack in the earth.

The Holuhraun eruption did not occur underneath the ice cap, so there wasn't ash fallout. The airspace was closed three nautical miles around the eruption area up to 1,524 meters (5,000 feet)—meaning it did not affect commercial flights flying over Iceland.

The eruption ended in late February 2015 after six months of fiery lava shooting up from the earth. Locally, the event was referred to as a "tourist eruption," as tourists from around the world clamored to get a glimpse of the lava. But the only people allowed close to the site were journalists and scientists.

mountain huts (rooms from 17,000ISK, www.fi.is) are open during the summer; they have cooking facilities and guests can access a geothermal nature pool. Laugafell and the region are accessible by **Route F821.**

Askja
Route F88

Askja is a caldera in the remote, awe-inspiring Dyngjufjöll Mountains. Essentially huge volcanic craters, calderas are formed by collapsing land after a volcanic eruption. At 1,519 meters (4,983 feet), Askja emerges from the **Ódáðahraun lava field,** and the terrain is quite rocky. **Víti** is a tremendous pale blue lake-filled crater that emerged after the great eruption of the Askja volcano in 1875. It's possible to take a dip in the water, which reaches a temperature of about 30°C (86°F).

Askja is one of the most popular destinations in the highlands. There are two **mountain huts** (the Dreki huts, www.ffa. is) on **Route F88,** about 100 kilometers (62 miles) from the Ring Road. From there, it's an 8-kilometer (5-mile) drive up into the Askja caldera. It is a **walk** of about 2.5 kilometers (1.5 miles) from the **car park** to Víti. Keep in mind that the roads are usually only open for about three months, from late June until September. Depending on the weather, the open period could be longer or shorter.

Kverkfjöll

Route F910 to Route F902, GPS N 64.7475, W 16.6315
Reaching 1,764 meters (5,787 feet), the Kverkfjöll volcano includes two calderas that are filled with ice. The area is striking for its range of colors, with a deep black background that gives way to gorgeous blues and icy white. The main attractions are the **ice caves** that were created by hot springs, slowly melting the ice into interesting shapes. Stay safe, however, and please observe the caves from the outside; you never know when the ice mass could give way. To get to Kverkfjöll, take **Route F910** southeast to **Route F902.**

SPORTS AND RECREATION
★ Hiking Askja
Distance: *11.5 km (7.1 mi)*
Hiking Time: *2 hours*
Information and Maps: *www.visiticeland.is*
Trailhead: *Parking lot (N 65.0140, W 16.4500),*
which can be reached by Route 1 to Route F88
Passionate hikers will want to walk the rim of Askja. It offers some slopes and ultra-rocky terrain along with spectacular views of lava fields, mountains, and the mighty **Víti crater.** It's about a 30-minute moderate hike, 2.5 kilometers (1.5 miles) one-way, from the **car park** up to the caldera. The landscape is punishing, and devoid of vegetation, but the muted colors of brown and gray are striking against spots of snow and the blue water in the crater. The highest point in Askja is 1,516 meters (4,973 feet). The rim is about 6.5 kilometers (4 miles) around, which takes about an hour to walk. If you are not planning to hike the rim, you can just explore near the car park. To reach the car park, take **Route 1** to **Route F88.**

While the trail is well maintained, the main challenge is weather. If the forecast calls for wind, it's best to skip the planned hike.

Do not underestimate the power of Iceland's wind, especially in the highlands.

FOOD AND ACCOMMODATIONS
Make sure to book your accommodation ahead of time.

THE HIGHLAND CENTER HRAUNEYJAR
Route F26, tel. 354/487-7782, www.
thehighlandcenter.is, open year-round, 36,000ISK
The Highland Center Hrauneyjar offers 99 rooms ranging from doubles with shared bathroom facilities to double rooms with private bathrooms and free Wi-Fi. There are also triple rooms available as well as sleeping bag accommodation for a cheaper price. The GPS coordinates are N 64.1964, W 19.2655. Rooms are sparsely decorated with a bed, desk, and small table. It's not luxury, but it's the only option other than mountain huts. Along with the guesthouse, Hrauneyjar has a **restaurant** (7am-8pm daily) open year-round, a **gas station,** and a tourist shop that offers food, maps, and fishing permits. It's a good idea to stop here to pick up essentials (like food, water, and gas) even if you don't plan to stay at the guesthouse.

LAUGAFELL HUTS
GPS N 65.0269, W 18.3321, tel. 354/462-2720, www.
ffa.is, 8,000ISK
The Laugafell huts are located about 15 kilometers (9 miles) northeast of Hofsjökull glacier and 20 kilometers (12 miles) southwest from the end of the Eyjafjarðardalur valley. The huts can be reached by Route F752 or F881 from Route F26 or by F821. Accommodations are basic, with gas available for cooking and restrooms near the swimming pool. It costs 8,000ISK to stay the night, and showers cost an additional 500ISK. The huts are open only during the summer months.

1: lava formations at Ódáðahraun **2:** the Víti crater on Mount Askja **3:** the Dreki huts at Drekagil gorge **4:** glacier caves at Kverkfjöll

Navigating the Arctic Desert Safely

Every year there are tourists that arrive in the highlands looking for a once-in-a-lifetime adventure but find themselves unprepared. Safety needs to be your top priority. Some tourists need to be rescued, and then there are those who don't make it out alive. Do not underestimate the weather in Iceland, even in the summer. Keep these things in mind—some may seem like common sense, but they're still important to note.

- Have an appropriate **rental car. A four-wheel drive approved for F roads** is required in the highlands, and if the trail calls for a **super jeep,** take heed.

- **Have enough gas for your trip.** Gas stations are few and far between in the highlands.

- **Dress the part.** Make sure you have waterproof layers, warm clothing, and sturdy footwear.

- **Bring adequate food and water.** Don't count on buying food along the journey.

- Have **maps,** a **compass,** and a **charged mobile phone** on hand.

- If you find yourself in trouble, the **emergency number** in Iceland is **112.**

NÝIDALUR

tel. 354/860-3334, www.fi.is, 9,000ISK, tent camping outside 2,000ISK

There are mountain huts along the valley Nýidalur that sleep 79 people; the GPS coordinates are N 64.7355, W 18.0725. The area can be reached by Route F26. The huts have cooking facilities, toilets, and hot showers. It costs 9,000ISK per night to stay inside the huts, and 2,000ISK for tent camping outside in an open field. Shower use costs 500ISK. The huts are open July-August.

DREKI HUTS

GPS N 65.0417, W 16.5948, tel. 354/822-5190, www.ffa.is, www.nat.is, 9,000ISK

The mountain huts closest to Askja are at Drekagil gorge. The Dreki huts can be reached by Route F88 from the Ring Road east of Lake Mývatn or by Route F910 from Route F26. There are two residential huts on the site that can accommodate 60 people. The huts have gas available for cooking and there are toilets and shower facilities. The Dreki huts are an ideal base for those interested in exploring the Askja caldera, which is an 8-kilometer (5-mile) drive from the huts. It costs 9,000ISK to stay the night. Showers cost

an additional 500ISK. The huts are open only during the summer months.

GETTING THERE AND AROUND
By 4WD Vehicle

Route F26 is not for the faint of heart. It cannot be emphasized enough that you must have a proper vehicle to navigate this road—an **F-road-approved four-wheel drive.** Weather is cruel to this road, and there are rivers to ford, large uneven sections, gravel, and potholes. The 200-kilometer (124-mile) route roams from **Mount Hekla** in the south to the glorious waterfall **Goðafoss** in the north. The route is not a year-round destination, and the road typically opens at the **end of June.** It could open later if the region had a particularly harsh winter with a lot of snowfall. To check road closures and the opening date, visit the **Icelandic Road and Coastal Administration** website (www.road.is).

Another important detail to keep in mind is that the only **gas station** along Route F26 is at **Hrauneyjar.** Be prepared and fill up before your journey. Also make sure you have all **food, water,** and **supplies** that you need. Depending on where you are staying the day before, you can stock up in Reykjavík before you head out, or at a town in the south.

By Bus
To get to the region by bus, check out the schedule of Reykjavik Excursions (tel.

354/562-1011, www.re.is), which offers trips early July-late August. The 10-hour trip costs 8,500ISK each way and the tour departs from Reykjavík. You can purchase a bus pass that allows you to hop off and on the bus. It is necessary to book in advance.

Route F35 (Kjölur)

For a less treacherous route to the highlands, Route F35 is your best bet. The majority of the route is flat and can be accessible up until October (depending on the weather, of course). As elsewhere in the highlands, an F-road-approved four-wheel drive vehicle is required. Be safe, monitor weather reports, and be aware of road conditions.

SIGHTS
★ Langjökull Glacier
Route F35
At 952 square kilometers (368 square miles), Langjökull (Long Glacier) is the second-largest ice cap in Iceland after Vatnajökull. The ice is quite thick, up to 580 meters (1,900 feet) deep. The highest point of the ice cap is about 1,450 meters (4,757 feet) above sea level. The rocky terrain and snowy patches are vast and haunting.

Route F35 runs along the east side of Langjökull, between it and Hofsjökull. From Reykjavík, you head east on Route 1. Before you reach the town of Selfoss, take a left turn on F35 and continue past Gullfoss for about 37 kilometers (23 miles).

★ Hveravellir Nature Reserve
Route F35, tel. 354/452-4200,
www.hveravellir.is
Situated in the western highlands, the Hveravellir Nature Reserve is one of the last great wilderness spots in Europe. It's about 90 kilometers (56 miles) north of Gullfoss on Route F35. Hveravellir is a natural geothermal hot spot with smoking fumaroles and bubbling water holes, and it's a special

experience to see geothermal energy at work. It's also a popular place to hike.

There are private rooms in one of two huts, called the New Hut and the Old Hut (28,800ISK per room, linens and breakfast included), dormitories (7,500ISK pp), and a campsite (1,900ISK pp) available within the reserve. One bathing-friendly, waist-deep pool is situated close to the mountain huts, and it's a safe place to take a dip.

Kerlingarfjöll
GPS N 64.6834, W 19.2999, Route F35, tel.
354/664-7000, www.kerlingarfjoll.is
The mountain range Kerlingarfjöll (Women's Mountains) shows all the characteristics of a matured caldera, including volcanic formations and geothermal hot spots. In short, this is a geology buff's dream. The towering peaks were created by eruptions from a large caldera lying under the mountains; while the caldera is still considered active, it has been silent for tens of thousands of years. Visitors will see steep slopes and pointy peaks dotted with ice, leading into a hotbed of geothermal activity. While the earth steams below, aboveground it's quiet and desolate.

Accommodations are available at Kerlingarfjöll, which has double rooms (38,800ISK), private cabins (58,080ISK), a campsite for tents (2,00ISK), and dorms (7,680ISK pp). The breakfast buffet is 2,500ISK per person.

To get to Kerlingarfjöll from Gullfoss, drive north on F35. For 15 kilometers (9 miles) the road is asphalt, and the remaining 38-kilometer (24-mile) section is gravel.

Hofsjökull Glacier

GPS N 64.8167, W 18.8167, east of Vatnajokull,
between Vididalur and Hofsdalur

Hofsjökull (Temple Glacier) is the third-largest glacier in Iceland after Vatnajökull and Langjökull. It is situated in the western highlands, north of the mountain range **Kerlingarfjöll**. The glacier covers an area of 925 square kilometers (357 square miles), reaching 1,765 meters (5,790 feet) at the top. It's vast and can be quite windy. Also, visitors will have to be careful of huge crevasses in the ice.

HIKING

Hikers have many choices for roaming the interior. These popular options vary in scenery and degree of difficulty.

Hveradalir

GPS N 64.6453, W 19.2825.

Hiking the geothermal area Hveradalir (Hot Springs Valley) is wildly popular, and for good reason. The valley offers views of mountains, vast expanses of desert-like earth marked by steam vents (reminding visitors that the land is very much alive), and hot springs. Hveradalir is accessible off **Route 1.**

NEÐRI-HVERADALIR HIKE

Distance: *3 km (2 mi)*
Hiking Time: *3 hours*
Information and Maps: *www.visiticeland.is*
Trailhead: *Neðri-Hveradalir car park*

A moderate hike begins at the car park by Neðri-Hveradalir (Lower Hveradalir) and takes you through the geothermal area Hveradalir, where ice and fire meet. The route is a 3-kilometer (2-mile) loop and takes about three hours. Hikers will view the stark white glacial landscape and see the steam rise out of the ground near the numerous hot springs. Muted colors of brown and black in a desert-like landscape give way to pockets of stark white snow in some regions

---

1: Hveravellir Nature Reserve 2: Langjökull Glacier

and lush green vegetation in others. Every few meters you'll want to stop and take in the views, and everything seems to warrant a photo.

ÁSGARÐSÁ RIVER HIKE

Distance: *11.2 km (7 mi) round-trip*
Hiking Time: *2.5 hours*
Information and Maps: *www.visiticeland.is*
Trailhead: *Keis parking lot*

For a longer, more demanding hike, start at the car park called Keis, toward the bottom of Hveradalir, where you follow the Ásgarðsá River for 4.5 kilometers (2.8 miles). The hike is an 11.2-kilometer (7-mile) loop. Being so close to the river, you will see vegetation, which is a rare sight in much of the highlands. During the hike, there will be points where you have to cross water, so dress accordingly. Hikers will pass hills and geothermal hot spots as the river twists and turns. Overall, it's a five-hour hike and moderately difficult.

Kerlingarfjöll

Distance: *7 km (4 mi)*
Hiking Time: *6 hours*
Information and Maps: *www.visiticeland.is*
Trailhead: *Kastali parking lot*

For a more difficult walk, start at the car park called Kastali and continue to 1,432-meter (4,698 feet) Mount Lodmundur, then to the highest peak of Kerlingarfjöll, Mount Snækollur, at 1,460 meters (4,790 feet). The trail is rocky and there are quite a few slopes, but the payoff is the gorgeous views of the barren landscape below and mountains in the distance. It's one of the best overviews of the highlands. This is a 7-kilometer (4-mile) hike, in a loop, which takes about six hours.

GETTING THERE AND AROUND
By 4WD Vehicle

The 200-kilometer (124-mile) Kjölur route (Route F35) begins near the picturesque waterfall **Gullfoss** in the south and extends to **Blönduós** in the northwest. This route

Crossing a River

4WD car crosses a river in Iceland

When driving in the highlands you will likely come across a river or two. They can range from small creeks to large rivers that vary in depth. Below are a few tips that you should keep in mind when you arrive at a river crossing.

- Never cross a river unless you are **100 percent confident** of how to do it. If you are unsure or uncomfortable crossing, wait for another vehicle to cross first.

- Look for the best place to ford, where it is most **shallow.**

- Note that rivers tend to have less volume **earlier in the day.**

- Wade into the river with two or three other people, clasping arms, to **gauge the depth** of the river.

is not a year-round destination: The road typically opens the **middle of June,** but it could be later if the winter was harsh. The road closes in **September,** but how early in September depends on the weather. You need an **F-road-approved four-wheel-drive vehicle** for the journey. Be sure to gas up before you head to the highlands, as there are no gas stations in the region. It's best to get supplies in Reykjavík or a large town in the south. Depending on the duration of your trip, it might be necessary to bring **gas cans.**

By Bus
SBA
tel. 354/550-0700, www.sba.is

SBA operates summer buses between **Akureyri** in the north and **Reykjavík** along the Kjölur route. The 10-hour, one-way trip, which is only available **late June through early September,** costs 17,900ISK. You can purchase a **bus pass** that allows you to make stops along the route. Be sure to have a copy of the most recent **bus schedule.** It tends to change.

Ring Road Road Trip

This recommended itinerary takes you counter-
clockwise around Iceland. The Ring Road (Route 1) encircles the island, connecting many of the most popular attractions. Paved for most of its 1,332-kilometer (828-mile) length, the Ring Road is the most accessible route around the country. Driving along, you'll encounter breathtaking landscapes ranging from towering mountains to barren lava fields to glaciers looming in the distance.

The Ring Road is popular for a reason: the loop is a convenient way to see the best of Iceland's nature, starting with the most popular attractions in the south to lesser-known gems around the island. For travelers who have at least 10 days, driving the Ring Road is ideal, the best

Planning the Drive 283
Day 1: Reykjavík and the
     Blue Lagoon 287
Day 2: The Golden
     Circle 288
Day 3: The South Coast . 290
Day 4: The Glacial East . . 291
Day 5: The Eastfjords to
     Mývatn 292
Day 6: Detour to
     Húsavík 293
Day 7: The North 294
Day 8: Driving to
     Snæfellsnes 296
Day 9: Snæfellsjökull
     National Park and
     Borgarnes 298
Last Day 299

Highlights

Look for ★ to find recommended sights, activities, dining, and lodging.

Whale Watching

Húsavík

Krafla Volcano

Akureyri

Akureyri Botanical Gardens

Norwegian
Sea

Egilsstaðir

Kirkjufell

Grundarfjörður

North
Atlantic
Ocean

Borgarnes

Reykjavík

Blue Lagoon

Grindavík

Flúðir

Gullfoss

Vatnajökull

Höfn

Jökulsárlón

0   50 mi
0   50 km

Reynisfjara

© MOON.COM

★ **Blue Lagoon:** The famous Blue Lagoon lives up to the hype as a place to relax after your flight to the island (page 287).

★ **Gullfoss:** If you see one waterfall in Iceland, let it be this spectacular example along the Golden Circle route (page 288).

★ **Reynisfjara:** Explore one of Iceland's most beautiful glacial, black sand beaches (page 290).

★ **Jökulsárlón:** Stand in awe of this icy, otherworldly glacial lake (page 291).

★ **Krafla Volcano:** Get up close to one of Iceland's powerful volcanoes (page 292).

★ **Whale-Watching in Húsavík:** Tiny Húsavík has earned its reputation as the whale-watching capital of the island (page 293).

★ **Akureyri Botanical Gardens:** The "capital" of the North is rightfully proud of its pretty, eclectic botanical gardens (page 294).

★ **Kirkjufell:** This conical mountain is one of the most striking sights in Iceland (page 296).

use of time to see as much as possible without backtracking to one or two bases.

The suggested itinerary can be supplemented with the many other different options in the destination chapters. Some of the can't-miss sites include the Golden Circle attractions, Seljalandsfoss and Skógafoss waterfalls in the south, Skaftafell and Jókulsárlón in the east, the Mývatn area and Akureyri in the north, and Snæfellsnes in the west. For activities, it's highly recommended to take a whale-watching tour in Húsavík and take a boat tour among the icebergs at Jókulsárlón.

Planning the Drive

SEASONAL CONSIDERATIONS AND ROAD CONDITIONS

Because the weather can be so challenging, it's ideal to plan a trip around the Ring Road in the **summer (June-August)** and the shoulder months **(May and September).** Iceland's weather is known for being notoriously changeable and this, of course, impacts a Ring Road drive. Sunny skies can give way to fog in seconds, rain comes and goes, and drivers must be aware of windspeeds that can be dangerous.

The **summer** is the most popular time to undergo a Ring Road trip as the weather is most favorable and the landscape is lush and green. The good weather draws a high number of tourists, but the Ring Road rarely feels crowded, with the most traffic in the south.

Despite snow removal during the **winter,** snowfall, ice, and high winds can make driving very challenging. It's important to frequently check the weather forecast and road conditions as windstorms can strike any time of year, making driving hazardous.

Keep in mind that it's always necessary to check **road conditions** before you head out in your car. Weather changes rapidly in Iceland, and you do not want to be unprepared. You should check weather and road conditions at the beginning of each day before hitting the road. Important websites to look at include www.road.is and www.vedur.is.

RENTING YOUR CAR

If you are planning a summer ring road trip, a **2WD** car will be adequate, though having a **4WD** vehicle wouldn't hurt. In the winter, you will want a car with **studded tires** for potentially icy roads. Campervan and motorhome rentals should be limited to the summer months as that is when campsites are open.

For regular cars, the Ring Road can be driven in any size car. It comes down to preference: Some travelers prefer a larger vehicle. In Iceland, you will find a number of international rental car agencies including **Hertz, Avis,** and **Budget,** as well as local rental agencies. It's best to book your rental directly instead of through third parties. A rental for a small car starts at 18,000ISK per day and a large SUV can start at 42,000ISK per day. It is best to book ahead, at least three months before your trip.

Deciding what kind of **insurance** to get is extremely important (sand and ash insurance, for instance). Collision damage waiver insurance is included in the price of the rental and it is recommended to get additional **gravel protection insurance.** When collecting your car, you should **take photos of existing damage** to the vehicle, and make sure you understand your rental agreement and insurance policy. Check all the lights, tires, and make sure there's a **spare tire. GPS devices** can be rented through your car

---

Previous: the Ring Road; the Blue Lagoon; walkway near Selfoss on the Golden Circle.

Ring Road Road Trip

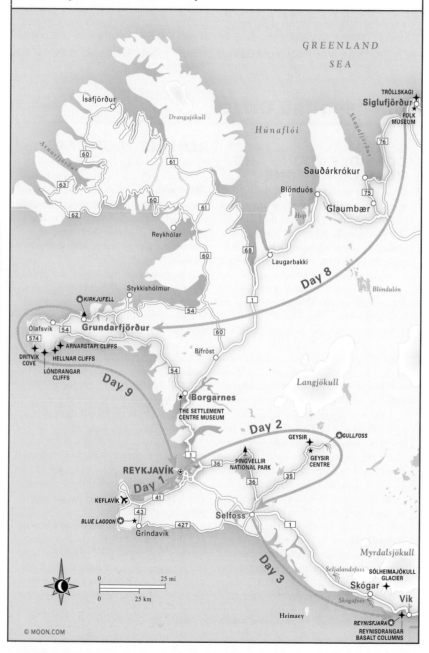

GREENLAND SEA

TRÖLLSKAGI
Siglufjörður
FOLK MUSEUM
76

Ísafjörður

Drangajökull

Húnaflói

Skagafjörður

Sauðárkrókur
Blönduós
75
Glaumbær
60
63
Arnarfjörður
62
60
61
61
Reykhólar
Hóp
68
60
Laugarbakki
Day 8
Blöndulón
Stykkishólmur
KIRKJUFELL
54
1
Ólafsvík 54
574 Grundarfjörður
ARNARSTAPI CLIFFS
60
DRITVÍK COVE HELLNAR CLIFFS
Bifröst
Langjökull
LÓNDRANGAR CLIFFS
Day 9
54
Borgarnes
THE SETTLEMENT CENTRE MUSEUM
Day 2
GEYSIR
GULLFOSS
REYKJAVÍK
36
ÞINGVELLIR NATIONAL PARK
GEYSIR CENTRE
35
KEFLAVÍK
41
36
43
Selfoss
1
BLUE LAGOON
427
Grindavík
Myrdalsjökull
Seljalandsfoss
SÓLHEIMAJÖKULL GLACIER
Day 3
Skógar
Skógafoss
Vik
Heimaey
REYNISFJARA
REYNISDRANGAR BASALT COLUMNS

Day 1

0   25 mi
0   25 km

© MOON.COM

DAY 1: Reykjavík
DAY 2: Reykjavík–Selfoss
DAY 3: Selfoss–Vík
DAY 4: Vík–Höfn
DAY 5: Höfn–Lake Mývatn
DAY 6: Lake Mývatn–Húsavík
DAY 7: Húsavík–Siglufjörður
DAY 8: Siglufjörður–Stykkishólmur
DAY 9: Stykkishólmur–Reykjavík

rental agency for a small fee. However, **paper maps** are preferable to GPS devices.

WHAT TO PACK

Packing for a road trip can seem daunting, so here is a handy guide.

* **Paper maps,** which can be purchased at gas stations or tourist information centers (GPS optional)

* **Reusable water bottle**

* **Snacks** for the car

* **Sturdy walking shoes**/boots with good tread

* Layers and **waterproof outerwear**

* **Bathing suit** for swimming pools/hot springs

* **Mobile phone, chargers** and **adapters**

GETTING GAS

Gas stations are located around the ring road, but there are pockets where they become scarce, namely between **Vík** in the south and **Mývatn** in the north. It's a good idea to **fully fill your tank** when you have the opportunity.

For a medium size car, it costs about 10,000ISK to fill up a tank with petrol. At the time of writing, one liter of petrol costs about 200ISK per liter and diesel costs 193ISK per liter. You can check up-to-date gas prices at www.gsmbensin.is.

Unmanned gas stations are popular in rural areas. You must have a **4-digit PIN** for your credit card to fill up at these gas stations. If you don't have a card with a PIN, contact your bank ahead of your visit.

DRIVING LAWS

There are a few rules travelers should be aware of when driving the Ring Road.

* **Off-road driving is strictly prohibited** and there are **hefty fines** from authorities.

* All passengers in a vehicle must **wear a seat belt.**

* **Talking on a mobile phone** while driving is prohibited.

* **Driving under the influence** is illegal and fines start at 80,000ISK.

* Drivers must **use headlights at all times,** even in bright daylight.

Speed Limits

Speeding **fines** are high, and can be collected through the rental car company, which will have an imprint of your credit card. Fines can range from 30,000ISK to 200,000ISK. There are **speed cameras** along the Ring Road. The speed limits are:

* 90km/h (56mph) on paved roads (like the Ring Road)

* 80km/h (50mph) on gravel roads

* 50km/h (31mph) or less in residential areas

CELL PHONE SERVICE

Iceland has surprisingly good cell phone service across the island, even in the highlands. You can purchase **SIM cards** at Keflavik Airport, as well as shops around the country. The three main cell phone providers in Iceland are **Vodafone, Siminn,** and **Nova.** Always make sure your mobile phone is **fully charged.** In case of an emergency, the national emergency number is **112.**

FOOD, ACOMMODATIONS, AND CAMPING

Accommodation along the Ring Road ranges from budget-friendly hostels to luxury hotels. It is highly recommended to **book accommodation in advance,** as options are limited in many parts of the island.

For food, it is recommended to have a rough itinerary for your road trip to highlight the locations of **restaurants, cafes,** and **supermarkets** along your route, as choices in rural areas can be few and far between. If you are staying in self-catering accommodation, it makes sense to buy food from supermarkets. For restaurants in the countryside, it is not necessary to make reservations. **Camping season** kicks off on June 1 and lasts until mid-September. During this time, campsites are open, most with **showers, electricity,** and an **area to prepare food;** all have **toilets,** and some have **washing machines.** It is not recommended to camp the rest of the year, as most campsites are closed. Wild camping in Iceland is against the law (without permission from the landowner). Campsites have different prices and facilities as they are operated independently. A campsite can range from 1,200-2,500ISK per night. You can stay at campsites in a tent or you can park your campervan or motorhome. If you are planning to camp, be sure to bring a **three-season tent** and a **warm sleeping bag.**

PLANNING YOUR TIME

To do the Ring Road justice, you should allocate at least **10 days** to the trip. It is possible to drive it in less time, but that would mean more time in the car and less time for sightseeing and activities. The shortest amount of time needed would be **7 days** in the summer, cutting down on time in the Eastfjords and the Snæfellsnes peninsula detour in the west. In the winter, 10 days should be the minimum, as the unpredictable weather may require a buffer day or two. You can expect to drive on average 200 kilometers (124 miles) per day, depending on the attractions and activities planned.

Advance bookings are necessary for the **Blue Lagoon** and the **Glacier Lagoon boat tour** at Jökulsárlón.

Day 1: Reykjavík and the Blue Lagoon

AFTERNOON

Driving time: 25 minutes
Driving distance: 21.5 km (13.4 mi)
Directions: Route 41 to Route 43 south to the Blue Lagoon

After landing at **Keflavík International Airport** (Keflavíkurflugvöllur, tel. 354/425-6000) in the morning or afternoon, pick up your **rental car** and head south on Route 43.

★ Blue Lagoon

Svartsengi, tel. 354/420-8800, www.bluelagoon. com, 8am-9pm daily Aug. 19-May 30, 7am-11pm May 31-June 27, and 7am-midnight June 28-Aug. 18, must be booked in advance

Make a stop at the Blue Lagoon near Grindavík to soak in the soothing, geothermally heated water.

EVENING

Driving time: 50 minutes
Driving distance: 49 km (30 mi)
Directions: Route 43 north to Route 41 east to

Reykjavik; Route 41 becomes Route 40; turn on Route 49 west to get to Reykjavík city center

Revived, you're ready to drive to Reykjavík to explore the capital city.

Reykjavík

In the early evening, walk along **Tjörnin** (The Pond) before visiting the thriving harbor area, **Grandi.** Stop by the glass-paneled **Harpa Concert Hall** (Austurbakki 2, tel. 354/528-5000, www.harpa.is, 9am-10pm daily) and visit the *Sun Voyager* (Sæbraut) metal sculpture, just down the coast to the south, which resembles a Viking ship.

For dinner, stop by **Noodle Station** (Laugavegur 103, tel. 354/551-3198, 11am-10pm daily, 1,680ISK) for one of the cheapest, most satisfying meals you can find in Reykjavík. You'll spend the night at **Hótel Frón** (Laugavegur 22A, tel. 354/511-4666, www.hotelfron.is, rooms from 23,000ISK), conveniently located to many of the city's best bars.

DAY 1 INDEX

- Keflavík International Airport, page 74
- Blue Lagoon, page 95
- Grandi, page 42
- Harpa Concert Hall, page 44
- *Sun Voyager,* page 44
- Noodle Station, page 58
- Hótel Frón, page 71

Day 2: The Golden Circle

MORNING

Driving time: 50 minutes
Driving distance: 48 km (30 mi)
Directions: Route 49 east turns into Route 1 (the Ring Road); Route 1 to Route 36 east to Þingvellir National Park

From Reykjavík, set off on a tour of the Golden Circle, a trio of must-see sights.

Þingvellir National Park

Þingvellir National Park is a geological wonder and also the birthplace of democracy in Iceland. The **Þingvellir Interpretive Center** (tel. 354/482-2660, www.thingvellir.is, 9am-8pm daily June-Aug., 9am-5pm Sept.-Apr., free) gives a great overview of the national park's history and geographical significance, along with maps for hiking trails. Spend 1-2 hours roaming this UNESCO World Heritage site's main sights, including **Almannagjá** (All Man's Gorge) and **Lögberg** (Law Rock).

AFTERNOON

Driving time: 1 hour
Driving distance: 70 km (73 mi)
Directions: Route 36 to Routes 365, 37, and 35 northeast to Geysir and Gullfoss

Geysir

Take Route 36 east, which turns into Route 365 and leads to a roundabout to Route 37 to visit the geothermal area of Geysir, about a 50-minute drive. Though the famous "Geysir" hasn't erupted since 2005, the nearby hot spring **Strokkur** erupts every 5-7 minutes. Have lunch in the cafeteria at **Geysir Center** (Biskupstungnabraut, tel. 354/519-6020, www.geysircenter.com, 9am-10pm daily June 1-Aug. 31 and 9am-6pm Sept. 1-May 31), a large visitor's center where you can also shop for souvenirs.

★ Gullfoss

After lunch, head east on Route 35 for 10 minutes to visit nearby Gullfoss, Iceland's most famous and most photographed waterfall. Watch white water thrash and tumble down the two-tiered falls.

EVENING

Driving time: 1 hour
Driving distance: 72 km (45 mi)
Directions: Route 35 southwest to Route 1 southeast to Selfoss

Selfoss

After a day of sightseeing, drive to Selfoss, the largest town in South Iceland, where you will have dinner and spend the night at **Hotel Selfoss** (Eyrarvegur 2, tel. 354/480-2500, www.selfosshotel.is, rooms from 26,000ISK).

DAY 2 INDEX

- Þingvellir National Park, page 99
- Geysir, page 104
- Gullfoss, page 106
- Selfoss, page 111

Day 3: The South Coast

MORNING

Driving time: *1.5 hours*
Driving distance: *100 km (62 mi)*
Directions: *Route 1 east to Route 249 north to Seljalandsfoss; Route 1 east to Skógafoss*

Seljalandsfoss

From Selfoss, drive along the spectacular south coast on Route 1, with your first stop at Seljalandsfoss, a beautiful waterfall about an hour's drive east. Turn left on Þórsmerkurvegur (Route 249), where a car park for Seljalandsfoss is clearly signed. At Seljalandsfoss, you can actually walk behind the falls on a footpath at the base of the waterfall. Explore the area for about an hour, and be sure to snap some photos.

Skógafoss

After visiting Seljalandsfoss, continue on Route 1 east for another 30 minutes to Skógafoss. Turn left on Skógar, then left again on Skógafoss, where you'll see the car park for the massive 60-meter (197-foot) waterfall in the village of **Skógar.**

AFTERNOON AND EVENING

Driving time: *45 min*
Driving distance: *46 km (29 mi)*
Directions: *Route 1 east to Route 215 south to Reynisfjara; Route 1 east to Vík*

★ Reynisfjara

Next, on Route 1 head to Reynisfjara beach near the village of Vík. This is about a 30-minute drive east, turning right toward the coast on **Reynishverfisvegur (Route 215).** This is perhaps the most famous black sand beach in Iceland. Explore the **Reynisdrangar basalt columns,** cliffs, and a sea cave; there's enough here to while away a few hours.

Vík

Backtrack to Route 1 and head east to the tiny town of Vík, where you'll spend the rest of the day. Have a late lunch at cozy **Halldórskaffi** (Víkurbraut 28, tel. 354/487-1202, www.halldorskaffi.is, noon-9pm daily year-round, entrées from 2,790ISK), just off the Ring Road. After lunch, take a fun one-hour zipline tour offered by **True Adventure** (Suðurvíkurvegur 5, tel. 354/698-8890, www.trueadventure.is, 14,900ISK), headquartered just on the other side of the Ring Road in Vík, a 12-minute walk or 2-minute drive.

Have dinner at **Suður-Vík Restaurant and Café** (Suðurvikurvegur 1, tel. 354/487-1515, noon-10pm daily, entrées from 2,850ISK, right next to True Adventure. Add some much-needed food diversity to your time in Iceland with their perfectly spiced Thai dishes. Spend the night at spacious, contemporary **Icelandair Hotel Vík** (Klettsvegi 1, tel. 354/487-1480, icelandairhotels.com/en/hotels/vik, rooms from 21,000 ISK).

DAY 3 INDEX

- Seljanlandsfoss, page 122
- Skógafoss, page 123
- Reynisfjara, page 126
- Vík, page 125

Day 4: The Glacial East

MORNING

Driving time: *2 hours*
Driving distance: *140 km (86 mi)*
Directions: *Route 1 east to Vatnajökull National Park*

Vatnajökull National Park

Get ready to see some icebergs today, as you drive the Ring Road to Vatnajökull National Park, which is just under 2 hours east of Vík on Route 1. Turn left on Skaftafellsvegur, which turns into Hæðavegur.

Vatnajökull National Park is the home of Europe's largest ice cap, specifically **Skaftafell,** the southern part of Vatnajökull, which used to be its own national park. Stop by **Skaftafellsoffa** (Skaftafellsvegur, tel. 354/478-1627, www.vatnajokulsthjodgardur. is, 10am-6pm daily Jan.-Feb., 9am-6pm daily Mar.-May, 8am-7pm daily June-Aug., 9am-6pm daily Sept.-Oct., 10am-6pm daily Nov.-Dec.), the national park office, for information about the many footpaths and hiking trails in the region. Plan to spend the morning here hiking and taking in some of the park's many vistas and waterfalls.

AFTERNOON

Driving time: *1 hour*
Driving distance: *58 km (36 mi)*
Directions: *Route 1 east to Jökulsárlón*

★ Jökulsárlón

Continue on Route 1 for about an hour to Jökulsárlón, a glacial lagoon, where you will see huge chunks of ice floating in the water and if you're lucky, a curious seal or two. Take a 40-minute boat tour of the lagoon, which you should book in advance, with **Glacier Lagoon** (Jökulsárlón Ehf, tel. 354/478-2222, www.icelagoon.is, 10am-5pm daily in May, 9am-7pm daily June-Sept., 10am-5pm daily in Oct., 5,800ISK) to get close to icebergs and even get a chance to taste the ice.

EVENING

Driving time: *1 hour*
Driving distance: *80 km (40 mi)*
Directions: *Route 1 east to Route 99 South to Höfn*

Höfn

Drive another hour on Route 1 to the sleepy town of Höfn, gateway for tourists seeking to visit the glacier, where you can have a fantastic lobster dinner at **Humarhofnin** (Hafnarbraut 4, tel. 354/478-1200, www. humarhofnin.is, langoustine entrées from 65,900ISK, other entrees from 2,900ISK) and spend the night in the brightly decorated **Nýibær Guesthouse** (Hafnarbraut 8, tel. 354/478-1736, www.hostel.is, rooms from 24,000ISK).

DAY 4 INDEX

- Skaftafell, Vatnajökull National Park, page 264
- Jökulsárlón, page 263
- Höfn, page 259

Day 5: The Eastfjords to Mývatn

MORNING

Driving time: *3 hours*
Driving distance: *211 km (131 mi)*
Directions: *Route 1 north to Stöðvarfjörður and Route 955 to Fáskrúðsfjörður*

Petra's Mineral Collection

Fjarðarbraut 21, Stöðvarfjörður, tel. 354/475-8834, www.steinapetra.is, 9am-6pm daily May 1-Sept. 30, closed Oct. 1-Apr 30. and Feb.-Apr., 1,500ISK, free for children 13 and under

Today's long drive takes you north to the spectacular Eastfjords, dotted with small fishing villages, gorgeous landscapes, and quirky attractions. About 2.5 hours in, make a stop at Petra's Mineral Collection, right off the Ring Road in **Stöðvarfjörður** to check out an enormous collection of geodes, minerals, and found objects.

Fáskrúðsfjörður

Continue just over 25 minutes to nearby Fáskrúðsfjörður to stroll one of the most unique towns in Iceland, distinguished by its French influence. Stop for lunch at **Café Sumarlína** (Búðavegur 59, tel. 354/475-1575, www.sumarlina.is, 11am-10pm daily, entrées from 2,650ISK).

AFTERNOON

Driving time: *3 hours*
Driving distance: *257 km (159 mi)*
Directions: *Route 1 north to Egilsstaðir and west to Krafla turnoff and Námaskarð*

Lagarfljót

Continue about an hour north on Route 1 to **Egilsstaðir** and the long and narrow lake Lagarfljót. Get out of the car to stretch your legs and take a look at the dramatic lake.

★ Krafla

Drive another 2 hours northwest toward the **Lake Mývatn** area, turning off the Ring Road just before you get to the lake to visit the Krafla volcano with its huge, 300-meter (984-foot) crater, **Víti**. A paved road leads up to the lava fields, where you can hike and take in hot springs and mud pools.

Námaskarð

Less than 2 kilometers (0.9 miles) west of the turnoff for Krafla on Route 1 is the sulfurous, multicolored Námaskarð pass (15 km/9 mi northeast of Mývatn on Route 1). A short walking path encircles the mud pools.

EVENING

Driving time: *25 minutes*
Driving distance: *20 km (12 mi)*
Directions: *Route 1 west to Lake Mývatn area; Route 848 south to Vogafjós Restaurant and Hotel Laxá*

Lake Mývatn

MÝVATN NATURE BATHS

tel. 354/464-4411, www.myvatnnaturebaths.is, 9am-midnight daily May 15-Sept. 30, noon-10pm daily Oct. 1-May 14, Jan. 1-Apr. 30 4,500ISK, May 1-Sept. 30 5,300ISK, Oct. 1-Dec. 31 4,500ISK

Back on Route 1, head west toward Lake Mývatn on for 1.7 kilometers (1 mile), then make a left at the turnoff for Mývatn Nature Baths, where you can have a relaxing evening soak.

VOGAFJÓS RESTAURANT

Vogar, tel. 354/464-4303, www.vogafjos.is, 11am-10pm daily summer, 10am-9:30pm daily winter, dinner entrées from 4,150ISK

For dinner, continue west on Route 1 and turn south on Route 848 to head to **Vogar.** dine at cute, quirky Vogafjós Restaurant.

HOTEL LAXÁ

Olnbogaás, tel. 354/464-1900,
www.hotellaxa.is, rooms from 26,690ISK
After dinner, head south on 848 to go halfway around the lake, about 16 kilometers (10
miles) from the restaurant. Spend the night at
Hotel Laxá, a modern hotel that offers huge
windows in rooms that overlook the wonders
of Mývatn.

DAY 5 INDEX

• Fáskrúðsfjörður, page 253

• Egilsstaðir, page 238

• Lagarfljót, page 241

• Krafla, page 217

• Námaskarð, page 217

• Mývatn Nature Baths, page 215

• Vogafjós Restaurant, page 220

• Hotel Laxá, page 221

Day 6: Detour to Húsavík

MORNING

Driving time: *45 minutes*
Driving distance: *62 km (38 mi)*
Directions: *Route 1 along west side of Lake
Mývatn to Route 845 and Route 85 north Húsavík*

★ Whale-Watching

From Lake Mývatn, take a 45-minute detour off Route 1 to Route 87, then Route 85
to **Húsavík,** a placid seaside town known
for its spectacular whale-watching. Take a
morning whale-watching tour with **Gentle
Giants** (tel. 354/464-1500, www.gentlegiants.
is, 10,400ISK adults, 4,400ISK children 7-15,
free for children 6 and under, 3-hour tour) to
get a glimpse of the giant mammals of the sea.
Afterward, stroll along the **harbor** and have
lunch at **Salka Restaurant** (Garðarsbraut 4,
tel. 354/464-2551, 11:30am-10pm daily, entrées from 2,800ISK).

AFTERNOON

Driving time: *50 minutes*
Driving distance: *62 km (39 mi)*
Directions: *Route 85 east to Ásbyrgi turnoff*

Ásbyrgi

From Húsavík, head back on Route 85
and drive east for 50 minutes to Ásbyrgi, a
horseshoe-shaped gorge with towering rock

walls and raw nature. Follow the 1-kilometer
(0.6-mile) **footpath** starting from the parking lot; it takes 30-60 minutes depending on
how often you pause to soak in the natural
beauty of the region. At the bottom of the canyon you can see small lakes, thick trees, and
interesting rock formations.

EVENING

Driving time: *50 minutes*
Driving distance: *62 km (39 mi)*
Directions: *Route 85 west to Húsavík*

Húsavík

Head back to Húsavík, have dinner at **Gamlí
Baukur** (Hafnarstett 9, tel. 354/464-2442,
www.gamlibaukur.is, 9am-9pm daily, entrées from 2,700ISK), and spend the night
at nautical-themed **Fosshotel Húsavík**
(Ketilsbraut 22, tel. 354/464-1220, www.is-
landshotel.is, rooms from 18,000ISK).

DAY 6 INDEX

• Húsavík, page 222

• Gentle Giants, page 223

• Salka Restaurant, page 225

• Ásbyrgi, page 227

• Gamlí Baukur, page 225

• Fosshotel Húsavík, page 226

Day 7: The North

MORNING

Driving time: 1.5 hours
Driving distance: 83 km (52 mi)
Directions: Route 85 south to Route 845 south to Route 1 south to Goðafoss; Route 1 west to Akureyri

Goðafoss

Drive 40 minutes south on Route 85 to 845 and finally back to the Ring Road and get ready to see the "waterfall of the Gods": Goðafoss, one of the most beautiful waterfalls on the island. Spend a couple of hours roaming the area and soaking in the views.

Akureyri

From Goðafoss, hop back on Route 1 for 30 minutes, heading west to Akureyri, the charming unofficial capital of north Iceland.

★ AKUREYRI BOTANICAL GARDENS

Eyrarlandsholt, tel. 354/462-7487, www.lystigardur. akureyri.is, 8am-10pm Mon.-Fri., 9am-10pm Sat.-Sun. June-Sept., free

Be sure to visit the Akureyri Botanical Gardens, one of the northernmost botanical gardens in the world. The gorgeous grounds boast native and international species alike.

CITY CENTER

Make your way to the city center (a few minutes' drive or a 10-minute walk from the Botanical Garden) to check out the **Akureyrarkirkja** church (Eyrarlandsvegur, tel. 354/462-7700, www.akureyrarkirkja.is, 10am-4pm Mon.-Sat., 4pm-7pm Sun. June 15-Aug. 15, free) and have lunch at **Berlín Akureyri** (Skipagata 4, tel. 354/772-5061, entrees from 1,350ISK).

AFTERNOON AND EVENING

Driving time: 1 hour
Driving distance: 78 km (48 mi)
Directions: Route 82 north turns into Route 76 to Siglufjörður

Tröllaskagi Peninsula

From Akureyri, set off for a drive north on Route 82 along the western side of Tröllaskagi Peninsula. You'll be following **Eyafjördur,** Iceland's longest fjord, so the scenery boasts breathtaking views of mountains and jagged cliffs.

Siglufjörður

After just over an hour, you'll reach the pretty town of Siglufjörður. Check out the **harbor** area and visit the fascinating **Herring Era Museum** (Snorragata 10, tel. 354/467-1604, www.sild.is, 10am-6pm daily June-Aug., 1pm-5pm daily May and Sept., by appointment rest of the year, 1,800ISK). The **Folk Music Center** (Norðurgata 1, tel. 354/467-2300, www.folk-musik.is, noon-6pm daily June-Aug., by request rest of year, 800ISK) is also worth a stop.

Have dinner at the unmissable **Hannes Boy** (Gránugata 23, tel. 354/461-7734, www.hannesboy.is, 11:30am-9pm daily, entrées from 2,690ISK) on the harbor and spend the night at hip **Siglunes Guesthouse** (Laekjargata 10, tel. 354/467-1222, www.hotelsiglunes.is, rooms from 18,000ISK).

DAY 7 INDEX

- Goðafoss, page 215
- Akureyri, page 203
- Tröllaskagi Peninsula, page 192
- Siglufjörður, page 196

1: Botanical Gardens in Akureyri 2: Icelandic fishing boat in Siglufjörður bay

Day 8: Driving to Snæfellsnes

The long journey to the Snæfellsnes Peninsula will take nearly the entire day.

MORNING

Driving time: *1.5 hours*
Driving distance: *107 km (66 mi)*
Directions: *Route 76 west and south to Route 75 west to Skagafjörður*

Skagafjörður

Take Route 76 out of Siglufjörður—this entails heading north at first, but ultimately, you'll be going south and west toward the Snæfellsnes Peninsula. Stop in Skagafjörður, a region known for its large number of horses, along the way. Take a break from driving with a visit to the **Skagafjörður Folk Museum** (tel. 354/453-6173, www.glaumbaer.is, 10am-4pm Mon.-Fri. Apr 1.-May 19, 9am-6pm daily May 20-Sept. 20, 10am-4pm daily Sept. 21-Oct. 20, open by request rest of year, 1,700ISK adults, free for children under 17), where you can learn about the turf houses Icelanders used to call home.

AFTERNOON AND EVENING

Driving time: *4 hours*
Driving distance: *285 km (177 mi)*
Directions: *Route 1 west to Route 54 west to Route 56 north to Route 54 west to Kirkjufell*

★ Kirkjufell

Route 54 is a semi-elliptical road that runs around the Snæfellsnes Peninsula. Since you will be approaching from the south, you will hit the peninsula on the southern stretch of 54, then cut across to the northern stretch to check out the beautiful mountain of Kirkjufell near **Grundarfjörður**. Kirkjufell is popular with photographers in Iceland thanks to its unique shape. When viewed from the south, the mountain looks very thin, coming to a point at the top, resembling a fin. Wander the picturesque beaches around the mountain and take pictures of it from every angle.

Grundarfjörður

Stay in the tiny town of Grundarfjörður for the evening. After a full day of driving, head to **Grundarfjörður Swimming Pool** (Borgarbraut 19, tel. 354/430-8564, 7am-9pm Mon.-Fri., 10am-6pm Sat.-Sun. 900ISK) for a relaxing soak and mingling with the locals. Then head to **Kirkjufell Hotel** (Nesvegur 8, tel. 354/438-6893, www.kirkjufellhotel.is, rooms from 19,000ISK), which is more than just where you'll spend the night—the in-house **restaurant** (breakfast 7am-10am, dinner 5pm-9pm daily, entrées from 2,800ISK) has a reputation for excellent seafood.

DAY 8 INDEX

- Skagafjörður, page 187
- Hraunfossar, page 148
- Kirkjufell, page 159
- Grundarfjörður, page 157

Day 9: Snæfellsjökull National Park and Borgarnes

MORNING

Driving time: *1 hour*
Driving distance: *52 km (32 mi)*
Directions: *Route 54 west to Route 574 west to Snæfellsjökull National Park*

Snæfellsjökull National Park

This morning, drive on Route 54 to Route 574 around Snæfellsjökull National Park. From Grundarfjörður, the most direct route is to take the northern stretch of Route 54 to Route 574 and approach the park from the north. Some of the more picturesque landmarks are on the southern end of the park: **Dritvík Cove** and **Lóndrangar Cliffs,** as well as **Hellnar** and **Arnarstapi Cliffs,** known for their rich bird life. These sites are all within minutes of each other, so plan to spend the entire morning driving short distances, wandering footpaths, and enjoying the vistas of this beautiful national park, with Snæfellsjökull glacier looming in the background.

AFTERNOON

Driving time: *1.5 hours*
Driving distance: *134 km (83 mi)*
Directions: *Route 54 east to Borgarnes*

Borgarnes

On your way back to Reykjavík, make a stop at the lovely town of Borgarnes. Have a pizza lunch at **La Colina** (Hrafnaklettur 1b, tel. 354/437-0110, 5pm-9pm Mon.-Fri., noon-9pm Sat.-Sun., entrées from 2,100ISK) and visit **The Settlement Center** museum (Brákarbraut 13-15, tel. 354/437-1600, www.landnam.is/eng, 10am-9pm daily, 2,500ISK adults, 1,900ISK students/seniors, free for children under 14), where you can learn about the sagas, Iceland's rich literary and historical tales.

EVENING

Driving time: *1 hour*
Driving distance: *76 km (47 mi)*
Directions: *Route 1 south to Route 49 west to Reykjavík*

Reykjavík

Back on the Ring Road, drive to Reykjavík. Spend a low-key evening in the city. For sweeping panoramic city views, visit either the church tower of **Hallgrímskirkja** (Hallgrímstorg, tel. 354/510-1000, www.hallgrimskirkja.is, 9am-9pm daily May 28-Sept. 30, 9am-5pm daily Oct. 1-May 27) or **Perlan (The Pearl)** (Öskjuhlíð, tel. 354/562-0200, www.perlan.is); a small fee is charged to access viewing decks at both sites.

Do as the locals do, and enjoy a relaxing swim at the pool **Laugarsdalaug** (Sundlaugavegur 30, tel. 354/411-5100, 6:30am-10pm Mon.-Fri., 8am-10pm Sat.-Sun., 1,000ISK). Afterward, head to **Fish Market** (Aðlstræti 12, tel. 354/578-8877, www.fiskmarkadurinn.is, 5:30pm-10:30pm daily, entrées from 4,990ISK) for dinner, then to **Hotel Frón** (Laugavegur 22A, tel. 354/511-4666, www.hotelfron.is, rooms from 23,000ISK) for the night.

DAY 9 INDEX

- Snæfellsjökull National Park, page 151
- Borgarnes, page 143
- Hallgrímskirkja, page 37
- Perlan, page 45
- Laugardalslaug, page 47
- Fish Market, page 58
- Hotel Frón, page 71

Last Day

REYKJAVÍK

Spend as much time in Reykjavík as possible before heading back to Keflavík for your flight. If you only have time for a quick coffee, check out Reykjavík's oldest coffeehouse, **Mokka** (Skólavörðustígur 3A, tel. 354/552-1174, www.mokka.is, 9am-6:30pm daily, 500ISK), or pick up one of the city's famous hot dogs at ★ **Bæjarins Beztu Pylsur** (Tryggvatagata 1, tel. 354/511-1566, www.bbp.is, 10am-1am Sun.-Thur., 10am-4:30am Fri.-Sat., 450ISK).

KEFLAVÍK AIRPORT

Driving time: 50 minutes
Driving distance: 49 km (30 mi)
Directions: Route 41 west to Reykjavik

Drive back to **Keflavík** to drop off your rental car and catch your flight back home. Congratulations on completing your Ring Road Road Trip!

LAST DAY INDEX

· Mokka, page 62

· Bæjarins Beztu Pylsur, page 60

· Keflavík International Airport, page 74

Background

The Landscape........300
History 304
Government and
    Economy 306
People and Culture 308

The Landscape

GEOGRAPHY

Iceland is the westernmost European country, situated in the North Atlantic between North America and Europe. Iceland is east of Greenland and south of the Arctic Circle, atop the northern Mid-Atlantic Ridge. It lies 859 kilometers (534 miles) from Scotland and 4,200 kilometers (2,610 miles) from New York City. The area of Iceland is 103,022 square kilometers (39,777 square miles), and a frequent comparison among Icelandic tour guides is that Iceland is roughly the size of the U.S. state Kentucky.

Geology

Iceland is a volcanic island constantly in flux, with magma breaking through fissures and periodic eruptions that redesign the rocky landscape. Iceland's land is made up of igneous rock, most of which is basalt, which forms from cooling magma. Most of Iceland's mountains were formed with basalt that has been carved by water and ice erosion. Some of the most well-known mountains in Iceland are Esja, Hekla, Snæfellsjökull, and Öræfajökull. Earthquakes are a common occurrence, but large tremors are rarely felt.

VOLCANOES

Volcanic eruptions are a growing source of tourism for the country. Local travel companies offer helicopter, jeep, and airplane tours when an eruption occurs. Most of Iceland's volcanic eruptions, such as the 2014-2015 Holuhraun eruption, are fissure vents, where lava seeps out of the cracks in the earth's crust. Holuhraun produced fountains of lava shooting out of the earth, delighting photographers and keeping volcanologists busy trying to determine if the nearby Bárðarbunga volcano would erupt. The three most active volcanoes on the island are Katla, Hekla, and Eyjafjallajökull. Eyjafjallajökull erupted in 2010, grounding air travel in Europe for days thanks to a large ash cloud. Most of Iceland's eruptions are small, and it's rare that they cause travel disruptions.

Residents have learned to adapt to eruptions, and most volcanoes are away from residential areas. In the case of the 2014-2015 Holuhraun eruption, the region near Vatnajökull was evacuated of locals, and tourists and animals were moved from the area. There were no deaths or major injuries. The main threat was from toxins in the air, and those close to the region were asked to stay indoors and turn up their heating if they were sensitive to air quality. There have not been any eruptions since 2015.

Air

When there isn't an eruption, Iceland's air is some of the cleanest and purest you will experience, as pollution is low and the Gulf Stream produces a strong, steady wind that blows toxins away. The main source of pollution on the island is from industry, mainly aluminum smelters.

Water

Like the air, Iceland's water is remarkably pure. There's clean, tasty drinking water on tap and geothermally heated water that fills swimming pools and provides hot water in homes. Snow can fall in any month of the year, but large snowfalls are uncommon in the Reykjavík area, at least during the last couple of decades. Ice covers about 11 percent of the country, mostly in the form of Iceland's largest glaciers: Vatnajökull, Hofsjökull, Langjökull, and Mýrdalsjökull. Melting ice from the glaciers and snowmelt form the rivers. Some of the major rivers include Krossá, Hvítá, Hofsá, and Lagarfljót.

Iceland's water is at the center of some of the country's tourist attractions. The human-made Blue Lagoon near Grindavík allows visitors to bathe in geothermally heated water, which soothes and heals the skin. Locals and tourists enjoy hot springs throughout the country, and spectacular waterfalls with roaring water tumble over basalt rock and earth. The largest and most visited waterfalls in Iceland are Gullfoss, Dettifoss, Goðafoss, Seljalandsfoss, and Skógafoss.

Climate

Iceland isn't as cold as you may think. The Gulf Stream swirls along the western and southern coasts and works to moderate Iceland's climate. But "moderate" doesn't mean "calm." The Gulf Stream is responsible for Iceland's frequent weather changes—as in lots of wind and rain.

Previous: horses grazing in southern Iceland

The biggest challenge of the climate is the unpredictability. The "summer" tourist season runs from the end of May to the beginning of September, and during that time, the climate ranges from rainy May days to the midnight sun in July to the possibility of snow in parts of the country in September. The winter climate brings colder temperatures, dark days, whipping winds, and the possibility of seeing northern lights flicker and dance on clear nights.

The climate is similar around the island, with the exception of the highlands, which become inaccessible from mid-September to early-June. The roads to the highlands are closed due to heavy snow conditions.

Weather

Weather in Iceland is not casual conversation, but serious business. Weather forecasts are frequent but largely hit or miss. The weather can change rapidly, from calm winds and sunny skies to rain, snow, sleet, and back again, all in the same hour. It's unpredictable, frustrating, exhilarating, and confusing for many tourists, but Icelanders have learned to adapt and go with the flow. As a result, plans tend to be loose for locals, whether it's for meeting friends for coffee or going for a job interview. If the weather acts up, Icelanders understand.

Some of the most extreme weather you could experience on this island is wind—the type of wind in winter that could knock you off your feet. If the weather forecast is showing strong winds, especially in the countryside, alter your plans accordingly. Do not underestimate the wind and be sure to heed any storm advisories. Be safe, smart, and prepared. The changing conditions are part of the experience of traveling to Iceland, and the key is being prepared with layers of clothing, proper footwear, and waterproof outerwear.

Daylight

Due to Iceland's proximity to the Arctic Circle, the island has almost endless daylight during the summer months from the

Average Temperatures in Reykjavík

- **January:** 30.9°F / -0.6°C
- **February:** 33.3°F / 0.7°C
- **March:** 36°F / 2.2°C
- **April:** 41.4°F / 5.2°C
- **May:** 42.8°F / 6°C
- **June:** 51.3°F / 10.7°C
- **July:** 55°F / 12.8°C
- **August:** 51.8°F / 11°C
- **September:** 46.4°F / 7.9°C
- **October:** 42.4°F / 5.8°C
- **November:** 37.6°F / 3.1°C
- **December:** 34.3°F / 1.3°C

midnight sun. The long days, about 20-22 hours of daylight in June and July, are magical, but it's a good idea to bring a sleep mask as some travelers find it difficult to sleep. The winter, however, has the opposite challenges. Days are much shorter, with just 4-5 hours of daylight in December. While this can be great for northern lights viewing, it limits your time seeing attractions.

Northern Lights

The biggest winter attraction in Iceland is the aurora borealis (northern lights). People travel from around the world to catch a glimpse of the green, white, blue, and red lights dancing in the night sky. There's something very special about bundling up in your warmest winter gear, trekking outside main towns to avoid bright lights, and hunting for northern lights. The natural phenomenon is caused by solar winds, which blow electronic particles into molecules of atmospheric gases, causing an emission of bright light. The best time to see northern lights is from September to March,

Sunrise and Sunset in Reykjavík

- **January 1:** 11:19am - 3:45pm
- **February 5:** 9:55am - 5:30pm
- **March 5:** 8:21am- 6:59pm
- **April 1:** 6:42am - 8:23pm
- **May 5:** 4:39am - 10:12pm
- **June 5:** 3:15am - 11:39pm
- **June 21:** 2:54am - 12:05am
- **July 1:** 3:07am - 11:55pm
- **August 5:** 4:50am - 10:14pm
- **September 5:** 6:16am - 8:36pm
- **October 1:** 7:37am - 6:57pm
- **November 5:** 9:24am - 4:58pm
- **December 3:** 10:51am - 3:44pm
- **December 21:** 11:22am - 3:30pm

and there are forecasts predicting visibility on the **national weather website** (www.vedur. is). When the forecast is favorable, it's best to drive (or take a tour bus) to a dark area and look up. Northern lights tours are offered by **Reykjavík Excursions** (www.re.is).

PLANTS

Don't be fooled by photos of the vast, barren lava fields; there is in fact life thriving on Iceland's land. The most common plants in Iceland are the hundreds of species of moss found throughout the country, clinging to rocks, basalt columns, and the earth. It's common to find Icelandic moss, maritime sunburst lichen, dulse, rockweed, and several species of algae in Iceland. Visitors will notice the lack of trees throughout Iceland, but that wasn't always the case. The lack of trees is due to a combination of Vikings using the trees to build their homes and boats, and

as fuel. Additionally, volcanic eruptions and lava flows have led to deforestation, as well as sheep contributing to soil erosion.

Iceland has an abundance of rhubarb plants and bilberry shrubs (which Icelanders refer to as blueberries). Berry-picking season runs from late July to early August, but the season can be delayed if the winter was particularly bad.

As for flowers, the pale-pink glacier poppy is the country's national flower, and other common flowers are sea mayweed, alpine bartsia, meadow buttercup, and arctic poppy. Others include wood cranesbill, oysterplant, purple lupine, and bluegrass.

ANIMALS

Iceland may not be known for its land mammals—other than sheep, cows, horses, reindeer, and the arctic fox—but animals in the ocean and sky are varied and ample. Sheep, cows, and horses can be found in every region of the island, but reindeer are only found in east Iceland. There are no reptiles or amphibians on the island.

Fish

Fish are the lifeblood of Iceland: They sustain its inhabitants and serve as the country's biggest trade resource. The waters surrounding Iceland support cod, haddock, catfish, mussels, halibut, plaice, lumpfish, monkfish, skate, and Greenland shark. Native to Icelandic river waters are salmon, trout, and arctic char.

Seals

Several species of seals call Iceland home, with harbor seals and gray seals being the most common. There are seal-watching sites in the north of Iceland; at Hvammstangi, there's a seal center that's a museum, point of information, and seal-watching enterprise. Harbor seals are more common to spot because they spend more time on land, whereas gray seals prefer the ocean. Harp, ringed, hooded, and bearded seals are also spotted in Iceland, but these are rarer.

Whales

Whale-watching is a spectacular way to spend an afternoon in Iceland, and there are several species to see, depending on where in Iceland you set out on your excursion. High season for whales around Iceland is May to October, and 14 species of cetaceans have been seen off the coasts of the island: blue, fin, minke, pilot, humpback, sei, orca, sperm, bottlenose, beluga, and narwhal whales, as well as white-beaked dolphins, white-sided dolphins, and harbor porpoises. The best places for whale watching are Reykjavik in the south, Snæfellsnes in the west, and Húsavík and Akureyri in the north.

Birds

Bird-watchers are delighted when they visit, as there are more than 300 species of birds in Iceland. The island is a stopover for birds migrating between North America and Europe, and common species are ravens, eider ducks, arctic terns, Iceland gulls, white gulls, black-headed gulls, skuas, white-tailed eagles, gannets, fulmars, kittiwakes, and oystercatchers.

The bird that has become synonymous with Iceland is the adorable puffin, with its black and white body, bright orange feet, and colorful red, blue, and orange beak. Puffins are remarkable swimmers and divers, able to dive underwater and surface with as many as 10 small fish in their beaks in under a minute. While exceptional in water, puffins are clumsy in flight and are known for their uneven landings on land. It's part of their charm. Millions of puffins call Iceland home, although their numbers have dwindled over the years. It's possible to see puffins during the summer in areas including the Westman Islands, Grímsey, and the Látrabjarg cliffs in the Westfjords. Puffins are not aggressive, and if you get too close, they will fly away.

History

SETTLEMENT

Iceland has the distinction of being the last country in Europe to be settled. The country has had impeccable record-keeping, and for that reason, it's known that the first permanent resident in Iceland was Ingólfur Arnarson, who built a farm in Reykjavík in the year 874. The earliest settlers were emigrants from Norway who opposed the king, Harald, due to a blood feud, and they wanted to make a new life in a new land. The Norwegians brought along their slaves from Ireland and Scotland, which means Icelanders are a blend of Norse and Celtic stock.

As word got out about the new land, within a few decades most of the coastline was claimed, with farms and fishing stations popping up. A government wasn't formed until 930, when the Alþing (parliament) was created, but in the meantime the new settlers determined that each farmstead should have a self-appointed chief. Once the Alþing was established in Þingvellir, a legislative body was elected.

CONVERSION TO CHRISTIANITY

Christianity came to Iceland, some say, by force. By the 10th century, the island faced mounting political pressure from the king of Norway, Olaf Tryggvason, to convert to Christianity or face the consequences, meaning war. As the end of the first millennium grew near, many prominent Icelanders had accepted the new faith.

By the year 1000, the Alþing was divided into two religious groups: modern Christians and pagans. The two groups were steadfast in their beliefs, and a civil war seemed likely. The law speaker, Þorgeir Þorkelsson, was called upon for a decision. (The law speaker was appointed to office and was required to recite the law during parliamentary meetings.)

Historical Timeline

874	Ingólfur Arnarson, Iceland's first permanent settler, builds a farm in Reykjavík
930	Alþing (parliament) is established at Þingvellir
1000	Law speaker Þorgeir Þorkelsson decrees Iceland a Christian country
1380	Iceland becomes part of the Kalmar Union, making it effectively a colony of Denmark
1602	Danish government forbids Iceland to trade with countries other than Denmark
1904	Hannes Hafstein becomes the first Minister of Icelandic Affairs
1915	Iceland creates its own flag
1918	Iceland becomes a sovereign state from Denmark
1941	25,000 British troops leave military base near Keflavík, replaced by 40,000 American troops
1944	Referendum confirms Icelandic independence from Denmark
1949	Iceland joins NATO
1980	Vigdís Finnbogadóttir is elected president, the first woman in the world to become an elected head of state
1994	Iceland joins the European Economic Area
2008	Iceland's three major banks fail in the midst of the global financial crisis
2017	Iceland surpasses 2 million visitors a year

Þorgeir decided that Iceland would be a Christian country, but that pagans could still celebrate their rituals in the privacy of their farms. Þorgeir was baptized in Þingvellir, and Christianity became the law of the land. Christian churches were built, a bishop was established in 1056, and the majority of today's religious Icelanders are Christian.

DANISH RULE

Iceland remained under Norwegian kingship rule until 1380, when the death of Olav IV put an end to the Norwegian male royal line. Norway (and by extension, Iceland) became part of the Kalmar Union, along with Denmark and Sweden, with Denmark as the dominant nation. At this time, Iceland effectively became a colony of Denmark, with the king owning the land and the church's money. Iceland's government now answered to Denmark and did so for the next several hundred years.

Iceland was still very much centered on fishing and farming, and it was quite isolated from the dealings in mainland Europe. In 1602, the Danish government, which was pursuing mercantilist policies, decreed that Iceland was forbidden to trade with countries other than Denmark. The Danish trade monopoly would remain in effect until 1786.

INDEPENDENCE

Iceland began inching toward independence when it was granted a Minister of Icelandic Affairs in 1904, who would be based in Reykjavík. Hannes Hafstein was the first to serve in the minister position, and his place in Iceland's history is prominent. During this time, Iceland became more autonomous, building up Reykjavík's harbor, founding the University of Iceland, and eventually creating its own flag in 1915.

Over the next couple of decades, Iceland was taking more control of its affairs, and when World War II started, there was an economic opportunity for the island. Iceland was invited to join the Allied war effort by Great Britain, but Iceland's government refused, declaring its neutrality. Britain pushed for Iceland's cooperation, but ultimately British naval forces arrived in Iceland, began building a base near Keflavík, and occupied the country for its proximity to North America. In all, 25,000 British soldiers occupied Iceland, which created a significant number of jobs for Icelanders. The British left in 1941, but more than 40,000 American troops replaced them, continuing the economic win for Iceland. There were jobs, opportunity, an American radio station, and lots of money flowing into the tiny island nation.

Denmark took a step back from Iceland's affairs during World War II, and Icelanders eventually held a referendum on its independence. Almost 99 percent of the population voted in the referendum, 97 percent of which voted for independence. On June 17, 1944, Iceland became totally independent of Denmark. American troops maintained the Keflavík NATO base until 2006.

MODERN-DAY ICELAND

An independent Iceland plodded along, building up its fishing resources, investing in infrastructure, and looking toward the future. During years of rule by the center-right Independence Party, banks were deregulated in the early 2000s and Iceland's financial sector began taking off at a rapid pace. Iceland was being lauded for its financial acumen, but it all imploded in 2008, when the country's three major banks failed, sending Iceland into one of the deepest financial crises seen in modern Europe.

In the years since, tourism has helped Iceland recover. Iceland today is reaping the benefits of increased tourism. People from around the world have become aware of and infatuated with Iceland for its raw nature, volcanic eruptions, and culture.

Government and Economy

GOVERNMENT

Iceland's democracy dates back to the year 930, when the Alþing (parliament) was formed, but its modern constitution was signed on June 17, 1944, when Iceland achieved independence from Denmark. The Alþing, which consists of 63 seats, meets four days a week near Austurvöllur in the center of Reykjavík. Nine judges make up the High Court of Iceland and are appointed by the president. Iceland's president serves more of a ceremonial role, while the prime minister holds most of the executive powers. Other high-level cabinet positions are the Minister of Finance and Minister of Foreign Affairs.

Political Parties

Iceland's political parties number in double digits, with 11 parties running for seats in the 2017 election. However, in the Alþing, eight parties hold seats: the Independence Party, the Progressive Party, the Social Democratic Alliance, the Left-Green Movement, the Pirate Party, the Center Party, the People's Party, and the Reform Party.

The Left-Green Movement (Vinstri Græn) is a left-wing party while the Independence Party (Sjálfstæðisflokkurinn) is a center-right party that was formed in 1929 after a merger of the Conservative and Liberal parties. The current prime minister, Katrín Jakobsdóttir, who worked in media before getting into politics, has served as leader of the party since 2013. The Independence Party was in power in the years leading up to the economic collapse of 2008. It was voted out of the majority in 2009 but regained seats, and power, in 2013. The Social Democratic Alliance, Bright Future, Left-Green Movement, and Pirate Party are the more liberal political parties on the island. Iceland's sitting president, Guðni Th. Jóhannesson, who took office in 2016, is a historian and former docent at the University of Iceland. Guðni is unaffiliated with any political party. He replaced Ólafur Ragnar Grímsson, who served five terms.

Elections

Iceland holds parliamentary elections every four years. The country has a multi-party system, which means they must form coalition governments. Iceland also elects a head of state every four years.

Defense

Iceland does not have a military, but is a member of NATO and hosted British and American troops in Keflavík during and after World War II. American troops remained in Iceland, on the NATO base, until 2006. Iceland's Coast Guard oversees crisis management and protection along the coasts of Iceland and has been known to participate in daring rescues at sea. The Icelandic police force consists of fewer than 1,000 officers, who maintain the peace. The crime rate is exceptionally low in Iceland, and police officers do not carry handguns.

ECONOMY

Iceland's economy is perhaps best known to tourists for taking a dive during the 2008 financial crisis. The island's economy has rebounded from the collapse, with tourism playing a significant role in this recovery. Alternative energy helps, too.

Banking Crisis

In early 2008, Iceland's currency began floundering compared to the euro, and that was the first international signal that there was deep trouble lurking in Iceland's financial sector. By the autumn, all three of Iceland's major banks had failed, lifting the veil on Iceland's house of cards. Following the collapse, unemployment soared, pension funds shrank, and inflation skyrocketed to more than 70 percent. Loans taken out in

foreign currency became unmanageable to thousands of Icelanders, credit lines were cut off, and capital controls were put in place that restricted how much money Icelanders could move out of the country. It was dire. The IMF made an emergency loan of $2.1 billion in November 2008.

Tourism

An increase in tourism helped Iceland recover from its 2008 economic collapse. The island became more affordable to visit and the headlines about the country's economic troubles made headlines around the world, shining a light on Iceland. By 2017, more than 2 million tourists visited Iceland a year, a sharp contrast from the 50,000 a year in the early 2000s. In fact, tourism is now the country's second-biggest revenue source after fish. Tourism comprises 10 percent of Iceland's GDP, and more than two million tourists visited Iceland in 2018. Most of Iceland's tourists come from the United States, Great Britain, the Nordic countries, Germany, France, and Switzerland. Tourism from Asian countries is also increasing. The issue going forward is how to keep tourism sustainable and protect Iceland's land from too much traffic.

Fishing

It's no secret that fish are the lifeblood of Iceland. They nourish its residents and are Iceland's number one export. Iceland's biggest trading partners are within the European Union, which is interesting because the reason to oppose joining the EU, for many, is for Iceland to maintain complete control of its fishing stock. Cod is the most common fish export.

Energy

One of the perks of living on a volcanic island is having a hotbed of geothermal energy. About 98 percent of the island's energy comes from geothermal and hydroelectric sources, which means low costs and low pollution. The pollution that does inhabit Iceland's airspace stems from an increasing number of aluminum smelters that have popped up in the last couple of decades. Foreign aluminum providers look to Iceland for its cheap energy and vast open land. The smelters do create jobs and revenue for the country, but it's a trade-off that many Icelanders remain unhappy about.

Currency

Iceland maintains its own currency, as it is not a member of the European Union. The Icelandic króna has a small circulation and is pegged to the euro. The notes are 500, 1,000, 5,000, and 10,000. Following the financial crisis, inflation soared more than 70 percent, and Iceland's currency took a hit. The uncertainty was a maddening time for many Icelanders. Inflation is still high, and exchange rates rise and fall. Capital controls were created in 2008 that limit how much money Icelanders can move out of the country, but they were lifted in 2017.

People and Culture

POPULATION

Nearly 360,000 people call Iceland home, and more than two-thirds live in the capital city, Reykjavík, and its suburbs. Outside of Reykjavík, Hafnarfjörður, and Kopavogur, the most populated towns in Iceland include Keflavík and Selfoss in the south, Akureyri in the north, Akranes and Borgarnes in the west, and Höfn and Egilsstaðir in the east. About 90 percent of the island population is composed of native Icelanders, but the foreign-born population continues to grow with the inflow of migrant workers and refugees.

Native Icelanders have a genetic makeup that combines Gaelic and Norse heritage, and many Icelanders consider themselves Nordic instead of Scandinavian. Social lives center on family, as Icelanders tend to be a close-knit bunch. It often seems like all Icelandic people either know one another, or have friends in common.

LANGUAGE

The official language of Iceland is Icelandic, which is considered a Germanic language. Icelanders like to think of their language as poetic and musical, and maintaining their tongue is an important part of Icelandic culture. Most Icelanders speak English and are happy to converse with tourists in English, but they are proud of their mother tongue and enjoy when foreign tourists give the language a go, even just a few words. The closest language to Icelandic is Faroese, which roughly 50,000 people speak, and the other close language spoken by a larger group is Norwegian. Many Icelanders can understand Norwegian, Swedish, and Danish due to some similarities. Learning Icelandic is a challenge for many foreigners because of the complex grammar and accent.

Alphabet

The Icelandic alphabet has 32 letters, including letters not known in the English language, such as Ð and Þ. The letter Ð represents the sound "th" as in "this," while Þ represents "th" as in "thin."

ICELANDIC NAMES

Iceland has a strident naming committee that must approve names parents wish to give their newborns, in the spirit of maintaining Icelandic culture. For that reason, you will find a lot of common first names, including Bjorn, Jón, Ólafur, Guðmundur, and Magnús for males, and Guðrun, Sara, and Anna for females. Very few Icelanders have surnames; instead, Iceland follows a patronymic system in which children are given their father's first name followed by -son or -dottir. If a man named Einar has a son named Johannes and a daughter named Anna, their names will be Johannes Einarsson and Anna Einarsdottir.

RELIGION

Icelanders have an interesting relationship with religion. Most of the country identifies as Lutheran (about 70 percent), but most Icelanders aren't known to attend church regularly or be very vocal about their religious beliefs. While the majority of the country identifies as Christian, Iceland is considered a progressive nation. There is no separation of church and state in Iceland; the National Church of Iceland is subsidized by Icelanders through a church tax. However, non-Lutherans can choose to have their church tax donated to designated charities.

Of Iceland's religious minorities, Catholics are the largest group at about 4 percent, and there are about 1,000 Muslims estimated to call Iceland home, as well as about 100 Jews. There is not a single synagogue in Iceland, as the Jewish population has not requested one, but a rabbi has relocated from New York to Reykjavík with his wife and children in 2018. A mosque was approved by Reykjavík in 2014, and construction is ongoing as of 2019. The pagan Norse religion Ásatrúarfélagið has grown in membership in recent years to about 4,500.

ARTS
Music

Music plays an important role in Icelandic society. There's an emphasis on children learning to play instruments, with music schools around the country. It seems that everyone in Iceland is in at least one band. The earliest Icelandic music is called *rímur,* which is a sort of chanting style of singing that could include lyrics ranging from religious themes to descriptions of nature. Choirs are also very common in Iceland, and there are frequent performances in schools and churches that are usually well attended by the community.

As for modern music, Iceland boasts quite a few bands that have gained a following abroad. Of course, there's Björk, who put Iceland on the musical map back in the 1980s with her band, the Sugarcubes, and later her solo career. Icelanders tend to be quite proud of Björk, as both an artist and an environmentalist. Sigur Rós, who have been recording since 1994, have become an indie favorite. Of Monsters and Men, Kaleo, Ólafur Arnalds, Amiina, Samaris, and GusGus are taking the world by storm. Reykjavík has cool venues in which to check out local bands and DJs, and some great record shops to pick up the newest and latest Icelandic releases.

Literature

Iceland has a rich literary history. The sagas, considered the best-known examples of Icelandic literature, are stories in prose describing events that took place in Iceland in the 10th and 11th centuries, during the so-called Saga Age. Focused on history, especially genealogical and family history, the sagas reflect the conflicts that arose within the societies of the second and third generations of Icelandic settlers. The authors of the sagas are unknown; *Egil's Saga* is believed to have been written by Snorri Sturluson, a 13th-century descendant of the saga's hero, but this remains uncertain. Widely read in school, the sagas are celebrated as an important part of Iceland's history.

Icelanders are voracious readers and love to write novels, prose, and poetry. The nation's most celebrated author is Halldór Laxness, who won a Nobel Prize for Literature in 1951 for his cherished novel *Independent People.* His tales have been translated into several languages and center on themes near and dear to Icelanders—nature, love, travel, and adventure. Other authors who have been translated into English (and other languages) include Sjón, Arnaldur Indriðason, and Einar Már Guðmundsson, to name just a few.

Knitting

Icelanders have been knitting for centuries, and it remains a common hobby today. Wool from Icelandic sheep has been keeping Icelanders warm for generations, and a traditional, modern sweater design emerged in the 1950s or so in the form of the *lopapeysa*. A *lopapeysa* has a distinctive yoke design around the neck opening, and the sweater comes in a variety of colors, with the most common being brown, gray, black, and off-white. Icelanders knit with *lopi* yarn, which contains both hairs and fleece of Icelandic sheep. The yarn is not spun, making it more difficult to work with than spun yarn, but the texture and insulation are unmistakable.

Essentials

Transportation

Transportation 311
Visas and Officialdom . .315
Recreation 316
Festivals and Events 317
Food 318
Accommodations 319
Health and Safety 321
Practical Details 322
Travel Tips 325

GETTING THERE
Air
Keflavík International Airport (KEF, tel. 354/425-6000, www.ke-fairport.is), about 50 minutes west of Reykjavík, frequently gets kudos for being one of the best airports in Europe, and the plaudits are well deserved. Flying into Iceland is a pretty seamless experience. The country's main carrier, **Icelandair** (www.icelandair.com), serves more than 30 destinations in the United States, Canada, and Europe. Iceland's accessibility has been the country's main selling point as a travel

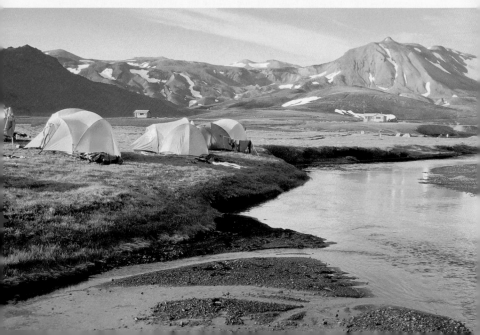

destination because it is just five hours from New York City and about three hours from London. Icelandair cleverly introduced an option years ago that allows North American travelers going on to Europe to stop over in Iceland for no extra cost. You can spend up to seven days exploring Iceland, and then continue on to your destination in Europe. The summer season is obviously the most expensive, with round-trip tickets that exceed $1,200 from North America. But Icelandair offers great deals during the winter months, when you can grab a round-trip ticket for around $700.

FROM NORTH AMERICA

In addition to Icelandair, travelers from North America have many options, including **Delta** from various cities in the US, **United Airlines** from Newark, **Air Canada** from Toronto and Montreal, and **American Airlines** from Dallas.

FROM EUROPE

There are several direct flights to Iceland from Europe, and common flight routes include **British Airways** from London, **EasyJet** from London, Manchester, and Edinburgh, **Norwegian** from Oslo and London, **SAS** from Copenhagen and Oslo, **Wizz Air** from London, Vienna, Prague and multiple cities in Poland, **Finnair** from Helsinki, and Icelandair from numerous cities in North America and Europe.

FROM AUSTRALIA AND NEW ZEALAND

There are no direct flights to Iceland from Australia or New Zealand; travelers will likely need to make a few connections. Common ones include first stopping in Singapore, Hong Kong, or Doha, Qatar, en route to one of the European hubs, where you can board a flight to Keflavík from there.

FROM SOUTH AFRICA

There are no direct flights to Iceland from South Africa; travelers should book a flight via one of the European travel hubs, such as London or Frankfurt, before connecting to their flight to Iceland. There are also common connections to Iceland from Cape Town and Johannesburg through Doha and Istanbul.

Boat

For those traveling from mainland Europe, a ferry can be a great option, especially if you want to bring a car, camper, or bicycle for the trip. **Smyril Line** (www.smyril-line.fo) is a Faroese company that runs the ferry *Norröna*, which goes to Iceland from Denmark, and the Faroe Islands. The ferry, which takes 19 hours from the Faroes and 36 hours from Denmark, drops you off in Seyðisfjörður, in East Iceland, which is convenient for those traveling with cars and who want to spend time in the countryside. But, if you want to stay in the south, where Reykjavík and Golden Circle attractions are, a ferry may not be the best option. The timetable tends to change frequently, so check the website for the latest information.

GETTING AROUND
Air

Iceland is surprisingly easy, if expensive, to get around by plane—if the weather is cooperating, that is. **Reykjavík City Airport** (tel. 354/569-4100, www.isavia.is) connects travelers to Akureyri, Egilsstaðir, Isafjörður, Vopnafjörður, Grímsey, and Þórshöfn. **Air Iceland Connect** (tel. 354/570-3000, www.airicelandconnect.com) and **Eagle Air** (tel. 354/562-4200, www.eagleair.is) fly year-round.

Car

If you plan to stay in Reykjavík for most of your trip or want to do short day trips in the southern or western parts of the country, it's not necessary to rent a car; you can book tours and travel by bus. However, having access to a car gives you the ultimate freedom of seeing the island on your own schedule. But if you want a rental car and the freedom that comes with it, expect to pay dearly, especially in the summer months. Icelanders drive on the right side of the road.

CAR RENTAL

Car rental prices remind you that you are very much on an island with very little price competition. In short, it's wildly expensive to rent a car (depending on the model of the car and season, it can be $200 per day with insurance), and gas prices are sky high compared to many other counties (approximately $6.50 per gallon).

You can rent a car in advance or at the rental office at **Keflavík International Airport,** at **BSÍ bus station,** or within Reykjavík once you're settled. In the busy summer tourist season, it is recommended to **arrange your rental in advance** because some dealers sell out early.

Choosing the right car for your trip depends on what you want to see and where you plan to go. If you plan on staying close to Reykjavík and traveling on well-paved roads, such as the Ring Road, a **compact car** is the best and cheapest option. However, if you plan on going out to the countryside or to the highlands, don't try to get away with renting the cheap option. If you try to bring a compact car into a region that requires **four-wheel drive,** expect damage to the car at best, and being stranded and needing to be rescued at worst. Be smart and be prepared.

Car rental companies provide "full insurance" for each rental, which is the basic third-party insurance option. For an additional fee, drivers have access to "extra insurance" that includes a collision damage waiver. However, be aware that you will *not* be covered for damage caused by rocks, snow, wind, ice, and all the other elements that could damage a vehicle. If you have any damage to a car, you will

be charged . . . *a lot.* Be sure to choose the right insurance for the region you plan to travel to. **Gravel insurance** is extra, and commonly purchased; if you're planning to travel on unpaved roads, it's recommended.

CAMPERVAN RENTAL

Traveling around Iceland by campervan is a popular option in season. This lets you explore at your own pace and frees you from worry over hotel reservations. However, there are important things to consider when traveling by campervan. Note that wild camping is strictly prohibited in Iceland and carries steep fines. Travelers must stay at **campsites,** where you will have access to facilities like toilets, showers, and cooking areas. Another important issue to consider is that traveling by campervan only makes sense during the summer months when campsites are open; many begin closing in early September. Additionally, campervans do not fare well in Iceland's windy winter conditions on icy roads. High winds can blow campervans off the road, leading to serious accidents; campervan companies that rent during the winter months are trying to take advantage of tourists. Here are a couple of reputable options:

- **Happy Campers** (Stapabraut 21, Keflavik 260, tel. 354/578-7860, www.happycampers.is, from 30,000ISK/day for two including insurance)

- **CampEasy** (Smiðjuvegur 72, Kópavogur, tel. 354/571-1310, www.campeasy.com, from 28,000ISK/day for two including insurance)

RULES OF THE ROAD

Always drive with **headlights** on (day and night). Do not drive off-road (expect heavy fines). Always wear your seat belt, and watch out for sheep and birds in the countryside.

Do not drink and drive. The law forbids any driving under the influence of alcohol, and police aggressively monitor drunk driving.

Do not speed. Always remember that roads are unpredictable and car accidents involving foreign drivers are quite common. You can be traveling on a quiet, scenic paved road that suddenly turns into an unpaved, rough section, and lose control of the car quite easily. The maximum speed limit for the entire island is 90 kph (55 mph), but in towns and residential areas, it can be much less. Always respect the limit. If you do speed and are caught by a police officer, expect a huge fine and a stern talking to. Don't risk it.

Monitor the weather forecast. Driving in Iceland can range from peaceful to harrowing, depending on the weather. To check road conditions, visit the **Icelandic Road and Coastal Administration** website (www.vegagerdin.is). If there is an advisory due to wind, rain, snow, or a volcanic eruption (it happens), stay off the road. Such advisories are to be taken seriously.

ROAD CONDITIONS

Road conditions in Iceland can change quite quickly, as the weather is unpredictable. As a rule, always check road conditions before you head out on a trip. The best way to get information about road conditions and the weather is to call **1777** (or tel. 354/522-1100). The line is open 8am-4pm in the summer and 6:30am-10pm in the winter.

The **Ring Road (Route 1)** is the most accessible and popular route around Iceland. It runs 1,332 kilometers (828 miles) and connects many of the country's most popular tourist attractions. The Ring Road is paved for most of its length, but there are still stretches in East Iceland with an unpaved gravel surface.

F roads are unpaved tracks that may only be driven in vehicles with four-wheel drive. Some F roads have river crossings, so trying to navigate them with a compact car is dangerous. In recent years, the Icelandic government has made a commitment to improving some gravel roads. You can check on road conditions at **www.road.is**.

GPS NAVIGATION

GPS coordinates are a popular way to navigate Iceland. You can input coordinates into navigational apps or GPS units to obtain directions. However, it's important to keep in mind that sometimes roads are closed, so do some research on the route you plan to take, and don't just rely on the shortest-distance option. You don't want to wind up stranded. Carry physical maps in addition to a GPS device.

Bus

The bus system in Iceland is surprisingly adequate, especially in Reykjavík.

BSÍ (Vatnsmýrarvegi 10, tel. 354/580-5400, www.bsi.is) is the main bus station in Reykjavík and serves as the first destination for many visitors to the city, as BSÍ is the initial stop on the **Fly Bus** (tel. 354/580-5400, www.flybus.is) from Keflavík International Airport. One-way tickets on the Fly Bus cost 2,999ISK. (For an extra fee, the Fly Bus can connect to several locations in downtown Reykjavík close to hotels and guesthouses.) BSÍ also serves as a main departure site for many day-tour bus trips, such as those to the Blue Lagoon and Golden Circle, offered by companies such as **Reykjavík Excursions** (tel. 354/580-5400, www.re.is).

Strætó (tel. 354/540-2700, www.straeto.is) operates the city bus system in Reykjavík, with bright yellow buses running on numbered routes. The routes are quite comprehensive, linking downtown Reykjavík to outlying neighborhoods. Tourists can pay exact change for one-way trips (470ISK) or purchase a book of 20 tickets for 9,100ISK. Strætó's blue long-distance buses depart from Mjódd station, traveling to several regions around the country.

SBA-Norðurleið (tel. 354/550-0700, www.sba.is) is another bus company that offers day tours and bus service throughout the country.

There is a "bus passport" available through **Reykjavík Excursions** (tel. 354/580-5400, www.re.is) that allows unlimited travel on buses throughout the country for a specific period of time (7-15 days). The bus passport is available from June to September and starts at 65,000ISK. It's quite convenient for those traveling the Ring Road without a rental car, and many tourists love that it allows you to meet fellow travelers along the way.

Taxi

Outside of Reykjavík, taxis are not an option to get around the island. Towns and villages are small and taxis are nonexistent. For Reykjavík, the two things you need to know about taxis is that they are expensive, and you have to call ahead for one (for instance, a ride from the BSÍ bus station to Harpa takes about eight minutes and costs roughly 2,000ISK). **Hreyfill** (tel. 354/588-5522, www.hreyfill.is) and **BSR** (tel. 354/561-0000, www.taxireykjavik.is) are two popular taxi companies in the city. You can also reserve taxis with Hreyfill through an app. Taxis arrive 5-10 minutes after you call, and the price on the meter is inclusive—you don't tip in Iceland. Cab prices rival those in New York City: It's rare to spend less than 2,000ISK on a taxi ride, even for short distances. Rideshare apps like Uber and Lyft are not available in Iceland.

Cycling

Cycling in Iceland is a favorite pastime among locals and tourists. While seeing Iceland by bicycle can be exhilarating and budget-friendly, the downside is that the weather is unpredictable, even in the summer. There are summers that are relatively dry and sunny, but realistically, you need to be prepared for rain, and lots of it. Some cyclists are lured by gorgeous landscape photos and the thrill of long summer days, but are challenged by keeping themselves dry and motivated. Also, bike theft is rampant on the island, so you must be vigilant in keeping your bicycle and gear under lock and key. The plus side, however, is that you get to see the country powered by your own two feet, and you have the freedom to control how long you stay at sites without being tied to a tour bus. There are numerous well-kept **bike paths** throughout the country, and brochures with trail information are available at tourist information offices. The best advice is to plan, plan, and plan some more for challenging roads and unpredictable weather. Bicycles can be rented in Reykjavík with **Reykjavík Bike Tours** (www.icelandbike.com) starting at 3,500ISK for 4 hours.

Hitchhiking

Hitchhiking is common practice, and legal, in Iceland, as it's a safe country with lots of drivers. If you are attempting to hitch along busier routes such as along the Reykjanes Peninsula, you will likely have more luck; in more remote destinations, it can be hit or miss. It's not advisable to be dependent on hitching in the winter months, because roads are less frequently traveled and the weather can be punishing. If you do score a ride, make sure you offer some **cash for gas.** It's just good form.

Visas and Officialdom

PASSPORTS AND VISAS

Visitors to Iceland must have a valid passport that will not expire within three months of your scheduled departure. Tourists from the United States, Canada, South Africa, Australia, and New Zealand do not need a visa if they are traveling to Iceland for fewer than 90 days. If you want to stay longer, you need to apply for a residence permit at the Icelandic immigration office (www.utl.is). For Europeans, Iceland is part of the Schengen Agreement, which allows free travel between Iceland and European Economic Area (EEA) and European Union (EU) countries; visas are not necessary.

Icelandic Embassies and Consulates Abroad

Iceland has embassies in a number of countries, including:

- **Canada:** 360 Albert St., Suite 710, Ottawa, ON K1R 7X7, tel. 613/482-1944, www.iceland.is/ca
- **United Kingdom:** 2A Hans St, London SW1X 0JE, tel. 20/7259-3999, www.iceland.is/uk
- **United States:** 2900 K St. NW, Suite 509, Washington, DC 20007, tel. 202/265-6653, www.iceland.is/us

Foreign Embassies and Consulates in Iceland

If you have an emergency while traveling in Iceland and require assistance (for example, if you lose your passport), contact your embassy for help. Embassies in **Reykjavík** include:

- **Canada:** Túngata 14, tel. 354/575-6500, rkjvk@international.gc.ca

- **United Kingdom:** Laufásvegur 31, tel. 354/550-5100, info@britishembassy.is
- **United States:** Laufásvegur 21, tel. 354/595-2200, reykjavikconsular@state.gov

Customs

Getting through customs in Iceland is quite easy compared to most other countries in Europe.

Travelers can import **duty-free** alcoholic beverages and tobacco products as follows: 1 liter of spirits, 1 liter of wine, and 1 carton or 250g of tobacco products; or 1 liter of spirits, 6 liters of beer, and 1 carton or 250g of tobacco products; or 1.5 liters of wine, 6 liters of beer, and 1 carton or 250g of tobacco products; or 3 liters wine and 1 carton or 250g of tobacco products. The minimum age for bringing alcoholic beverages into Iceland is 20 years; for tobacco, it's 18 years.

Iceland has a zero-tolerance policy on drugs, and all meat, raw-egg products, and unpasteurized dairy will be confiscated.

For additional information, visit the official **customs website** (www.tollur.is).

Recreation

Iceland truly is a nature buff's playground. There is much to do, and locals are thrilled to have you explore their treasured land—safely and responsibly. If you are heading out on a hike or a climb, report your whereabouts. Also, be sure to closely monitor weather conditions, bring all the water and gear you need with you, and be careful. Iceland's rescue team is often called upon to save unprepared tourists in completely avoidable situations. Have fun, but be safe.

HIKING

Hiking is by far the most popular outdoor activity on the island; its stretches of land beg to be explored. Hikers have their choice of terrain, whether they're looking for vast lava fields, steep mountains, or enormous glaciers.

The key is to be well prepared, safe, and smart. Monitor weather conditions, have all the proper equipment with you, and alert authorities about your plans at **www.safetravel.is**. In case something happens during your trip, the search and rescue teams will know where to look for you. While hiking is a beautiful way to explore the island, most emergency calls to the rescue service are due to ill-prepared tourists finding themselves in a predicament on a hiking expedition gone wrong. It cannot be overstated that you must respect Iceland's raw and sometimes treacherous nature.

Detailed maps are available at regional tourist information offices as well as online at the **Ferðafélag Íslands (Icelandic Touring Association)** (www.fi.is).

FISHING

Fishing is how many Icelanders make their living, so who has fishing rights can be political. Your best bet is to sign up for a tour with a local operator who handles the necessary permit as well as bait and gear. A good place to start is through the tour operator **Iceland Fishing Guide** (www.icelandfishingguide.com), which offers fishing tours in Iceland's lakes, rivers, and streams. You have a chance at catching salmon, trout, and arctic char, depending on the tour location.

SWIMMING

Swimming is a big part of Icelandic culture. That may sound strange given the chilly temps compared to, say, Spain or Florida, but an Icelander's local swimming pool is part of his or her social scene. If you visit a pool, you will notice groups of Icelanders, friends and family, sitting in hot tubs, sunrooms, or in the children's pool with their little ones. They love the water and they love to socialize. Pools are heated, and many have extensive facilities that include a gym, sauna, and several hot tubs. There are more than 120 swimming pools in Iceland, and they are well used, no matter the weather. Even outdoor pools can be full when there is a light snowfall.

The part about Iceland's swimming culture that frazzles some tourists is the communal showering that takes place before and after your swim. In the gender-divided locker rooms, you will see Icelanders showering stark naked—that's right, sans bathing suit—and you're expected to do the same. You must thoroughly clean yourself before you join the pool. At larger pools, there are often attendants who make sure that visitors shower. Locals are used to shy visitors and find it amusing, but at the end of the day, it just doesn't matter. After a couple of visits to the pool, you get used to it.

Towels and lockers are available at the local pools, and some rent out bathing suits as well. Some pools have fitness centers as well as an area to purchase soft drinks.

Festivals and Events

There's always something going on in Iceland—and whether it's the Viking Festival in June celebrating the country's roots, or the huge Iceland Airwaves music festival in the autumn, there's something for everyone.

FEBRUARY

- **Reykjavík Food & Fun Festival** (Reykjavík): During this three-day festival at the end of February, world-renowned chefs occupy kitchens at trendy Reykjavík restaurants, using fresh local ingredients and lots of imagination.

MARCH

- **DesignMarch (HönnunarMars)** (Reykjavík): Typically held in early March over four days, DesignMarch showcases the newest and best Icelandic design in pop-up shops, lectures, and fun events around the city.

APRIL

- **Reykjavík Blues Festival (Blúshátíð í Reykjavík)** (Reykjavík): For a week in early April, blues music enthusiasts from around the world descend on Reykjavík for this annual festival that features **international** musicians and local artists.

- **AK-Extreme** (Akureyri): Dedicated to winter extreme sports, AK-Extreme is an annual snowboard and music festival held in the northern city of Akureyri over four days in mid-April.

- **Reykjavik International Literary Festival** (Reykjavík): Every April,

Reykjavík celebrates local and international authors during this five-day festival. The program includes discussions, readings, workshops, meet and greets, and lectures.

MAY

- **Reykjavík Arts Festival (Listahátíð í Reykjavík)** (Reykjavík): For two weeks over late May and early June, Reykjavík is treated to exhibitions and outdoor installations of local and international artists.

JUNE

- **Viking Festival** (Hafnarfjörður): Just outside Reykjavík, the annual Viking Festival in mid-June has fun reenactments of fights with traditional dress and weaponry, as well as food, music, and a market. The weeklong festival is great for kids.

AUGUST

- **Reykjavík Jazz Festival (Jazzhátíð Reykjavíkur)** (Reykjavík): It may seem unexpected, but Icelanders have an affinity for jazz music, and they put on a great annual festival over five days in mid-August

that features local and international musicians.

- **Culture Night (Menningarnótt)** (Reykjavík): Held at the end of August, this daylong event is the biggest and most popular festival in Iceland, with more than 100,000 people participating. There's live music, food, and art to celebrate the end of the summer and Iceland's rich culture.

SEPTEMBER

- **Reykjavík International Film Festival** (Reykjavík): Beginning at the end of September, this 11-day festival showcases short films, documentaries, and features from more than 40 countries.

NOVEMBER

- **Iceland Airwaves** (Reykjavík): The largest music festival of the year hits Iceland in late October and early November. More than 200 local and international artists perform at the five-day festival, which has attracted bands including Kraftwerk, The Flaming Lips, and local band Of Monsters and Men.

Food

TYPICAL FARE

Descriptions of Icelandic food depends on who you ask. Certainly, fish and lamb take center stage. Typical fare can range from light to hearty. Local produce means what can survive outdoors (potatoes, rhubarb, moss) and what is grown in greenhouses (tomatoes, cucumbers, broccoli, etc.). Most of Iceland's food is imported, and it isn't cheap.

Local fish includes cod (fresh and salted), salmon, lobster, mussels, halibut, trout, and haddock. A classic Icelandic dish is whitefish cooked in a white sauce with potatoes and onions. A popular snack is hardfish, which is like a whitefish jerky, where the fish is dried and seasoned.

As for meat, lamb is the most prevalent, but there is plenty of beef, pork, and chicken in the Icelandic diet. Some Icelanders also indulge in horse and whale meat as well.

Hot dogs are wildly popular among Icelanders. Called *pylsur,* Icelandic hot dogs are done up in a traditional bun with chopped onions, mustard, ketchup, crispy fried onions, and pickled mayonnaise. They're delicious.

Dairy is an important part of Icelanders' diets, including milk, cheese, butter, and the yogurt-like soft cheese called *skyr,* which you should try. It's very tasty and chock-full of protein. Icelanders are also known to eat ice cream all year long, despite the weather.

There are quite a few popular ice cream shops around Reykjavík, and the ice cream sections in supermarkets offer an astounding number of locally produced choices.

Once a year, Icelanders celebrate the traditional foods of the nation, which sustained their ancestors through the ages. The winter festival, called Þorrablót, features svið (singed lamb head), blood pudding, lamb intestines and stomach, ram's testicles, fermented shark, seal flippers, hardfish, and rye bread. The food that gets the most attention from foreigners is rotten shark or *hákarl,* which is meat from Greenland shark. The flesh is put through an interesting process: it's buried for at least two months and then is hung for another three or four months to cure. If you dare, *hákarl* is available in small containers for sale throughout Iceland. It's an experience you will not forget—if not the taste, then definitely the smell.

RESTAURANTS

Reykjavík is home to some excellent fine-dining establishments and casual eateries, but eating cheaply in Reykjavík, or on the island as a whole, is not easy. Hours tend to change depending on the season, but for the most part restaurants open their doors for lunch around 11:30am, and kitchens tend to close around 9pm.

Outside of Reykjavík and Akureyri, you will find a lot of fish and lamb restaurants that focus on local cuisine, but inside the two main cities, you have a lot to choose from. You will find sushi, tapas, Indian, hamburger joints, noodle bars, kebab houses, and Italian restaurants, to name a few. International cuisine has been growing in popularity over the last 20 years, and new and interesting spots are always cropping up. If you have your heart set on a certain restaurant, it would be best to reserve ahead, but walk-ins are possible. **Tipping** is not expected in Iceland, but it is not considered an insult to tip.

DRINKING

The water in Iceland is pure and some of the tastiest in the world. Drinking from the tap is common and safe, and bottled water is frowned upon. Iceland is also a coffee-drinking nation. If you're a tea drinker, you will find some basic choices in coffee shops, but Icelanders are crazy about their coffee.

As for alcohol, given the expensive prices, beer is often the drink of choice when going out to a bar. And, believe it or not, beer is still relatively new to Iceland. A countrywide alcohol ban went into effect in 1915; the ban was relaxed in phases, with first wine and then strong liquors permitted, and beer eventually became legal to sell in 1989. Outside of bars, alcohol is available only at the government-run shops called **Vínbúðin.**

Accommodations

HOTELS

Iceland is not known for posh hotels offering every luxury that you desire. However, there is a good mix of "upscale" accommodations, mid-level boutiques, and budget hotels. The "fanciest" options on the island are in Reykjavík, namely 101 Hotel and Hótel Borg, which cater to guests who are willing to pay for top-notch service and amenities. Reykjavík also has mid-range boutique or family-run options if you are looking for something a bit more formal than a guesthouse.

Outside of Reykjavík, hotels tend to be of the local chain-hotel ilk in the form of **Fosshotels** (www.fosshotel.is), **Hótel Edda** (www.hoteledda.is), and **Icelandair Hótels** (www.icelandairhotels.is). They are clean, comfortable, and reliable options.

When they compare hotel prices to those in other European countries, some tourists feel that they don't get their money's worth. In fairness, Iceland is a more popular destination than it was 20 years ago, but it's still not meant to be a budget destination. In short, accommodations do cost a lot. Be prepared for shocking rates, especially in the summer months.

GUESTHOUSES

The most prevalent form of accommodations on the island is the guesthouse. Guesthouses range from comfortable bed-and-breakfasts that offer shared bathrooms and cooking facilities to more design-conscious options that are chic, modern, and fun. Some guesthouses in Reykjavík can still have "hotel-like" prices, as the competition for scoring a room in the high season has become almost a contact sport. Outside Reykjavík, however, guesthouses could be a good way to save a little money, depending on where you book. Always book a room in advance, as it's not recommended to leave where you will lay your head to chance.

HOSTELS

Hostels are another great option for the budget traveler, but as in guesthouses, beds tend to fill up, so make sure you book far in advance, especially in the summer. Some hostels in Reykjavík, like Kex Hostel and Loft Hostel, cater to young, music-conscious travelers, and beds are almost an afterthought. There is frequently live music in the lounge areas, and the bar is always packed with locals and tourists. Other hostel options cater to a more mature crowd looking to avoid the high hotel rates. Hlemmur Square would be a good option for those travelers. Outside of Reykjavík, hostels are prevalent and it's key to book ahead.

SLEEPING BAG ACCOMMODATIONS

Some guesthouses and hostels around Iceland offer travelers sleeping bag accommodations, which can be great for the budget traveler. For a low price, guests are allowed to sleep in their sleeping bags and have access to shared bathroom facilities.

MOUNTAIN HUTS

Not to be confused with emergency huts, mountain huts are similar to cabin-style accommodation, with many providing a cozy, hostel-like atmosphere with bunk beds. Huts have running water, and there is usually a shared dining hall. As tourism in Iceland has increased, it has become necessary to book in advance to guarantee a place.

For more information, visit the website of **Icelandic Touring Association (Ferðafélag Íslands)** (www.fi.is), which runs several mountain huts around the country.

CAMPING

Camping can be a great option for some travelers, but be prepared. If you're going it alone with a tent, make sure you're ready for any type of weather—it can be unpredictable (even in summer), and you may be on the island during a good week, but maybe not.

There are campsites around the country that allow for tents as well as campers and caravans. Facilities vary; some campsites have top-notch cooking areas and steaming-hot showers, while others have adequate cooking facilities and just toilets.

Be advised that wild camping is strictly prohibited in Iceland, so travelers must stay in campsites. Those who break the law face steep fines.

Most campsites are open mid-May to mid-September. It's not necessary to book a site well in advance. To see a list of campsites, visit www.nat.is/camping/camping_sites.htm.

The main camping information centers in Iceland are:

- **Reykjavík:** info@visitreykjavik.is
- **Leifsstöð** (Keflavík Airport): touristinfo@reykjanesbaer.is
- **Reykjanesbær** (Southwest Iceland): Icelandreykjanes@reykjanesbaer.is

- **Borgarnes** (West Iceland): tourinfo@vesturland.is
- **Ísafjörður** (Westfjords): info@vestfirdir.is
- **Varmahlíð** (Northwest Iceland): upplysingar@skagafjordur.is
- **Akureyri** (North Iceland): tourinfo@est.is

- **Egilsstaðir** (East Iceland): info@east.is
- **Seyðisfjörður** (East Iceland): ferdamenning@sfk.is
- **Höfn** (Southeast Iceland): tourinfo@hornafjordur.is
- **Hveragerði** (South Iceland): tourinfo@hveragerdi.is

Health and Safety

MEDICAL SERVICES

The Icelandic health-care system is top-notch, with hospitals in each large town and health clinics in smaller villages and hamlets. Most doctors, nurses, and emergency medical staff speak English. Non-EU citizens must pay for health services provided. If you are having a medical emergency, dial the number **112.** **Pharmacies** (called *apótek*) hold everything from prescription medication to aspirin. Some tourists from North America find it frustrating that cold medicine and aspirin cannot be bought in supermarkets, just at the pharmacy. Pharmacies are typically open 10am-9pm Monday-Friday, 10am-4pm Saturday, and are closed on Sunday and public holidays.

WEATHER

Weather is the number one safety concern in Iceland, trumping everything from violent crime to volcanic eruptions. The main danger is how fast weather can change. It could be a bright, sunny day when you head out on a trek in the highlands, but there could be a storm brewing that will bring high winds, rain, hail, and snow. And the storm could pass as quickly as it arrived. The joke among locals is that if you don't like the weather in Iceland, wait five minutes. The best defense against inclement weather is to closely monitor weather forecasts and obey advisories. You can check frequently updated forecasts at **www.vedur.is.** Icelanders deal with the weather by being flexible and never confirming plans far in advance. They learn to adapt after a lifetime of battling gale-force winds.

EMERGENCY HUTS

Iceland's emergency huts are strictly for emergencies. Don't even think of staying in one unless you are, in fact, experiencing an emergency. The huts are painted bright orange and are based in isolated areas. Inside the hut, you will find, water, food, bedding, and an emergency radio that will allow you to call for help. The huts can be located on maps, usually depicted as a red house. If you find yourself amid a storm, hunker down in an emergency hut and call for help by dialing the emergency number **112.**

CRIME

Crime is quite low in Iceland and is mostly limited to theft and vandalism; violent crime is rare. Be vigilant in protecting your possessions (especially bicycles) and trust your instincts. If you're out at night on Laugavegur in downtown Reykjavík on weekends, you might encounter loud and drunk locals or tourists. If you are a victim of a crime, contact the police by dialing the emergency number, **112;** all police officers are proficient in English.

Practical Details

WHAT TO PACK

How you pack depends on where you plan to go and what you're going to do on the island. If you're going for a "city-break" long weekend to Reykjavík, you can afford to pack light; however, if you plan on an extended stay that includes camping, packing light is not an option. Here are some suggestions and tips for your time in Iceland.

Clothing

The key to dressing warm and being comfortable in Iceland is **layers.** Depending on the weather, it can be cotton T-shirt, fleece or sweater, parka or windbreaker, and perhaps a hat, scarf, and gloves. If it's summer and the sun is shining, it's common to see locals wearing a T-shirt in 15°C (60°F) weather. It's important to keep comfortable and add layers if the temperature warrants it. If you're out hiking, wearing **waterproof gear** along with proper hiking attire is key. Make sure fabrics are breathable and comfortable and underlayers are cotton.

Formal attire in Iceland is reserved for work or funerals; if you want to bring a nice outfit along for a "fancy" dinner, by all means, pack something, but you won't find stringent dress codes anywhere on this island. Lastly, a **bathing suit** is necessary. Chances are you'll want to take a dip in a pool or hot spring.

OUTERWEAR

Because the temperature varies so much depending on time of day, season, and where you are in the country, it's a good idea to bring a **hat, scarf,** and **gloves.** As for jackets, the best advice is to bring something waterproof; whether it's a **windbreaker** for summer or a **parka** for winter, you are likely to encounter rain at some point on your trip. If you need to go shopping for warmer layers in Iceland, expect to pay. Clothes are not cheap in Iceland.

FOOTWEAR

Again, if you are staying in Reykjavík for the duration of your trip, and don't plan to climb mountains, you don't need to invest in an expensive pair of hiking boots. That said, if you do plan to be outdoors quite a bit, **hiking boots** are a great idea. You will need a pair of shoes that can withstand rain, rocks, ice, mud, puddles, sand, and sometimes snow. It's recommended to buy boots in your home country because shoes can be expensive in Iceland, and it's not the best idea to break in a brand-new pair of boots if you plan to do a lot of walking and/or climbing. Comfort is key. **Socks** are also important to consider. You want socks that are breathable yet thick enough to keep you comfortable in your shoes/boots.

Camping Gear

If camping is in your plan, don't scrimp on the quality of the **tent** you bring. And, make no mistake, you should bring the tent with you, as quality tents are, you guessed it, expensive in Iceland. You will need something waterproof that can endure punishing winds. A **sleeping bag** is necessary for campers, but it's also great to have a sleeping bag for guesthouses and hostels, some of which offer sleeping bag accommodations at a much lower price. Be sure to call ahead to see if they're available. Because of the likelihood of encountering rain, a sleeping bag made from a synthetic material is the best option, and it should be able to withstand -9°C (15°F) temperatures in the summer and -18°C (0°F) in the winter. If you decide to camp, be sure to monitor weather conditions and be safe.

MONEY
Exchange Rates

The official currency of Iceland is the **króna** (abbreviated kr or ISK). The króna fluctuates often; at the time of writing, the exchange rate

Budgeting

Iceland is not a cheap place to visit. Don't be fooled by the news stories that declared Iceland cut prices to accommodate tourists after its economic crisis of 2008. That period was brief, and Iceland remains an expensive destination. Prices on accommodations, food, gas, and everyday necessities remain high, compared to many other countries. Here is a list showing prices of common items:

- **Milk (1 L):** 156ISK

- **Loaf of bread:** 347ISK

- **Dozen eggs:** 615ISK

- **Apples (1 kg):** 291ISK

- **Potatoes (1 kg):** 255ISK

- **Coke/Pepsi:** 306ISK

- **Meal for two:** 12,000ISK

- **Domestic beer:** 1,200ISK

- **Bottle of wine:** 2,500ISK

- **Pack of cigarettes:** 1,390ISK

- **Bus ticket (one-way):** 470ISK

- **Gasoline (1 L):** 223ISK

was 125ISK to US$1, 93ISK to CAD$1, 153ISK to GBP1, 138ISK to EUR1, 84ISK to AUD$1, 79ISK to NZD$1, and 814ISK to 100ZAR.

There are banknotes in the amount of 500, 1,000, 5,000, and 10,000 and coins in the amount of 1, 5, 10, 50, and 100 kronur. Coins are handy for having exact change for the bus.

Currency exchange is available at the airport and banks as well as tourist information offices. **ATMs** are available at all banks as well as supermarkets and other shops.

Banks

Banking hours are 9:15am-4pm Monday-Friday, and ATMs are available 24/7. There may be a limit on the amount of cash you can withdraw per your home bank's policy.

Credit Cards

Your best bet to get the most favorable exchange is to use your credit card. Cash overall is not a popular payment method; locals are known to use debit and credit cards for just about every transaction. Using plastic is so common in Iceland that many tourists will not need cash for anything; you can pay for parking, public toilets, and even campsite fees with a credit card. However, you may want to carry a little cash on you if you plan on **tipping** a guide for an excursion; guides will gladly accept any currency.

VISA and MasterCard are the two main credit cards accepted in Iceland. Please note that Iceland uses the chip and PIN system, which requires a 4-digit PIN for transactions, including at unmanned gas stations. If your card does not have a PIN, it's best to contact your home bank or credit card issuer before traveling to Iceland. ATMs are widely available in Iceland.

OPENING HOURS

Most businesses in Iceland operate between 9am and 6pm during weekdays and 10am and 4pm on Saturdays. Many shops are closed on

Sundays, with the exception of grocery stores and some shops that choose to have limited hours.

Public Holidays

Businesses in Iceland close on the following holidays:

- January 1: **New Year's Day**
- March or April: **Maundy Thursday**
- March or April: **Good Friday**
- March or April: **Easter Sunday**
- March or April: **Easter Monday**
- First Thursday after April 18: **First day of summer**
- May 1: **Labor Day**
- May or June: **Ascension Day**
- May or June: **Whitsun**
- May or June: **Whit Monday**
- June 17: **Icelandic National Day** (commemorates achieving independence from Denmark in 1944)
- First Monday in August: **Trading Day**
- December 24: **Christmas Eve**
- December 25: **Christmas Day**
- December 26: **Second day of Christmas**
- December 31: **New Year's Eve**

COMMUNICATIONS
Phones and Cell Phones

The country code for Iceland is **354.** There are no area codes; if you are calling from within the country, just dial the seven-digit phone number and you will connect.

Icelanders love their mobile phones, and for that reason pay phones became obsolete several years ago. You can purchase **international phone cards** at local shops (called *sjoppas*) as well as at post offices and gas stations. SIM cards are also available from providers **Vodafone** (www.vodafone.is) and **Siminn** (www.siminn.is) and can be purchased from phone retail shops, gas stations, and the airport.

Cell phone coverage in the countryside is surprisingly strong. You can buy phone credit refills for any amount, but 1,000 or 2,000ISK is recommended.

Most European mobile phones work on Iceland's network, but most North American phones use a different standard. You may need to contact your service provider to unlock your mobile phone for use abroad.

Internet Access

Iceland is wired, with Wi-Fi hot spots all over the country, even in the remote highlands. Hotels typically have free Wi-Fi, as do many coffeehouses.

Printed and Online News

Given its small population, it's refreshing to see Reykjavík is such a die-hard newspaper town. Locals have several Icelandic-language print publications and websites to choose from, but publishers haven't forgotten about English-language readers. The *Reykjavík Grapevine* (www.grapevine.is) is the unofficial guide to music, museum exhibitions, restaurant reviews, and just about every cultural event in the city. The website is updated daily, and the free print edition comes out every two weeks in the summer and monthly in the winter. *Iceland Review* (www.icelandreview.com) is the main English-language glossy magazine on the island. You will find in-depth features on travel, culture, and business issues as well as gorgeous photography.

RUV (www.ruv.is) is Iceland's national public-service broadcasting organization, which consists of one television channel and two radio stations. RUV's television programs feature news, dramas, and documentaries, as well as programming from foreign countries, including the United States, Denmark, and Sweden.

Shipping and Postal Service

You can buy stamps and send letters or packages in the post office. It costs about 300ISK to mail a letter from Iceland to the United States. Business hours in Reykjavík are typically

9am-5pm Monday to Friday, but post offices in the countryside may have shorter hours. More information about post office services, locations, and hours can be found here: www.postur.is/en.

MAPS AND TOURIST INFORMATION

Visit Iceland (www.visiticeland.com) is the main tourist information website for the country. The website has information on accommodations and activities for each region in Iceland.

To properly navigate Iceland, you need maps. That's a given. Lucky for you, they are available all over the island. You can pick up all-inclusive maps for the entire island as well as regional maps, road maps, and hiking maps at tourist information centers, bookstores, and gas stations. If you have the chance to purchase maps before your trip, do so, as they will likely be a lot cheaper in your home country. However, if you plan to stay in Reykjavík for the duration of your trip, it's not necessary to buy a map, because quite a few free maps do a nice job detailing downtown Reykjavík.

WEIGHTS AND MEASURES

Iceland uses the **metric system.** With regard to electricity, the standard voltage is **230 V** and the standard frequency is **50 Hz.** The power sockets that are used are type F, for plugs with two round pins. If you forget to bring an **adapter,** they can be purchased in most bookstores and tourist shops.

TIME ZONE

Iceland uses Greenwich mean time (GMT). However, the country does not observe daylight saving time, so Iceland is either four or five hours ahead of New York time, depending on the time of year.

As for the amount of daylight, what you've heard is true. The summers are full of long days, and darkness reigns supreme in the winter. To give you an idea of what that means, here are daylight hours for Reykjavík at different times of year:

- **January 1:** sunrise 11:20am, sunset 3:45pm
- **April 1:** sunrise 6:45am, sunset 8:20pm
- **July 1:** sunrise 3:05am, sunset midnight
- **October 1:** sunrise 7:30am, sunset 7pm

Travel Tips

TAX-FREE SHOPPING

As tourists encounter high prices for everything from accommodations to food, it only seems fair that you get a break when it comes to shopping.

A refund of local Value-Added Tax (VAT) is available to all visitors in Iceland. The refund will result in a reduction of up to 15 percent of the retail price, provided departure from Iceland is within three months after the date of purchase.

The fine print is that the refund does not apply to food or accommodations and the purchase must exceed 4,000ISK (VAT included) per store. Shops will provide you with a **tax-free form** (ask the store clerk

for a "tax-free check"). Make sure you secure the forms and redeem the rebate at the cash-refund office at Keflavík Airport before your flight. There, you will get an immediate cash refund.

You can also submit the receipts and paperwork by mail for a rebate on your credit card. This, of course, can take considerably longer.

TIPPING

Tipping is very new to Iceland. Workers in bars, restaurants, and hotels, as well as taxi drivers, earn a living wage and are not dependent on tips. In recent years, tip jars have cropped up in coffeehouses and bars, but it's just tourists who tend to tip.

OPPORTUNITIES FOR STUDY AND EMPLOYMENT

Iceland's two universities are **Háskóli Íslands** (University of Iceland) and **Háskólinn Í Reykjavík** (Reykjavík University). Both schools offer a limited number of programs in English. For more information on programs and requirements visit www.hi.is and www.en.ru.is. There are not volunteer opportunities at the universities and a semester lasts about five months.

While individuals from around the world study at the universities, the Icelandic job market is more complicated. If you are a citizen of an EU/EEA country, you can move to Iceland and look for a job as there are immigration agreements in place. However, if you are a citizen from outside the EU/EEA, it is much more difficult to secure a job. Your prospective employer must prove that the position cannot be filled by an Icelander or EU/EEA candidate. Therefore, non-European citizens working in Iceland tend to fill specialist jobs like computer programming, and science and medical-related jobs, which are few and far between. For more information on immigration and employment matters visit www.utl.is.

ACCESS FOR TRAVELERS WITH DISABILITIES

Iceland has taken great strides in making as many tourist-related sites as wheelchair-accessible as possible. Visitors in wheelchairs will find that most museums, swimming pools, and restaurants provide access, as do transportation services. For instance, Keflavík International Airport and all domestic airlines can accommodate travelers in wheelchairs, and many buses come with automatic ramps to allow for easy boarding.

For more information on accessible travel, get in touch with the organization **Þekkingarmiðstöð Sjálfsbjargar** (tel. 354/550-0118, www.thekkingarmidstod.is). While the website is almost entirely in Icelandic only, information on traveling in Iceland has been translated into English (www.thekkingarmidstod.is/adgengi/accessible-tourism-in-iceland), and employees are happy to assist in English.

For information on services available to deaf travelers, contact the **Icelandic Association of the Deaf** (www.deaf.is), and for services for the sight-impaired, contact the **Icelandic Association of the Blind** (www.blind.is).

TRAVELING WITH CHILDREN

Children are the center of Icelandic society, and tourists traveling with children will feel right at home, whether in restaurants or museums or on child-appropriate tours. The island is a safe place for children, and many foreign travelers raise an eyebrow at how carefree parents can appear—whether it's a child walking around a shop, or an unaccompanied pram outside a coffeehouse. It's not irresponsible parenting, just a reflection on how safe Iceland is. While Iceland is safe, it needs to be said to always take care to watch out for the elements, whether it's high winds, a slippery surface, or cracks in a walking path.

As for attractions and restaurants, there are frequently **child rates** for museums and tours, and children's options on menus. Discounts can be as great as 50 percent for children under the age of 16.

WOMEN TRAVELING ALONE

Iceland is regularly ranked as being one of the best countries in the world in which to be a woman and a mother. Icelanders are proud to have elected the first woman president in the world as well as the first openly gay prime minister (a woman). However, Iceland is not a utopia. Women are subject to incidents of theft, intimidation, and physical violence. Always keep your wits about you, and if you are a victim of crime, contact the police at the emergency number 112.

LGBTQ TRAVELERS

Iceland is a leader in equality, and Reykjavík is one of the most gay-friendly cities in Europe. What many travelers find refreshing is that there is not just tolerance for gay, lesbian, bisexual, and transgendered individuals, but overwhelming love and acceptance of their fellow Icelanders. For instance, the gay pride festival, **Reykjavík Pride,** which takes place every August, attracts approximately 100,000 participants, for a country of just 320,000 people. As for laws, the LGBT community is protected from discrimination, gay marriage was legalized in 2010, and hate crimes are few and far between. For such a small population, it's hard to say there's a "gay scene," but there is one gay bar in Reykjavík, Kiki Queer Bar. More information can be found at the **Pink Iceland** website (www.pinkiceland.is).

TRAVELERS OF COLOR

Iceland is one of the least diverse countries in Europe, with immigrants accounting for around 11 percent of the population. While diversity isn't common, Iceland is one of the safest countries on earth for its residents and tourists. There are no immediate safety concerns for travelers of color.

Resources

Glossary

austur: east
bær: farm
bíll: car
bíó: movie theater
bjarg: rock, cliff
dalur: valley
ey: island
fjall: mountain
fjörður: fjord
fljót: river
flugvöllur: airport
foss: waterfall
gata: street
geysir: erupting hot spring
gistiheimilið: guesthouse
herbergi: room
hestur: horse
höfn: harbor
hradbanki: ATM
hraun: lava field
huldufólk: hidden people

Ísland: Iceland
jökull: glacier
kirkja: church
kort: map
laug: swimming pool
lopapeysa: Icelandic knitted sweater
lundi: puffin
norður: north
safn: museum
sími: telephone
stræti: street
strætó: bus
suður: south
sumar: summer
tjörn: pond
torg: town square
vatn: water
vedur: weather
vestur: west
vetur: winter

Icelandic Phrasebook

Icelandic is not the easiest language to understand. It's a North Germanic language that is related to Norwegian, Danish, and Swedish, but it has the added difficulty of declensions that the other languages lack. Icelandic nouns are declined in four cases, which stumps many people. Fortunately, just about everyone in Iceland speaks English.

The Icelandic alphabet has 32 letters, including letters not known in the English language, such as Ð and Þ. The letter Ð represents the sound "th" as in "this," while Þ represents "th" as in "thin."

PRONUNCIATION

Pronunciation can be very tricky, but Icelanders are thrilled when tourists give their language a shot. Be warned, though; if you attempt to speak an Icelandic phrase, your accent will tell them you're a foreigner, and they most likely will answer you in English.

Vowels

Some vowels in Icelandic have accent marks that modify the sound of each vowel. Vowels can come in long or short forms. In Icelandic, all vowels can be long or short. Vowels are long when they are in single-syllable words or when they form the penultimate syllable in two-syllable words.

A a like the "a" in "land"
Á á like "ow" in "cow"
E e like the "e" in "set"
É é like "ye" in "yet"
I i like "i" in "sit"
Í í like "ee" in "feet"
O o like the "o" in "not"
Ó ó like the "o" in "flow"
U u like the "u" in "put"
Ú ú like the "oo" in "soon"
Y y like the "i" in "sit"
Ý ý like the "ee" in "feet"
Æ æ like the "i" in "file"
Ö ö like the "ur" in "lure"

Consonants

Ð ð like "th" in "this"
J j like "y" in "year"
R r rolled, like Spanish "r"
Þ þ like "th" in "that"

BASIC AND COURTEOUS EXPRESSIONS

Hello Halló
Good morning Góðan dag
Good evening Gott kvold
How are you? Hvað segir þú?
Very well, thank you Mjog gott, takk fyrir
Good Allt gott
Not OK, bad Ekki okei
So-so Bara fint
OK Allt í lagí
And you? En þú?
Thank you Takk fyrir
Goodbye Bless
Nice to see you Gaman að sjo þig
See you later Sjamust

Please Takk
Yes Ja
No Nei
I don't know. Ég veit ekki.
Just a moment. Augnablik.
Excuse me. Afsakið.
What is your name? Hvað heiti þu?
Do you speak English? Talar þú ensku?
I don't speak Icelandic well. Ég tala ekki íslensku vel.
I don't understand. Ég skil ekki.
How do you say ... in Icelandic? Hvernig segir þú ... á íslensku?
My name is ... . Ég heiti ... .
What's your name? Hvað heitir þú?

TERMS OF ADDRESS

I ég
you þú
he/him hann
she/her hún
we við
they þeir
girl stelpa
boy strakur
man madur
woman kona
wife eiginkona
husband eiginmaður
friend vinur
son sonur
daughter dóttir
brother bróðir
sister systir
father pabbi
mother mamma
grandfather afi
grandmother amma

FOOD

I'm hungry. Ég er svangur.
menu matseðil
May I have ...? Get ég fengið ...?
glass glas
fork gaffall
knife hnifur
spoon skeið
breakfast morgunmatur

lunch *hádegisverður*
dinner *kvöldmatur*
the check *reikninginn*
soda *gos*
coffee *kaffi*
tea *te*
water *vatn*
beer *bjór*
wine *vín*
white wine *hvítvín*
red wine *rauðvín*
milk *mjólk*
juice *safi*
cream *rjómi*
sugar *sykur*
eggs *eggjum*
cheese *osti*
yogurt *jógúrt*
almonds *möndlu*
cake *kaka*
bread *brauð*
butter *smjör*
salt *salt*
pepper *pipar*
garlic *hvítlaukur*
salad *salat*
vegetables *grænmeti*
carrot *gulrót*
corn *korn*
cucumber *agúrka*
lettuce *kál*
mushroom *sveppir*
onion *laukur*
potato *kartöflu*
spinach *spinat*
tomato *tómatar*
fruit *ávöxtum*
apple *epli*
orange *appelsína*
fish *fiski*
meat *kjöti*
lamb *lamb*
beef *nautakjöti*
chicken *kjúklingi*
pork *svínakjöt*
bacon *beikon*
ham *skinka*

ACCOMMODATIONS

hotel *hótel*
guesthouse *gistihúsið*
Is there a room? *Áttu laus herbergi?*
May I see the room first? *Má ég sjá*
herbergið fyrst?
What is the rate? *Hvað kostar það?*
Is there something cheaper? *Ódýrara*
herbergi?
single room *einsmanns herbergi*
double room *tveggjamanna herbergi*
bathroom *klósetti*
shower *sturtu*
towels *handklæði*
soap *sapa*
toilet paper *salernispappír*
sheets *rúmfötum*
key *lykill*
heater *hitari*
manager *framkvæmdastjóri*

SHOPPING

money *peningar*
What is the exchange rate? *Hvað er*
gengið á?
Do you accept credit cards? *Tekur þú*
greiðslukort?
How much does it cost? *Hvað kostar það?*
expensive *dýr*
cheap *ódýr*
more *meira*
less *minna*
a little *smá*
too much *of mikið*

HEALTH

Help me! *Hjálp!*
I am ill. *Ég er veikur.*
I need a doctor. *Ég þarf lækni.*
hospital *sjúkrahús*
pharmacy *apótek*
pain *verkir*
fever *hiti*
headache *höfuðverkur*
stomachache *magaverki*
burn *brunablettur*
cramp *krampa*
nausea *ógleði*

vomiting *uppköst*
antibiotic *sýklalyf*
pill *pilla*
aspirin *aspirín*
ointment *smyrsli*
cotton *bómull*
condoms *smokkur*
toothbrush *tannbursta*
toothpaste *tannkrem*
dentist *tannlæknir*

TRANSPORTATION

Where is the ...? *Hvar er ...?*
How do I get to ...? *Hvernig kemst ég til ...?*
the bus station *strætóstöðin*
the bus stop *strætóstopp*
Where is the bus going? *Hvert fer þessi strætó/rúta?*
taxi *taxi*
boat *bátur*
airport *flugvöllurinn*
I'd like a ticket to ... *Einn miða, aðra leiðina til ...*
round-trip to ... *Einn miða, báðar leiðir til ...*
Stop here. *Hætta hér.*
I want to rent a car. *Get ég leigt bíl.*
entrance *inngangur*
exit *útgangur*
to the; toward the *til*
right *hægri*
left *vinstri*
straight ahead *beint áfram*
past the ... *framhjá ...*
before the ... *á undan ...*
opposite the ... *á móti ...*
Watch for the ... *Leita að ...*
intersection *gatnamót*
street *stræti*
north; south *norður; suður*
east; west *austur; vestur*

STREET SIGNS

Stop *Stans*
One Way *Einstefna*
Yield *Biðskylda*
No Parking *Engin Bílastæði*
Speed Limit *Hámarkshraði*

AT THE GAS STATION

gas station *bensínstöð*
gasoline (petrol) *bensín*
diesel *disel*
garage *verkstæði*
air *loft*
water *vatn*
oil change *olíu breyting*
tow truck *draga vörubíl*

VERBS

to buy *að kaupa*
to eat *að borða*
to climb *að klifra*
to do or make *að gera*
to go *að fara*
to love *að elska*
to want *að vilja*
to need *að þurfa*
to read *að lesa*
to write *að skrifa*
to stop *að hætta*
to arrive *til koma*
to stay *að vera*
to leave *að fara*
to look for *að leita*
to give *að gefa*
to carry *að bera*
to have *að hafa*

NUMBERS

zero *null*
one *einn*
two *tveir*
three *þrir*
four *fjorir*
five *fimm*
six *sex*
seven *sjo*
eight *atta*
nine *niu*
10 *tiu*
11 *ellefu*
12 *tólf*
13 *þrettán*
14 *fjórtán*
15 *fimmtán*
16 *sextán*

17	sautján
18	átján
19	nítján
20	tuttugu
21	tuttugu og einn
30	prjatiu
40	fjorutiu
50	fimmtiu
60	sextiu
70	sjotiu
80	attatiu
90	niutiu
100	hundrað
101	hundrað og einn
200	tvö hundruð
500	fimm hundrað
1,000	þúsund
100,000	hundrað þúsund
1,000,000	milljón

TIME

What time is it? *Hvað er klukkan?*
It's one o'clock. *Klukkan er eitt.*
morning *morgunn*
afternoon *eftir hádegi*
evening *kvöld*
night *nótt*
midnight *miðnætti*

DAYS AND MONTHS

Monday *mánudagur*
Tuesday *þriðjudagur*
Wednesday *miðvikudagur*
Thursday *fimmtudagur*
Friday *föstudagur*
Saturday *laugardagur*
Sunday *sunnudagur*
day *dagur*
today *i dag*
tomorrow *a morgun*
yesterday *í gær*
January *janúar*
February *febrúar*
March *mars*
April *april*
May *mai*
June *juni*
July *juli*
August *ágúst*
September *september*
October *október*
November *nóvember*
December *desember*
early *snemma*
late *seint*
later *seinna*
before *áður en*

Suggested Reading

Guðmundsson, Einar Már. *Angels of the Universe*. 1997. This is a startling tale of a young man struggling with mental illness, set in Iceland in the 1960s. The protagonist, Paul, retreats into his own fantasy world, while friends and family come along for the ride. The book is disturbing at times, funny at others, and almost impossible to put down. It was made into a film in 2000, which was wildly popular in Iceland.

Helgason, Hallgrímur. *101 Reykjavík*. 2007. The protagonist, Hlynur, is a lazy, unemployed twentysomething who lives with his mother, watches a lot of pornography, and hangs out in bars in downtown Reykjavík. His life takes a turn when a former girlfriend announces she is pregnant and Hlynur becomes obsessed with his mother's lesbian lover. It's a fun, unexpected tale that was made into a popular movie in Iceland.

Indriðason, Arnaldur. *Jar City*. 2006. Arnaldur is Iceland's leading mystery author. He pens about one book a year, which is great since his tales are so addicting. *Jar City* was the first of Arnaldur's books to feature detective Erlendur Sveinsson, who is a complicated man with a troubled relationship with his family and an obsession with solving

Reykjavík's violent crimes. Other characters include his partner, Sigurður Óli, and a female colleague, Elínborg.

Kellogg, Robert. *The Sagas of Icelanders.* 2001. This huge volume includes 10 sagas and 7 shorter tales that give a wonderful overview of Iceland's history and literature. If you're looking for a short introduction, this isn't it. It's comprehensive and glorious.

Laxness, Halldór. *Independent People.* 1946. Laxness remains Iceland's sole recipient of the Nobel Prize for Literature for his novel *Independent People.* The tale follows the life of a Bjartur, a sheep farmer, as he grapples with life, loss, and the sacrifices he made to achieve independence. If you're going to read one Icelandic novel, this should be it.

Internet Resources

Discover North Iceland
www.northiceland.is
This is the regional tourism guide for North Iceland, which includes information on towns including Akureyri, Mývatn, and Húsavík. You will find events listings, accommodations information, and a large list of tour operators.

Icelandic Tourist Board
www.inspiredbyiceland.com
Iceland's tourist board provides a website with pages and pages of information for travelers. The site offers information on festivals, shopping, national parks, and outdoor activities like hiking, bird-watching, whale-watching, and catching the northern lights in the wintertime. There's also information on accommodations, tour operators, and maps.

Iceland Review
www.icelandreview.com
Iceland's main English-language magazine provides features on everything from culture to travel to politics. The website is worth checking out for in-depth articles as well as columns written by locals.

Reykjavík Grapevine
www.grapevine.is
Reykjavík's go-to English-language newspaper, which is published every two weeks in

the summer and monthly in the winter, also maintains a website. You can bone up on local news as well as check out a listings section that details concerts, art exhibitions, and bars.

Visit East Iceland
www.east.is
Covering everywhere from Egilsstaðir to the Eastfjords, this tourism guide lists camping options, weather advisories, outdoor activities, and tour operators.

Visit South Iceland
www.south.is
Covering the south as well as the Reykjanes Peninsula, this tourism site offers detailed information on driving routes, maps, accommodations options, and tour operators. This region encompasses the Golden Circle as well as the Blue Lagoon.

Visit West Iceland
www.west.is
This is a regional tourism guide for the western section of the country, including Akranes, Borgarnes, Snæfellsnes, and the Westfjords. The site lists upcoming festivals and events, tour operators, and travel information for the region.

Index

A

accessibility: 326
accommodations: 20–21, 287, 319–321. See also
    specific place
Aðalvík Bay Hike: 177
Afrettadalur Valley: 248
Agricultural Museum of Iceland
    (Landbúnaðarsafn Íslands): 143
air quality: 301
air travel: 21, 202, 212, 226, 241, 299, 311–312
AK-Extreme: 208, 317
Akrafjall: 141
Akranes: 139–143
Akranes Folk Museum (Safnasvæðið á Akranesi):
    141
Akranes Lighthouse (Akranesviti): 19, 139
Akureyrarkirkja: 204, 294
Akureyri: accommodations 211–212; around 213–
    215; bars and nightlife 210–211; entertainment
    and events 208; food and dining 208–210;
    getting there and around 212–213;
    information and services 212; map 203; Ring
    Road Road Trip 294; sights 203–207; sports
    and recreation 207–208; top experience 203
Akureyri Botanical Gardens (Lystigarður
    Akureyrar): 203–204, 294
Akureyri Museum (Minjasafnið á Akureyri): 206
Akureyri Museum of Industry (Iðnaðarsafnið á
    Akureyri): 206
Álfaborg: 245
Almannagjá: 100, 101
Alþingishúsið: 42
animals: 303–304. See also Reykjavík Zoo
    (Fjölskyldu- og Húsdýragarðinum); wildlife-
    watching
apartments. See accommodations
architecture: Akureyrarkirkja 204, 294; Culture
    House (Safnahúsið) 36–37; Hallgrímskirkja
    37–41; Harpa 44; Höfði House (Borgartún) 44;
    Langabúð 256; Nordic House (Norræna Húsið)
    41; Perlan 31, 45–46, 298; Reykjavík City Hall
    (Ráðhús Reykjavíkur) 42
Arctic Circle: 200
Arctic Coast Way: 181
Arnarstapi Cliffs: 151
Árnason, Jónas: 236
Árnason, Jón Múli: 236
art events/galleries: Center for Visual Arts
    (Sjónlistamiðstöðin) 204; Hafnarborg Center of
    Culture and Fine Art 81; Reykjavík Arts Festival

(Listahátíð í Reykjavík) 49, 318; Skaftfell Center
    for Visual Art (Myndlistarmiðstöð Austurlands)
    248. See also museums
arts: 309–310. See also art events/galleries;
    museums
Ásbyrgi: 227, 293
Ásgarðsá River: 279
Askja: 273, 274
Ásmundarsafn: 36
Aurora Reykjavík: 45
Auroras Iceland: 254
autumn activities and travel: 18, 50–52
Aviation Museum (Flugsafn Íslands): 206

B

banks: 323
Bárðarbunga: 273, 301
Bardúsa-Verslunarminjasafn (Merchant Museum):
    184–185
Barnafoss (Children's Falls): 148
bars and nightlife: 67–70, 210–211, 319. See also
    breweries
Bath Mountain (Laugafell): 272–273
beaches: Diamond Beach 264; Djúpalónssandur
    beach 152; Katla Geopark 126; Rauðisandur
    172; Skaftafell (Vatnajökull National Park—
    South) 264
beer: 319. See also breweries
Beer Spa, The (Bjórböðin): 193
Beluga Whale Sanctuary: 130
biking: 46, 75, 110, 129, 219–220, 315
Bird and Mineral Museum (Fuglavefur
    Djupavogs): 256
birds: 304
bird-watching: Borgarfjörður Eystri 245;
    Djúpivogur 256–258; Flatey 162; Grímsey
    Island 175, 201; Heimaey 132; Höfn 259; Hrísey
    195; Látrabjarg Peninsula 172; Mývatn 219;
    Patreksfjörður 171; Reykjavík 46; Seyðisfjörður
    249; Stykkishólmur 161; Vopnafjörður 236
Bjarnarhöfn Hákarlasafnið (Bjarnarhöfn Shark
    Museum): 160
Bjarnarhöfn Shark Museum (Bjarnarhöfn
    Hákarlasafnið): 160
Bjórböðin (The Beer Spa): 193
Blaa Kirkjan (Blue Church): 246
Bláa Lónið (Blue Lagoon): 20–21, 23, 28, 85, 95–96,
    287–288
Black Falls (Svartifoss): 266
Blönduós: 186–187

Blue Church (Blaa Kirkjan): 246
Blue Lagoon (Bláa Lónið): 20–21, 23, 28, 85, 95–96, 287–288
blues music: 49, 317
Blúshátíð í Reykjavík (Reykjavík Blues Festival): 49, 317
boating and boat tours: 85, 130–132, 188
boat travel: 202, 213, 312
Bobby Fischer Center: 111
Borgarfjörður Eystri: 24, 244–246
Borgarnes: 143–145, 298
Borgarnes Museum (Safnahús Borgarfjarðar): 144
Borgartún (Höfði House): 44
Bowie, David: 141
Breiðafjörður: 162
Breiðdalsvík: 255
Brekka Settlement: 249
breweries: The Beer Spa (Bjórböðin) 193; gastropubs/breweries 62, 66; Old Harbor Brewery Tour 47; The Pub Crawl 47. See also bars and nightlife
Bridge Between Continents: 94
Brimnes: 248–249
BSÍ: 314
Bulandsnes Peninsula: 256
Bustarfell: 235
bus travel: 213, 277, 280, 314–315
Byggðasafn Garðskaga (Folk Museum): 94
Byggðasafnið Dalvík (Heritage Museum of Dalvík): 193
Byggðasafn Skagfirðinga (Skagafjörður Folk Museum): 189, 296
Byggðasafn Vestfjarða (Westfjords Heritage Museum): 164–165

C

calderas: 273, 274, 277
campervan rental: 313
camping: 320–321; Djúpivogur 258; Egilsstaðir 241; Garður 94; Golden Circle 102; Grindavík 98; Hólmavík 175; Hrísey 195; Jökulsárgljúfur (Vatnajökull National Park—North) 228; packing tips 322
car insurance: 283, 313
car rentals: 271, 276, 283–286, 313
car travel: 21, 283–286, 312–314. See also Ring Road
Cave People, The: 103
caves: 146, 152
cell phones: 286, 324
Center for Visual Arts (Sjónlistamiðstöðin): 204
children, traveling with: 326
Children's Falls (Barnafoss): 148
Christianity, Iceland's conversion to: 304–305
Christmas Garden (Jólagarðurinn): 206–207

churches and cathedrals: Akureyrarkirkja 204, 294; Blaa Kirkjan (Blue Church) 246; Flatey Church 162; Grímseyjarkirkja 199–200; Hallgrímskirkja 31, 37–41, 298; Húsavíkurkirkja 223; Ingjaldshólskirkja 155; Skálholt church 113; Þingeyrakirkja 186–187; Víðimýrarkirkja 188
climate: 301–302
color, travelers of: 327
Columbus, Christopher: 155
crafts: 310
credit cards: 323
crime: 321
Crime Lava Field (Óðáðahraun): 272
cross-country skiing: 23
cultural centers: Hafnarborg Center of Culture and Fine Art 81; Nordic House (Norræna Húsið) 41; Reykjavík Culture Night 50; Snorrastofa 146
culture: 29, 50, 308–310
Culture House (Gamla Sjúkrahúsið) (Ísafjörður): 165
Culture House (Safnahúsið) (Reykjavík): 36–37
Culture House at Húsavík (Safnahúsið á Húsavík): 223
Culture Night (Menningarnótt): 318
currency: 308, 322–323. See also money and budget tips
customs: 316
cycling: 46, 75, 110, 129, 219–220, 315

D

Dalvík: 24, 192–194
David Bowie Wall: 141
daylight: 302, 303, 325
Deildartunguhver: 146
Dellusafnið (Nonsense Museum): 167
DesignMarch (HönnunarMars): 49, 317
Dettifoss: 228
Diamond Beach: 264
Dimmuborgir: 217
disabilities, access for travelers with: 326
diving tours: 102
Djúpalónssandur beach: 152
Djúpivogur: 256–258
ðnaðarsafnið á Akureyri (Akureyri Museum of Industry): 206
Drangajökull glacier: 166
Drangey: 192
Drangsnes: 175–176
Dritvík Cove: 152
driving laws: 286, 313–314. See also car travel
Dvergasteinn (Dwarf Boulder): 248
Dverghamrar (Dwarf Cliffs): 129
Dwarf Boulder (Dvergasteinn): 248
Dwarf Cliffs (Dverghamrar): 129

INDEX

Dynjandi: 170
Dyrhólaey: 126

E

East Iceland and Eastfjords: 230–233;
  Borgarfjörður Eystri 244–246; Breiðdalsvík
  255; Eskifjörður 251–253; Fljótsdalur Valley
  238–244; highlights 231; itinerary ideas 233–
  235; map 232, 234, 245; Neskaupstaður 253;
  planning tips 17–18, 233; Reyðarfjörður 251;
  Ring Road Road Trip 291–293; Seyðisfjörður
  246–251; Vatnajökull Region 259–267;
  Vopnafjörður 235–238; wildlife-watching 24
East Iceland Emigration Center
  (Vesturfaramiðstöð Austurlands): 236
East Iceland Heritage Museum (Minjasafn
  Austurlands): 238
East Iceland Maritime Museum (Sjóminjasafn
  Austurlands): 252
economy: 307–308
Egilsstaðir: 238–241; around 241–242
Einar Jónsson: 41
Einar Jónsson Museum: 41
Eldey Island: 94
Eldfell: 130, 132
Eldfjallasafn (Volcano Museum): 160–161
Eldheimar: 130
electricity: 325
embassies and consulates: 316
emergency huts: 321
emergency services: 73–74, 276, 321
employment opportunities: 326
entry requirements: 20, 315–316
Esja: 31
Eskifjörður: 251–253
EVE Fanfest: 49
Exploration Museum (Könnunarsögusafnið):
  222–223
Eyafjördur: 294
Eyjafjallajökull: 122–123, 301
Eysteinsdalur Valley Hike: 156

F

fall activities and travel: 18, 50–52
Fardagafoss: 242
Fáskrúðsfjörður: 253–254, 292
ferry travel: 21, 132
festivals and events: 317–318; AK-Extreme 208,
  317; Culture Night (Menningarnótt) 318; Dalvík
  194; DesignMarch (HönnunarMars) 49, 317;
  EVE Fanfest 49; French Days festival 254; The
  Great Seal Count 185; Grímsey Day 200–201;
  Herring Festival 196; Hrísey Family Festival
  195; Iceland Airwaves 318; Reykjavík 49–52;
  Reykjavík Arts Festival (Listahátíð í Reykjavík)

49, 318; Reykjavík Blues Festival (Blúshátíð
  í Reykjavík) 49, 317; Reykjavík Food & Fun
  Festival 317; Reykjavík International Film
  Festival 318; Reykjavík International Literary
  Festival 49, 317–318; Reykjavík Jazz Festival
  (Jazzhátíð Reykjavíkur) 318; Reykjavík Pride
  (Hinsegin Dagar) 50, 327; summer solstice
  festival 200; Viking Festival 318
Fimmvörðuháls Trail: 26, 123–125
Fischer, Bobby: 111
fish and fishing: 46, 92, 96, 102, 168, 196, 207, 236,
  249, 294, 303, 307, 317
Fisherman Memorial: 96
Fjaðrárgljúfur: 85, 128–129
Fjölskyldu- og Húsdýragarðinum (Reykjavík
  Zoo): 45
Fjörukráin (Viking Village): 81
Flatey: 162–164
Flatey Church: 162
Flateyri: 167–168
Fljótsdalur Valley: 238–244
Flugsafn Íslands (Aviation Museum): 206
Fly Bus: 314
Folk Museum (Byggðasafn Garðskaga): 94
Folk Museum (Gamlabúð): 259
Folk Museum of Vestmannaeyjar: 130
Folk Music Center (Þjóðlagasetrið Siglufjörður):
  196, 294
food: 57–66, 286–287, 318–319. See also specific
  place
French Days festival: 254
French Fishermen in Iceland: 254
Friðbjarnarhús: 206
F roads: 276, 314
Fuglabjarganes: 236
Fuglasafn Sigurgeirs (Sigurgeir's Bird Museum):
  219
Fuglavefur Djupavogs (Bird and Mineral
  Museum): 256

G

Galdrasafnið á Hólmavík (Museum of Sorcery and
  Witchcraft): 174
Gamla Bókabúðin (Old Bookstore): 167
Gamlabúð (Folk Museum): 259
Gamla Sjúkrahúsið (Culture House): 165
gardens. See parks, gardens, and nature reserves
Garður: 93–94
gas stations: 271, 276, 280, 286
Geirmundartindur: 141
geography: 300–303
geology: 301
Geosea Geothermal Sea Baths: 223
geothermal sites: Geosea Geothermal Sea Baths
  223; Geysir 85, 103, 104–106, 288; Hveradalir
  (Hot Springs Valley) 279; Hveragerði 108–111;

Hveravellir Nature Reserve 277; Krýsuvík 98; Laugafell (Bath Mountain) 272–273; Laugarvatn Fontana 103; Mývatn Region 215–222. *See also* hot springs and pools
Gerðarsafn (Kópavogur Art Museum): 80
geysers: 85, 103, 104–106, 254–255, 288
Geysir: 85, 103, 104–106, 288
Ghost Centre, The: 115
Glacier Lagoon (Jökulsárlón): 263–264, 291
glaciers: Drangajökull glacier 166; Eyjafjallajökull 122–123, 301; Fimmvörðuháls Trail 26, 123–125; Hofsjökull Glacier 279; Húsafell 149; Hveravellir Nature Reserve 277; Jökulsárlón (Glacier Lagoon) 263–264, 291; Katla Geopark 126; Langjökull Glacier 149, 277; Laugavegurinn Trail 26, 85; Lónsöræfi 242–244; Snæfellsjökull glacier 151, 152; tours 23; Vatnajökull Glacier 263; Vatnajökull National Park 264–267, 291
Gljúfrasteinn: 78
Glymur: 141
goats: 145–146
Goðafoss: 215, 294
Golden Circle: 23, 99, 100, 288
golfing: Akranes 142; Akureyri 207–208; Borgarnes 144; Dalvík 193; Egilsstaðir 240; Eskifjörður 252; Höfn 260; Hólmavík 174; Húsafell 149; Hveragerði 110; Sauðárkrókur 191; Selfoss 113
government: 306–307
GPS navigation: 314
Grasagardur Reykjavíkur (Reykjavík Botanical Garden): 45
great seal count: 185
Grettisból: 184
Grímsey Day: 200–201
Grímsey Island: 175–176 (Westfjords), 199–202 (North Iceland)
Grímseyjarkirkja: 199–200
Grindavík: 95–98
Grótta Lighthouse: 19, 76
Grundarfjörður: 24, 157–160, 296
Grundarfjörður Heritage Center (Sögumiðstöðin): 159
Gudnason, Svavar: 259
guesthouses: 320. *See also* accommodations
Gullfoss: 106–107, 288
Gullfoss waterfall: 85
Gunnar Gunnarsson: 239
Gunnarsson, Gunnar: 239

H

Hafnarborg Center of Culture and Fine Art: 81
Hafnarfjörður: 81–83
Hafnarfjörður Museum: 81
Hafnarhús: 36
Háifoss: 118
Haihnukur: 141

Halldór Laxness: 78, 235
Hallgrímskirkja: 31, 37–41, 298
Hallgrimur Pétursson: 37–41
Hallormsstaður: 242
Harpa: 31, 44
health and safety: 202, 271, 276, 316, 321, 326
Heimaey: 24, 85, 130–133
Heimilisiðnaðarsafnið (Textile Museum): 186
Hekla: 301
Hekla Center: 116
Helgafell: 161
Hellissandur: 155–156
Hellissandur Maritime Museum (Sjómannagarður): 155
Hellnar Cliffs: 152
Hengifoss: 242
Heritage Museum of Dalvík (Byggðasafnið Dalvík): 193
Herring Era Museum (Síldarminjasafn Íslands): 196, 294
Herring Festival: 196
Hið Íslenzka Reðasafn (Icelandic Phallological Museum): 41
Highlands: 268–271; getting there and around 271; highlights 269; map 270; planning tips 18, 271; Route F26 (Sprengisandur) 272–277; Route F35 (Kjölur) 277–280; safety tips 271, 276
hiking: 316; Akranes 141; Akureyri 207; best day hikes 26; Borgarfjörður Eystri 245; Dalvík 194; Djúpivogur 256–258; Drangsnes and Grímsey Island 177; Esja 31; Eskifjörður 252; Fimmvörðuháls Trail 123–125; Fjaðrárgljúfur 85; Háifoss 118; Heimaey 132; Hellissandur 156; Highlands 271, 274, 279; Húsafell 148–149; Hveragerði 109–110; Landmannalaugar 120–122; Laufás 215–216; Laugavegurinn Trail 85; Mount Hekla 116; Mount Snæfell 242–244; Mývatn 219–220; Reyðarfjörður 251; Reykjavík 78–79; Seyðisfjörður 248; Skaftafell (Vatnajökull National Park—South) 266; Snæfellsjökull National Park 154; Þingeyri 168–170; Þingvallavatn 101–102; Vopnafjörður 236–237; Westfjord Alps Hike 168–170
Hinsegin Dagar (Reykjavík Pride): 50, 327
history: 304–306
hitchhiking: 315
Hjálparfoss: 118
Hof: 208
Höfði House (Borgartún): 44
Höfn: 259–263, 291
Hofsa River: 236
Hofsjökull Glacier: 279
holidays: 324
Hólmatungur: 227
Hólmavík: 174–175
Holuhran eruption and lava field: 273, 301

338

HönnunarMars (DesignMarch): 49, 317
Hornafjörður Art Museum (Listasafn Hornafjarðar): 259
Hornstrandir Nature Reserve: 176–177
Hornstrandir Peninsula: 176–177
horseback riding: 23, 81, 102, 113, 170, 187, 188, 240
hospitals: 212, 321
hostels: 320. See also accommodations
hotels: 319–320. See also accommodations
hot springs and pools: 28; Akranes 141–142; Blue Lagoon 20–21, 23, 28, 85, 95–96; Djúpivogur 256–258; Drangsnes 175; Geosea Geothermal Sea Baths 223; Hveradalir (Hot Springs Valley) 279; Hveragerði 108–109; Laugafell (Bath Mountain) 272; Laugarvatn Fontana 103; Mývatn Nature Baths (Jarðböðin) 28, 215–217, 292; reservations 20–21; Reykholt 146; in winter 23. See also geothermal sites
Hot Springs Valley (Hveradalir): 26, 279
Hound Falls (Hundafoss): 264–266
House of Shark-Jörundur, The (Jörundur Hus): 195
Hraunfossar (Lava Waterfalls): 148
Hrísey: 194–196
Hrísey Family Festival: 195
Húnaflói: 184–187
Hundafoss (Hound Falls): 264–266
Húsafell: 148–151
Húsavík: 24, 222–226, 293
Húsavíkurkirkja: 223
Húsavík Whale Museum (Hvalasafnið á Húsavík): 222
Hvalasafnið á Húsavík (Húsavík Whale Museum): 222
Hveradalir (Hot Springs Valley): 26, 279
Hveragerði: 108–111
Hveragerði Botanical Garden: 108
Hveragerði Stone and Geology Exhibition: 108
Hveravellir Nature Reserve: 277
Hverfjall: 217
Hversdagssafn (Museum of Everyday Life): 166
Hvítserkur: 185
Hvolsvöllur: 116–118

I

Iceland, birth of: 99, 101
Iceland Airwaves: 50–51, 318
Icelandic Goat Center (Íslenska Geitin): 145–146
Icelandic language: 308, 328–332
Icelandic Lava Show: 126
Icelandic Museum of Rock 'n' Roll: 90
Icelandic Mythical Walk: 47
Icelandic names: 308–309
Icelandic Opera (Íslenska Óperan): 48
Icelandic Phallological Museum (Hið Íslenzka Reðasafn): 41

Icelandic Seal Center (Selasetur Íslands): 24, 184
Icelandic Symphony Orchestra (Sinfóníuhljómsveit Íslands): 48
Icelandic Wartime Museum: 251
Icelandic Wonders: 115
ice skating: 207
Imagine Peace Tower: 76
information and services: 73–74, 325. See also specific place
Ingjaldshólskirkja: 155
insurance: 283, 313
internet access: 324
internet resources: 333–334
Into the Arctic (Norðurslóð): 206
Into the Glacier: 149
Ísafjörður: 164–167
Íslendingur (Icelander): 91
Íslenska Geitin (Icelandic Goat Center): 145–146
Íslenska Óperan (Icelandic Opera): 48

JK

Jarðböðin (Mývatn Nature Baths): 28, 215–217, 292
Jazzhátíð Reykjavíkur (Reykjavík Jazz Festival): 50, 318
jazz music: 50, 318
jeep tours: 220
Jóhannes Kjarval: 36
Jökulsárgljúfur (Vatnajökull National Park—North): 227–229
Jökulsárlón (Glacier Lagoon): 263–264, 291
Jólagarðurinn (Christmas Garden): 206–207
Jónas Árnason: 236
Jón Múli Árnason: 236
Jónsson, Einar: 41
Jónsson, Ríkarður: 256
Jón Sveinsson: 204
Jörundur Hus (The House of Shark-Jörundur): 195
Josafat Hinriksson Maritime Museum: 253K
Kaldbakur peak: 168
Katla: 301
Katla Geopark: 126
kayaking: 166
Keflavík Airport: 286, 299, 311, 325
Kerið crater: 111
Kerlingarfjöll (Women's Mountains): 277, 279
Kirkjubæjarklaustur: 128–129
Kirkjufell: 296
Kjarval, Jóhannes: 36
Kjarvalsstaðir: 36
Kjarvalsstofa: 245
knitting: 55–56, 310
Könnunarsögusafnið (Exploration Museum): 222–223
Kópavogur: 80–81
Kópavogur Art Museum (Gerðarsafn): 80

Krafla lava fields: 217, 292
Krýsuvík: 98
Kverkfjöll: 274

L

LÁ Art Museum (Listasafn Árnesinga): 108
Lagarfljót: 241, 292
Lagarfljótsormur: 241
Lake Mývatn: 219, 292
Landbúnaðarsafn Íslands (Agricultural Museum of Iceland): 143
Landmannalaugar: 118–122
Landnámssetur (Settlement Center): 143, 298
Langabúð: 256
Langjökull Glacier: 149, 277
language: 308, 328–332
Látrabjarg Peninsula: 24, 172–174
Laufás: 213–215
Laugafell (Bath Mountain): 272–273
Laugarvatn: 101, 103–104
Laugarvatn Fontana: 103
Laugavegurinn Trail: 26, 85
Lava Centre: 85, 117
lava fields: Blue Lagoon (Bláa Lónið) 20–21, 23, 28, 85, 95–96, 287–288; Dimmuborgir 217; Djúpalónssandur beach 152; Holuhran lava field 273; Hraunfossar (Lava Waterfalls) 148; Katla Geopark 126; Kirkjubæjarklaustur 128–129; Krafla lava fields 217, 292; Laugavegurinn Trail 26, 85; Mount Hekla 26, 116; Ódáðahraun (Crime Lava Field) 272; Prestahraun lava field 156; Reykjanes Peninsula 90, 101; Snæfellsnes Peninsula 154, 156; Þingvellir National Park 101; Vikrar lava fields 118. See also volcanoes
Lava Waterfalls (Hraunfossar): 148
Laxnes Farm: 79
Laxness, Halldór: 78, 235
LGBTQ+ events/nightlife: general discussion 327; Kiki Queer Bar 68; Reykjavík Pride (Hinsegin Dagar) 50, 327; Reykjavík Queer City Walk 47
lighthouses: Akranes Lighthouse (Akranesviti) 19, 139; Garður 93–94; Grímsey Island 200; Grótta Lighthouse 19, 76; Reykjavík Lighthouse 44
Listahátíð í Reykjavík (Reykjavík Arts Festival): 49, 318
Listasafn Árnesinga (LÁ Art Museum): 108
Listasafn Hornafjarðar (Hornafjörður Art Museum): 259
Listasafn Íslands (National Gallery of Iceland): 31, 42
Listasafn Reykjavíkur (Reykjavík Art Museum): 36
literature: 309
Ljósmyndasafn Reykjavíkur (Reykjavík Museum of Photography): 42
local, living like: 29
Lögberg: 100–101

Lóndrangar Cliffs: 152
Lónsöræfi: 242–244
Lower Hveradalir (Neðri-Hveradalir): 279
Lystigarður Akureyrar (Akureyri Botanical Gardens): 203–204, 294

M

maps: 325
marimo: 219
medical services: 74, 212, 321
Menningarnótt (Culture Night): 318
Merchant Museum (Bardúsa-Verslunarminjasafn): 184–185
Minjasafn Austurlands (East Iceland Heritage Museum): 238
Minjasafnið á Akureyri (Akureyri Museum): 206
mobile phones: 286, 324
money and budget tips: 20, 308, 322–323. *See also* currency
Mosfellsbær: 76–80
Motorcycle Museum of Iceland (Mótorhjólasafnið): 206
mountain huts: 273, 274–276, 320
Mount Akrafjall: 26
Mount Askja: 26
Mount Esja: 26, 78–79
Mount Hekla: 26, 116
Mount Hengill: 109
Mount Holmatindur: 252
Mount Kaldbakur: 215–216
Mount Kirkjufell: 159
Mount Snæfell: 24, 242–244
Mount Strútur: 149
Múlastofa Cultural Center: 236
Museum House (Safnahúsið): 253
Museum of Everyday Life (Hversdagssafn): 166
Museum of Icelandic Folk and Outsider Art (Safnasafnið): 204–206
Museum of Natural History: 253
Museum of Sorcery and Witchcraft (Galdrasafnið á Hólmavík): 174
museums: Agricultural Museum of Iceland (Landbúnaðarsafn Íslands) 143; Akranes Folk Museum (Safnasvæðið á Akranesi) 141; Akureyri Museum (Minjasafnið á Akureyri) 206; Akureyri Museum of Industry (Iðnaðarsafnið á Akureyri) 206; Into the Arctic (Norðurslóð) 206; Ásmundarsafn 36; Aviation Museum (Flugsafn Íslands) 206; Bird and Mineral Museum (Fuglavefur Djupavogs) 256; Bjarnarhöfn Shark Museum (Bjarnarhöfn Hákarlasafnið) 160; Borgarnes Museum (Safnahús Borgarfjarðar) 144; Center for Visual Arts (Sjónlistamiðstöðin) 204; Culture House (Safnahúsið) 36–37; Culture House at Húsavík (Safnahúsið á Húsavík) 223; East Iceland

Heritage Museum (Minjasafn Austurlands) 238; Einar Jónsson Museum 41; Exploration Museum (Könnunarsögusafnið) 222–223; Folk Museum (Byggðasafn Garðskaga) 94; Folk Museum (Gamlabúð) 259; Folk Museum of Vestmannaeyjar 130; French Fishermen in Iceland 254; Hafnarfjörður Museum 81; Hafnarhús 36; Hellissandur Maritime Museum (Sjómannagarður) 155; Heritage Museum of Dalvík (Byggðasafnið Dalvík) 193; Herring Era Museum (Síldarminjasafn Íslands) 196, 294; Hornafjörður Art Museum (Listasafn Hornafjarðar) 259; House of Shark-Jörundur, The (Jörundur Hus) 195; Húsavík Whale Museum (Hvalasafnið á Húsavík) 222; Icelandic Museum of Rock 'n' Roll 90; Icelandic Phallological Museum (Hið Íslenzka Reðasafn) 41; Icelandic Wartime Museum 251; Josafat Hinriksson Maritime Museum 253; Kjarvalsstaðir 36; Kópavogur Art Museum (Gerðarsafn) 80; LÁ Art Museum (Listasafn Árnesinga) 108; Merchant Museum (Bardúsa-Verslunarminjasafn) 184–185; Motorcycle Museum of Iceland (Mótorhjólasafnið) 206; Museum House (Safnahúsið) 253; Museum of Icelandic Folk and Outsider Art (Safnasafnið) 204–206; Museum of Natural History 253; Museum of Sorcery and Witchcraft (Galdrasafnið á Hólmavík) 174; National Gallery of Iceland (Listasafn Íslands) 31, 42; National Museum of Iceland (Þjóðminjasafn Íslands) 41; Natural History Museum (Náttúrúfræðistofa) 80; Nonnahús 204; Nonsense Museum (Dellusafnið) 167; Norwegian House (Norska Húsið) 160; Pakkhús Museum 156; Reykjanes Art Museum 90; Reykjavík Art Museum (Listasafn Reykjavíkur) 36; Reykjavík Museum of Photography (Ljósmyndasafn Reykjavíkur) 42; Saga Museum 44; Saltfish Museum (Saltfisksetur) 96; Settlement Center (Landnámssetur) 143, 298; Sheep Farming Museum (Sauðfjársetur á Ströndum) 174; Sigurgeir's Bird Museum (Fuglasafn Sigurgeirs) 219; Skagafjörður Folk Museum (Byggðasafn Skagfirðinga) 189, 296; Skagafjörður Transportation Museum (Samgönguminjasafn Skagafjarðar) 189; Skógar Folk Museum (Skógasafn) 123; Technical Museum of East Iceland (Tækniminjasafn Austurlands) 246; Textile Museum (Heimilisiðnaðarsafnið) 186; Tryggvi Olafsson Art Collection 253; 1238: The Battle of Iceland 191; Viking Maritime Museum 45; Viking World (Vikingaheimar) 91; Volcano Museum (Eldfjallasafn) 160–161; Westfjords Heritage Museum (Byggðasafn Vestfjarða)

164–165; Whales of Iceland 45; in winter 23. See also art events/galleries
music: bars and nightlife: 68–70; Folk Music Center (Þjóðlagasetrið Siglufjörður) 196, 294; Harpa 31; Iceland Airwaves 50–51, 318; in Icelandic culture 309; Icelandic Museum of Rock 'n' Roll 90; Reykjavík Blues Festival (Blúshátíð í Reykjavík) 49, 317; Reykjavík Jazz Festival (Jazzhátíð Reykjavíkur) 50, 318; shopping 53; Tvísöngur 246–248. See also performing arts
Myndlistarmiðstöð Austurlands (Skaftfell Center for Visual Art): 248
Mývatn Nature Baths (Jarðböðin): 28, 215–217, 292
Mývatn Region: 215–222

N
Námaskarð: 217–219, 292
names: 308–309
National Gallery of Iceland (Listasafn Íslands): 31, 42
National Museum of Iceland (Þjóðminjasafn Íslands): 41
national parks: Jökulsárgljúfur (Vatnajökull National Park—North) 227–229; Skaftafell (Vatnajökull National Park—South) 264–267, 291; Snæfellsjökull National Park 151–155, 298; Þingvellir National Park 19, 85, 99–103, 288
National Theater of Iceland (Þjóðleikhúsið): 49
Náttúrúfræðistofa (Natural History Museum): 80
Natural History Museum (Náttúrúfræðistofa): 80
nature reserves. See parks, gardens, and nature reserves
Neðri-Hveradalir (Lower Hveradalir): 279
Neskaupstaður: 253
news, printed and online: 324
nightlife. See bars and nightlife
Nonnahús: 204
Nonsense Museum (Dellusafnið): 167
Nordic House (Norræna Húsið): 41
Norðurslóð (Into the Arctic): 206
Norræna Húsið (Nordic House): 41
Norska Húsið (Norwegian House): 160
northern lights: 19, 23, 45, 302–303
North Iceland: 178–181; Akureyri 203–213; around Akureyri 213–215; Grímsey Island 199–202; highlights 179; Húnaflói 184–187; Húsavík 222–226; itinerary ideas 182–183; Jökulsárgljúfur (Vatnajökull National Park—North) 227–229; map 180, 183; planning tips 17, 181; Ring Road Road Trip 294; Skagafjörður 187–192; Tröllaskagi 192–199
Norwegian House (Norska Húsið): 160
Núpsstaðarskógar: 266

OP

Ódáðahraun (Crime Lava Field): 272
Oddar: 149
Ólafsvík: 156–157
Old Bookstore (Gamla Bókabúðin): 167
Old Harbor Brewery Tour: 47
opening hours: 323–324
Öxará (Axe) River: 101P
packing tips: 286, 322
Pakkhús Museum: 156
parking: 212–213
parks, gardens, and nature reserves:
  Akureyri Botanical Gardens (Lystigarður
  Akureyrar) 203–204, 294; Christmas Garden
  (Jólagarðurinn) 206–207; Hornstrandir Nature
  Reserve 176–177; Hveragerði Botanical
  Garden 108; Hveravellir Nature Reserve
  277; Jökulsárgljúfur (Vatnajökull National
  Park—North) 227–229; Reykjavík Botanical
  Garden (Grasagardur Reykjavíkur) 45;
  Skaftafell (Vatnajökull National Park—South)
  264–267, 291; Skalanaes Nature Reserve 248;
  Snæfellsjökull National Park 151–155, 298;
  Svarfaðardalur Nature Reserve 192; Þingvellir
  National Park 19, 85, 99–103, 288; Vestdalseyri
  Nature Reserve 248
passport: 20, 315–316
Patreksfjörður: 171–172
performing arts: Akureyri 208; bars and
  nightlife 68–70; Icelandic Opera (Íslenska
  Óperan) 48; Icelandic Symphony Orchestra
  (Sinfóníuhljómsveit Íslands) 48; National
  Theater of Iceland (Þjóðleikhúsið) 49; The
  Secret Cellar 49. See also music
Perlan: 31, 45–46, 298
Petra's Stone & Mineral Collection (Steinasafn
  Petru Stöðvarfirði): 254, 292
Pétursson, Hallgrimur: 37–41
pharmacies: 212, 321
phones: 286, 324
planning tips: 16–21; itinerary ideas 284–285,
  287–299; practical details 322–325. See also
  specific place
plants: 303
political parties: 306–307
population: 308
postal service: 324–325
power sockets: 325
Prestahraun lava field: 156
Pub Crawl, The: 47
public holidays: 324
public transportation: 21, 75, 213, 314–315
puffin-watching: 24

R

Ráðhús Reykjavíkur (Reykjavík City Hall): 42
rafting: 188
Rauðhóll: 154
Rauðisandur: 172
Rauðubjörg lookout point: 253
reindeer-watching: 24
religion: 304–305, 309
reservations: 20–21
Reyðarfjörður: 251
Reykholt: 145–148
Reykjadulur hike: 85, 110
Reykjanes Art Museum: 90
Reykjanesbær: 90–94
Reykjanes Maritime Center: 90
Reykjanes Peninsula and the South: 84–87;
  Garður 93–94; Geysir 85, 103, 104–106, 288;
  Grindavík 95–98; Gullfoss 106–107; highlights
  85; itinerary ideas 88–90; Laugarvatn 101,
  103–104; map 86, 89, 91; planning tips 16, 87;
  Reykjanesbær 90–94; Þingvellir National Park
  19, 85, 99–103
Reykjavík: 30–32; accommodations 70–73;
  around 76–83; bars and nightlife 67–70;
  entertainment and events 48–52; food and
  dining 57–66; highlights 31; information and
  services 73–74; itinerary ideas 32–33; map
  34–35, 38–40, 77; orientation 32; planning tips
  16, 32; Ring Road Road Trip 287–288, 298–299;
  shopping 52–57; sights 36–46; sports and
  recreation 46–48; sunrise and sunset 303;
  travel 74–75; walking tours 37, 47; wildlife-
  watching 24
Reykjavík Art Museum (Listasafn Reykjavíkur): 36
Reykjavík Arts Festival (Listahátíð í Reykjavík):
  49, 318
Reykjavík Blues Festival (Blúshátíð í Reykjavík):
  49, 317
Reykjavík Botanical Garden (Grasagardur
  Reykjavíkur): 45
Reykjavík City Hall (Ráðhús Reykjavíkur): 42
Reykjavík Culture Night: 50
Reykjavík Dance Festival: 50
Reykjavík Excursions: 314–315
Reykjavík Food & Fun Festival: 51, 317
Reykjavík Food Walk: 47
Reykjavík Grapevine: 73
Reykjavík International Film Festival: 50, 318
Reykjavík International Literary Festival: 49,
  317–318
Reykjavík Jazz Festival (Jazzhátíð Reykjavíkur):
  50, 318
Reykjavík Lighthouse: 44
Reykjavík Museum of Photography
  (Ljósmyndasafn Reykjavíkur): 42

Reykjavík Music Walk: 47
Reykjavík Pride (Hinsegin Dagar): 50, 327
Reykjavík Queer City Walk: 47
Reykjavík Welcome Card: 75
Reykjavík Zoo (Fjölskyldu- og Húsdýragarðinum): 45
Reynisdrangar: 126
Reynisfjara: 126, 290
Ríkarður Jónsson: 256
Ring Road: 281–283; highlights 282; planning tips 18, 283–287; road conditions 314 river crossing: 280 road rules: 286, 313–314. See also car travel
Route F26 (Sprengisandur): 272–277
Route F35 (Kjölur): 277–280

S
safety: 202, 271, 276, 316, 321, 326
Safnahús Borgarfjarðar (Borgarnes Museum): 144
Safnahúsið (Culture House): 36–37
Safnahúsið (Museum House): 253
Safnahúsið á Húsavík (Culture House at Húsavík): 223
Safnasafnið (Museum of Icelandic Folk and Outsider Art): 204–206
Safnasvæðið á Akranesi (Akranes Folk Museum): 141
Saga Museum: 44
Saltfish Museum (Saltfisksetur): 96
Samgönguminjasafn Skagafjarðar (Skagafjörður Transportation Museum): 189
Sauðárkrókur: 189–192
Sauðfjársetur á Ströndum (Sheep Farming Museum): 174
Saxa: 254–255
seal count, great: 185
seals and seal-watching: 24, 184, 185, 303
season: festivals and events by 49–52, 317–318; planning Ring Road Road Trip 283; travel tips by 18–20, 233, 271
Secret Cellar, The: 49
Secret Lagoon: 28, 107
Secret Solstice: 50
Sela River: 236
Selasetur Íslands (Icelandic Seal Center): 24, 184
Selfoss: 111–115, 288
Seljalandsfoss: 122, 290
Seltjarnarnes: 76
services. See information and services
Settlement Center (Landnámssetur): 143, 298
settlement of Iceland: 304
Seyðisfjörður: 246–251
Sheep Farming Museum (Sauðfjársetur á Ströndum): 174
shipping: 324–325

shopping: Borgarnes 144; Kópavogur 80; Laugarvatn 103–104; Mosfellsbær 79; Reykjavík 52–57; tax-free 325
Siglufjörður: 196–199, 294
Sigurgeir's Bird Museum (Fuglasafn Sigurgeirs): 219
Síldarminjasafn Íslands (Herring Era Museum): 196, 294
Sinfóníuhljómsveit Íslands (Icelandic Symphony Orchestra): 48
Sjómannagarður (Hellissandur Maritime Museum): 155
Sjóminjasafn Austurlands (East Iceland Maritime Museum): 252
Sjónlistamiðstöðin (Center for Visual Arts): 204
Skaftafell (Vatnajökull National Park—South): 264–267, 291
Skaftfell Center for Visual Art (Myndlistarmiðstöð Austurlands): 248
Skagafjörður: 187–192, 296
Skagafjörður Folk Museum (Byggðasafn Skagfirðinga): 189, 296
Skagafjörður Transportation Museum (Samgönguminjasafn Skagafjarðar): 189
Skalanaes Nature Reserve: 248
Skálholt church: 113
Skeiðarársandur: 264
skiing: 23, 196–197, 207, 249, 252
Skógafoss: 123, 290
Skógar: 123–125
Skógar Folk Museum (Skógasafn): 123
Skógasafn (Skógar Folk Museum): 123
Skriðuklaustur Center of Culture & History: 239
Sláturhúsið: 240
sleeping bag accommodations: 320. See also accommodations
Snæfellsjökull glacier: 151, 152
Snæfellsjökull National Park: 151–155, 298
Snæfellsnes Peninsula: 134–137; Akranes and inland 139–143; Flatey 162–164; Grundarfjörður 157–160; Hellissandur 155–156; highlights 135–137; itinerary ideas 137–139; map 136; Ólafsvík 156–157; planning tips 17, 137, 151; Ring Road Road Trip 296; Snæfellsjökull National Park 151–155; Stykkishólmur 160–162; Westfjords 164–177
Snorri Sturluson: 145
Snorralaug: 146
Snorrastofa: 146
snowmobiling: 23
Sögumiðstöðin (Grundarfjörður Heritage Center): 159
Sólfar (Sun Voyager Sculpture): 31, 44
South Coast: Eyjafjallajökull 122–123; Hveragerði 108–111; Hvolsvöllur 116–118; Kirkjubæjarklaustur 128–129; map 109; Mount

Hekla 116; Ring Road Road Trip 290; Selfoss 111–115; Seljalandsfoss 122; Skógar 123–125; Stokkseyri 115–116; Þjórsárdalur 117–118; Þórsmörk and Landmannalaugar 118–122; Vík: 125–128
souvenirs: 56
spas: 48, 110, 193
sports and recreation: 316–317; biking 46, 75, 110, 129, 219–220, 315; diving tours 102; horseback riding 23, 81, 102, 113, 170, 187, 188, 240; ice skating 207; kayaking 166; skiing 23, 196–197, 207, 249, 252; winter activities 23; ziplining 126–128. See also camping; festivals and events; fish and fishing; golfing; hiking; specific place; swimming; wildlife-watching
spring activities and travel: 20, 49
Steinasafn Petru Stöðvarfirði (Petra's Stone & Mineral Collection): 254, 292
Stöðvarfjörður: 254–255, 292
Stokkseyri: 115–116
Stöng: 118
Strætó: 314
Strokkur geyser: 85
study opportunities: 326
Sturluson, Snorri: 145
Stykkishólmur: 160–162
suggested reading: 332–333
summer activities: 49–50, 116, 120, 176–177, 201, 287
summer climate: 302
summer solstice festival: 200
summer travel: 18, 283
Sun Voyager Sculpture (Sólfar): 31, 44
super jeeps: 271, 276
Svarfaðardalur Nature Reserve: 192
Svartifoss (Black Falls): 266
Svavar Gudnason: 259
Sveinsson, Jón: 204
swimming: 28, 29, 317; Akureyri 207; Dalvík: 193; Djúpivogur 256–258; Drangsnes 175–176; Egilsstaðir 240; Eskifjörður 252; Flateyri 168; Grímsey Island 201; Grindavík 96; Grundarfjörður 159, 296; Hafnarfjörður 81; Heimaey 132; Höfn 259–260; Hólmavík 174; Húsafell 149; Húsavík 223, 225; Hveragerði 108–109; Hvolsvöllur 117; Ísafjörður 166; Kópavogur 80; Laugarvatn 103; Mosfellsbær 79; Mývatn 220; Ólafsvík 156–157; Patreksfjörður 171; Reykjanesbær 92; Reykjavík 47–48; Sauðárkrókur 191; Selfoss 113; Seyðisfjörður 249; Siglufjörður 198; Skagafjörður 188; Stykkishólmur 161; Þingeyri 170; Þjórsárdalur 118; Vopnafjörður 237. See also hot springs and pools
Syðsta Súla: 102

T
Tækniminjasafn Austurlands (Technical Museum of East Iceland): 246
Tannery Visitor Center: 191
tax-free shopping: 325
taxis: 75, 213, 315
Technical Museum of East Iceland (Tækniminjasafn Austurlands): 246
tephra craters: 217
Textile Museum (Heimilisiðnaðarsafnið): 186
Thieves' Falls (Þjófafoss): 266
Thor's Woods (Þórsmörk): 118–122
time zone: 325
tipping: 323, 325
Tjörnin: 31, 42
top experiences: 10–15; Akureyri 203; Blue Lagoon 95–96; Dettifoss 228; Goðafoss 215; Golden Circle 99; hot springs and pools 28; Jökulsárgljúfur (Vatnajökull National Park—North) 227; Jökulsárlón (Glacier Lagoon) 263–264; Laugavegurinn Trail 120–121; northern lights 19; Reykjavík bars and nightlife 67; Ring Road Road Trip 281–299; Skaftafell (Vatnajökull National Park—South) 264–267; Snæfellsjökull National Park 151–155; swimming 28; wildlife-watching 24
tourist information: 325
tours: 21, 47, 220, 271–272
travel: entry requirements 20, 315–316; getting there and around 21, 311–315; tips for 325–327. See also specific place
trekking. See hiking
Trölladyngja (Troll's Volcano): 272
Tröllaskagi Peninsula: 294
Tröllskagi: 192–199
Troll's Volcano (Trölladyngja): 272
Tryggvi Olafsson Art Collection: 253
Tvísöngur: 246–248
1238: The Battle of Iceland: 191

UV
universities: 326
Varmahlíð: 187–188
Varmárlaug: 79
Vatnajökull Glacier: 263
Vatnajökull Region: Höfn 259–263; Jökulsárlón (Glacier Lagoon) 263–264; Skaftafell (Vatnajökull National Park—South) 264–267; Vatnajökull Glacier 263
Vatnaveröld Swimming Pool: 92
Vatnshellir lava cave: 152
Vatnsnes Peninsula: 24, 184–186
Vestdalseyri Nature Reserve: 248
Vesturdalsa River: 236
Vesturfaramiðstöð Austurlands (East Iceland

344

Emigration Center): 236
video gaming: 49
Viðey Island: 76
Viðeyjarstofa: 76
Víðimýrarkirkja: 188
Vík: 125–128, 290
Vikingaheimar (Viking World): 91
Viking Festival: 318
Viking Maritime Museum: 45
Viking Village (Fjörukráin): 81
Viking World (Vikingaheimar): 91
Vikrar lava fields: 118
visas: 20, 315–316
Viti: 273, 274
volcanoes: 301; Bárðarbung 273, 301; Eldfell
    130; Eyjafjallajökull 122–123, 301; Hekla 301;
    Katla Geopark 126, 301; Krafla 292; Kverkfjöll
    274; Mount Hekla 116; Trölladyngja 272;
    Vatnajökull Glacier 263; Volcano Museum
    (Eldfjallasafn) 160–161. See also lava fields
Volcano Museum (Eldfjallasafn): 160–161
Vopnafjörður: 235–238

WZ
water: 301, 319
waterfalls: Dynjandi 170; Fardagafoss 242; Glymur
    141; Goðafoss 215, 294; Gullfoss 106–107, 288;
    Hengifoss 242; Húsafell 148; Seljalandsfoss
    290; Skaftafell (Vatnajökull National
    Park—South) 264–266; Skógafoss 123, 290;
    Þjórsárdalur 118
weather: 302, 314, 321
weekend getaways: 22–29
weights and measures: 325
Westfjord Alps Hike: 168–170
Westfjords: 17, 164–177
Westfjords Heritage Museum (Byggðasafn
    Vestfjarða): 164–165
whales and whale-watching: 24, 46, 92, 157, 159,
    193, 223–225, 293, 304
Whales of Iceland: 45
wheelchair accessibility: 326
wildlife: 303–304
wildlife-watching: 24, 46; Borgarfjörður Eystri
    245; Dalvík 193; Djúpivogur 256–258; Flatey
    162; Grímsey Island 175, 201; Grundarfjörður
    159; Heimaey 132; Höfn 259; Hrísey 195;
    Húsavík 223–225, 293; Látrabjarg Peninsula
    172; Mývatn 219; Ólafsvík 157; Patreksfjörður
    171; puffin-watching 24; reindeer-watching
    24; Reykjanesbær 92; Reykjavík 46; seal-
    watching 24, 184, 185, 303; Seyðisfjörður
    249; Stykkishólmur 161; Vatnsnes Peninsula
    185; Vopnafjörður 236; whales and whale-
    watching 24, 46, 92, 157, 159, 193, 223–225,
    293, 304
winter climate: 302
Winter Lights Festival: 51
winter travel: 19–20, 23, 283
Women's Mountains (Kerlingarfjöll): 277, 279
women traveling alone: 326
ziplining: 126–128
zoo: 45

Þ
Þingeyrakirkja: 186–187
Þingeyri: 168–171
Þingvallavatn Lake: 101
Þingvellir Interpretive Center: 99–100
Þingvellir National Park: 19, 85, 99–103
Þjóðlagasetrið Siglufjörður (Folk Music Center):
    196, 294
Þjóðleikhúsið (National Theater of Iceland): 49
Þjóðminjasafn Íslands (National Museum of
    Iceland): 41
Þjófafoss (Thieves' Falls): 266
Þjórsárdalur: 117–118
Þórsmörk (Thor's Woods): 118–122

List of Maps

Front Map
Iceland: 4–5

Discover Iceland
chapter divisions map: 17

Reykjavík
Intinerary Ideas: 34–35
Reykjavík: 38–39
Central Reykjavík: 40
Around Reykjavík: 77

Reykjanes Peninsula and the South
Reykjanes Peninsula and the South: 86
Itinerary Ideas: 89
Reykjanes Peninsula: 91
The Golden Circle: 100
The South Coast: 109

**Snæfellsnes Peninsula
and the Westfjords**
Snæfellsnes Peninsula and the Westfjords: 136
Itinerary Ideas: 138
Akranes and Snæfellsnes Peninsula: 140
The Westfjords: 165

North Iceland
North Iceland: 180
Itinerary Ideas: 183
Akureyri: 203
Mývatn Region: 216

East Iceland and the Eastfjords
East Iceland and the Eastfjords: 232
Itinerary Ideas: 234
Fljótsdalur Valley: 239
The Eastfjords: 245
The Vatnajökull Region: 260

The Highlands
The Highlands: 270

Ring Road Road Trip
Ring Road Road Trip: 284–285

Photo Credits

Title page photo: Sova004 | Dreamstime.com; page 2 © Saletomic | Dreamstime.com; page 3 © Dieniti | Dreamstime.com; page 6 © (top left) Bjorn Ludviksson; (top right) Svobodapavel | Dreamstime.com; (bottom) Rndmst | Dreamstime.com; page 7 © (top) Jenna Gottlieb; (bottom left) Jenna Gottlieb; (bottom right) Lee Chee Keong | Dreamstime.com; page 8 © (top) Leonardospencer | Dreamstime.com; page 9 © (top) Anna Pakutina/123rf.com; (bottom left) Branislav Petkovic/123rf.com; (bottom right) Iaceo | Dreamstime.com; page 10 © Shaiith | Dreamstime.com; page 12 © (top) Pitchathorn Chitnelawong | Dreamstime.com; (bottom) Derwuth | Dreamstime.com; page 13 © (top) Banepetkovic | Dreamstime.com; (middle) Alexeys | Dreamstime.com; (bottom) Regardeauloin | Dreamstime.com; page 14 © Frank Fichtmueller | Dreamstime.com; page 15 © (top) Maksym Topchii | Dreamstime.com; (middle) Vitaliy Mateha | Dreamstime.com; (bottom) Mathiasrhode | Dreamstime.com; page 16 © (bottom) Jarcosa | Dreamstime.com; page 21 © (top) 1tommas | Dreamstime.com; page 22 © (bottom) Supoj Taechapanyasin | Dreamstime.com; page 25 © (bottom) Oleksandr Korzhenko | Dreamstime.com; page 27 © (bottom) Ganna Stryzhekin | Dreamstime.com; page 30 © Hannamariah | Dreamstime.com; page 31 © (top left) Jenna Gottlieb; (top right) Bjorn Ludviksson; page 43 © (top) Bjorn Ludviksson; (left middle) Lilja Hauksdottir; (right middle) Bjorn Ludviksson; (bottom) Rudi1976 | Dreamstime.com; page 51 © (top left) Bjorn Ludviksson; (top right) Bjorn Ludviksson; (bottom) Jenna Gottlieb; page 54 © (top) Bjorn Ludviksson; (bottom) Bjorn Ludviksson; page 60 © Julia H Midland | Dreamstime.com; page 61 © Marcin Kadziolka | Dreamstime.com; page 63 © (top) Bjorn Ludviksson; (bottom) Bjorn Ludviksson; page 69 © (top left) Bjorn Ludviksson; (top right) Bjorn Ludviksson; (bottom) Bjorn Ludviksson; page 78 © Barbora Arnostova | Dreamstime.com; page 82 © (top) Alaskagm | Dreamstime.com; (bottom) Rudi1976 | Dreamstime.com; page 84 © Tomaz Kunst/123rf.com; page 85 © (top left) Juliengrondin | Dreamstime.com; (top right) Bjorn Ludviksson; page 95 © Dgmate | Dreamstime.com; page 105 © (top) Bjorn Ludviksson; (bottom) Jenna Gottlieb; page 107 © Pitchathorn Chitnelawong | Dreamstime.com; page 112 © (top) Stacey Katz; (bottom) Milan Surkala/123rf.com; page 114 © Bjorn Ludviksson; page 119 © (top) Stacey Katz; (bottom) Bjorn Ludviksson; page 124 © (top) Sumos | Dreamstime.com; (bottom) Jenna Gottlieb; page 127 © (top) Bjorn Ludviksson; (bottom) Jenna Gottlieb; page 131 © (top) Anouk Stricher | Dreamstime.com; (bottom) Stacey Katz; page 134 © Jenna Gottlieb; page 135 © (top left) Jenna Gottlieb; (top right) Jenna Gottlieb; page 147 © (top left) Jenna Gottlieb; (top right) Bjorn Ludviksson; (bottom) Bjorn Ludviksson; page 150 © (top) Bjorn Ludviksson; (bottom) Bjorn Ludviksson; page 153 © (top) Maldesowhat | Dreamstime.com; (bottom) Oleksandr Korzhenko | Dreamstime.com; page 158 © (top) Wasin Pummarin/123rf.com; (bottom) Stacey Katz; page 163 © (top) Bjorn Ludviksson; (left middle) Bjorn Ludviksson; (right middle) Jenna Gottlieb; (bottom) Bjorn Ludviksson; page 169 © (top) Jenna Gottlieb; (bottom) Victorflowerfly | Dreamstime.com; page 173 © (top) Stacey Katz; (bottom) Jenna Gottlieb; page 176 © Frédéric Maillard | Dreamstime.com; page 178 © Stacey Katz; page 179 © (top left) Neurobite | Dreamstime.com; (top right) Lilja Hauksdottir; page 185 © Santirf | Dreamstime.com; page 190 © (top) Stacey Katz; (bottom) Parys | Dreamstime.com; page 197 © (top) Rudolft | Dreamstime.com; (left middle) Lilja Hauksdottir; (right middle) Lilja Hauksdottir; (bottom) Vampy1 | Dreamstime.com; page 201 © Deserttrends | Dreamstime.com; page 205 © (top left) Rndmst | Dreamstime.com; (top right) Anna Pakutina | Dreamstime.com; (bottom) Checco | Dreamstime.com; page 214 © (top) Dalish | Dreamstime.com; (bottom) Jenna Gottlieb; page 218 © (top) Bjorn Ludvikssn; (bottom) Lilja Hauksdottir; page 224 © (top left) Tatonka | Dreamstime.com; (top right) Jenna Gottlieb; (bottom) Lilja Hauksdottir; page 228 © Shaiith | Dreamstime.com; page 230 © Zimu Liu | Dreamstime.com; page 231 © (top left) Macsim | Dreamstime.com; (top right) Bjorn Ludviksson; page 243 © (top left) Yggdrasill33 | Dreamstime.com; (top right) Neurobite | Dreamstime.com; (bottom) Filip Fuxa | Dreamstime.com; page 247 © (top) Jenna Gottlieb; (bottom) Selenasoro | Dreamstime.com; page 257 © (top) Stacey Katz; (bottom) Oleksandr Korzhenko | Dreamstime.com; page 262 © (top) Lilja Hauksdottir; (left middle) Bogdan | Dreamstime.com; (right middle) Jenna Gottlieb; (bottom) Shaiith | Dreamstime.com; page 265 © (top) Jenna Gottlieb; (bottom) Stacey Katz; page 268 © Bjorn Ludviksson; page 269 © (top left) Daniloforcellini | Dreamstime.com; (top right) Luciany | Dreamstime.com; page 273 © Gisbal | Dreamstime.com; page 275 © (top) Dmitry Naumov | Dreamstime.com; (left middle) Martinmolcan | Dreamstime.com; (right middle) Oleksandr Korzhenko | Dreamstime.com; (bottom) Fyletto | Dreamstime.com; page 278 © (top) Icerock | Dreamstime.com; (bottom) Icerock | Dreamstime.com; page 280 © Selitbul

Trips to Remember

BALI & LOMBOK
CHANTAE REDEN

ECUADOR
& THE GALÁPAGOS ISLANDS
BETHANY PITTS

ICELAND
JENNA GOTTLIEB

TRIP OF A LIFETIME
MACHU PICCHU
TED DUDLEY

MOROCCO

NEW ZEALAND
JAMIE CHRISTIAN DESPLACES

NORWAY

TRIP OF A LIFETIME
PATAGONIA
WAYNE BERNHARDSON

PRAGUE, VIENNA & BUDAPEST
JENNIFER WALKER
AUBURN SCALLON

ROME, FLORENCE & VENICE
ALEXEI J. COHEN

ZION & BRYCE
W. C. MCRAE, JUDY JEWELL

Epic Adventure

CAMINO DE SANTIAGO
SACRED SITES,
HISTORIC VILLAGES,
LOCAL FOOD & WINE

BEEBE BAHRAMI

ROUTE 66
Road Trip

JESSICA DUNHAM

YELLOWSTONE TO GLACIER NATIONAL PARK
Road Trip

JACKSON HOLE, CODY, THE GRAND TETONS
& THE ROCKY MOUNTAIN FRONT

CARTER G. WALKER